CHSPE CALIFORNIA HIGH SCHOOL PROFICIENCY EXAM

TestWare® Edition

Maria Suzanne Scafuri
Teacher
Cathedral School for Boys
San Francisco, CA

Stephen Hearne, Ph.D.
Professor of Psychology
Skyline College
San Bruno, CA

Research & Education Association
Visit our website: www.rea.com

Research & Education Association
61 Ethel Road West
Piscataway, New Jersey 08854
E-mail: info@rea.com

**California High School Proficiency Exam
with TestWare® on CD**

Printed in the United States of America

Library of Congress Control Number 2013936009

ISBN-13: 978-0-7386-1156-3
ISBN-10: 0-7386-1156-5

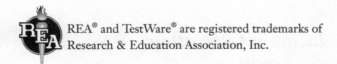

Table of Contents

About Research & Education Association

Founded in 1959, Research & Education Association (REA) is dedicated to publishing the finest and most effective educational materials—including study guides and test preps—for students in middle school, high school, college, graduate school, and beyond.

Today, REA's wide-ranging catalog is a leading resource for teachers, students, and professionals. Visit *www.rea.com* to see a complete listing of all our titles.

Acknowledgments

We would like to thank Larry Kling, Vice President, Editorial, for his editorial direction; John Cording, Vice President, Technology, for coordinating the design and development of the TestWare®; Pam Weston, Publisher, for setting the quality standards for production integrity and managing the publication to completion; Alice Leonard, Senior Editor, for project management; Diane Goldschmidt, Senior Editor, for post-production quality assurance; Christine Saul, Senior Graphic Artist, for cover design.

We also gratefully acknowledge Transcend Creative Services for typesetting, Ellen Gong for proofreading, and Stephanie Reymann for indexing the manuscript.

Introduction

The CHSPE and You

Congratulations on making the decision to take the CHSPE! As a California high school student, you may have any of several reasons for taking the exam. Perhaps you want to leave school early to start working in a vocational trade or take part in a family business, or maybe you've decided that high school just isn't right for you. On the other hand, many students who take the CHSPE continue to attend school even after they've earned the equivalent of a high school diploma.

Whatever your reasons for taking the CHSPE, this test prep will provide you with all the information you need to score high and pass the test. Prepared by California teachers, our review chapters and practice exams reinforce the English-language arts and mathematics material that you need to know for test day.

If you are eligible to take the CHSPE, you can earn the legal equivalent of a high school diploma. The CHSPE consists of two sections: an English-language arts section and a mathematics section. If you pass both sections of the exam, the California State Board of Education will award you a Certificate of Proficiency, which by state law is equivalent to a high school diploma (although not equivalent to completing all the coursework required for regular graduation from high school).

Students who are interested in military service should check with their recruiter in advance for details about applying the Certificate of Proficiency to military enlistment. If you are planning to attend a university or college, contact the individual institutions to verify their entrance requirements.

Please note that passing the CHSPE **does not** exempt minors from attending school. Minors who have a Certificate of Proficiency must **also** have verified parent or guardian permission to stop attending high school. Many students who pass the CHSPE continue to attend school. Talk to your guidance counselor or school administrator for more information about leaving school after passing the CHSPE.

The CHSPE and the Law

The California High School Proficiency Examination (CHSPE) is a testing program established by California law. Legally, all persons and institutions subject to California law that require a high school diploma must accept the certificate as satisfying the requirement. The U.S. Office of Personnel Management accepts the Certificate of Proficiency in applications for federal civilian employment.

Students who leave high school after passing the CHSPE and are no more than 18 years old may re-enroll in the school district in which they were registered with no adverse consequences. If they do re-enroll, they may be required to meet new or additional requirements established since they were previously enrolled. Students who re-enroll and then leave school again may be denied re-admittance until the beginning of the following semester.

Dropping out of school after registering for the CHSPE or while awaiting test results is unlawful for students under 18 years old. It may also result in failing grades for courses in which they are enrolled.

Eligibility to Take the CHSPE

You may take the CHSPE only if, on the test date, you

- are at least 16 years old, or
- have been enrolled in the tenth grade for one academic year or longer, or

- will complete one academic year of enrollment in the tenth grade at the end of the semester during which the next regular test administration will be conducted. (Regular test administrations are the fall and spring administration each school year.)

An Overview of the Test

CHSPE English-Language Arts Section

Format and Scoring

The CHSPE English-Language Arts section includes two subtests: Language and Reading. You must get a passing score on both subtests to pass the English-Language Arts portion of the CHSPE. The two tests do not have to be passed at the same test administration and can be taken separately.

The Language subtest consists of 48 multiple-choice questions and a writing task, both of which must be completed at the same administration. The multiple-choice questions measure language mechanics and expression. The writing task requires you to write an essay which will be scored on the basis of your writing skills, not on your knowledge of the subject.

The Reading subtest has a total of 84 multiple-choice questions: 54 reading comprehension questions and 30 vocabulary questions. The chart below breaks down the number of test questions in each content cluster assessed on the Language and Reading subtests.

Number of Test Questions by Content Cluster in English-Language Arts

Language Subtest		
Area	Content Cluster	Number of Questions
Mechanics	Capitalization	8
	Usage	8
	Punctuation	8
Expression	Sentence Structure	10
	Prewriting	5
	Content and Organization	9
Total Questions		48
Writing	Writing Task	1

Reading Subtest		
Area	Content Cluster	Number of Questions
Comprehension	Initial Understanding	10
	Interpretation	20
	Critical Analysis	14
	Strategies	10
Vocabulary	Synonyms	12
	Multiple Meaning Words	6
	Context Clues	12
Total Questions		84

Your score for the multiple-choice questions on both sections of the English-Language Arts test is based on the number of questions you answer correctly; you do not lose points for incorrect answers. Your essay in response to the writing task is scored on a 6-point scale, with 1 the lowest score and 6 the highest. The essay is scored independently by at least two trained scorers, resulting in two scores. Your writing task score is the average of the two scores.

Multiple-choice results on both subtests of the CHSPE English-Language Arts section are reported using scale scores that typically range from 250 to 450. Raw scores (i.e., the number of questions answered correctly) are converted to scale scores to correct for any differences in difficulty across test forms. Regardless of the particular test form taken, or the particular test date on which the test is taken, equal scale scores represent essentially the same level of performance.

Score Combinations for Passing the CHSPE English-Language Arts Section

Writing Task Score	Multiple-Choice Score Required to Pass
2 or lower	You cannot pass.
2.5	365
3	350
3.5	342

CHSPE Mathematics Section

Format and Scoring

The mathematics section of the CHSPE has 50 multiple-choice questions that assess skills in the following content areas (specific skills for each content area are listed in the appendix):

- Number sense and operations
- Patterns, relationships, and algebra
- Data, statistics, and probability
- Geometry and measurement

The questions also assess the following mathematical process skills:

- Communication and representation
- Estimation
- Mathematical connections
- Reasoning and problem solving

CHSPE Mathematics: Number of Questions per Content Area

Content Area	Number of Questions
Number sense and operations	9
Patterns, relationships, and algebra	15
Data, statistics, and probability	12
Geometry and measurement	14
Total Questions	50

The mathematics section of CHSPE is scored in the same way as the multiple-choice questions of the language arts section. The raw score (i.e., the number of test questions you answer correctly) is converted to a scale score to adjust for any differences in difficulty across test forms. Regardless of the particular test form taken, or the date on which a test is taken, scale scores represent the level of performance.

A scale score of 350 or higher is passing. That translates into a raw score of about 30 or more correctly answered questions.

Calculators

You will be allowed to use a calculator while working on the CHSPE Mathematics section. All problems can be solved without the use of a calculator. If you wish to use a calculator, however, you may bring a solar-powered or battery-powered basic, nonstatistical, nonscientific, nonprogrammable calculator. A basic calculator has 25 or fewer buttons and can perform no more than the four standard mathematical functions of addition, subtraction, multiplication, and division. Calculators with percentage signs, square root, and negative signs are also acceptable, as well as calculators that have simple memory such as M+, M−, MC, MR.

Time

You have a total of three and a half hours to take the CHSPE. You determine how much time you want to spend on each section. You do not have to pass the entire test on the same day. Once you pass a section or subtest, you do not have to take it again. You do have to pay the entire test fee each time you take the test.

Taking the CHSPE

When and Where Can I Take the CHSPE?

The CHSPE is given three times a year (in March, June, and October) at more than 60 test centers throughout California. Visit *http://www.chspe.net/about/locations/* to find a test location near you.

How Do I Register for the CHSPE?

To register for the exam, you must submit a registration form with proof of eligibility and a cashier's check or money order for payment. Be sure to register as early as possible to increase your chances of getting a seat at a test site in your preferred location. Registration procedures and a registration form are included in the Information Bulletin on the CHSPE website: *http://www.chspe.net/about/bulletin/*.

Do I Have to Take All Three Sections of the CHSPE on the Same Day?

No. On the day of the test you can decide to take either of the English-Language subtests, or the Mathematics section, or any combination of the three. Remember though, the test fee is the same regardless of which parts of the test you take. To receive a Certificate of Proficiency you must pass the English-Language Arts section and the Mathematics section. You do not have to retake a section or subtest that you previously passed. There is no limit to the number of times you may take the CHSPE, but you must register and pay the test fee each time.

When Will I Get My Scores?

CHSPE test scores will be posted online about a month after the exam. You can access your results online by providing an email address and password when you register for the exam. Your official score results will be mailed to you a few days after the unofficial results have been posted online.

For more information and the latest updates on the CHSPE, visit *http://www.chspe.net/*.

Studying for the CHSPE

When confronted with taking a test like the CHSPE, everyone has a different reaction. Some people are nervous about the time length, while others are concerned about content material. Some people even look forward to taking these kinds of tests because they are like a rite of passage from one level of schooling to the next. Others like the fact that the test, other than the essay on the language arts section, is all multiple-choice questions. Whether you feel confident or unnerved, REA's *California High School Proficiency Exam* is here to help you. Studying the review chapters, taking the practice tests using our TestWare® on CD, and reading through the answer explanations will help you fine-tune your knowledge of the material on the test while also familiarizing yourself with the test's format. This preparation will ensure that you do your best.

STUDY PLAN

REA's 4-Week CHSPE Study Schedule

This study schedule will help you prepare for the CHSPE. Although the schedule is designed for 4 weeks, it can be condensed into 2 weeks by combining two weeks of study into one. If you choose the 4-week schedule, plan to study for *at least* one hour a day. CHSPE test-takers who are following a 2-week program need to set aside *at least* two hours for studying every day.

Find a study routine that works for you and stick to it! Some people like to get up early and study for an hour or two before going to school. Others might choose to study during their lunch break, at the library, or at home after school. Whatever schedule you choose, be sure to study every day—even on weekends.

Week	Activity
1	Read our introduction to the CHSPE. Be sure you understand the format and know exactly what is tested on the exam. Start your study routine by taking the Pretest to determine your strengths and weaknesses. Give yourself 3 1/2 hours after school, on a weekend, or at another convenient time to take the exam. You will need to concentrate, so take the Pretest at a time and place where you will not be disturbed. After you have finished the test, record your scores. This will help you track your progress as you study. Later in the week, study the detailed explanations for the questions you answered incorrectly. Take notes and pay attention to sections where you missed a lot of questions. You will need to spend more time reviewing the related material.
2	This week, focus on the English-Language Arts and Writing Reviews and become familiar with all the topics discussed. Study our examples and answer the practice questions as you complete the review for each subtest. The more practice you get now, the better prepared you'll be for the actual CHSPE. Read the suggestions and examples provided in the Writing Section, and make sure you understand everything. Now is also a good time to review any supplemental materials (such as a writing and/or grammar handbook) that will help you write clearer, better-focused essays. Try a few practice essays on your own and ask a teacher, parent, or friend to give you feedback.
3	This week study the Mathematics Review. Go through each section slowly and pay close attention to our examples and practice questions. Later this week, take Practice Test 1 on CD. Record your scores for each section and see how well you did. Study the detailed explanations of answers for any questions you answered incorrectly. Make sure you understand why you answered the question wrong, so you can improve your test-taking skills. If you find yourself in need of extra review or don't fully understand a topic, consult your textbook or ask a classmate or teacher for additional help.
4	This week, take Practice Test 2 on CD. After you finish the test, review the explanations for the questions you answered incorrectly. Use your remaining study time to revisit any sections of the CHSPE in which you need improvement. Re-read the review sections or retake the Pretest and see how much you've improved in just a matter of weeks!

Congratulations! You've studied hard and you're ready for the CHSPE!

Test-Taking Tips

Taking an important test like the CHSPE might make you nervous. These test tips will help alleviate your test-taking anxieties.

Tip 1. Become comfortable with the format of the test. When you are practicing, stay calm and pace yourself. After simulating the test only once, you will boost your chances of doing well, and you will be able to sit down for the actual CHSPE with much more confidence.

Tip 2. Familiarize yourself with the directions on the test. This will not only save time but will also help you avoid anxiety (and the mistakes anxiety causes).

Tip 3. Read all of the possible answers. Just because you think you have found the correct response, do not automatically assume that it is the best answer. Read through each choice to be sure that you are not making a mistake by jumping to conclusions.

Tip 4. Use the process of elimination. Go through each answer choice and eliminate as many as possible. If you can eliminate two answer choices, you will give yourself a better chance of getting the item correct since there will be only two choices left from which to make your guess. Do not leave an answer blank; it is better to guess than to not answer a question on the CHSPE as there is no penalty for incorrect answers.

Tip 5. Skip difficult questions. Be sure to mark which questions you skipped in your test booklet and come back to them later. Answer as many questions as you can, then come back to the questions you skipped. Work at a steady pace and avoid focusing on any one question too long.

Tip 6. Be sure that the answer circle you are marking corresponds to the number of the question in the test booklet. The test is graded automatically, and marking one answer in the wrong space can throw off your answer key and your score. Be careful to mark your answers in accurate sequence.

The Day of the Test

Here are a few things to keep in mind so you'll be prepared for the CHSPE.

Before the Test

Check your CHSPE registration information to find out what time to arrive at the testing center. Get directions if you need to and make sure you arrive early. This will allow you to collect your thoughts and relax before the test, and will also spare you the anguish that comes with being late. (If you arrive late, you might not be admitted to the test center.)

Before you leave for the test center, make sure that you have your admission ticket, several sharpened No. 2 pencils with erasers, and two forms of identification, one of which must contain a recent and recognizable photograph, your name, and signature (i.e., driver's license). All documents must be originals (no copies). You will not be admitted to the test center, and you will forfeit your test fees if you do not have proper identification. (More information about proper forms of ID is listed in the official registration booklet.)

Dress comfortably, so you are not distracted by being too hot or too cold while taking the test.

You may wear a watch to the test center. However, you may not wear a calculator watch or one that makes noise.

Do not bring cell phones, smart phones, pagers, and other electronic listening, recording, music, or photographic devices into the test center. Dictionaries, textbooks, notebooks, highlighters, scratch paper, briefcases, tote bags, purses, or packages are also not permitted. If you bring or use prohibited materials, you will be dismissed from the exam and your scores will be voided.

During the Test

Procedures will be followed to maintain test security. Once you enter the test center, follow all of the rules and instructions given by the test supervisor. If you do not, you risk being dismissed from the test and having your scores cancelled.

When all of the materials have been distributed, the test instructor will give you directions for filling out your answer sheet. Fill out this sheet carefully since this information will be printed on your score report.

After the Test

When you finish your test, hand in your materials and you will be dismissed. Then, go home and relax—you deserve it!

Good luck on the CHSPE!

PRETEST

PRETEST

PRETEST
ENGLISH-LANGUAGE ARTS SECTION

Language Subtest

DIRECTIONS: Look at the underlined words in each sentence. You may see a mistake in punctuation, capitalization, or word usage. If you spot a mistake in the underlined section of a sentence, select the answer that corrects the mistake. If you find no mistake, choose D, *Correct as is*.

1. Every person on the team is doing <u>there</u> best to win the game.
   - (A) his
   - (B) they're
   - (C) their
   - (D) Correct as is.

2. By the beginning of next term, the governor <u>will be</u> in office for two years.
   - (A) will have been
   - (B) have been
   - (C) is
   - (D) Correct as is.

3. He <u>did not keep no</u> record of the event.
   - (A) does not keep no
   - (B) did not keep any
   - (C) did not keep none
   - (D) Correct as is.

4. The man bought the present <u>for him</u> daughter.
   - (A) for her
   - (B) for his
   - (C) for himself
   - (D) Correct as is.

5. The musicians <u>requires</u> microphones for their performance.
   - (A) are require
   - (B) will requires
   - (C) require
   - (D) Correct as is.

6. The director <u>said, "It won't take long to finish.</u>"
   - (A) said "It won't take long to finish"
   - (B) said it won't take long to finish".
   - (C) said it wont, "take long to finish".
   - (D) Correct as is.

GO TO NEXT PAGE

7. <u>Maddie and me</u> had hamburgers for lunch.
   - (A) Me and Maddie
   - (B) Maddie and I
   - (C) Maddie and myself
   - (D) Correct as is.

8. <u>Lets make</u> a castle in the sand.
   - (A) Lets us make
   - (B) Let's us make
   - (C) Let's make
   - (D) Correct as is.

9. When I went to the concert, <u>I will bought a shirt</u>.
   - (A) I will buy a shirt.
   - (B) I would buy a shirt.
   - (C) I bought a shirt.
   - (D) Correct as is.

10. Everyone received a donut <u>accept</u> Tommy.
    - (A) accepted
    - (B) except
    - (C) excepting
    - (D) Correct as is.

11. The recipe called <u>for carrots, peas, onions, and, celery</u>.
    - (A) for, carrots, peas, onions, and, celery.
    - (B) for carrots; peas; onions; and celery.
    - (C) for carrots, peas, onions, and celery.
    - (D) Correct as is.

12. The letter was sent to <u>dr. Smith</u> and his associates.
    - (A) Dr. Smith
    - (B) Dr Smith
    - (C) dr. smith
    - (D) Correct as is.

13. Trina works for <u>Chico state university</u>.
    - (A) chico state university.
    - (B) Chico State University.
    - (C) Chico State university.
    - (D) Correct as is.

14. The first song of the evening was <u>sung at</u> a famous opera singer.
    - (A) sung by
    - (B) sung in
    - (C) sang for
    - (D) Correct as is.

15. Heidi was born on <u>September 2 1967</u>.
    - (A) september 2 1967
    - (B) September, 2, 1967
    - (C) September 2, 1967
    - (D) Correct as is.

16. The expedition ended on the top of <u>Mt. McKinley</u>.
    - (A) mt mckinley
    - (B) MT. mckinley
    - (C) Mt McKinley
    - (D) Correct as is.

17. When the play was over, the <u>teams shaken</u> hands.
    - (A) teams shaking
    - (B) teams shook
    - (C) teams will shake
    - (D) Correct as is.

18. The guitar <u>was bought</u> at the local music store.
    - (A) were bought
    - (B) was buying
    - (C) buys
    - (D) Correct as is.

GO TO NEXT PAGE ➡

19. He <u>was enjoyed</u> the Sunday crossword before the alarm went off outside.
    (A) was enjoying
    (B) had enjoying
    (C) is enjoying
    (D) were enjoying

20. <u>"Are you ready?" asked the teacher</u>.
    (A) "Are you ready?", asked the teacher.
    (B) "are you ready" asked the teacher
    (C) "Are you ready"? asked the teacher.
    (D) Correct as is.

21. There are three names on <u>the wall: Jim, Suzanne, and Bernard</u>.
    (A) the wall Jim Suzanne and Bernard.
    (B) the wall: Jim, Suzanne and Bernard.
    (C) the wall; Jim, Suzanne and Bernard.
    (D) Correct as is.

22. <u>Because the exam was very challenging, I did just fine</u>.
    (A) Being the exam was very challenging, I did just fine.
    (B) Since the exam was very challenging, I did just fine.
    (C) Even though the exam was very challenging, I did just fine.
    (D) Correct as is.

23. <u>Jeremy is a student who is talkative, witty, has intelligence and friendly</u>.
    (A) Jeremy is a student who is talking, witty, has intelligence and friendly.
    (B) Jeremy is a student who is talkative, witty, intelligent, and friendly.
    (C) Jeremy is a student who is talkative, witty, intelligence and friendly.
    (D) Correct as is.

24. <u>One of the oldest religions is hinduism</u>.
    (A) One of the oldest Religions is hinduism.
    (B) One of the oldest religion is Hinduism.
    (C) One of the oldest religions is Hinduism.
    (D) Correct as is.

25. When Liz returns from the store, <u>she gave her receipt to</u> her boss.
    (A) she will give her receipt to
    (B) she will give her receipt at
    (C) she is giving her receipt to
    (D) Correct as is.

26. <u>I enjoyed the movie for its story, dialogue and musical scoring</u>.
    (A) I enjoyed the movie for its story, dialoguing and music score.
    (B) I enjoyed the movie for its story, dialogue, and musical score.
    (C) I enjoyed the movie for its story, dialogue and music scored.
    (D) Correct as is.

27. The <u>apple placed on the table</u> by the man in the coat.
    (A) apple placing on the table
    (B) apple was placed on the table
    (C) apple was place on the table
    (D) Correct as is.

28. Luca, Anton and I <u>am</u> the only people going to the restaurant.
    (A) is
    (B) was
    (C) are
    (D) Correct as is.

GO TO NEXT PAGE ➡

29. Bella plays tennis every day because she wanted to get better.
    (A) played tennis every day because she does wants
    (B) plays tennis every day because she wants
    (C) plays tennis every day because she will wanted
    (D) Correct as is.

30. Sophie bought her dog on tuesday june 22.
    (A) Tuesday june 22.
    (B) tuesday June 22.
    (C) Tuesday, June 22.
    (D) Correct as is.

31. No one believed that she could do it; however, she managed to finish the task.
    (A) No one believed that she could do it however she managed to finish the task.
    (B) No one believed that she could do it however, she managed to finish the task.
    (C) No one believed that she could do it; however: she managed to finish the task.
    (D) Correct as is.

32. If the soccer team wins this next game, they will win the last four in a row.
    (A) If the soccer team wins this next game, they will have won the last four in a row.
    (B) If the soccer team wins this next game, they could have win the last four in a row.
    (C) If the soccer team wins this next game, they will be winning the last four in a row.
    (D) Correct as is.

33. Marley sped down the hall, knocks over the chair, and runs into class.
    (A) Marley is speeding down the hall, knocking over the chair, and ran into class.
    (B) Marley sped down the hall, knocks over the chair, and ran into class.
    (C) Marley sped down the hall, knocked over the chair, and ran into class.
    (D) Correct as is.

34. He put the cheese in the refrigerator next to the tortillas.
    (A) cheese next by the refrigerator
    (B) cheese unto the refrigerator
    (C) cheese between the refrigerator
    (D) Correct as is.

35. In the spring we will plant tree in the park.
    (A) we will planting tree
    (B) we will plant trees
    (C) we will plants trees
    (D) Correct as is.

36. After she wrote the story, which won first prize she started working on the sequel.
    (A) After she wrote the story, which won first prize, she started working on the sequel.
    (B) After she wrote the story, which won first prize she started, working on the sequel.
    (C) After she wrote the story: which won first prize she started working on the sequel.
    (D) Correct as is.

GO TO NEXT PAGE ➡

37. <u>Once Mary arriving at the store</u>, she counted the money in the register.

(A) Once Mary arrive at the store,

(B) Once Mary arrived at the store,

(C) Once Mary arrives at the store,

(D) Correct as is.

38. <u>The fish prepared well</u>.

(A) The fish is preparing well.

(B) The fish was prepares well.

(C) The fish is prepared well.

(D) Correct as is.

39. <u>Eating at the bar is my least favorite place in
a restaurant</u>.

(A) Eats at the bar is my least favorite place
in a restaurant.

(B) Eats at the bar are my least favorite
place in a restaurant.

(C) Eating at the bar are my least favorite
place in a restaurant.

(D) Correct as is.

40. <u>The items on the shopping list included:
apples, oranges, peanuts butter, and milk</u>.

(A) The items on the shopping list included; apples, oranges, peanuts butter, and
milk.

(B) The items on the shopping list included, apples, oranges, peanuts butter, and
milk.

(C) The items on the shopping list included: apples, oranges, peanuts, butter, and
milk.

(D) Correct as is.

41. <u>"Yes" said Dan. "I will swim this afternoon."</u>

(A) "Yes," said Dan. "I will swim this afternoon."

(B) "Yes." Said Dan. "I will swim this
afternoon."

(C) "Yes, said Dan. I will swim this afternoon."

(D) Correct as is.

42. <u>Both the mother and father's cameras were
in good condition</u>.

(A) Both the mother's and father's cameras
were in good condition.

(B) Both the mothers' and fathers' camera
were in good condition.

(C) Both the mother's and father camera
were in good condition.

(D) Correct as is.

43. If chefs want to cook in the production
kitchen, <u>he should enter immediately</u>.

(A) you should enter immediately.

(B) they should enter immediately.

(C) she should enter immediately.

(D) Correct as is.

44. <u>The Northern states include Vermont and
Maryland</u>.

(A) The northern states include Vermont
and Maryland.

(B) The Northern States include Vermont
and Maryland.

(C) The northern States include Vermont
and Maryland.

(D) Correct as is.

GO TO NEXT PAGE

45. Brian and Michelle went to the mall with <u>Maddie and I.</u>

    (A) I and Maddie.

    (B) Maddie and me.

    (C) they and Maddie.

    (D) Correct as is.

46. Adele asked us to <u>brought</u> the drinks to the party.

    (A) bring

    (B) brung

    (C) brings

    (D) Correct as is.

47. When the lessons were finished, <u>the painters has learned how to trim properly.</u>

    (A) the painters had learned how to trim properly.

    (B) the painters have learned how to trim properly.

    (C) the painters is learning how to trim properly.

    (D) Correct as is.

48. <u>The tournament this Winter will be held on the main green.</u>

    (A) The tournament this winter will be held on the main green.

    (B) The Tournament this winter will be held on the main green.

    (C) The Tournament this Winter will be held on the main green.

    (D) Correct as is.

PRETEST
ENGLISH-LANGUAGE ARTS SECTION

Writing Task

DIRECTIONS: Carefully read the writing task and review the "Writer's Checklist" below. You must be specific and explain your reasons for your opinion.

Writing Topic
Many home and business owners complain that skateboard riders use their parking lots, driveways, and sidewalks to practice tricks, which can be disturbing to customers and house occupants. Should skateboard riders be confined only to skate parks? Be sure to explain your answer with specific examples.

Writer's Checklist
The following "Writer's Checklist" (© 2008 by NCS Pearson, Inc.) will be provided with the CHSPE writing task.

- Did I write about the topic?
- Did I express my ideas in complete sentences?
- Did I give enough details to explain or support my ideas?
- Did I include only those details that are about my topic?
- Did I write my ideas in an order that is clear for the reader to follow?
- Did I write a topic sentence for each paragraph?
- Did I use a capital letter at the beginning of each sentence and for all other words that should be capitalized?
- Did I use the correct punctuation at the end of each sentence and within each sentence?
- Did I spell words correctly?
- Did I print or write clearly?

GO TO NEXT PAGE ➡

Reading Subtest

DIRECTIONS: Read the passages in this section, then read each question about the passage. Decide which is the best answer to the question and mark the answer you have chosen on your answer sheet.

THE RED WHEELBARROW
by William Carlos Williams (1883–1963)

1   so much depends
        upon

        a red wheel
5   barrow

        glazed with rain
        water

        beside the white
10   chickens.

1. This short poem would best be described as an example of

(A) imagery.

(B) metaphor.

(C) simile.

(D) irony.

2. The word "glazed" in line 6 would best be described as

(A) lined.

(B) coated.

(C) sprinkled.

(D) dotted.

GO TO NEXT PAGE

3. How many stanzas are in this poem?

(A) One

(B) Two

(C) Three

(D) Four

4. Which statement best describes this poem?

(A) The rhyme scheme is unusual for such a short poem.

(B) The imagery is striking for such a short poem.

(C) The author uses alliteration to make a visual statement to the reader.

(D) The author uses onomatopoeia to create tone.

Excerpt from *Harrison Bergeron*
by Kurt Vonnegut (1922–2007)
In the following selection, Vonnegut shows the reader what life may be like in an "equal" future.

1   The rest of Harrison's appearance was Halloween and hardware. Nobody had ever worn heavier handicaps. He had outgrown hindrances faster than the H-G men could think them up. Instead of a little ear radio for a mental handicap, he wore a tremendous pair of earphones, and spectacles with thick wavy lenses. The spectacles were intended to make

5   him not only half blind, but to give him whanging headaches besides.

Scrap metal was hung all over him. Ordinarily, there was a certain symmetry, a military neatness to the handicaps issued to strong people, but Harrison looked like a walking junkyard. In the race of life, Harrison carried three hundred pounds.

And to offset his good looks, the H-G men required that he wear at all times a red

10   rubber ball for a nose, keep his eyebrows shaved off, and cover his even white teeth with black caps at snaggle-tooth random.

5. In line 1, Harrison Bergeron's image is described as "Halloween and hardware." This is most likely to mean

(A) he is in a Halloween costume.

(B) he is carrying nails and screws in a basket.

(C) he is dressed in a crazy assortment of hardware that has a ghoulish appearance.

(D) he is carrying various tools with him.

6. In line 4, the word "spectacles" is used twice. The meanings of these words are

(A) glasses, a nuisance.

(B) glasses, glasses.

(C) a nuisance, glasses.

(D) a nuisance, a nuisance.

GO TO NEXT PAGE ➡

7. In the first paragraph, "handicaps" are discussed in detail. What do "handicaps" most likely mean in this selection?
   (A) Items made to help him physically
   (B) His physical deformities
   (C) His emotional problems
   (D) Impediments to hold back his true potential

8. Who would best represent the "H-G men" in line 9?
   (A) Firemen
   (B) Nurses
   (C) Policemen
   (D) Teachers

9. In line 5, Vonnegut writes that the handicaps give Harrison "whanging headaches." The best way to describe "whanging" would be
   (A) mild.
   (B) severe.
   (C) average.
   (D) ceaseless.

10. In the second paragraph, Vonnegut says that the handicaps usually have "a certain symmetry, a military neatness" to them. This description most likely implies that the handicaps are
   (A) precise.
   (B) sloppy.
   (C) elegant.
   (D) simple.

11. In the second paragraph, Vonnegut says that Harrison is in a "race of life." This is most likely to mean
   (A) his existence as compared to others.
   (B) a contest that runs his life.
   (C) a foot race that is run with other people.
   (D) a race to see who can live the longest.

12. In the last paragraph, Vonnegut describes Harrison's modified facial features. These features would be described mostly as
   (A) clownish.
   (B) handsome.
   (C) pale and tired.
   (D) angry.

DIRECTIONS: Refer to the chart to answer questions 13 through 22.

Features	Car #1	Car #2	Car #3
MSRP Including Destination Charge	$12,955	$13,830	$12,685
Fuel Economy (city miles per gallon)	29	26	27
Fuel Economy (highway miles per gallon)	36	31	34
Doors	2	4	4
Body Style	Liftback	Hatchback	Wagon
Transmission Type	Manual	Manual	Manual
Seating Capacity	5	4	5
Front Airbags	Standard	Standard	Standard

(chart cont'd)

GO TO NEXT PAGE

PRETEST

Features	Car #1	Car #2	Car #3
Side Airbags	Standard	No	Standard
Roll-Sensing Side Curtain Airbags	Standard	Standard	Not Available
Power Windows	Standard	Optional	Not Available
Power Door Locks	Optional	Optional	Not Listed
Power Mirrors	Optional	Standard	Not Available
PowerTrain Warranty Miles	65,000	60,000	100,000
PowerTrain Warranty Months	60	60	60
Basic Warranty Miles	36,000	36,000	36,000
Basic Warranty Months	36	36	36
MSRP Including Delivery Charge	$12,955	$13,830	$12,685

13. "Body Style" most likely means
  (A) where the car was designed.
  (B) how many doors the car has.
  (C) how many people can sit in the car.
  (D) the overall style of the car.

14. "Seating Capacity" most likely means
  (A) how big the inside of the car is.
  (B) the minimum number of people who can sit in the car safely.
  (C) the maximum number of people who can sit in the car safely.
  (D) the number of cup holders in the car.

15. Which answer best defines basic warranty miles and warranty months?
  (A) Warranty miles refer to an established number of miles for the car to be serviced without charge to the owner. Warranty months are the months the warranty is in effect.
  (B) Warranty miles refer to the miles left before the car needs service. Warranty months are the months the warranty is in effect.

  (C) Warranty miles refer to the miles driven by the owner. Warranty months are the number of months left on the life of the car.
  (D) Warranty miles refer to the miles left before the car needs service. Warranty months are the number of months left on the life of the car.

16. How many seatbelts would Car #2 most likely have in it?
  (A) 2
  (B) 3
  (C) 4
  (D) 5

17. Which car is the worst deal for the money?
  (A) Car #1
  (B) Car #2
  (C) Car #3
  (D) They are all the same.

GO TO NEXT PAGE ➡

18. If an option is labeled as "Not Listed," it is most likely to mean

(A) it is not available at all.

(B) it may be available, but it is not listed on this sheet.

(C) it is available but not listed on the sheet.

(D) it is available at no extra cost.

19. If an option is listed as "Standard," it is most likely to mean

(A) it is an option a lot of people choose.

(B) it is included as part of the base price.

(C) it is a simple option.

(D) it is an advanced choice made by the car manufacturer.

20. What is the difference in price of the car with the highest highway gas mileage as compared to the car with the lowest highway gas mileage?

(A) $875

(B) $1,130

(C) $1,330

(D) $1,375

21. Which two cars have the best PowerTrain Warranty Miles?

(A) Car #1 and Car #2

(B) Car #2 and Car #3

(C) Car #1 and Car #3

(D) Car #2 and Car #3 are the same.

22. Which car has the most standard options?

(A) Car #1

(B) Car #2

(C) Car #3

(D) Car #1 and #3 have the same options.

DIRECTIONS: Refer to the following passage to answer questions 23–29.

Excerpt from Presidential Address to Joint Session of Congress on February 24, 2009
by President Barack Obama

1   You see, the flow of credit is the lifeblood of our economy. The ability to get a loan is how you finance the purchase of everything from a home to a car to a college education, how stores stock their shelves, farms buy equipment, and businesses make payroll.

But credit has stopped flowing the way it should. Too many bad loans from the housing
5   crisis have made their way onto the books of too many banks. And with so much debt and so little confidence, these banks are now fearful of lending out any more money to households, to businesses, or even to each other. And when there is no lending, families can't afford to buy homes or cars. So businesses are forced to make layoffs. Our economy suffers even more, and credit dries up even further.

10   That is why this administration is moving swiftly and aggressively to break this destructive cycle, to restore confidence, and restart lending.

GO TO NEXT PAGE

23. In line 1, Obama states that "the flow of credit is the lifeblood of our economy." "Lifeblood" in this sentence is most likely to mean

    (A) a liquid that runs through veins.

    (B) a life-sustaining element for humans.

    (C) a life-sustaining element for commerce.

    (D) the beginning of the economy.

24. In line 4, Obama states that "credit has stopped flowing the way it should." When he says that credit "flows," he most likely means

    (A) it moves like electricity.

    (B) it moves like blood in the veins.

    (C) it moves like dirt in a vacuum.

    (D) it moves like music.

25. "Credit dries up" most likely means

    (A) increases.

    (B) becomes scarcer.

    (C) becomes a desert.

    (D) elevates.

26. In line 5, it says that banks have "books." The definition of "books" is most likely to mean

    (A) novels.

    (B) accounting files.

    (C) banking customer addresses.

    (D) housing and job information.

27. In line 11, Obama says that the administration wants to restore "confidence." "Confidence" most likely means

    (A) self-esteem.

    (B) a secret told in private.

    (C) trust.

    (D) life.

28. In Obama's speech, he implies that credit is important to the American people because

    (A) Americans use credit for simple purchases.

    (B) Americans need to stop using credit.

    (C) Americans do not need credit for large purchases such as homes, cars, and boats; it is only a myth that it is needed at all.

    (D) the entire infrastructure of American living is based around credit and the ability to give and receive loans.

29. In this speech, Obama makes which following connection?

    (A) With credit limits, spending increases, and more people have jobs.

    (B) With no lending, families cannot spend money on homes or transportation and business increases everywhere else.

    (C) With no lending, families cannot spend money on homes or transportation and businesses suffer and mandate layoffs.

    (D) When banks fail, the American people can rally together to create a new economy.

GO TO NEXT PAGE ➡

DIRECTIONS: Refer to the following passage to answer questions 30–37.

Excerpt from *Lord of the Flies*
by William Golding (1911–1993)
William Golding's famous book, THE LORD OF THE FLIES, tells a story about a group of boys stranded on an island who must fend for themselves until they are rescued. Stranded on the island for several months, many of the boys' emotional and physical states deteriorate, leaving each one vulnerable to each other and the elements.

1   Here, on the other side of the island, the view was utterly different. The filmy enchantments
       of mirage could not endure the cold ocean water and the horizon was hard, clipped blue. Ralph
       wandered down to the rocks. Down here, almost on a level with the sea, you could follow with
       your eye the ceaseless, bulging passage of the deep sea waves. They were miles wide, apparently
5   not breakers or the banked ridges of shallow water. They traveled the length of the island with
       an air of disregarding it and being set on other business; they were less a progress than a mo-
       mentous rise and fall of the whole ocean. Now the sea would suck down, making cascades and
       waterfalls of retreating water, would sink past the rocks and plaster down the seaweed like shin-
       ing hair: then, pausing, gather and rise with a roar, irresistibly swelling over point and outcrop,
10   climbing the little cliff, sending at last an arm of surf up a gully to end a yard or so from him in
       fingers of spray.
            Wave after wave, Ralph followed the rise and fall until something of the remoteness of the
       sea numbed his brain. Then gradually the almost infinite size of this water forced itself on his
       attention. This was the divider, the barrier. On the other side of the island, swathed at midday
15   with mirage, defended by the shield of the quiet lagoon, one might dream of rescue; but here,
       faced by the brute obtuseness of the ocean, the miles of division, one was clamped down, one
       was helpless, one was condemned, one was—

30. In this passage, on line 1, Golding describes the ocean and the horizon as "filmy enchantments." "Enchantments" can best be defined as
(A) ghosts.
(B) figments.
(C) stories.
(D) lies.

31. On line 2, the horizon is described as "hard." "Hard" would be best described here as
(A) solid.
(B) fuzzy.
(C) metal.
(D) defined.

32. On lines 5–6, Golding states, "They traveled the length of the island with an air of disregarding it and being set on other business." Which element of figurative language is best represented in this line?
(A) Alliteration
(B) Irony
(C) Personification
(D) Metaphor

GO TO NEXT PAGE ➡

33. On lines 8–9, Golding describes the surf as something that would "plaster down the seaweed like shining hair." This phrase is an example of

   (A) metaphor.

   (B) simile.

   (C) personification.

   (D) alliteration.

34. On line 14, Ralph describes the scene as "the divider, the barrier." What is the barrier metaphorically?

   (A) His blood from his veins

   (B) The island from the water

   (C) Being stranded and freedom

   (D) The fruit from the skin

35. In lines 13–14, Golding writes, "Then gradually the almost infinite size of this water forced itself on his attention." "Infinite" means never-ending. Why would Ralph describe the ocean as "almost infinite" if he knows that it is just an ocean with land on the other side?

   (A) To show how incredibly uneducated he is

   (B) To show his frustration of the size of the beach

   (C) To show how loud the waves crashing is to his ears

   (D) To portray his dismay at his predicament and the barrier of the ocean to his surroundings

36. On line 16, Golding writes that Ralph is "faced by the brute obtuseness of the ocean." "Obtuseness" could best be defined as

   (A) small.

   (B) angular.

   (C) circular.

   (D) wide.

37. On line 17, Golding writes that Ralph is "faced by the brute obtuseness of the ocean." "Brute" could best be defined as

   (A) simple.

   (B) barbaric.

   (C) smooth.

   (D) gentle.

DIRECTIONS: Refer to the following passage to answer questions 38–42.

Excerpt from *A Tale of Two Cities*
by Charles Dickens (1812–1870)

1   It was the best of times, it was the worst of times, it was the age of wisdom, it was the age of foolishness, it was the epoch of belief, it was the epoch of incredulity, it was the season of Light, it was the season of Darkness, it was the spring of hope, it was the winter of despair, we had everything before us, we had nothing before us, we were all going direct to Heaven, we were all

5   going direct the other way—in short, the period was so far like the present period, that some of its noisiest authorities insisted on its being received, for good or for evil, in the superlative degree of comparison only.

GO TO NEXT PAGE ➡

38. This entire paragraph is an example of which element of figurative language?

(A) Metaphor

(B) Simile

(C) Irony

(D) Characterization

39. In line 2, "epoch of incredulity" would most likely mean

(A) an age of unbelievable things.

(B) an age of incredible things.

(C) an age of realism.

(D) an age of fantasy.

40. Why are "Light" and "Darkness" capitalized?

(A) Because they are more important than the other words

(B) Because there is a mistake in the sentence

(C) Because they are metaphorical to something sacred

(D) Because they are more ironic capitalized

41. "The best of times" and "the worst of times" are which type of phrases?

(A) Comparative

(B) Contradictory

(C) Complete

(D) Absolute

42. The mood of this paragraph explains the time of the piece as

(A) uncertain.

(B) realistic.

(C) important.

(D) unexplainable.

DIRECTIONS: Refer to the table to answer questions 43–48.

Years of Service	BA+0	BA+15	BA+30	BA+45	BA+90	BA+135	MA+0	MA+45	MA+90 or PhD
0	34,426	35,356	36,319	37,285	40,383	42,378	41,274	44,372	46,369
1	34,889	35,832	36,808	37,816	40,946	42,931	41,733	44,863	46,847
2	35,331	36,283	37,269	38,354	41,476	43,481	42,195	45,316	47,321
3	35,786	36,747	37,743	38,864	41,979	44,033	42,632	45,746	47,801
4	36,232	37,235	38,238	39,397	42,531	44,599	43,091	46,225	48,295
5	36,693	37,701	38,713	39,937	43,059	45,169	43,558	46,681	48,791
6	37,167	38,153	39,200	40,484	43,591	45,713	44,036	47,144	49,264
7	37,999	39,000	40,061	41,415	44,568	46,748	44,932	48,084	50,265
8	39,218	40,273	41,359	42,825	46,021	48,281	46,341	49,538	51,797
9		41,591	42,731	44,250	47,521	49,858	47,765	51,038	53,374
10			44,120	45,749	49,063	51,478	49,265	52,580	54,993
11				47,291	50,677	53,141	50,807	54,194	56,656
12				48,784	52,335	54,872	52,410	55,851	58,389
13					54,034	56,646	54,069	57,550	60,162
14					55,740	58,486	55,778	59,368	62,003
15					57,191	60,008	57,227	60,911	63,615
16 or more					58,334	61,207	58,372	62,129	64,887

Additional information: BA=Bachelor's Degree, MA=Master's Degree

Numbers after the letters refer to college credits, i.e., "BA + 15" means a Bachelor's degree plus 15 college credits.

GO TO NEXT PAGE

43. How many years of service would a person with a Bachelor's degree need to make $37,999?

    (A) 5
    (B) 6
    (C) 7
    (D) 8

44. How much money would a person make who has a Master's degree plus 45 credits and has served the district for 9 years?

    (A) Less than $49,000
    (B) More than $52,000
    (C) Less than $52,000
    (D) More than $54,000

45. What degree would a person need to make the most money on the salary schedule?

    (A) BA + 45
    (B) MA + 45
    (C) PhD
    (D) MA +15

46. What assumption could be made about a PhD who has over 16 years experience?

    (A) Their salary continues to increase.
    (B) Their salary decreases.
    (C) Their salary stays the same as year 16.
    (D) They are expected to quit or retire.

47. What is the best explanation for 0 years of service?

    (A) This person is a student.
    (B) This person has no experience.
    (C) This person is over-qualified.
    (D) This person is already a teacher.

48. Why does a person with a BA +135 credits and 0 years experience make more than a person with an MA and 0 years experience?

    (A) The person with the BA has more experience than the person with the MA.
    (B) The person with the BA has more college credits than the person with the MA.
    (C) The person with the BA has already worked in a school however, the person with the MA has not.
    (D) The person with the BA has committed to getting a higher academic degree.

GO TO NEXT PAGE ➡

DIRECTIONS: Refer to the flowchart to answer questions 49–54.

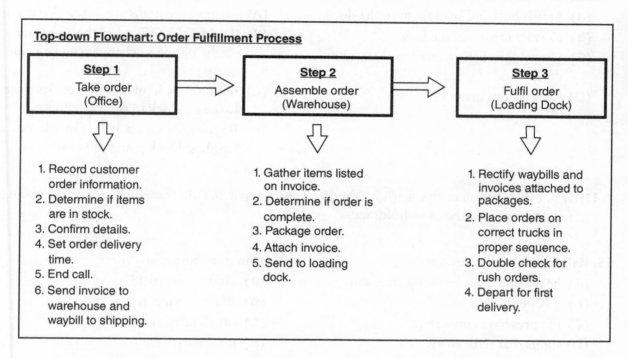

Top-down Flowchart: Order Fulfillment Process

Step 1
Take order
(Office)

1. Record customer order information.
2. Determine if items are in stock.
3. Confirm details.
4. Set order delivery time.
5. End call.
6. Send invoice to warehouse and waybill to shipping.

Step 2
Assemble order
(Warehouse)

1. Gather items listed on invoice.
2. Determine if order is complete.
3. Package order.
4. Attach invoice.
5. Send to loading dock.

Step 3
Fulfil order
(Loading Dock)

1. Rectify waybills and invoices attached to packages.
2. Place orders on correct trucks in proper sequence.
3. Double check for rush orders.
4. Depart for first delivery.

49. Why is the second step of Step 2 important to fulfilling the order?

(A) Picking the right size package saves on shipping.

(B) Attaching the invoice makes sure it is shipped to the correct address.

(C) The order must be checked for completion before it is sent out.

(D) The orders need to go on the trucks in the correct sequence.

50. Which department is in charge of incoming orders?

(A) The Customer Department

(B) The Office

(C) The Warehouse

(D) The Loading Dock

51. The Loading Dock is responsible for how many steps?

(A) 4

(B) 5

(C) 6

(D) 7

52. Why is the third step of Step 1 important to fulfilling orders?

(A) Packaging the orders correctly is important for customer satisfaction.

(B) Comfirming details with the customer ensures customer satisfaction.

(C) Sending orders to the dock makes sure that the items get out to the customers on time.

(D) Recording the customer information correctly is very important to satisfaction.

GO TO NEXT PAGE

53. The first step in Step 3 is to "rectify way-bills." What does this mean?

   (A) Attach bills and send them to the dock.

   (B) Correct errors on the lists.

   (C) Cancel bills before sending them to the dock.

   (D) Rush-stamp the bills.

54. Why should the Office be responsible for determining if an item is in stock?

   (A) Because the items are in the Warehouse

   (B) Because the Office has the customer on the phone so changes can be made quickly

   (C) Because the items are moved from the Loading Dock to the Warehouse

   (D) Because the Office is able to ask the Loading Dock if an item is in stock

DIRECTIONS: Select the word or group of words that has the same, or nearly the same, meaning as the word that is in **boldface**.

55. **Ballast** most nearly means

   (A) heavy metal used to stabilize a ship.

   (B) a sail on a ship.

   (C) life preservers on a ship.

   (D) songs that tell a story.

56. **Abhor** most nearly means

   (A) hate.

   (B) adore.

   (C) worship.

   (D) distemper.

57. **Counterfeit** most nearly means

   (A) foreign.

   (B) obscure.

   (C) fake; false.

   (D) dim.

58. **Enfranchise** most nearly means

   (A) explode.

   (B) give voting rights.

   (C) enlist.

   (D) laughable.

59. **Hamper** most nearly means

   (A) hinder; obstruct.

   (B) allow to happen.

   (C) small, furry animal.

   (D) tear apart.

60. **Kindle** most nearly means

   (A) to start a fire.

   (B) to comfort.

   (C) to develop.

   (D) to begin a meeting.

61. **Noxious** most nearly means

   (A) open; airy.

   (B) harmful; poisonous; lethal.

   (C) closed; locked.

   (D) stupid; unintelligent.

62. **Placid** most nearly means

   (A) faulty.

   (B) horrible.

   (C) calm; peaceful.

   (D) energetic; tense.

GO TO NEXT PAGE ➡

63. **Remuneration** most nearly means
    (A) to count again.
    (B) to spread rumors.
    (C) payment for work done.
    (D) gift to charity.

64. **Hubbub** most likely means
    (A) lovely.
    (B) horrible.
    (C) chaos.
    (D) calm.

65. **Limpid** most likely means
    (A) strong.
    (B) soft.
    (C) hard.
    (D) liquid.

66. **Drivel** most likely means
    (A) exceptional.
    (B) smart.
    (C) photogenic.
    (D) nonsensical.

67. **Transfusion** most likely means
    (A) to bind together.
    (B) act of taking blood and moving it.
    (C) quietly moving.
    (D) steaming.

68. **Incalculable** most likely means
    (A) greater than estimated.
    (B) less than needed.
    (C) as much as expected.
    (D) between what was thought.

69. **Ballistic** most likely means
    (A) forcefully moving.
    (B) sitting on a stable surface.
    (C) inching along.
    (D) walking.

70. **Devout** most likely means
    (A) flippant.
    (B) careful.
    (C) important.
    (D) religious feeling of commitment.

71. **Decadent** most likely means
    (A) pious.
    (B) luxurious.
    (C) careful.
    (D) important.

72. **Autonomy** most likely means
    (A) self-government.
    (B) togetherness.
    (C) runs like a car.
    (D) sporty.

73. **Banal** most likely means
    (A) creative.
    (B) boring.
    (C) original.
    (D) scholastic.

GO TO NEXT PAGE ➡

DIRECTIONS: In each of the sentences below, the word in **boldface** may be unfamiliar to you. Use the other words in the sentence to help you decide what the word in **boldface** means.

74. The **cursory** manner in which she prepared her project did nothing to help her grade.
    (A) enlivened.
    (B) angry.
    (C) sad.
    (D) hasty.

75. Though the sailor really wanted to stay on the mainland, the captain's **distemper** made him run onboard.
    (A) pleasant attitude.
    (B) command.
    (C) snappish attitude.
    (D) question.

76. Hannah's **smart** outfit was perfect for tea.
    (A) neat.
    (B) sloppy.
    (C) outdated.
    (D) intelligent.

77. Alexandra decided that the **indigo** pants were the most flattering for her figure.
    (A) black.
    (B) red.
    (C) baggy.
    (D) blue.

78. Rufus and Buck **capered** with the puppies in the yard.
    (A) jogged.
    (B) rolled.
    (C) walked.
    (D) frolicked.

79. The dentist's **emphatic** reply made the toothless patient feel better.
    (A) forceful.
    (B) sad.
    (C) angry.
    (D) melancholy.

80. Opal and Judy found Beau's reply about the dance **irrelevant** to the current problem.
    (A) not needed.
    (B) stupid.
    (C) smart.
    (D) enlightened.

81. Melissa's **ebullience** overshadowed the rest of the class.
    (A) cubes used for flavoring.
    (B) bubbly attitude.
    (C) melancholy attitude.
    (D) intelligent replies.

GO TO NEXT PAGE ➡

82. Kaitlin **incinerated** all of the evidence against her.

   (A) wrote.

   (B) saved.

   (C) burned.

   (D) planted.

83. Besides being able to vote, the opportunities to drive and **imbibe** alcoholic beverages are the big milestones of life.

   (A) bottle.

   (B) can.

   (C) slurp.

   (D) drink.

84. With the **inundation** of the flu and other winter illnesses, doctor offices have been very busy with appointments.

   (A) rush.

   (B) trickle.

   (C) beginning.

   (D) end.

GO TO NEXT PAGE ➡

PRETEST
MATHEMATICS SECTION

1. What is the value of the expression 2.4×10^3?
   - (A) 2.400
   - (B) 24
   - (C) 240
   - (D) 2,400

2. Simplify: $\dfrac{3!}{4!}$
   - (A) $\dfrac{1}{2}$
   - (B) .75
   - (C) $\dfrac{1}{4}$
   - (D) 12

3. A businessman has a meal at a nice restaurant. He likes to tip 15% when the service is excellent. How much money will he tip on a $40 meal?
   - (A) $4.50
   - (B) $6.00
   - (C) $6.75
   - (D) $7.00

4. In one classroom, there are 5 boys and 15 girls. What is the ratio of the number of boys to the total number of students?
   - (A) 1:2
   - (B) 2:3
   - (C) 1:3
   - (D) 1:4

5. Which of the following points lies on the line expressed by the equation $2x + 3y = 12$?
   - (A) (3, 2)
   - (B) (2, 3)
   - (C) (1, 4)
   - (D) (6, 1)

6. The points (1, 1), (2, 3), (4, 1), and (5, 3) are the vertices of a polygon. What type of polygon is formed by these points?
   - (A) Triangle
   - (B) Square
   - (C) Parallelogram
   - (D) Trapezoid

7. Simplify: $\dfrac{15x^2y^4}{3xy^2}$
   - (A) $5x^3y$
   - (B) $5xy^6$
   - (C) $5x^3y^6$
   - (D) $5xy^2$

8. What is the next number in this sequence?
   2, 5, 11, 23, 47, 95, ____
   - (A) 105
   - (B) 174
   - (C) 191
   - (D) 203

9. General admission tickets to a music concert hall regularly cost $32. They are on sale for 20% off. What is the sale price of the tickets?
   - (A) $25.60
   - (B) $26.00
   - (C) $27.25
   - (D) $28.00

10. What is the slope of the following line?

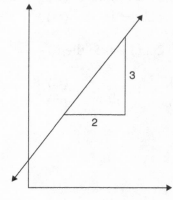

   - (A) $-\dfrac{2}{3}$
   - (B) $\dfrac{3}{2}$
   - (C) $\dfrac{2}{3}$
   - (D) $-\dfrac{3}{2}$

GO TO NEXT PAGE ➡

11. The fraction $\dfrac{4}{16}$ is equal to which value?

   (A) $\dfrac{1}{8}$ **(C)** $\dfrac{3}{6}$

   (B) .38   **(D)** .25

12. Estimate: 216×192

   (A) 400   **(C)** 40,000

   (B) 4,000   **(D)** 400,000

13.

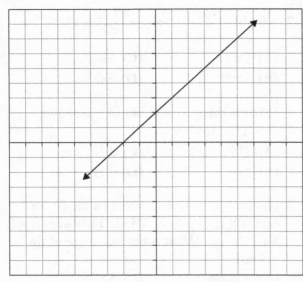

What is the equation of the line shown on the graph?

   (A) $y = 2x + 1$ **(C)** $y = x - 2$

   (B) $y = 2x - 1$ **(D)** $y = x + 2$

14. If $x = 2$ and $y = 5$, then $\dfrac{xy + 4}{2} - 3 =$

   (A) 4.   **(C)** 8.

   (B) 6.   **(D)** 10.

15. The absolute value of -7 is

   (A) $-\dfrac{1}{7}$.   **(C)** $\dfrac{1}{7}$.

   (B) 7.   **(D)** -7.

16. Four cards are shown below: a heart, a diamond, a moon, and a sun.

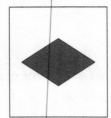

If you randomly select a single card, what is the probability that it is **not** a heart?

   (A) .25   **(C)** .75

   (B) .33   **(D)** 1.25

GO TO NEXT PAGE ➡

17.

Delivery Company	Customer Complaints	Months in Business
SPEEDY	100	25
ON TIME	10	2

ON TIME Delivery Company used the data in the table above to support their claim, "We have one-tenth the number of customer complaints that SPEEDY Delivery Company has." Why is this claim misleading?

(A) On the average, SPEEDY has more complaints.

(B) The claim should say "one-fourth" of the number of complaints.

(C) The claim should say "one-fifth" of the number of complaints.

(D) On the average, ON TIME has more complaints per month.

18. How many different ways can you order three books on a shelf where order matters?

(A) 3   (C) 5
(B) 4   (D) 6

19. Solve for x: $4x + 4 = 7$

(A) $\dfrac{3}{4}$ (C) $\dfrac{1}{4}$

(B) $\dfrac{1}{2}$ (D) $\dfrac{4}{3}$

20. What is the solution to the following system of equations?
$y = 2x - 3$
$y = 3x$

(A) $(4, -5)$ (C) $(-3, -9)$
(B) $(3, 0)$ (D) $(6, 2)$

21. Given the similar figures of a rectangle below, find the length of the missing side.

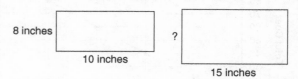

8 inches

10 inches

?

15 inches

(A) 6 inches   (C) 10 inches
(B) 9 inches   (D) 12 inches

22. What is the slope of a line through two points with coordinates of $(4, 2)$ and $(6, 8)$?

(A) -3 (C) $\dfrac{1}{3}$

(B) $-\dfrac{1}{3}$ (D) 3

23. Evaluate:

$a^2 + \dfrac{3b}{12} + 10$ for $a = 7$ and $b = -4$

(A) 42   (C) 63
(B) 58   (D) 71

GO TO NEXT PAGE ➡

24. Solve: $\dfrac{x}{3} - 2 = 8$

(A) 18   (C) 24

(B) 21   (D) 30

25. The graph shows the relationship between the number of CDs purchased and the total cost. What is the price of each CD?

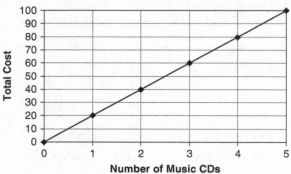

(A) $15   (C) $25

(B) $20   (D) $30

26. What expression does the graph represent?

(A) $x > 3$ (C) $x < 3$

(B) $x \geqslant 3$ (D) $x \leqslant 3$

27. On a math quiz, Jim is asked to write down the mathematical expression for the words "five more than three times a number." Jim incorrectly answers $8x$. Which expression should he have used?

(A) $3x + 5$ (C) $5x + 3$

(B) $5(3x)$ (D) $5x$

28. The chart shows the English test scores of three students.

	Test 1	Test 2	Test 3	Test 4
Peter	10	7	5	4
Paul	3	6	9	10
Mary	9	8	10	5

What is Mary's average score?

(A) 7   (C) 9

(B) 8   (D) 10

29. A fair coin is flipped twice. What is the probability of getting 2 heads?

(A) 10%   (C) 50%

(B) 25%   (D) 75%

30. Which of the graphs below could be the graph for the equation $y = x^2$?

(A)

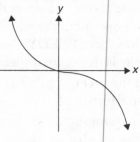

(B)

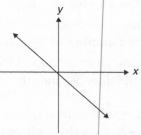

(C)

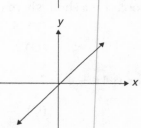

(D)

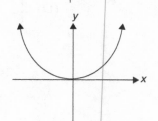

GO TO NEXT PAGE ➡

31. In the triangle, what is the measurement of the missing angle?

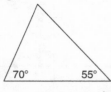

(A) 35°   (C) 55°

(B) 45°   (D) 65°

32. What is the value of *x* in the triangle?

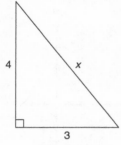

(A) 5   (C) 7

(B) 6   (D) 12

33. A purse contains four different coins. How many different combinations of three coins can you choose, where order does not matter?

(A) 3   (C) 6

(B) 4   (D) 9

34. Ashley scored the following number of points in her high school basketball games: 6, 0, 3, 7, 12, 2, 5. What is her median number of points scored?

(A) 2   (C) 7

(B) 5   (D) 12

35.

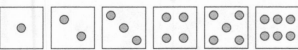

A die has six sides. What is the probability of rolling a 2 or a 3 in one throw of a fair die?

(A) $\frac{1}{6}$ (C) $\frac{1}{2}$

(B) $\frac{1}{3}$ (D) $\frac{2}{3}$

36. Tom flipped a coin 10 times, and each time it came up tails. If he flips the coin 1 more time, what is the probability that it will come up heads?

(A) $\frac{1}{2}$ (C) $\frac{3}{4}$

(B) $\frac{4}{5}$ (D) $\frac{9}{10}$

37. In the figure, if the measure of angle *q* is 55°, what is the measure of angle *m*? Assume parallel lines.

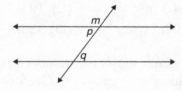

(A) 35°   (C) 70°

(B) 55°   (D) 125°

38. The scaled drawing of the tennis court uses the scale 1 inch = 24 feet.

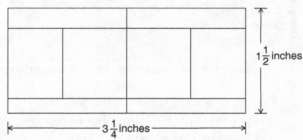

What is the length in feet of the tennis court?

(A) 66 feet   (C) 80 feet

(B) 78 feet   (D) 92 feet

GO TO NEXT PAGE ➡

39. What is the area of the shaded region in the figure?

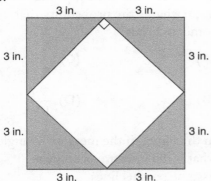

(A) 4.5 in²   (C) 18 in²

(B) 9 in²   (D) 32 in²

40. The graph shows the number of oranges produced by a grower in California for the years 1997, 1999, and 2001.

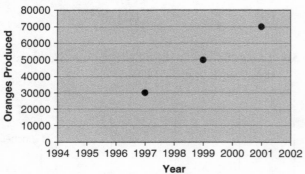

From this graph, which of the following was the most probable number of oranges produced by this grower in 1995?

(A) 0   (C) 20,000

(B) 10,000   (D) 30,000

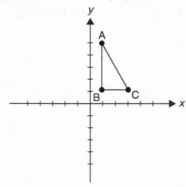

41. Which of the following triangles $A'B'C'$ is the result of the image of triangle ABC reflecting the triangle ABC across the y-axis?

(A)

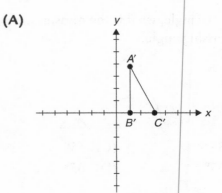

(B)

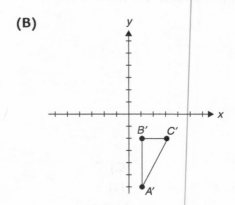

(C)

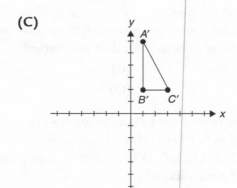

(D)

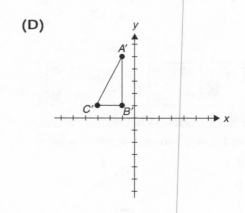

GO TO NEXT PAGE ➡

42. The graph represents the high temperature for five days of the week.

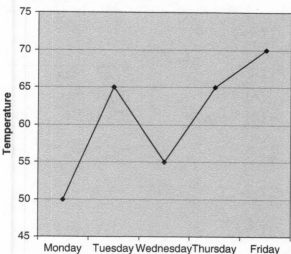

Which day had the greatest increase in temperature over that of the previous day?

(A) Tuesday   **(C)** Thursday

(B) Wednesday   **(D)** Friday

43. What is the area in square units of the figure shown?

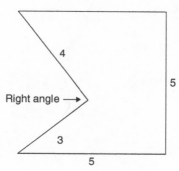

(A) 12   **(C)** 19

(B) 18   **(D)** 20

44. In a certain class, the number of boys, b, is equal to four times the number of girls, g. Which of the following equations expresses this relationship?

(A) $4b = g$ **(C)** $gb = 4$

(B) $4b = gb$ **(D)** $4g = b$

45. Solve: $10 - 4 \times 2$

(A) -8 **(C)** 12

(B) 2   **(D)** 28

46.

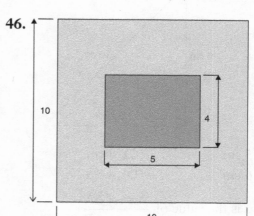

A rectangular duck pond is on a square lot. The rest of the lot is a flower garden. In the scaled drawing shown, each unit represents 10 feet. How many square feet is the flower garden?

(A) 1,400   **(C)** 7,500

(B) 4,000   **(D)** 8,000

47. What is the approximate circumference of the circle shown?

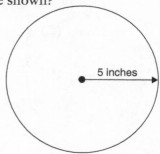

(A) 10 inches   **(C)** 31 inches

(B) 16 inches   **(D)** 78 inches

GO TO NEXT PAGE ➡

PRETEST

48. On the right triangle shown, what is the length of the missing side?

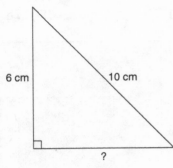

6 cm   10 cm

?

(A) 5 cm   (C) 8 cm

(B) 6 cm   (D) 9 cm

49. What is the value of $\dfrac{\text{Area of } \Delta A}{\text{Area of } \Delta B}$

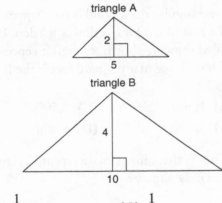

triangle A

2

5

triangle B

4

10

(A) $\dfrac{1}{8}$ (C) $\dfrac{1}{2}$

(B) $\dfrac{1}{4}$ (D) $\dfrac{3}{4}$

50. Given the similar figures of a rectangle below, find the length of the missing side.

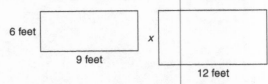

6 feet

9 feet

x

12 feet

(A) 8 feet   (C) 10 feet

(B) 9 feet   (D) 11 feet

STOP

Pretest Answer Key

Question Number	Correct Answer
ENGLISH-LANGUAGE ARTS SECTION: LANGUAGE SUBTEST	
1.	(A)
2.	(A)
3.	(B)
4.	(B)
5.	(C)
6.	(D)
7.	(B)
8.	(C)
9.	(C)
10.	(B)
11.	(C)
12.	(A)
13.	(B)
14.	(A)
15.	(C)
16.	(D)
17.	(B)
18.	(D)
19.	(A)
20.	(D)
21.	(D)
22.	(C)
23.	(B)
24.	(C)

Question Number	Correct Answer
25.	(A)
26.	(B)
27.	(B)
28.	(C)
29.	(B)
30.	(C)
31.	(D)
32.	(A)
33.	(C)
34.	(D)
35.	(B)
36.	(A)
37.	(B)
38.	(C)
39.	(D)
40.	(C)
41.	(A)
42.	(A)
43.	(B)
44.	(A)
45.	(B)
46.	(A)
47.	(A)
48.	(A)
ENGLISH-LANGUAGE ARTS SECTION: READING SUBTEST	
1.	(A)
2.	(B)
3.	(D)
4.	(B)
5.	(C)
6.	(B)
7.	(D)
8.	(C)
9.	(B)

Question Number	Correct Answer
10.	(A)
11.	(A)
12.	(A)
13.	(D)
14.	(C)
15.	(A)
16.	(C)
17.	(B)
18.	(B)
19.	(B)
20.	(A)
21.	(C)
22.	(A)
23.	(C)
24.	(B)
25.	(B)
26.	(B)
27.	(C)
28.	(D)
29.	(C)
30.	(B)
31.	(D)
32.	(C)
33.	(B)
34.	(C)
35.	(D)
36.	(D)
37.	(B)
38.	(C)
39.	(A)
40.	(C)
41.	(B)
42.	(A)
43.	(C)
44.	(C)
45.	(C)
46.	(C)

Question Number	Correct Answer
47.	(B)
48.	(B)
49.	(C)
50.	(B)
51.	(A)
52.	(B)
53.	(B)
54.	(B)
55.	(A)
56.	(A)
57.	(C)
58.	(B)
59.	(A)
60.	(C)
61.	(B)
62.	(C)
63.	(C)
64.	(C)
65.	(B)
66.	(D)
67.	(B)
68.	(A)
69.	(A)
70.	(D)
71.	(B)
72.	(A)
73.	(B)
74.	(D)
75.	(C)
76.	(A)
77.	(D)
78.	(D)
79.	(A)
80.	(A)
81.	(B)
82.	(C)
83.	(D)
84.	(A)

Question Number	Correct Answer
MATHEMATICS SECTION	
1.	(D)
2.	(C)
3.	(B)
4.	(D)
5.	(A)
6.	(C)
7.	(D)
8.	(C)
9.	(A)
10.	(B)
11.	(D)
12.	(C)
13.	(D)
14.	(A)
15.	(B)
16.	(C)
17.	(D)
18.	(D)
19.	(A)
20.	(C)
21.	(D)
22.	(D)
23.	(B)
24.	(D)
25.	(B)
26.	(B)
27.	(A)
28.	(B)
29.	(B)
30.	(D)
31.	(C)
32.	(A)
33.	(B)
34.	(B)
35.	(B)
36.	(A)

Question Number	Correct Answer
37.	(D)
38.	(B)
39.	(C)
40.	(B)
41.	(D)
42.	(A)
43.	(C)
44.	(D)
45.	(B)
46.	(D)
47.	(C)
48.	(C)
49.	(B)
50.	(A)

ENGLISH-LANGUAGE ARTS SECTION

Language Subtest

1. **(A)** his
   "His" is the singular possessive. "Everyone" is a singular noun; therefore, the pronoun should be singular. "They're" is a contraction while "their" is plural possessive.

2. **(A)** will have been
   The beginning of the sentence gives the time of the statement—the "beginning of next term." Therefore, the future tense is represented here.

3. **(B)** did not keep any
   For this sentence, "did not keep any" is the only appropriate choice. The other choices all represent double negatives: double negatives are when two negative statements are represented in the same verb phrase. This is considered incorrect and inferior diction.

4. **(B)** for his
   "For his" is correct because "man" takes a male possessive adjective. Because it is "his" daughter, the incorrect choices would not make sense.

5. **(C)** require
   The subject of this sentence, musicians, is plural; therefore, the verb must be plural as well to agree with the subject. All of the other choices do not agree with the plural verb.

6. **(D)** Correct as is.
   The correct form is represented in the original sentence. The comma is represented after the verb "said," "it" is capitalized, and the end punctuation is included inside the end quotation marks.

7. **(B)** Maddie and I
   For this sentence, there is a dual subject: Maddie and I. "I" is always used as a subject in a sentence, and it cannot be used as an object. "Me" is an object pronoun and should not be used as a subject pronoun. "Myself" is reflexive and it is never used as a subject alone.

8. **(C)** Let's make

"Let's" is a contraction of "let us." Contractions always have an apostrophe because they are the blending of two words.

9. **(C)** I bought a shirt

The first verb, "went," gives an indication of the past. Therefore, "bought" is the only correct answer. "Will buy" is future tense, and "would buy" implies the possibility of something happening in the future.

10. **(B)** except

"Accept" is the consent to receive something. "Excepting" is a progressive tense verb, but it must have a helping verb to be correct. "Except" means not to include something; therefore, except is the best choice.

11. **(C)** for carrots, peas, onions, and celery

This sentence is an example of how to correctly write items in a list with commas. There are four items in this list, and each item needs to be separated by a comma.

12. **(A)** Dr. Smith

"Dr." is a title, and it should be capitalized. "Smith" is the last name; therefore, it should be capitalized as well.

13. **(B)** Chico State University

This is an example of capitalization rules for an organization. All of the words need to be capitalized in the name for it to be correct.

14. **(A)** sung by

Prepositions express a relation to another word or element. In this example, the opera singer sings a song; therefore, "by" is the only correct choice because the singer is actually doing the singing.

15. **(C)** September 2, 1967

This example shows how to use commas correctly in a date. The comma goes after the day and before the year only. No other commas are needed.

16. **(D)** Correct as is.

"Mt. McKinley" is a proper noun and the full name of a mountain; therefore, both the "Mt." (the abbreviation for "mount") and "McKinley" are capitalized.

17. **(B)** teams shook

This sentence is in the past; therefore, the correct verb must be in the past tense. Also, "teams" is plural, so the verb must also be plural so the agreement is correct. "Teams shook" is the only correct choice because it has the plural subject and the correct past plural form of the verb "shake."

18. **(D)** Correct as is.

This sentence is in the past tense and the subject is singular. In this example, "was bought" is the only correct choice because it fulfills these two requirements.

19. **(A)**   was enjoying

This sentence shows time happening in two different areas of the sentence. The man was working on his crossword, and THEN the alarm went off. The distinction is important because the man's action is in the past. It happened BEFORE the alarm went off. Therefore, it uses the past progressive verb tense, "was enjoying": it was an action that was happening before the alarm went off.

20. **(D)**   Correct as is.

This sentence is an example of using correct quotation marks with a question mark in the dialogue. The question mark goes on the inside of the end quotation marks in the dialogue; a comma is not needed because the question mark fulfills the punctuation requirement.

21. **(D)**   Correct as is.

Commas and colon use are covered in this question. The colon shows that there is a list following the colon; in this case, the names. The three names are a list, and there is a comma separating each name, including the commas before the "and" and after "Suzanne."

22. **(C)**   Even though the exam was very challenging, I did just fine.

The beginning of each sentence is headed by a conjunction. Each conjunction gives a different meaning to the overall sentence. The one that makes the most sense is **(C)**. **(A)** implies that the exam was very hard, so it doesn't show WHY the person "did just fine." **(B)** implies that because the exam was hard, the person "did just fine," which doesn't make sense.

23. **(B)**   Jenny is a student who is talkative, witty, intelligent, and friendly.

This example is another lesson about using commas correctly in a list. There are four adjectives that describe Jenny. Each one is separated by a comma, including the one before the "and."

24. **(C)**   One of the oldest religions is Hinduism.

"Hinduism" is a religion. Religions are capitalized because they are proper nouns. "Religion," however, is not a name nor does it have special significance in this sentence. Therefore, it should not be capitalized.

25. **(A)**   she will give her receipt to

This sentence explains that something will happen in the future once "Liz returns from the store." Therefore, the tense of the verb should be in future tense. Secondly, the use of the preposition "to" is correct because Liz is giving the receipt "to" her boss directly. "At" would show that Liz is giving the receipt to a place rather than a person.

26. **(B)**   I enjoyed the movie for its story, dialogue, and musical score.

This question is another lesson about using commas correctly in a list. There are three adjectives that describe the movie. Each one is separated by a comma, including the one before the "and." Additionally, score is modified by "musical." "Musical" is an adjective and adjectives modify nouns. "Music," on the other hand, is a noun and would not be the correct answer.

27. **(B)**   apple was placed on the table
In this sentence, the correct form of the verb is the past tense. "Placed" in this sentence needs a helping verb to make sense; therefore, "was placed" is the correct choice.

28. **(C)**   are
There are three subjects in this sentence: Luca, Anton, and I. Because there is a plural subject, the verb must be plural as well. Also, the sentence is in the present tense, so only a present tense, plural verb would be correct.

29. **(B)**   plays tennis every day because she wants
This sentence has two verbs in it and both of the verbs are in the same tense. To show continuity, both of the verbs must be in the same tense. "Plays" is a present tense, singular verb. The only correct choice is "wants."

30. **(C)**   Tuesday, June 22.
There should always be a comma after the specific day in the American style. One should put a comma after the day of the week, Tuesday in this case (and a proper noun, which is always capitalized) to distinguish that day from the rest of the date.

31. **(D)**   Correct as is.
Anytime a conjunction is in the middle of a sentence, it is always preceded by a semi-colon and followed by a comma. This is a semi-colon rule of punctuation.

32. **(A)**   If the soccer team wins this next game, they will have won the last four in a row.
This sentence takes on the complex verb tense future perfect. The beginning phrase "if the soccer team wins this next game" tells us that the tense is something that could happen in the future. Therefore, the verb tense in the second part of the sentence must align with the first verb. Therefore, "will have won" is the best choice.

33. **(C)**   Marley sped down the hill, knocked over the chair, and ran into the class.
In this sentence, a list of actions are separated by a comma. However, two of the verbs are in the present tense ("runs" and "knocks") while "sped" is in past tense. All of the verb tenses must be the same, so the only correct choice is **(C)**.

34. **(D)**   Correct as is.
This sentence tests preposition usage. "In" is a preposition that says something is put inside of something else. **(A)** is "next by," which is completely incorrect. "Next to" would imply the cheese was placed beside the refrigerator. "Unto" means "to" which would imply that the cheese was brought to the refrigerator, but not put inside of it. Finally, "between" implies that the cheese would be placed in an area with the refrigerator on one side, while there would be something else on the other side.

35. **(B)**   we will plant trees
This sentence shows an object, "tree," and the plural subject "we." However, there are two problems with this sentence. "We," being plural, must have a plural verb. "Will plant" is the best choice. Also, "tree," being singular, needs to have an article modifying it for the sentence to make sense. For example, "a tree" or "the tree" would be a good

choice. Since this is not an option, the best choice is to make "tree" plural. "The trees" is considered acceptable, but it was not an option. Therefore, **(B)** is the best choice.

36. **(A)** After she wrote the long story, which won first prize, she started working on the sequel.
This sentence has an appositive inside it. An appositive is a descriptive phrase that defines a noun. In this sentence, "which won first prize" is the appositive, and it modifies "story." Appositives can be removed from a sentence without changing the integrity of the original structure, and they should always be separated by commas.

37. **(B)** Once Mary arrived at the store.
To correctly answer this question, verb tense is the important element. Mary had to arrive at the store BEFORE she could count the money; therefore, the first verb must be in past tense. Also, since "Mary" is a singular noun, it will take a singular verb. "Arrived" is the best choice.

38. **(C)** The fish is prepared well
The skill tested here is verb tense. "Prepare" is a verb that usually takes a helping verb. "Is preparing" is the progressive tense, which means something is happening now. This tense does not fit this sentence. "Was prepares" is not a valid choice because the correct form would be "was prepared." "Is prepared" is the best answer.

39. **(D)** Correct as is.
"Eating" is a gerund, which is a noun that looks like a verb with an -ing ending. "Eating," in this case, is a thing, not an action, and it works as the subject in this sentence. Because it is singular, it also takes the singular verb "is."

40. **(C)** The items on the shopping list included: apples, oranges, peanuts, butter, and milk.
Comma and colon use are covered in this question. The colon shows that there is a list following the word "included"; in this case, the items on the grocery list. This sentence, however, is a little tricky. Notice that "peanuts" and "butter" follow closely together. Be careful not to think that the word is "peanut butter" and not include the needed comma. The comma is needed between these two words because it distinguishes the two items from each other.

41. **(A)** "Yes," said Dan. "I will swim this afternoon."
(A) is the best choice for this sentence because the comma after "yes" and before the end quotation mark is present. Additionally, "said" is not capitalized because it is still part of the sentence. Finally, "yes" must have end quotation marks because that part of the dialogue is finished.

42. **(A)** Both the mother's and father's cameras were in good condition.
This sentence tests knowledge of possessive. Though somewhat tricky, the word "cameras" tell you that that there is more than one camera. Therefore, each person had a camera. Because each person had a separate camera and owned in singularly, both "mother" and "father" are possessive.

43. **(B)** they should enter immediately.
The sample has an error in number. "Chefs" is plural; therefore, the following pronoun must also be plural. "His," however, is singular and is incorrect; "she" follows the same line of reasoning. "You" is a different point of view. Because the main part of the sentence is in third person point of view, "you" is an incorrect choice.

44. **(A)** The northern states include Vermont and Maryland.
"Northern" should only be capitalized if the author is using it as a name or designated location. For example, "Northern Hemisphere."

45. **(B)** Maddie and me.
The usage of "I" over "me" is regularly misused in these types of sentences. "Me" is an object pronoun. It can only be used in the object position: direct object, indirect object, or the object of a preposition. "I" is never used as an object. Consequently, "Maddie and me" is correct.

46. **(A)** bring.
"To bring" is an infinitive (the basic form of any verb. It is represented by the singular present tense and "to" is in front of it). Therefore, none of the other choices is valid.

47. **(A)** the painters had learned how to trim properly.
In the beginning of the sentence, "were finished" shows that the statement is in the past. Thus, the following verb must also be in past tense. "Painters" is plural, so the verb must be plural as well. As a result, "had learned" is the best choice.

48. **(A)** The tournament this winter will be held on the main green.
Neither "tournament" nor "winter" is used as a proper noun here. "Tournament" is not a name of an event in this sentence, and "winter" is simply used to describe a season.

PRETEST DETAILED EXPLANATIONS
ENGLISH-LANGUAGE ARTS SECTION
Writing Task

The following is an example of a well-written essay. This essay would earn a 5–6 on the Writing Rubric.

For the last few decades, the issues skateboards and business owner concerns have been a hot topic among skateboard enthusiasts. Though there are valid arguments for both sides, the facts show that though skateboarding is a sport that merits practice, the disruption it causes to business patrons and owners is a legitimate concern.

To practice skateboarding, one must have a smooth, even surface: cement walkways, stairs, parking lots, and winding walkways are the perfect environments for skateboard fans. Unfortunately, most areas with large expanses of cement are business locations, and these areas can become a local Mecca for neighborhood kids to practice their skateboarding tricks. Elderly customers or those with children are especially at risk from the runaway skateboard to someone falling off their board and accidently hitting them. Sometimes, even walking two by two or with packages can become an obstacle course of dodging boards, kids flying past on racing skateboards, or the random elbow or arm flinging into space. Many local business owners can easily become concerned that their patrons may get hurt, annoyed, or not be able to find parking, and therefore, they may look to other places to shop. Finally, the liability to the business owners can drastically increase their insurance costs, let alone their emotional distress should a child get seriously hurt outside of their stores.

In conclusion, although skateboarding is a entertaining, appealing sport, it is better practiced in a designated facility where the boarders can manipulate their environments safely, away from local shoppers and businesses. Besides, if the skateboard fans can practice freely, away from glass, passing cars, and local shoppers, they will be much more able to perfect their tricks and enjoy themselves with their friends without repercussions.

Reading Subtest

1. **(A)** imagery
   Imagery in poetry is the use of descriptive words that appeal to the senses. In this poem, Williams appeals to sight with the vivid contrasts in color. There is no metaphor or simile, a comparison of two unlike things. Irony is a twist in events.

2. **(B)** coated
   "Glazed" is defined as a substance that is smooth and shiny. The other choices are too light in substance ("dotted," "lined," and "sprinkled").

3. **(D)** Four
   There are four stanzas in this poem. Each stanza is separated from the one above it by a blank line.

4. **(B)** The imagery is striking for such a short poem.
   There is no rhyme scheme in this poem, and there is no instance of alliteration (the repetition of consonant sounds). "Onomatopoeia" is a word that sounds like what it is, as in "BAM" or "WHOOSH." Because there is so much description in this poem, imagery is the best answer.

5. **(C)** he is dressed in a crazy assortment of hardware that has a ghoulish appearance.
   "Halloween and hardware" is a very descriptive line to describe Harrison's appearance. "Halloween" evokes an image of ghosts and witches, and "hardware" implies tools. The tone of the piece is ominous; therefore, "ghoulish" is the best choice.

6. **(B)** glasses, glasses
   "Spectacles" is used in both instances as eyeglasses. A "spectacle" can also be an important event or nuisance, but nuisance does not fit in either meaning of spectacle.

7. **(D)** Impediments to hold back his true potential
   The definition of "handicap" is something that impairs one's performance. "Physical deformities" could be a viable option, but the context of the passage suggests that there is

nothing physically wrong with Harrison: he is made to look funny for a certain reason. Therefore, **(D)** is the best answer.

8. (C) Policemen
Though we don't know exactly what H-G men are in the story, it is implied that they are "controllers" of some sort that have requirements. Thus, "policemen" is the best choice.

9. (B) severe
The text says that Harrison has to wear very thick lenses in his glasses. He also has to wear other heavy handicaps. Therefore, "whanging" would most likely mean "severe" because it most aligns with the context of the passage.

10. (A) precise
"Military neatness" here is a descriptive phrase. "Military" usually implies a sense of order or structure. Therefore, "structured order" would most likely mean precise.

11. (A) his existence as compared to others
"Race" means to compete against others from one point to another. "Race of life" would mean that Harrison is competing against others in life, or his existence. Thus, "his existence as compared to others" is a better choice than **(B)** "a contest that runs his life." Life, in this selection, does not "run him." Rather, the competition is Harrison against others.

12. (A) clownish
The last paragraph describes Harrison as wearing "a rubber ball nose," having teeth "painted as snaggle-tooth random," and keeping his "eyebrows shaved off." If you picture this in your mind, a clown image definitely becomes prominent, and is a much better choice than the other answers.

13. (D) the overall style of the car
"Body style" is defined as shape and style of the body of a car. The other answers only describe certain aspects of the car (i.e., "car doors" and "how many people can sit in the car").

14. (C) the maximum number of people who can sit in the car safely
"Seating capacity" is easy to understand if you know the meaning of "capacity," which is the maximum contained amount. Further defining "capacity" by adding "seating." expands the definition to mean how many maximum seats are available in the car.

15. (A) Warranty miles refer to an established number of miles for the car to be serviced without charge to the owner. Warranty months are the months the warranty is in effect.
The best way to get this answer is to have prior knowledge of the word "warranty." The other answers do not make sense because a warranty is not defined by an owner—it is for the car itself. No matter who drives the car, the warranty is still in effect. Second, warranties are for miles, i.e., how many miles a car can be driven and what be covered for mechanical defects. Warranty months state the length of time the warranty miles are in effect.

16. **(C)** 4
    Knowing the seating capacity leads you to this answer. Since the car has four seats, four seatbelts is the best choice.

17. **(B)** Car #2
    To answer this question correctly, you must review the chart. Each car has a set of standards and options, as well as the total price. To make the best selection, you have to review all of the options for each car, determine which car has the most options, and then look at the price. Car #1 has the most standard features, has more PowerTrain warranty miles, gets the best gas mileage, and is slightly more expensive than Car #3. Car #3, though a little cheaper, has less PowerTrain warranty miles and fewer standard options. Car #2 gets less gas mileage, has less PowerTrain warranty miles, and is significantly more expensive than the other two cars.

18. **(B)** it may be available, but it is not listed on this sheet
    As the reader, we don't know, for sure, if the option noted as "not listed" is available or not. This particular chart may not have it listed, for reasons unknown to us. To conclusively say that the options are absolutely not available would be a mistake here.

19. **(B)** it is included as part of the base price
    "Standard" is defined as the "norm," or regular items something has without additions. Thus, the correct answer is that the car is made with that option already in place and would not be something optional to the buyer.

20. **(A)** $875
    Though this question is somewhat of a math problem, you have to discern which car has the most highway mileage and which has the lowest highway mileage. That is how you would find the difference in cost.

21. **(C)** Car #1 and Car #3
    The skill tested in this question is how to correctly discern which two cars have the best PowerTrain warranty miles. Car #1 has 65,000 and Car #3 has 100,000, both of which are higher than Car #2, which has 60,000.

22. **(A)** Car #1
    Car #1 has four standard options, while Car #2 has three. Car #3 has only two listed for sure.

23. **(C)** a life-sustaining element for commerce
    "Lifeblood" is defined as the blood necessary to support life. Because Obama uses the term "lifeblood" with economy, you have to think about what the "blood" of the economy would be. In this case, **(C)** is the best choice because "commerce" and "economy" are closely linked.

24. **(B)** it moves like blood in the veins
    Obama talks about credit and how it "flows" throughout his speech. Because he uses "lifeblood in the economy" earlier in the speech, the best answer is **(B)** Flowing "like dirt in a vacuum" implies suction, and electricity moves very, very fast. Music ebbs and swells and doesn't translate in meaning in this selection.

25. (B)   becomes scarcer

"Dries up" means to evaporate. Using this term with credit implies that credit is becoming less and less available. Since credit is not viscous or concrete like water (where **(C)** would be the best answer), the best choice for this question is **(B)**.

26. (B)   accounting files

Before computers, people would keep ledgers or notebooks of their accounting files and all of the math was done manually. The terms "books" has been kept for hundreds of years, whether accounts are computerized or not. This is an example of general knowledge of language in literature.

27. (C)   trust

"Confidence" in this selection is not self-esteem, which means how one feels about oneself. Nor is it a secret told to someone (i.e., "in confidence"). "Life" is not a viable option. "Confidence" in this statement means to "trust" that the administration is doing what is best for the nation. Inserting the other options for "confidence" would not make sense with the rest of the piece.

28. (D)   the entire infrastructure of American living is based around credit and the ability to give and receive loans

Obama's speech revolves around the middle class's need for credit for homes, cars, and businesses. Paragraph #2 discusses the need for loans and the consequences of fear when loans are denied to the public. Obama's speech implies that low confidence stops people from spending, which affects everything else until the whole system spirals out of control.

29. (C)   With no lending, families cannot spend money on homes or transportation and businesses suffer and mandate layoffs.

Obama's main statement in this speech is that people need to have credit to continue spending. Spending includes the purchase of houses and businesses, and business owners can buy supplies. Essentially, spending is described as a sort of food chain, where each element is dependent on the other for survival.

30. (B)   figments

Golding uses "enchantments" figuratively here. The "enchantments" are like mirages and things in fairy tales. They are not real things—they are only imaginary. Therefore, "figments" is the best choice.

31. (D)   defined

In this line, the line between the ocean and the sky is very defined. Golding describes the day as being clear, with the clouds and surrounding areas being clear. Obviously, the ocean is not "metal" or "fuzzy," so "defined" is the best answer.

32. (C)   personification

The wind is personified in this passage. The wind moves along to "do business" and with an "air of disregard," both human traits.

33. (B) simile

Here, there is a comparison between the seaweed and a woman's hair. It is a simile because of the comparison of two unlike things and the use of the word "like": "plaster down the seaweed like shining hair."

34. (C) Being stranded and freedom

The divider, in this case, is Ralph's freedom in civilization and being stranded on the island. The ocean is a defined barrier that keeps him from being able to go home.

35. (D) To portray his dismay at his predicament and the barrier of the ocean to his surroundings

Even though the ocean is, obviously, not infinite, to Ralph it might as well be. The ocean barrier is so big, so troublesome an obstacle, that he would not be able to overcome it without amazing strength and the help of others. An example you could think about here would be if you owed $10,000 and had to pay it right away. If you only had $100 and no way to pay the rest, that $10,000 might as well be $1,000,000. Ralph feels the same way about the ocean.

36. (D) wide

Because Ralph is looking at the great expanse of the ocean, the best choice would be "wide." We get these clues early on when Ralph describes the ocean as infinite. The word "obtuse" generally refers to an angle.

37. (B) barbaric

Golding gives connotation in the text that the best definition is "barbaric." The ocean and his surroundings are wild and unpredictable, and his environment keeps him from civilization. "Barbaric" is defined as "wild and uncivilized"—a perfect complement to "brute" in this piece.

38. (C) irony

Because the paragraph has opposing sentences put together, the best choice is "irony."

39. (A) age of unbelieving things

Incredulity means to be unbelieving, so the best choice is the "age of unbelievable things."

40. (C) Because they are metaphorical to something sacred

"Light" and "Darkness" are capitalized. "Heaven" is capitalized as well, giving the reader a clue that "Light" and "Darkness" are sacred in this sense.

41. (B) contradictory

"The best of times" and "the worst of times" are opposite in meaning, making them contradictory.

42. (A) uncertain

Because there are several contradictory phrases, the mood shows uncertainty, with the reader being unsure about the time period.

43. (C)   7
The chart shows that when a person has a BA degree and has worked for seven years, they make $37,999.

44. (C)   less than $52,000
The chart shows that a person who has a Master's degree plus 45 credits and 9 years of service would make $51,038.

45. (C)   PhD
With the given choices, the PhD makes the most money at $64,887.

46. (C)   Their salary stays the same as year 16.
Because the chart says "16 or more years," the salary is the same for 16 years or more of service.

47. (B)   This person has no experience.
With the given choices, 0 years of service would most likely mean no experience. A person can have a lot of experience and still be a student. Zero years of service is very unlikely to mean overqualified, and if the person was already a teacher, they would have years of service.

48. (B)   The person with the BA has more college credits than the person with the MA.
Because the salary schedule is based on credits when someone has 0 years experience, one must assume that more credits must be the only reason for a larger salary.

49. (C)   The order must be checked for completion before it is sent out.
The second step of Step 2 is "Determine if the order is complete."

50. (B)   The Office
The steps for the Office are to take the customer's orders before sending them to the Warehouse for processing.

51. (A)   4
There are four steps under Step 3—the ones the Loading Dock is responsible for completing.

52. (B)   Confirming detail with the customer ensures customer satisfaction.
The third step of Step 1 is to confirm details.

53. (B)   Correct errors on the lists.
"Rectify" means to correct, and "waybills" are lists of goods: in this case, the list of packages that need to be sent.

54. (B)   Because the Office has the customer on the phone so changes can be made quickly
If the Office has the customer on the phone, the changes are made most efficiently, which is important for customer service.

55. (A)   heavy metal used to stabilize a ship

56. **(A)** hate

57. **(C)** fake; false

58. **(B)** give voting rights

59. **(A)** hinder; obstruct

60. **(C)** to develop

61. **(B)** harmful; poisonous; lethal

62. **(C)** calm; peaceful

63. **(C)** payment for work done

64. **(C)** chaos

65. **(B)**   soft

66. **(D)** nonsensical

67. **(B)** act of taking blood and moving it

68. **(A)** greater than estimated

69. **(A)** forcefully moving

70. **(D)** religious feeling of commitment

71. **(B)** luxurious

72. **(A)** self-government

73. **(B)** boring

74. **(D)** hasty

75. **(C)** snappish attitude

76. **(A)** neat

77. **(D)**   blue

78. **(D)** frolicked

79. **(A)** forceful

80. **(A)** not needed

81. **(B)** bubbly attitude

82. **(C)** burned

83. **(D)** drink

84. **(A)** rush

PRETEST DETAILED EXPLANATIONS
MATHEMATICS SECTION

1. **(D)** This is scientific notation. Because the exponent is a 3, move the decimal point on 2.4 three places to the right and add zeros in the open spaces. The answer is 2,400.

2. **(C)** The exclamation point (!) is used in mathematics to represent factorial expressions: $\dfrac{3!}{4!} = \dfrac{3 \times 2 \times 1}{4 \times 3 \times 2 \times 1} = \dfrac{1}{4}$

3. **(B)** To solve this problem, first convert the percent to a decimal:

    $15\% = \dfrac{15}{100} = .15$

    Then multiply the cost of the meal by .15:

    $\$40(.15) = \$6.00$

4. **(D)** The total number of students is 20 (5 boys + 15 girls). So the ratio of boys to total number of students is 5:20, which simplifies to 1:4.

5. **(A)** Substitute each answer into the equation until you find a point that makes the equation true. $2(3) + 3(2) = 12$ is true. So the answer is (3, 2).

6. **(C)** Plot the points on an x, y graph. Then connect the nearest points. The figure created is called a parallelogram. A parallelogram is a figure with four sides whose opposite sides are parallel and equal.

7. **(D)** First simplify the constants by dividing 15 by 3, which equals 5. Then simplify the x and y variables by finding the difference between the exponents: for x, $2 - 1 = 1$, which leaves x^1, or simply x. For y, $4 - 2 = 2$, which leaves y^2. The final answer is $5xy^2$.

8. **(C)** The pattern is to double the number and then add 1. The last given number in the series is 95, so $95(2) + 1 = 191$.

9. **(A)** First calculate the discount:

$32 × 20\% = \$32(.2) = \$6.40$.

Then subtract the discount from the regular price:

$32.00 − \$6.40 = \$25.60$

10. **(B)** Slope is equal to the rise over the run, so the slope is $\frac{3}{2}$.

11. **(D)** This question asks you to simplify a fraction and then convert it to a decimal:

$$\frac{4}{16} = \frac{1}{4} = .25$$

12. **(C)** First round the numbers: 216 rounds down to 200; 192 rounds up to 200. Now multiply: $200 × 200 = 40,000$.

13. **(D)** The important parts in the equation of a line are the slope and the y-intercept. Slope is equal to the rise over the run. Using the rise-over-run formula, you see that the slope of this is line is 1. The y-intercept is 2. Therefore, the correct equation is $y = x + 2$.

14. **(A)** $\dfrac{xy + 4}{2} - 3 = \dfrac{(2)(5) + 4}{2} - 3 = 4$

15. **(B)** The absolute value of a number, other than 0, is positive. The absolute value of -7 is 7.

16. **(C)** There are four possible outcomes, and three of them satisfy the question. So the probability of not getting a heart is $\frac{3}{4}$, which in decimal form is .75.

17. **(D)** The number of complaints is not as important as the average number of complaints. This is because an average takes into consideration how long a company has been in business. SPEEDY Delivery Company has $\frac{100}{25}$ or an average of 4 complaints per month. However, ON TIME Delivery Company has $\frac{10}{2}$ or an average of 5 complaints per month.

Therefore, on average, ON TIME Delivery Company has more complaints per month. It is misleading for a company to say that they have fewer complaints than another company when they have not been in business as long.

18. **(D)** This question is asking for the number of permutations of three things from a set of three things. The answer is 3!: $3! = 3 × 2 × 1 = 6$.

19. **(A)** $4x + 4 = 7$

$4x = 7 - 4$

$4x = 3$

$\dfrac{4x}{4} = \dfrac{3}{4}$

$x = \dfrac{3}{4}$

20. **(C)** Solving a system of linear equations involves finding the point at which two lines intersect. One approach to this problem is to substitute each answer, one at time, into the two formulas given. The correct answer is the one that makes both of the equations true. In this case, the point $(-3, -9)$ makes both equations true (remember that the first number in the parentheses is the x value, and the second is the y value):

$$y = 2x - 3$$
$$-9 = 2(-3) - 3$$
$$-9 = -6 - 3$$
$$-9 = -9$$
$$y = 3x$$
$$-9 = 3(-3)$$
$$-9 = -9$$

21. **(D)** Set up this problem as a proportion. Write a proportion for the corresponding sides in which x represents the length of the missing side. Then solve for x:

$$\frac{x}{8} = \frac{15}{10}$$

$$10x = 15 \times 8$$

$$x = 15 \times \frac{8}{10}$$

$$x = 12 \text{ inches}$$

22. **(D)** Use the formula for the slope of a line through two points:

$$m = \frac{y_2 - y_1}{x_2 - x_1}$$

$$m = \frac{8 - 2}{6 - 4} = \frac{6}{2} = 3$$

The slope is equal to 3.

23. **(B)** Substitute the values given into the expression and simplify:

$$a^2 + \frac{3b}{12} + 10 = 7^2 + \frac{3(-4)}{12} + 10$$
$$= 49 - 1 + 10 = 58$$

24. **(D)** Solve for x:

$$\frac{x}{3} - 2 = 8$$

$$\frac{x}{3} = 10$$

$$x = 30$$

25. **(B)** The price of each CD is actually the slope of the line. The slope is rise over run. For each CD purchased, the cost goes up $20.

26. **(B)** The arrow is pointing in the "greater than" direction and it is a solid dot. This number line represents greater than or equal to 3, or in symbol form, $x \geq 3$.

27. **(A)** The words "five more than three times a number" can be turned into an expression. "Five more" means to add 5. "Three times a number" means to multiply by 3. Let x represent the number. The correct expression is $3x + 5$.

28. **(B)** The average of a given set of values is calculated by adding all the values and then dividing by the total number of values added. So, to calculate Mary's average test score, add her four test scores and then divide by 4:

$$9 + 8 + 10 + 5 = 32$$
$$\frac{32}{4} = 8$$

29. **(B)** There are four possible outcomes that can result from flipping a fair coin twice. Only one of these includes two heads. So the probability of getting two heads is $\frac{1}{4}$ or .25 or 25%.

30. **(D)** An equation that has an x-squared term will produce some type of a parabola.

31. **(C)** The sum of the angles of a triangle must equal 180°. To find the missing value, first add the two known measurements together and then subtract from 180:

$$55 + 70 = 125$$
$$180 - 125 = 55°$$

32. **(A)** Solve using the Pythagorean theorem, $a^2 + b^2 = c^2$, where c represents the hypotenuse, or the side opposite the right angle:

$$4^2 + 3^2 = c^2$$
$$16 + 9 = c^2$$
$$25 = c^2$$
$$c = \sqrt{25} = 5$$

33. **(B)** Use the formula for the combination of four different things taken three at a time:

$$_nC_k = \frac{n!}{k!(n-k)!}$$
$$_4C_3 = \frac{4!}{3!(4-3)!}$$
$$_4C_3 = \frac{4!}{3!(1!)}$$
$$_4C_3 = \frac{24}{6(1)}$$
$$_4C_3 = \frac{24}{6} = 4$$

34. **(B)** To find the median score, the scores must first be ordered from smallest to largest:

    0, 2, 3, 5, 6, 7, 12

    The median score is the one in the middle, in this case, 5.

35. **(B)** There are six possible and equally likely outcomes from rolling one fair die. Rolling a 2 or a 3 would cover two out of the six possibilities. Therefore, the probability of rolling a 2 or a 3 would be $\frac{2}{6}$ or $\frac{1}{3}$.

36. **(A)** Each flip of a fair coin is an independent event. Therefore, the probability of flipping a coin and getting heads is always $\frac{1}{2}$.

37. **(D)** In the figure, the measure of angle q is equal to the measure of angle p because they are alternate interior angles, which are always equal. So angle p measures 55°. Also, the sum of the measures of angle m and angle p must equal 180° because they are adjacent angles on a straight line and a straight line (or straight angle) measures 180°. Therefore, angle m is equal to 180° minus 55°:

    $180 - 55 = 125°$

38. **(B)** In the scaled drawing, length is equal to $3\frac{1}{4}$ inches or, in decimal form, 3.25 inches. The scale is "1 inch = 24 feet." To find the length in feet, multiply the number of inches by 24: $3.25 \times 24 = 78$ feet.

39. **(C)** The shaded region is made up of four separate triangles. Calculate the area of one triangle using the formula one-half its base times its height: $\frac{1}{2}bh$. In the given problem, the base is 3 and the height is 3:

    $\frac{1}{2}(3)(3) = \frac{1}{2}(9) = 4.5$

    This is the area of one triangle. Because there are four triangles in the shaded region, multiply this area by 4: $4.5(4) = 18$. The final answer is 18 square inches.

40. **(B)** The pattern that this data suggest is a straight line. If this imaginary line were extended down, the year 1995 would have a predicted value of 10,000.

41. **(D)** Find the side of the figure closest to the y-axis and measure the distance that this side is from the y-axis. A reflection of the figure will put this side the same distance from the y-axis, but on the other side. Also, notice the point labeled C. A reflection of this point across the y-axis will also be the same distance from the y-axis, but on the other side.

42. **(A)** The greatest increase in temperature over the previous day can be determined by looking for the longest line segment on the graph in the upward direction. The greatest increase over the previous day was Tuesday.

43. (C) Imagine that this figure is a square with a triangle missing. First calculate the area of the missing triangle using the formula $\frac{1}{2}bh$ (one-half the base times the height):

$$\frac{1}{2}bh = \frac{1}{2}(3)(4) = \frac{1}{2}12 = 6$$

Then calculate the area of the imaginary square using the formula s^2 (side times side):

$$s^2 = 5^2 = 25$$

Last, subtract the area of the triangle from the area of the square:

$$25 - 6 = 19$$

44. (D) The written expression "the number of boys, b, is equal to four times the number of girls, g" can be written as $4g = b$.

45. (B) The rule called "order of operations" tells us to do multiplication and division before addition and subtraction. Therefore, $10 - 4 \times 2 = 10 - 8 = 2$.

46. (D) For this problem, it is important to note that the measurements given are in units of 10 feet, so, for example, the side of the outer square marked "10" is 100 feet (10×10). To determine the square footage of the flower garden, first calculate the area of the duck pond using the formula for the area of a rectangle, lw (length times width):

$50 \times 40 = 2,000$ square feet

Next, calculate the area of the whole lot:

$100 \times 100 = 10,000$ square feet

Last, subtract the area for the duck pond from the whole lot to find the area of the flower garden:

$10,000 - 2,000 = 8,000$ square feet

47. (C) To find the circumference of a circle, use the formula $2\pi r$, or two times pi times the radius. Pi can be rounded to 3.14:

$$2\pi r = 2(3.14)(5) = 31.4$$

This is approximately equal to 31 inches.

48. (C) Solve using the Pythagorean theorem, $a^2 + b^2 = c^2$. Remember: c is the hypotenuse, or the side opposite the right angle:

$$a^2 + 6^2 = 10^2$$
$$a^2 + 36 = 100$$
$$a^2 = 100 - 36$$
$$a^2 = 64$$
$$\sqrt{64} = 8 \text{ cm}$$

49. (B) The formula for the area of a triangle is $\frac{1}{2}bh$ where b equals the base and h equals the height. The area of triangle A equals $\frac{1}{2}(5)(2) = 5$. The area of triangle B equals $\frac{1}{2}(10)(4) = 20$. Last, divide the area of triangle A by the area of triangle B and put this fraction into lowest terms: $\frac{5}{20} = \frac{1}{4}$.

50. (A) Set this problem up as a proportion. Write a proportion for the corresponding sides in which x represents the length of the missing side. Then solve for x:

$$\frac{x}{6} = \frac{12}{9}$$

$$x = \frac{12 \times 6}{9}$$

$$x = 8 \text{ feet}$$

STOP

ENGLISH-LANGUAGE ARTS REVIEW

English-Language Arts Review

Reading Comprehension

What Does the Reading Subtest Look Like?

The reading subtest of the CHSPE has 54 vocabulary and reading comprehension questions, all of which are multiple choice. The **vocabulary questions** assess synonyms, multiple-meaning words, and context clues as follows:

Synonyms—demonstrate the ability to recognize a synonym for a word used in context.

Multiple-meaning words—demonstrate the ability to determine the meaning of a given word with multiple meanings.

Context clues—demonstrate the ability to use context clues to assign meaning to an unknown word.

Reading comprehension is basically how well you understand what you've read. The **reading comprehension questions** on the CHSPE assess initial understanding, interpretation, critical analysis, and strategies using three types of text: literary (material typically read for enjoyment), informational (material typically found in textbooks and other sources of information), and functional (material typically encountered in everyday-life situations). The specific reading comprehension skills assessed are listed in the appendix.

The test includes six to eight separate texts, each with several related questions. The texts come from a range of genres, including poetry, nonfiction, fiction, charts and graphs, commentaries, and newspaper and magazine articles.

Now that you know what the reading subtest will look like, you need to review strategies that will help you read effectively and answer the questions correctly.

Responding to Literature

Read with purpose

As difficult as it can be to read something uninteresting to you, remember that you must read with purpose. Knowing your purpose will help you to interpret the information you have read and use it to your advantage.

Because you are studying for the CHSPE, your main purpose for reading the selections is clear: to score highly on the test questions. The next step is to find the subpurpose for each selection. Here are some questions to ask yourself to help you home in on that subpurpose:

- Why is it important for me to know this information?
- What is the point or main idea?
- How does this passage make me feel?

Literature can seem to be an overwhelming subject, especially if you are not an avid reader. Reading through this chapter should help settle some of your fears.

The two types of reading

There are two types of reading: general reading and practical reading. Each has a certain purpose or point that you, the reader, must discern from the words on the page. Let's look at each type separately.

General reading

General reading includes all types of common knowledge information, books, magazines, journals, congenial reading on the Internet, and other types of texts that you may read for pleasure at home, on the job, or just in passing. This type of common information is meant to entertain or inform you about nonessential information.

Although this type of reading is supposed to be pleasurable, some texts can still be difficult to remember or understand. One way to help you stay on task and remember what you've read is to read for the main idea. Ask yourself the following questions:

- What is the author trying to tell me?
- Why is this information important?

When reading for the main idea, think of yourself as a treasure hunter. You want to find the all-important point of the text, the author's reason for writing, but sometimes, that can be a really difficult adventure. Often, the main idea isn't even stated outright: it is implied, meaning that you have to figure it out for yourself based on what is stated outright. More than likely, you will encounter on the CHSPE selections ranging from easy, where the main idea is obvious, to difficult, where finding the main idea can be cumbersome.

Here are some strategies to help you as you read for the main idea:

Strategy 1—Ask yourself, "How can I relate to this piece?" One way to find the main idea is to put yourself in the main character's place. How would you feel if you were in the situation that the main character is in?

Strategy 2—Outline the story or text. Either in your mind or on your text booklet or scrap paper, write a quick outline of the selection. Sometimes, only one word is needed per paragraph or topic change. This provides a road map to the story, an easy way to review what you've read.

Strategy 3—Find repetition within the text. Do you see any patterns? A repetition of words? If you do, more than likely this has something to do with the main idea of the piece. Let's use the following example to practice Strategy 3:

<u>Because of the recent downturn in the economy, many people are</u> <u>returning to the kitchen to cook their own meals instead of going out to eat.</u> Grocery stores have many items that are cost efficient for large families, and there are many cookbooks available that offer easy-to-make, low-cost recipes. Many cooking shows cater to the frugal home cook, focusing on low-cost, healthy, easy, and quick-to-assemble meals. Inexpensive and easy-to-handle kitchen

gadgets are available to assist the untrained chef, making home cooking a viable alternative to eating out. Finally, the gathering around the table to share a meal and the day's events make going out seem less desirable. Who knew the changes in the economy could be such fun?

In this piece, a form of the word "cook" is used four times, and "low-cost" and its synonyms ("cheap," "cost efficient") are used four times. The main idea of this selection must have something to do with cooking cheaply. Now, go back and read the underlined sentence of the piece. We were right! The main idea is about cooking cheaply in today's economy.

If you were to use Strategy 2 and sketch an outline of this text, it would look something like this:

Bad economy makes cooking at home good
Grocery stores have a lot of items for cooking
Lots of cookbooks for reference
Many cooking shows to help
Kitchen gadgets cheaper and easier to use

Though the outline is simple and rough, you can see that there is a main idea and supporting examples that follow it.

Using Strategy 1, you can find the main idea by looking for associations between the text and your own life. In that case, you would jot down connections to your own life in the margins; your notes might look something like this:

Economy is bad and I have to cook all the time.
I like cooking because it brings my family together.
I have fun in the kitchen and going grocery shopping.
It has turned out to be a good thing!

You can see here that you still get the same main idea, but this time you did it by forming your own associations.

Let's take a look at another example:

One amazing place to visit in Mexico is Calafia. Calafia's complex includes the hotel with its panoramic views of the ocean, along with many terraces, bars, bazaars, discos, five restaurants, and four banquet rooms. Calafia's master architectural plan includes the Plaza de las Misiones, with replicas of the facades of 12 missions from the Missional Camino Real. At the Bahia del Descanso (Bay of Rest), you can admire the fantastic Beach Club built as an old fortress, the Christ of the Sea Chapel, and a full-size replica of the Spanish Galleon *Corona Aurea*. Calafia welcomes over thousands of tours, and many visitors come annually from around the world to enjoy Calafia's beauty and warm hospitality. Calafia has become a magical and spectacular historical village and tourist destination—the only one of its kind in Baja California.

Using Strategy 3, we find the name "Calafia" has been used six times, so we know that the piece has something to do with Calafia. But that doesn't help us too much. So let's move to Strategy 2 and do a quick outline:

Calafia is a place in Mexico.
It has restaurants, discos, bars, etc.
It is historical.
It has a beach club with a boat replica.
Many people go there.
It is a tourist spot.

Strategy 2 works much better for this selection, and our outline matches up with the underlined sentence above, giving us the correct main idea.

Practical reading

Practical reading is for gathering information. You do this at work, at home, and or while traveling. Charts, menus, recipes, direction booklets, maps, and some Internet sites are a few of the many examples of practical reading.

Imagine that you are eating out at a restaurant. Upon walking in the door, you are greeted with several opportunities for practical reading. The sign posted by the entrance, "Please wait to be seated," is the first. Once you are led to your seat, you are given a second practical reading text: the menu. On the left side of the menu you see the food options available, and on the right side, the prices. Sometimes, there are add-ons listed toward the bottom of the menu as well, along with their prices. You have to navigate the menu and all its information before making your final selection. After you finish your dinner, you read over the check. This tells you the items you ordered, the price for each, any taxes and service charges, and your total. Once again, this is an example of practical reading. And all this just for eating at a restaurant!

The CHSPE includes practical reading selections. Though these may appear to be easier to understand than the general reading texts, pay close attention to the questions and read through the entire piece before answering any questions. Here are some examples of practical reading selections that may appear on the CHSPE:

Warranties: These are documents outlining a manufacturer's guarantee for items you buy; they have directions and explanations for use and repair. These are generally wordy and dense.

Drug labels: You've heard the warnings on television, but have you ever read the insert label for an antibiotic? Many of us have scanned the backs of bottles of aspirin and other over-the-counter drugs. These labels list dangerous side effects, chemical composition, and dosage details, all important and essential information. Be careful with this type of example as all the information is very important.

Nutritional facts: Reading the back of a box of macaroni can be very enlightening. As people have become more weight conscious and concerned about fats and calories, many people are seen reading the nutritional facts label on the side of a package before putting it in their shopping carts. These labels detail the vitamin, mineral, fat, sugar, and protein content of the food, as well as the recommended serving size and usually the ingredients.

Maps: These are a graphic representations of all or part of a specific area. Whether geographic, topographic, weather-related, or of some other category, maps help us to visualize how one place connects to or relates to another.

Time schedules: Numbers are the critical element in time schedules. Generally, the CHSPE asks you to look at one side of a schedule and relate the information given there to information on another part of the schedule. Time schedules are usually formatted using horizontal and vertical columns.

Recipes: These give you a list of food items and specific amounts for each, and then instruct you on how to combine them to create a whole new food product. Proportions are important, as well as following the steps in the order given.

Charts: These can have pictures and/or diagrams that give you information. Usually, you have to determine how the pieces of information relate to each other.

Here are some strategies for approaching the practical reading selections on the CHSPE:

Strategy 1—Visualize. Have you ever tried to follow written directions to some complicated task, with no illustrations to refer to? Or have you ever had to follow directions composed only of illustrations, with no words for help? Having both a visual and words can be extremely helpful, so if only one is given, it helps to make up the other one. Here's an example:

How to Fold a Fitted Sheet

1. Slip your hands into the two top corners of the sheet, with the rough edges (wrong side) facing out.
2. With one hand inside each of the top two corners, bring your hands together and fold the left corner over the right corner so that you are now holding both corners in one hand.
3. With your free hand, grab another corner and fold it over the two on your other hand, rough side out. You now have three corners on one hand.
4. Do the same thing with the last corner, folding it over the other three with the rough side out.
5. Shake out folds and lay sheet on a table or hard surface.
6. Fold in half, and then in thirds. You should have a nice compact square.

Wow! Would these directions be easier with a diagram or a set of pictures? Could you imagine if it were just a set of pictures and no words? So, using Strategy 1, you have to visualize all of the steps as though you were actually completing the task. For some sets of directions, it can be difficult to visualize the first time. If necessary, take a moment to reread the directions so you can get a clearer picture of what is being explained. Just remember not to take too much time on any one question or text selection.

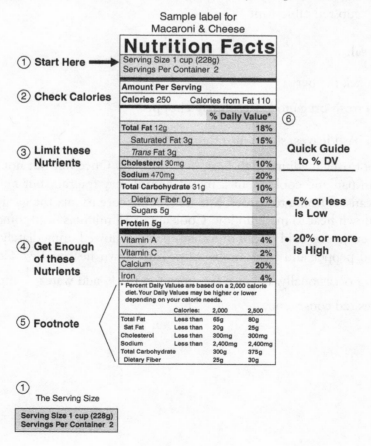

Strategy 2—Look for patterns in numbers or symbols. To illustrate this strategy, let's look at another common example, a nutrition label, in this case, from a box of macaroni and cheese:

This label uses shading, numbers, and symbols. The shading groups together like nutrients. There are two categories of numbers for each nutrient: grams (g) per serving and the percentage (%) of the recommended daily value. In this example, we can see that a serving of this mac and cheese includes 470 milligrams sodium, which is 20 percent of the daily value of sodium for the average person. That is a pretty high number. Asking yourself a question like "Is sodium a good thing or a bad thing?" would be a good idea here. Looking lower on the label, you see that calcium is also listed as 20 percent. Most of us know from previous knowledge that calcium is good for us, so now we have a reference.

Another good example of practical reading is the recipe. Let's take a look at the following recipe:

Mama's Marinara Sauce

Always a crowd pleaser, this marinara sauce is an easy recipe for the beginning chef. This recipe is made with alcohol, so if you are underage, please ask your parents for assistance!

2 tbsp olive oil

5 cloves of garlic, peeled and diced

2 large cans of chopped Roma tomatoes

1 small can of tomato paste

$\frac{3}{4}$ to 1 cup red table wine

$\frac{1}{2}$ tsp salt

1 tsp black pepper

$\frac{1}{4}$ cup fresh oregano leaves, finely chopped

8 fresh basil leaves, sliced into thin strips

In a large pot over medium-high heat, heat olive oil. Once hot but not scalding, add garlic. Stir garlic in pan and cook about 2 minutes until very fragrant but not too brown. Add in both large cans of Roma tomatoes. Stir well, being sure to mix the garlic through the tomatoes. Turn down heat to medium low. Cook about 15 minutes until tomatoes are bubbly and releasing their juices. Add in can of tomato paste, followed immediately by cup of red wine. Add salt and pepper and fresh herbs. Stir. Turn down heat to low. Cook for about a half hour, stirring occasionally. If sauce becomes too thick, add water $\frac{1}{2}$ cup at a time until you reach the desired consistency.

The most important part about working with recipes is proportion: measurements ensure a greater chance of success. When reading a recipe on the CHSPE, keep in mind that questions about proportion will likely be the first ones asked on the test. (If you aren't sure what a "cup" or "tsp" [teaspoon] or "tbsp" [tablespoon] looks like, check it out in the kitchen.)

Visualization is important for recipes because it enables you to "see," in your mind's eye, how much is supposed to go in the recipe. Adding 15 cloves of garlic instead of 5 cloves or adding a $\frac{1}{2}$ tablespoon of salt would change the flavor profile significantly and probably ruin the dish. Therefore, studying the ingredients carefully, looking at any notes or additional instructions, and reading through the steps while visualizing them will be very helpful in answering the questions correctly.

California Reading Standards

"Standards" is a term used often in education. Generally, a standard is a benchmark or goal that students should master at a particular grade level. Every state has a list of standards with which all public schools must comply and around which they must build their curriculum.

A number system is used to categorize the established educational standards. The lower numbers represent the simpler standards, and higher numbers, more complex standards.

The Basics of Literature

Genres in Literature

Literature genres are defined by form and style. Literary genres include horror, fantasy, thriller/action, mystery, romance, science fiction, Western, children, and young adult. All of these genres can be dramatic or comedic; therefore, there are no separate genre categories for these types.

Horror

Ghosts, goblins, killers, the inhuman, things that go bump in the night . . . all of these and more play roles in horror books. Sometimes, the horror is outright, with pages filled with blood and gore. Other times, it is the mood of the story that makes it terrifying. Horror books have defined protagonists and antagonists. The antagonist or evil element usually overpowers many in the story except for the main character. Even then, evil sometimes wins.

Fantasy

Many people confuse this genre with science fiction. Fantasy stories contain at least one "fantastic" element: it could be the setting (an imaginary land) or the characters (elves, goblins, etc.). Magic plays a huge role as do weapons, spells, and overall power. Though strength is very important for the protagonist's success, morality is key to winning in fantasy books.

Thriller/Action

Thrillers are suspenseful books that keep the reader on the edge of his or her seat. A successful thriller novel usually contains at least some of the following elements: an exotic or unusual setting, a striking event that summons extreme courage or test of will in the protagonist, and plot twists that keep the story, and the characters, moving. The protagonist will usually win in the end, but there are usually casualties.

Mystery

Books of this genre always contain a puzzle that is solved before the end of the story. Usually, the reader feels as if he or she is gathering the clues and deciphering the mystery alongside the investigator, a common character in these novels.

Romance

Romance literature is centered on love stories that are mostly written for women. Classic romance novels include a hunky man and a dainty, yet feisty woman who fall in love after a complicated series of conflicts. Modern romance novels follow a similar formula, but they are more sensitive to the independent role of women today. Many refer to modern romance novels as "chick lit."

Science fiction

This genre emphasizes the effect of science and technology—real or imagined—on the characters, setting, and/or plot. Often, science fiction stories take place on another planet or in the most distant future.

Western

Western literature is the only major genre that has a definite setting: these stories take place in the wild frontiers of North America and Mexico, during the mid- to late 1800s. There are sharply defined protagonists and antagonists in Westerns (the "good" guy and the "bad" guy), and the hero wins in the end.

Children

"Children's literature" refers specifically to literature for children under the age of 11. Books in this genre usually have lots of pictures and tell a straightforward story. Generally, the content is very light, without violence or harsh language.

Young adult

Young adult literature can be difficult to define and/or categorize. It does not fit into a typical genre "box," mostly because many of the issues addressed in these works are very adultlike. Young adult literature contains some romance, and simple to complex relationship problems and other conflicts. The protagonist is always between the ages of 11 and 18, the target reader age for this genre.

Setting

Setting is the time and location in which a story takes place. For some stories, the setting is very important and acts almost as an additional character, while for others, it is not a crucial factor. There are several aspects of setting to consider when examining how setting contributes to a story (some, or all, may be present in a story):

Place is the actual geographical location the characters inhabit. Work outward and move to the inner area to define the location. For example, a story may take place in Canada. Therefore, the setting could be Canada, Ontario, Bismarck (country, province, city).

Time is when the story takes place. What is the historical era, the time of day, the time of month, the time of year?

Weather can affect how the characters act and feel, where they go, what they wear. It can also indicate the time of year.

Social conditions include the characters' place within society and the state of the society in general. What is going on in the time period? Is it during elections? Is there social strife like war?

Mood or atmosphere refers to the general feeling the writer conveys. This marker of setting is the most abstract. The reader must look for clues in the text to analyze atmosphere. How does the author describe the day or night? The location?

Plot

Plot is the movement of the story from one set of conflicts to the next (rising action) to the climax and then the falling action to the resolution (denouement). Every story has plot. There are five basic elements to plot:

Introduction: The beginning of the story during which the characters and the setting are revealed

Rising action: The point at which the events in the story become complicated and the conflict in the story is revealed (events between the introduction and climax)

Climax: The highest point of interest and the turning point of the story, at which the reader wonders what will happen next; will the conflict be resolved or not?

Falling action: The events during which complications begin to resolve themselves. The reader learns whether the conflict is resolved or not (events between climax and denouement)

Denouement: The final outcome or untangling of events in the story that ultimately leads to the presence of a resolution or the absence of one

Graphically, a simple plot can look like this:

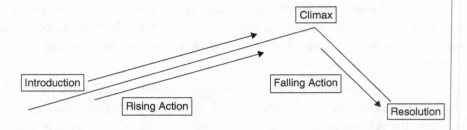

A longer story, a novel perhaps, may have several mini-climaxes, each complete with falling action. However, it will have one main climax, where everything in the story is changed because of its occurrence.

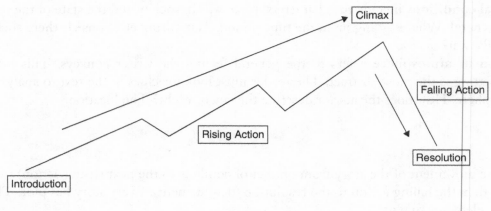

Conflict

Conflict is essential to plot. There would be no story without conflict. Conflict is a representation of forces acting against each other. The conflict can be either **internal**, in which the character struggles with a power outside him- or herself; or **external**, in which the struggle comes from within, forcing the character to make some decision that goes against his or her primal or usual urges.

There are three main types of conflict:

Man versus man (physical): The lead character struggles with his physical strength against other men, forces of nature, or animals.

Man versus society (social): The lead character struggles against ideas, practices, or customs of other people.

Man versus himself (psychological): The lead character struggles with him- or herself; with his or her own soul, ideas of right or wrong, physical limitations, choices, and so on.

Character

There are two meanings for the word "character":

1. The person, animal, or part of nature in a work of fiction
2. The characteristics or traits of a person, animal, or part of nature

Persons in a work of fiction

Works of fiction involve two main character types: protagonists and antagonists. The **protagonist** is the classic "hero" of a story or the character who opposes the "villain," the **antagonist**. The protagonist is the main character of the story on whom the story's main events and conflicts center.

The characteristics of a person

Characters must be realistic to the reader in order for the story to immerse the reader, touch him or her in a personal way, and/or have value to that person. That may seem an overly strong statement, but think about a book you've read that affected you in some way; your reaction to it was most likely because you could relate to the experience of one of the characters. This is the "magic" that occurs in books and why some stories become very successful while others do not.

Characterization is the information a writer gives the reader about the various characters in a story. The author may reveal a character in several ways:

- Physical appearance
- Feelings or dreams
- Thoughts and actions
- The thoughts and reactions of other characters

Characters are convincing if they are like real people. The more three-dimensional the character is in the text, the more believable and complex the character becomes.

Theme

Theme is probably the most difficult element to define in literature. Simply stated, theme is not a subject or a character but rather an element or dimension of the human experience. It is a statement of sorts about the subject of the story, and it can be a direct statement or something that is implied indirectly to the reader.

When you read literature, you must become a critical thinker. You have to ask yourself why the author wrote the text and what message or lessons he or she wanted to pass on to the reader. Sometimes, these answers will be crystal clear, and in other instances, you may have to think on the subject matter before making a decision. Either way, remember that every word the author chose, every scene, every name, every place were thought over carefully and edited and reedited before being published. Every element of the work is important!

The following sections discuss a few common themes in literature.

The individual in nature

In this element, man must explore how he functions in the world, his place in it, and his relationship to the earth. Many naturalist writers such as John Steinbeck and Henry David Thoreau wrote about themes in nature and man's struggle with and delight at how he fits into it.

The individual in society

The word "society" can be traded for the word "community" here. This theme focuses on how man fits into communities: family, neighborhoods, groups, towns, cities, countries, and ultimately, the world. Here, man finds his true identity: society shapes man and forms him into who he will become in the future.

Society here can also be the personal relationship between lovers and spouses. Generally, in classical literature, love is full of conflict. The misinterpretation of conversations, symbols, and situations leads to stresses in the relationship. Thematic elements in this area include lust, suspicion, disappointment, and loss of self, among other problems.

The individual and the gods

This theme has modern and classical interpretations. In the classical tradition, such as Greek myths and creation stories, man generally questions the power of the gods and learns a very hard lesson in the process. Vanity, greed, lust, anger, and other rash behaviors on both the human and the god "sides" are at the root of the problem in this theme.

The modern interpretation is different. Generally, it portrays the gods as benevolent entities that want to help foster good and healthy living among humans, reward positive change, and encourage free will. The lesson learned here is that in failing, man realizes his "humanness" and grows from the experience.

Growth and initiation

Growth is a popular theme in all of literature. The "hero cycle" is probably the most commonly used theme in this section. Look at the diagram below:

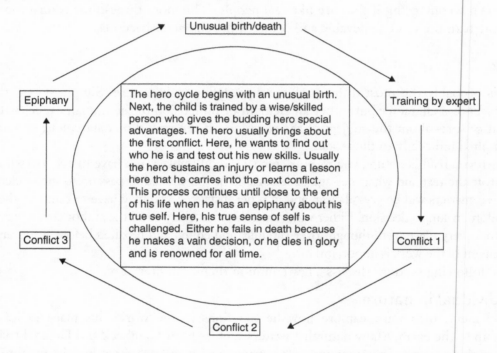

The hero cycle begins with an unusual birth. Next, the child is trained by a wise/skilled person who gives the budding hero special advantages. The hero usually brings about the first conflict. Here, he wants to find out who he is and test out his new skills. Usually the hero sustains an injury or learns a lesson here that he carries into the next conflict. This process continues until close to the end of his life when he has an epiphany about his true self. Here, his true sense of self is challenged. Either he fails in death because he makes a vain decision, or he dies in glory and is renowned for all time.

The hero cycle appears in classic and modern literature and in many movies. Luke Skywalker of *Star Wars* is a perfect example of a character who moves through the stages of the hero cycle.

Other growth themes include the movement from childhood to adulthood and crisis in adulthood. Young adult novels focus on teen challenges: the movement into adulthood is peppered with conflicts for which the main character is somehow unprepared but through which he or she ultimately matures. Crisis in adulthood generally refers to a moral or ethical challenge the main character must face and the growth that results from the experience.

Time, birth, death

The passage of time, marked by birth and death, is another popular literary theme. In literature, birth and death are symbols of change and growth that make the main character realize the precious fragility of life. Birth, the symbol of newness, can be shown through the actual birth of a character, through the change in seasons, or the "birth" of thought or new path in life. Death is an end marker. When a character dies, there is a realization of the superfluous frivolity of material goods and the horrible loneliness in the absence of love. The other characters will also have similar realizations.

Isolation

In literature with this theme, the main character is somehow isolated, either physically (external) or psychologically (internal). The isolation brings challenge and, as a result, knowledge of, for example, the self, society, or civilization.

Point of View

Point of view is defined as the angle from which the story is told. It is very important to determine the point of view in any piece of literature because the reader has to distinguish whether the voice is reliable. There can be more than one point of view in a story:

Innocent eye: The story is told through the eyes of a child (his/her judgment being different from that of an adult).

Stream of consciousness: The story is told through inner thoughts of a character. Readers feel as if they are inside the head of that character and know all the character's thoughts and reactions.

First person: The story is told by the protagonist or one of the characters who interacts closely with the protagonist or other characters (using pronouns "I," "me," "we," etc.). The reader sees the story through this one character's eyes as he or she experiences it and knows only what that one character knows or feels.

Omniscient: The author narrates the story by moving from character to character, event to event, having free access to the thoughts, feelings, and motivations of the characters and introducing information where and when he or she chooses. There are two main types of omniscient points of view:

Omniscient limited: The author tells the story in third person (using pronouns "they," "she," "he," "it," etc.). We know only what the character knows and what the author allows the character to tell us. We can see the thoughts and feelings of characters if the author chooses to reveal them to us.

Omniscient objective: The author tells the story in the third person but presents the information as though a camera is following the characters, going anywhere, and recording only what is seen and heard. There is no comment on the characters or their thoughts. No interpretations are offered. The reader is placed in the position of spectator without the author there to explain. The reader has to interpret events on his or her own.

Poetry

You hear poems every day: in music, on television, in advertising, in literature—poetry is all around us. Poetry is an art form. The poet uses words much as an artist uses paint: to create an image that invokes feelings in the reader.

There are many different types of poems. Some poems rhyme and some don't. They can be very short or hundreds of pages long. So how do you know if what you are hearing or reading is a poem? Poetry has a rhythm that is unlike prose (the writing you would find in a novel or a textbook). It embodies an expression of feelings and environment different from that of "regular" text, and poetry is written specifically to create a mental image in the reader. Poems are full of adjectives, so it is important to have a tight grasp on the nature of adjectives and how they work in a sentence.

Most poets use figurative language, or language that creates images in the mind of the reader. There are many literary devices in figurative language, and it is important to note that prose writers, like poets, use many of these devices, too:

Alliteration: the repetition of intial consonant sounds to make an impression on the reader; for example:

Peter Piper picked a peck of pickled peppers.

The repetition of the "p" sound enhances the phrase, making it humorous and interesting.

Assonance: the repetition of vowel sounds; the following example highlights both alliteration and assonance:

She sells seashells by the seashore.

The repetition of the long and short "e" sounds are examples of assonance. In terms of the images this assonance helps create, the long "e" sound is reminiscent of the cry of seagulls, while the "s" sound could be indicative of waves.

Metaphor: a comparison of two unlike things without using the words "like" or "as"; for example:

That man is a house!

The man is compared to a house to indicate his large size.

Simile: a comparison of two unlike things using the words "like" or "as"; for example:

The clouds look like ripples in water.

The clouds' appearance is compared to that of water ripples.

Note: Similes and metaphors are very similar, so be careful to look for the "like" or "as."

Personification: the attribution of human traits or characteristics to something that is not human; for example:

The chair screamed and groaned in agony when the fourth student stood on it.

Chairs are not human. They may make noise when overstressed, but the use of the "human" verbs "screamed and groaned" and emotion word "agony" make this personification.

Meter: a measured pulse in poetry. Meter is the "beat" of the poem. Some poems have structured meter, while others do not.

Rhyme: the effect created by matching sounds at the end of words. There are two types of rhyme—masculine and feminine. Masculine rhyme falls on one syllable: "fat," "cat," "rat." Feminine rhyme falls on two syllables: "defeated," "repeated." The following are the four sounds of rhyme:

exact: *fat, cat*

slant: *cat, cot; defeated, impeded*

identical: *two, too, to*

eye rhyme refers to words that look the same but don't rhyme: *proved, loved*

Rhyme scheme: the pattern created by rhyming words of a stanza or poem; for example:

> Jack and Jill
> went up the hill
> To fetch a pail of water.
> Jack fell down
> And broke his crown
> And Jill came tumbling after.

To find rhyme scheme, attach a letter of the alphabet to the end of each line. Each line that rhymes on the end word gets the same letter. Rhyme scheme for the above poem would look like this:

> Jack and Jill   A
> went up the hill   A
> To fetch a pail of water.   B
> Jack fell down   C
> And broke his crown   C
> And Jill came tumbling after.   D

The rhyme scheme for this poem is AABCCD. "Jill" and "hill" rhyme, so they get the same letter, as do "down" and "crown." Here is another example, one of Shakespeare's poems, called a sonnet:

Sonnet 18

> Shall I compare thee to a summer's day?   A   1
> Thou art more lovely and more temperate: B
> Rough winds do shake the darling buds of May,   A
> And summer's lease hath all too short a date: B
>
> Sometime too hot the eye of heaven shines,   C   5
> And often is his gold complexion dimm'd;   D
> And every fair from fair sometime declines,   C
> By chance or nature's changing course untrimm'd;   D
> But thy eternal summer shall not fade   E
>
> Nor lose possession of that fair thou owest;   F   10
> Nor shall Death brag thou wander'st in his shade,   E
> When in eternal lines to time thou growest: F
> So long as men can breathe or eyes can see,   G
> So long lives this and this gives life to thee.   G

Notice that lines 2 and 4 rhyme. Though "temperate" and "date" don't rhyme exactly, they are considered rhyming words. This type of rhyme is called slant rhyme.

> **Verse form:** the form or structure a poem takes. Ballads (stanzas with varied line counts; most songs are ballads) and sonnets (see example under "rhyme scheme") are fixed verse forms, meaning they have a specific, or fixed, number of lines and adhere to an established structure or pattern. In contrast, free verse has no pattern.
>
> **Sonnet:** A verse form of 14 lines that rhyme together in a particular way. There are two types of sonnets: Shakespearean and Petrarchan.
>
> **Canto:** the major division of a long poem (for example, Dante's *Inferno*, an epic poem, is split into cantos)

Literary Response and Analysis
Practice Questions

Each of the following reading selections is accompanied by an explanation summary and questions for practice. These sample texts are typical of those on the CHSPE test. Learning about literature takes years and is a labor of love for many people around the world. Don't get too down on yourself if you don't recognize all the vocabulary or understand all of the texts. Just keep reviewing and you will start to see improvement on your answers.

Practice 1

She Walks in Beauty
by George Gordon (Lord Byron) (1788–1824)

1
She walks in beauty, like the night
Of cloudless climes and starry skies;
And all that's best of dark and bright
Meet in her aspect and her eyes:
5
Thus mellow'd to that tender light
Which heaven to gaudy day denies.

One shade the more, one ray the less,
Had half impair'd the nameless grace
Which waves in every raven tress,
10
Or softly lightens o'er her face;
Where thoughts serenely sweet express
How pure, how dear their dwelling-place.

And on that cheek, and o'er that brow,
So soft, so calm, yet eloquent,
15
The smiles that win, the tints that glow,
But tell of days in goodness spent,
A mind at peace with all below,
A heart whose love is innocent!

In Byron's poem, he admires a beautiful woman, his cousin and future wife. Be careful when reading these lines—you should not stop at the end of the line if there is no punctuation. The first two lines, for example, would be confusing otherwise. Because he compares her to "cloud-less climes and starry skies" (2), one can guess that he thinks she is attractive, rather than ugly and plain. Lines 3 to 4 are interesting because he says "all that's best in dark and bright / Meet in . . . her eyes." Dark and bright are opposites; therefore, she is the apex of beauty in opposites.

In the next stanza, he addresses her hair and face. In lines 7 to 9, he describes her dark ("raven") hair and how it falls in waves around her face. Comparing her hair to a raven here is important; raven's feathers are shiny and luminescent, not dull and flat. Next he says that her face is where "thoughts serenely sweet express / How pure, how dear their dwelling-place." Her face is serene and sweet, meaning calm and quiet—a trait highly regarded in Byron's time. This calm quietness "lives" (dwells) on her face: her features reflect this peace.

In the last stanza, Byron deviates from her physical features and includes her character in the last three lines. First, he describes the beauty of her forehead, cheek, and brow as "calm" and "eloquent." In the last three lines, he describes her obvious innocence and goodness. There is no doubt that the theme of this poem is Byron's deep love for his cousin.

In line 1, Byron uses a

(A) metaphor.

(B) simile.

(C) personification.

(D) rhyme.

Correct Answer: (B)

A simile is comparison of two disparate things using "like" or "as." Byron uses the word "like" to compare the woman's beauty to the night: "She walks in beauty, **like** the night." A metaphor (A) is also a comparison of unlike things, but metaphors do not use "like" or "as." Byron does not use personification (C) or rhyme (D) in these lines.

Practice 2

In Athens, Greece, there lived a man named Academus. Plato, learned author and philosopher, chose Academus's beautiful gardens to host his lectures. Because Plato's students met in these gardens, they became know as "The Academy" and as "academics."

The Greeks gave much to the study of literature and the origin of language. In this selection, Academus's gardens are used by the philosopher Plato. Because philosophy is a study of thought, and Academus is a follower of Plato, it would follow that Academus is a person who is interested in learning. Also, Plato named these groups after Academus, which is another clue that Academus is fascinated by learning and study.

If something were described as "academic," you would expect it to mean

(A) scholarly.

(B) athletic.

(C) melodramatic.

(D) traumatic.

Correct answer: (A)

"Scholarly" is correct because the passage implies Academus's love of knowledge. "Athletic" **(B)** is used to describe that having to do with athletes or sports. "Melodramatic" **(C)** refers to stagelike emotions. "Traumatic" means filled with trauma or distress.

Practice 3

The Titans, a race of huge beings, were a group of immortal gods who lived before Zeus and Hera. Some famous Titans include Rhea, Ocean, Atlas, Hyperion, Prometheus, and Zeus's father, Cronus.

Cronos married his sister Rhea and had several children. He feared that his children would overthrow him, so every time Rhea had a child, Cronus would order her to bring the child to him and he would swallow it. With her last child, Zeus, Rhea wrapped a stone in a blanket and brought it to Cronus. He swallowed it without a second thought. Rhea took the child down to an island, where he was raised by a layman. When Zeus was old enough, he climbed up to Mount Olympus and forced his father to disgorge his brothers and sisters. Then he waged a heated war with Cronus and the rest of the Titans, overthrowing them and subjecting them to horrific punishments.

Greek literature is full of tragedy and action. Similar to fables and parables, these stories were originally told orally, and over time, they became full of action, magic, sex, comedy, and tragedy. The story of Cronos and Zeus is typical of Greek action. The original conflict (man versus man) is tragic; however, Zeus ends up saving the day—but he has to murder his father in the process. Thus, there is no real hero. These types of stories have become the archetypes for today's literature, and it is important to recognize that any conflict you see on television or in the theater, or read in a book has some basis in Greek and/or Roman literature.

A "heated war" most likely means

(A) war in the summer.

(B) war in the desert.

(C) war full of action and violence.

(D) war that is not as violent as a regular war.

Correct answer: **(C)**

Clearly, the context of the story and our knowledge of the main characters shows us that they are violent and ruthless: Cronos eats his children; Zeus overthrows his father and defeats his followers, then metes out "horrific punishments." Choice **(C)**, "war full of action and violence," is the best answer. The time of year when they fought is not mentioned; therefore, the setting answers, **(A)** and **(B)**, are incorrect. Choice **(D)**, "war that is not as violent as a regular war," doesn't make sense for these characters. This war was special, pitting vengeful son against cruel father. The text shows that the fight was violent, and the end result was additional punishment.

Practice 4

The following excerpt describes Mr. and Mrs. Bennet, a well-to-do British couple who live in the country. They have five daughters, and Mrs. Bennet's only resolve in life is to see her daughters married to wealthy men of high respect. Her doggedness was typical of the time period—Regency England (1800–1820)—when upper-class people centered their lives on a complicated infrastructure of manners, including "calling" visits, elaborate dinners and balls, and courtship rituals.

Excerpt from *Pride and Prejudice*
by Jane Austen (1775–1817)

Mr. Bennet was so odd a mixture of quick parts, sarcastic humour, reserve, and caprice, that the experience of three-and-twenty years had been insufficient to make his wife understand his character. Her mind was less difficult to develop. She was a woman of mean understanding, little information, and uncertain temper. When she was discontented, she fancied herself nervous. The business of her life was to get her daughters married; its solace was visiting and news.

Mr. Bennet was among the earliest of those who waited on Mr. Bingley. He had always intended to visit him, though to the last always assuring his wife that he should not go; and till the evening after the visit was paid she had no knowledge of it. It was then disclosed in the following manner. Observing his second daughter employed in trimming a hat, he suddenly addressed her with:

"I hope Mr. Bingley will like it, Lizzy."

"We are not in a way to know what Mr. Bingley likes," said her mother resentfully, "since we are not to visit."

"But you forget, mamma," said Elizabeth, "that we shall meet him at the assemblies, and that Mrs. Long promised to introduce him."

"I do not believe Mrs. Long will do any such thing. She has two nieces of her own. She is a selfish, hypocritical woman, and I have no opinion of her."

The first paragraph gives several key pieces of information to help you picture Mrs. Bennet. First, she is described as having "mean [average] understanding" and being of "little information," which tell us that Mrs. Bennet is not the smartest or most intuitive individual. The fact that she is of "uncertain temper" and given to acting "nervous" when discontent suggests a self-centered personality. This self-centeredness is underscored in the dialogue, where we hear her resentment that her husband (she thinks) will not allow the daughters to see Mr. Bingley: her husband has not done as she has asked, and thus, she is in a huff. She projects her displeasure onto Mrs. Long by describing her as "selfish" and "hypocritical" but then claims to have no opinion of her. Overall, the passage paints a picture of a not terribly bright and somewhat spoiled middle-aged lady of the manor who is given to childish, sulking behavior when she does not get her own way.

Mrs. Bennet's mood could best be described as

(A) friendly.

(B) agitated.

(C) melancholy.

(D) thoughtful.

Correct answer: **(B)**

The best way to find this answer is to review the adjectives that describe Mrs. Bennet. Paragraph 1 has several (here the adjectives are in bold):

> Her mind was less difficult to develop. She was a woman of **mean** understanding, **little** information, and **uncertain** temper. When she was **discontented**, she fancied herself **nervous**. The business of her life was to get her daughters married; its solace was visiting and news.

After looking at the adjectives, it is easy to see that "agitated" is the best choice. Even if you didn't know the meanings of all the boldface words, you can tell that Mrs. Bennet is indeed agitated by her "resentfully" delivered reply to Lizzy and her churlish remarks about Mrs. Long later in the passage.

> Why would Mrs. Long's nieces be a problem for Mrs. Bennet?
> **(A)** They could be competition for the Bennet girls.
> **(B)** They will not fit into the Bennet girls' clothes.
> **(C)** They will not be able to escape Lizzy's visit.
> **(D)** They will not be able to come to the assemblies.

Correct answer: **(A)**

The last sentence of paragraph 1 and Mrs. Bennet's quote at the end of paragraph 6 actually give this away. At the end of paragraph 1, we learn that the "business" of Mrs. Bennet's life "was to get her daughters married." Couple this quote with Mrs. Bennet's last quote: "I do not believe Mrs. Long will do any such thing. She has two nieces of her own. She is a selfish, hypocritical woman, and I have no opinion of her." When thinking that Mrs. Long's nieces may meet Mr. Bingley before her daughters, Mrs. Bennet reacts violently by calling Mrs. Long nasty names. Indeed, Mrs. Bennet is very worried that one of Mrs. Long's nieces will marry Mr. Bingley instead of one of her own daughters.

Practice 5

Excerpt from "The Most Dangerous Game"
by Richard Connell (1857–1912)

In Connell's most famous story, Rainsford, upon swimming to shore after falling off his passing vessel, has found himself on a large jungle island with a most unusual host. The general, a great hunter and marksman, has finally found an animal that gives the best hunt—humans. The general explains his rationale to Rainsford over a sumptuous dinner and informs Rainsford that the next morning, he will be hunted after given a decent head start. In this excerpt, Rainsford is hiding in the brush, having just laid a trap for the general.

> He knew his pursuer was coming; he heard the padding sound of feet on the soft earth, and the night breeze brought him the perfume of the general's cigarette. It seemed to Rainsford that the general was coming with unusual swiftness; he was not feeling his way along, foot by foot. Rainsford, crouching there, could not see the general, nor could he see the pit. He lived a year in a minute. Then he felt an impulse to cry aloud with joy, for he heard the sharp crackle of the breaking branches as the cover of the pit gave way; he heard the sharp scream of pain as the

pointed stakes found their mark. He leaped up from his place of concealment. Then he cowered back. Three feet from the pit a man was standing, with an electric torch in his hand.

"You've done well, Rainsford," the voice of the general called. "Your Burmese tiger pit has claimed one of my best dogs. Again you score. I think, Mr. Rainsford, I'll see what you can do against my whole pack. I'm going home for a rest now. Thank you for a most amusing evening."

Connell uses setting description to create mood for the reader. The tension is obvious as Rainsford hides in the brush waiting for the general to find him. Every sound, every smell, every movement is captured in exact detail, creating a rich sensory description for the reader. When you read selections like this one, be aware of the five senses: sight, taste, touch, smell, and sound. Rich scenes like these are excellent examples of imagery—where the reader is easily able to create a picture in his or her mind of the action, setting, and characters.

Connell writes in lines 4 to 5, "He lived a year in a minute." This line most likely means
(A) Rainsford is really tired.
(B) Rainsford is completely unaware of his surroundings.
(C) Rainsford is trying very hard to make enough noise to be heard.
(D) Rainsford experiences more in this one minute than he might in a year.

Correct answer: **(D)**

Rainsford is so very poised for action that he is acutely aware of his surroundings, making a minute seem like a very, very long time. You may have felt this as well at one time in your life when you waited excitedly for something to happen: those moments until your awaited event seem very, very long.

Which sentence from the passage best illustrates mood?
(A) "You've done well, Rainsford," the voice of the general called.
(B) He knew his pursuer was coming; he heard the padding sound of feet on the soft earth, and the night breeze brought him the perfume of the general's cigarette.
(C) Rainsford, crouching there, could not see the general, nor could he see the pit.
(D) Three feet from the pit a man was standing, with an electric torch in his hand.

Correct Answer: **(B)**

Because mood appeals to the five senses, the best choice is **(B)**. Choice **(B)** employs three senses: the smell of the cigarette, the feel of the breeze against him, and the sound of the padding of feet. The other choices each highlight only one sense: in choice **(A)**, sound, as Rainsford listens to the general call out to him; and in choices **(C)** and **(D)**, sight, as Rainsford strains to see the general in the dark.

Why would Rainsford want to "cry aloud with joy" when he is being pursed by the general?
(A) He wants to be found so the game can be over.
(B) He is actually thinking of trying to imitate a bird.
(C) He feels victorious, and he wants to yell in triumph.
(D) He is happy at his death.

Correct Answer: **(C)**

The answer to this question is found in the rest of the sentence. He wants to "cry aloud with joy" because "he heard the sharp crackle of the breaking branches as the cover of the pit gave way; he heard the sharp scream of pain as the pointed stakes found their mark." He thinks that his trap (the Burmese trap the general mentions in the last paragraph) has claimed the life of the general. Obviously, this conclusion makes him feel happy, as if he's "won" the "battle" between the general and him.

Practice 6

Excerpt from *A Midsummer Night's Dream* by William Shakespeare (1564–1616)

In this play within a play, we meet a group of simpleton laborers who have decided to prepare a wedding play for their prince, Theseus. Because this is a wedding, one would assume that the choice of play would be a romance or a comedy; however, these simple men have chosen the play of *Pyramus and Thisbe*, a tragic play of death, suffering, and suicide. Their choice alone is comedic, and in their great enthusiasm to play the characters "right," they do not want to frighten anyone with their "superior" acting skills. In this excerpt, the men are gathered together to practice the play, and they are concerned that the part of the lion will frighten the ladies in the audience.

1   SNOUT: Will not the ladies be afeard of the lion?
     STARVELING: I fear it, I promise you.
     BOTTOM: Masters, you ought to consider with yourselves: to
                              bring in—God shield us!—a lion among ladies, is a
5   most dreadful thing; for there is not a more fearful
                              wild-fowl than your lion living; and we ought to
                              look to't.
     SNOUT: Therefore another prologue must tell he is not a lion.
     BOTTOM: Nay, you must name his name, and half his face must
10   be seen through the lion's neck: and he himself
                              must speak through, saying thus, or to the same
                              defect,— 'Ladies,'—or 'Fair-ladies—I would wish
                              You,'—or 'I would request you,'—or 'I would
                              entreat you,—not to fear, not to tremble: my life
15   for yours. If you think I come hither as a lion, it
                              were pity of my life: no I am no such thing; I am a
                              man as other men are;' and there indeed let him name
                              his name, and tell them plainly he is Snug the joiner.

Though at first glance this passage may not radiate humor, when performed onstage, the results are uproariously funny. Shakespeare uses subtle humor hints to clue in the reader. Snout (a funny name in itself) wonders if the ladies in the audience will be afraid when they see a lion on stage, and he thinks they may mistake the actor for a real lion. Bottom (an even funnier name) rushes to the rescue, and he suggests that the actors perform a soliloquy stating that "Snug the joiner" is not really a lion at all, but an actor. Obviously, this makes the entire idea of someone actually performing anything on stage ridiculous because there is no suspension of disbelief. Furthermore, imagining someone dressed in a lion suit, who is reassuring the audience not to be afraid of him, is a comic scene indeed.

What is the best interpretation of lines 15 to 17: "If you think I come hither as a lion, it were pity of my life: no I am no such thing; I am a man as other men are"?

(A) I am a lion; take pity on me.

(B) I am not a lion, and I would be very sorry if I were to scare you. I am a man like any man.

(C) Take pity on lions. They are not men.

(D) Men are like lions, and I come to you as one.

Correct answer: **(B)**

Shakespeare's words can be difficult to decipher. The best method is to look at which words you do know and piece together what you think the sentence means. Let's look at the sentence below:

> If you think I come hither as a lion, it were pity of my life: no I am no such thing; I am a man as other men are.

If you put in bold all the words you absolutely know, the sentence would probably look like this:

> **If you think I come** hither **as a lion, it were** pity **of my life**: **no I am no such thing**; **I am a man as other men are.**

Almost all the words in the sentence are common in the English language. So lets break the quote into pieces and "translate" the pieces into simpler, modern-day language (in italics):

> **If you think I come** hither **as a lion**: *If I come to you as a lion.*
> **it were** pity **of my life**: *It is _____ of my life.*
> **no I am no such thing**: *No, I am not that thing.*
> **I am a man as other men are**: *I am a man like any other man.*

Breaking it down in this way, you can easily see that **(B)** is the obvious choice. Even if you don't know the meaning of "pity" and "hither," the quote still makes some sense. The other answer choices either interpret only part of the quote or misinterpret parts of it. Be careful when asked to look at Shakespearean quotes for this reason: there is usually more than one part to consider.

Excerpt from *Romeo and Juliet*
by William Shakespeare (1564–1616)

Romeo and Juliet is the tale of two young adults who fall in love and marry, unbeknownst to their parents, who are bitter rivals. Early in the day, right after Romeo marries Juliet in secret, Mercutio (Romeo's best friend) and Tybalt (Juliet's cousin) get into an argument and Tybalt kills Mercutio, infuriating Romeo, who then kills Tybalt. For this crime, Romeo is banished to Mantua, a neighboring town, and Juliet's parents, who arrange a marriage for Juliet to make her "happy" after the death of her cousin, tell her this sobering news. Juliet rebels against her parents, refusing the marriage, and her father gives her an ultimatum: either she does as he says or she will be disowned. In terror at her predicament and without Romeo's guidance and comfort, Juliet goes to Friar Lawrence, who gives her a vial of special poison that will make her appear dead so she will be taken to her family tomb (where Tybalt is buried, too), thus giving her a chance to escape with Romeo. In this excerpt, Juliet is about to drink the poison, and she has serious questions and thoughts about her upcoming experience.

1   JULIET: I have a faint cold fear thrills through my veins,
     That almost freezes up the heat of life:
     I'll call them back again to comfort me:
     Nurse! What should she do here?
5   My dismal scene I needs must act alone.
     Come, vial.
     What if this mixture do not work at all?
     Shall I be married then to-morrow morning?
     No, no: this shall forbid it: lie thou there.
10   (*Laying down her dagger*)
     What if it be a poison, which the friar
     Subtly hath minister'd to have me dead,
     Lest in this marriage he should be dishonour'd,
     Because he married me before to Romeo?
15   I fear it is: and yet, methinks, it should not,
     For he hath still been tried a holy man.
     How if, when I am laid into the tomb,
     I wake before the time that Romeo
     Come to redeem me? there's a fearful point!
20   Shall I not, then, be stifled in the vault,
     To whose foul mouth no healthsome air breathes in,
     And there die strangled ere my Romeo comes?
     Or, if I live, is it not very like,
     The horrible conceit of death and night,
25   Together with the terror of the place,—
     As in a vault, an ancient receptacle,
     Where, for these many hundred years, the bones
     Of all my buried ancestors are packed:
     Where bloody Tybalt, yet but green in earth,
30   Lies festering in his shroud; where, as they say,
     At some hours in the night spirits resort;—
     Alack, alack, is it not like that I,
     So early waking, what with loathsome smells,
     And shrieks like mandrakes' torn out of the earth,
35   That living mortals, hearing them, run mad:—
     O, if I wake, shall I not be distraught,
     Environed with all these hideous fears?
     And madly play with my forefather's joints?
     And pluck the mangled Tybalt from his shroud?
40   And, in this rage, with some great kinsman's bone,
     As with a club, dash out my desperate brains?
     O, look! methinks I see my cousin's ghost
     Seeking out Romeo, that did spit his body
     Upon a rapier's point: stay, Tybalt, stay!
45   Romeo, I come! this do I drink to thee.

Because plays are meant to be performed on a stage, the audience can't know what is going on in a character's mind (as you can in a book because it is written out for you). In order to convey this information, the actor performs a soliloquy—a dramatic speech that tells the audience a character's emotions and thoughts. Juliet's soliloquy is a great example for study because her worry about being locked up in a tomb is very valid. Who wouldn't be scared to wake up in a pitch-dark tomb where, next to you, is your cousin's rotting corpse (lines 29–30) and possibly ghosts lurking in the shadows (line 31)? What if, by lying in a dark, scary tomb, she goes insane from the terror of it all (lines 33–41)? And what if the plan (where Romeo and Friar Lawrence open the tomb to rescue her) doesn't work and she's locked in there forever (lines 17–22)? And what about the possibility that the potion she's about to drink will actually kill her instead of just putting her to sleep (lines 11–15)—that *is* a scary thought! But despite all of her concerns and defying insanity, ghosts, and awry plans, she decides to drink it anyway.

Pay close attention to the adjectives in soliloquies. Because they are all about emotions and plans, they include a great deal of description, which will also tell you the main character's mood and give details of the coming plans. For example, take a look at the bolded adjectives:

To whose **foul** mouth no **healthsome** air breathes in.

The two adjectives in this line are very strong. "Foul" and "healthsome," when used together, are opposites, which should clue you in as to how Juliet feels about the tomb. Look at the next example:

As in a vault, an **ancient** receptacle,
Where, for **these many hundred** years, the bones
Of **all my buried** ancestors are packed:
Where **bloody** Tybalt, yet but **green** in earth,
Lies **festering** in his shroud;

Even if you read only the adjectives in this section, you can easily discern what Juliet is talking about while she thinks about her fate.

Juliet's mood could be best described as
(A) cautious.
(B) cheerful.
(C) disappointed.
(D) low.

Correct answer: **(A)**

Juliet is indeed cautious. Her listing of all the things that can possibly happen to her in this scheme shows she is definitely considering all the negative possibilities. She wonders what the end result will be. Nevertheless, though she is cautious about moving forward, she does anyway. "Cheerful" **(B)** is obviously the opposite of how she feels in this scene. "Disappointed" **(C)** and "low" **(D)** do not fit well here. "Low" may have been a choice, but she is not sad, a synonym of "low"; rather, she is much more cautious and apprehensive about the upcoming events.

What is the best definition for the phrase "freezes up the heat of life" (line 2)?
(A) Surprise
(B) Fascination
(C) Death
(D) Fear

Correct answer: **(C)**

Juliet says in lines 1 to 2 that she is so scared, she has so much cold running "through her veins," it almost "freezes up the heat of life." "Heat" here means to be warm and alive. The cold would quiet it, thus killing the person who is living.

What does "madly" mean in line 38?

(A) Angry

(B) Sullen

(C) Insane

(D) Struggle

Correct answer: (C)

Juliet is describing what she would do if she suddenly lost her mind in terror of the tomb. The whole line means that she would, if going insane, pick up her ancestors bones and play with them. "Mad," in this sense, shows up often in literature; be careful when you come across it in your reading as it can have more than one meaning.

In lines 7 to 10, Juliet wonders if the potion will work at all, and then she lays down her dagger. What is the dagger for?

(A) To cut open the vial

(B) To use as protection against Romeo

(C) To remove a bone splinter

(D) To kill herself if she has to marry

Correct answer: (D)

Let's take a look at these lines:

What if this mixture do not work at all?
Shall I be married then to-morrow morning?
No, no: this shall forbid it: lie thou there.
(Laying down her dagger)

Being able to infer what is happening in a piece of literature is very important, but in Shakespeare, it is essential. She says that if the mixture doesn't work and she has to be married, that the dagger will "forbid" the marriage from happening. The only way a dagger could forbid something would be for someone to use it for force.

Writing

What Is the Writing Task Like?

The writing task on the English-Language Arts Section of the CHSPE is used to assess your writing abilities. It asks you to write a persuasive essay in which you express your opinion on the given issue and then support your position with a logical presentation of reasons and details to convince the reader to accept that position. Stating your opinion clearly and supporting it with relevant, appropriate examples is key to your success. There is no right or wrong answer to the question;

rather, your skill in writing your answer will be assessed with a grading rubric. You must achieve a score of 3 or higher to pass the writing subtest. The following table details the writing task rubric.

CHSPE Writing Task Rubric

SCORE	EXPECTATIONS
6	Essay addresses the writing task in an excellent manner. The essay • elaborates a central idea with appropriate specificity; is purposefully organized • demonstrates control of a variety of sentence structures; uses precise word choice • is generally free of errors in grammar, usage, and conventions
5	Essay addresses the writing task in an effective manner. The essay • elaborates a central idea with some degree of specificity; is well organized • demonstrates control of sentence structure; uses appropriate word choice • may have minor errors in grammar, usage, and conventions
4	Essay addresses the writing task in a competent manner. The essay • supports a central idea with some degree of specificity; is organized • demonstrates control of sentence structure; uses generally appropriate word choice • may have a few errors in grammar, usage, and conventions
3	Essay addresses the writing task in a basic manner. The essay • provides some relevant details in support of a central idea; has some organization • demonstrates basic control of sentence structure and word choice • may have errors in grammar, usage, and conventions, but errors do not cause confusion
2	Essay addresses the writing task in a limited manner. The essay • provides limited or irrelevant details; may not have a clear central idea or may be poorly organized • exhibits inadequate control of sentence structure and word choice • may have serious or repeated errors in grammar, usage, and conventions that may cause confusion
1	Essay may or may not address the writing task. The essay • provides little or no detail; may have no central idea • exhibits little or no control of sentence structure • may have pervasive errors that cause confusion

Example Essays

This section contains five sample essays, each a response to the same writing task. Each essay has been given a score according to the CHSPE writing rubric, and an explanation follows each essay so you can better understand the differences among these writing samples.

> The government is considering raising the age requirement for driver's licenses to 18 instead of 16. Do you think this is a wise decision?

Essay 1

Wow! Raising the age of the driver's license would not be good because lots of kids want to drive right after they turn 16 it would really be a sad thing. I know lots of people who wait and wait to get behind the wheel and they drive really good. I know that when I turned 16 I asked my for parents for a car and I got an old truck it's ok though because at least I have a ride. Some of my friends have to take the bus. So, it wouldn't be a good decision and lots of people would complain.

Score: 1

This essay does not address the question. It talks about getting a car, taking the bus, and so on. The only reason given in support of maintaining the current age requirement rather than raising it to 18 is that "lots of people . . . wait and wait" and people would "complain" if they were not allowed to get their license at 16.

There are limited to no specific details. The only real detail is that the writer received a truck.

There is little control of sentence structure. There are run-on sentences, comma errors, and word-choice problems.

The tone of the essay is confusing. Is the writer talking to adults or friends? The run-on sentences make following the text difficult.

Essay 2

It wouldn't be a good decision because their are lots of people who are good drivers even though they are 16. I am a good student and I have a job and I work really really hard so I am responsible. Sometimes I even have to watch my little sister, and if I can do that I can do anything! I signed up to take a course at school it was a driving course, so I could know all the right signs of the road and how to parallel park and drive on the highway. Also, I practiced a lot because I don't want to hurt anyone or get in an accident. Since I did all these things, I should get to drive at 16.

Score: 3

This essay addresses the question in a basic manner. It answers the question simply, but it presents only one point of view: that of the writer. As indicated by the use of "I" throughout the essay, the writer fails to consider how the change might affect others and/or society in general; therefore, the argument becomes less effective. The essay has basic organization: it includes an introduction and a conclusion sentence with some supportive details, although one of them is trivial.

The writing illustrates basic control of sentence structure but includes several punctuation errors and one important spelling error. The repetition of words also shows limited word choice.

Though the essay contains the errors just stated, these mistakes do not cause confusion to the reader. Therefore, this essay would receive a 3 rather than a 2.

Essay 3

Driving is a huge responsibility, and it should not be taken light. A good driver needs to have the right skills and things and also be mature. Some immature behaviors are things like driving and eating, putting on makeup, and talking on the phone or texting friends. Younger people sometimes blast music so they can't hear things good, and they also pack lots of kids into their car. All of these things are dangerous.

There are many accidents caused by kids who drink, do drugs, or other things and drive. Lots of kids this age go to parties were alcohol and drugs are readily available and then they think they are sober enough to drive themselves home. This is not the case, and sometimes people get killed or hurt because one kid made a wrong decision.

I think that 18 is a better age because the person is more mature and responsible. They won't want to endanger other people around them, and they will pay better attention to signs and road rules.

Score: 3

This essay is organized, has specific details, and approaches the topic from a "world" perspective, rather than from that of the writer alone ("I").

Though the writer has made a few minor spelling and grammar errors, none of them take away from the reading or comprehension of the piece.

The word choice holds back this essay, however. Notice the use of the word "things." Using specific words, actually telling the reader what you want to say, is vitally important with persuasive essays. In this case, what the reader may think of as "things" may be very different from what the writer intended. Notice the difference in the next example. It is the same essay, but editing it for word choice changes the score to a 4.

Essay 4

Driving is a huge responsibility, and it should not be taken light. A good driver needs to have the right skills [removed "and things"] and driving knowledge and also be mature. Some immature behaviors are [removed "things like"] driving and eating, putting on makeup, and talking on the phone or texting friends. Younger people sometimes blast music so they can't hear traffic noises good, and they also pack lots of kids into their car. All of these behaviors are dangerous.

There are many accidents caused by kids who drink and do drugs [removed "and other things"] and drive. Lots of kids this age go to parties were alcohol and drugs are readily available and then they think they are sober enough to drive themselves home. This is not the case, and sometimes people get killed or hurt because one kid made a wrong decision.

I think that 18 is a better age because the person is more mature and responsible. They won't want to endanger other people around them, and they will pay better attention to signs and road rules.

Score: 4

Replacing "things" with more concrete details or removing it to make the text less vague raises the score one point. If this piece had a few more good details and other grammatical and stylistic fixes, it could score a 5 or 6. Take a look at essay 5.

Essay 5

Driving is a huge responsibility, and it should not be taken lightly [**replaced adjective "light"**]. A good driver should have [**replaced "needs to have"**] the right skills and driving knowledge and also be a mature young adult [**replaced just "mature"**]. Some immature behaviors are driving and eating, putting on makeup, and talking on the phone or texting friends. Younger people sometimes blast music so they can't hear traffic noises well [**replaced adjective "good"**], and they sometimes [**deleted "also"**] pack lots of kids into their car. All of these behaviors are dangerous.

There are many accidents caused by kids who drink and do drugs and drive. Lots of kids this age go to parties where [**replaced "were"**] alcohol and drugs are readily available, [**added needed comma**] and then they think they are sober enough to drive themselves home. This is not the case, and sometimes people get killed or hurt because one kid made a wrong decision.

I think that 18 is a better age for driving [**added for clarity**] because the person is more mature and responsible. He or she [**replaced "they," a plural pronoun when a singular one is needed**] will not [**replaced "won't"**] want to endanger other people [**removed "around them"**] and [**removed comma and "they"**] will pay better attention to signs and road rules.

Score: 6

Replacing words, checking spelling, and clarifying material raises the essay to the maximum score. Grammatically sound, this essay explains the writer's position in an easy, understandable manner. The writer has varied the sentence structure and has paid special attention to subject-verb agreement.

The Basics of Writing

"There is magic in every beginning . . ." Hermann Hesse

There is magic in every new start, and anytime you are asked to write an essay, it is like a new beginning, filled with the magic of possibility. Though you will be asked to write an essay for the CHSPE, do not worry about the topics too much. As mentioned in the previous section, the writing task topics are opinion based; therefore, you should be able to answer the question based on the events in your life. Here are some typical questions:

The Constitution states that all Americans have the right to bear arms. However, should this clause be rewritten for today's society?

Many music CDs and video games are labeled "parental advisory." Who should decide what should or should not be censored? Write a letter to this person detailing your opinion on this subject.

Many people think that once a person reaches the age of 18 and can legally vote, that same person should be able to drink alcohol as well. Is this an appropriate correlation? Why or why not?

As you can see, these questions are thought provoking, and they require a personal answer. There is no right or wrong answer; rather, you will be graded on your writing structure, style, and organization. In the next section, we use the topic of "Teen Life" to explore these and other aspects of the writing process.

The Writing Process

Writing is a process, and there are four specific steps that will help you achieve greater writing success: prewriting, writing a draft, editing/reviewing, and publishing.

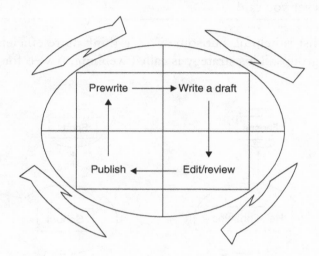

The arrows surrounding the diagram show that each step moves into the next step. Without the previous step or the one after, the writing process is incomplete. We will explore each step in detail in the next few pages.

Step 1: Prewrite

When you prewrite, you gather information in a very quick way. The technical term for this process is "brainstorming."

Anytime you are given a thought-provoking topic, brainstorm for two or three minutes to quickly gather ideas about your subject. There are a few methods for brainstorming. One way is to quickly create a list. Here's the list that might result after brainstorming on our topic, "Teen Life":

Teen Life

Technology	Travel	Lessons
Clothes	Sports	Hobbies
Friends	Clubs	TV
Entertainment	School	Parents
Money	Stress	Family
Jobs	Music	Siblings

As you can see, quickly listing a bunch of words about teen life is a fruitful exercise. Though there are only 18 elements listed here, you could most likely come up with more. If you are given a difficult topic and you come up with only 10 ideas or fewer, try brainstorming for another minute to see if anything else comes to mind.

Once you have a good inventory of ideas, look closely at your list. More than likely, you can group some of the items together. For example, "family" and "siblings" could go together, and "entertainment," "technology," and "music" could be grouped into one subject. The key is to look for *three* main topics. If you can find three topics (and more than likely, you can), you can group them together in a process called webbing or chunking.

Three is a magic number. It is not too many, nor is it too little. It is the perfect number of topics in a thesis statement, which is the key to any essay. Always try to give three examples in your writing whenever you can!

Writing out this list is helpful, but some people think more efficiently if they are able to move their ideas into groups. This strategy is called webbing. A web for Teen Life might look like this:

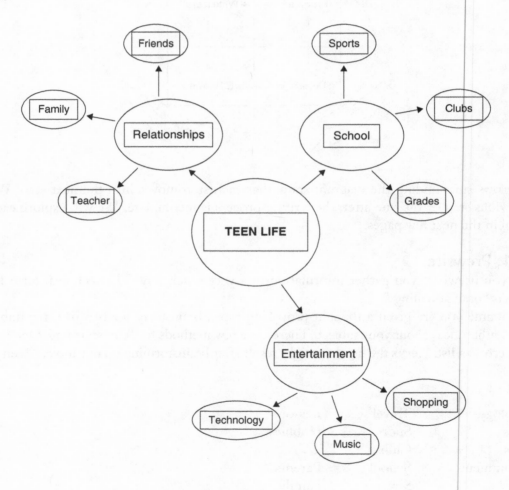

Looking at this web, you may suddenly realize some missing ideas. You can add them into your web at this point, but remember to keep your *three* main topics—in this case, relationships, school, and entertainment—distinct enough from each other so they have independent information. You do not want to have topics that are too similar: if they are too similar, then all the information should go into one paragraph instead of three.

Step 2: Write a draft

Now that you have your ideas organized, it's time to write a draft. With the CHSPE, you may take as long as you like to write your essay, but it's a good idea to limit yourself to about 45 minutes. If you write for longer than that, you risk the possibility of overshooting your topic, which will decrease your points. Forty-five minutes is enough time to create a well-developed, organized, yet succinct essay.

The thesis statement

A thesis statement is a sentence that provides the backbone for a piece of expository writing. A good thesis statement gives direction to a written piece, provides relevant details to the body paragraphs, and discusses the topic thoroughly. In essence, the thesis statement is the most important part of your essay: mastering the art of writing a thesis statement will not only help you organize your written work, it will also give polish to any written piece.

For this lesson, picture in your mind a three-pronged pitchfork.

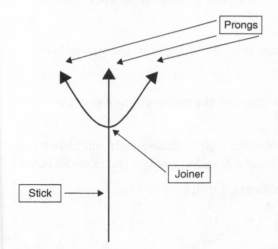

The pitchfork is a great visual aid to help you understand the thesis statement. All of the prongs on the pitchfork are essential to the pitchfork working properly, and there is space between each prong. Each prong is independent from the other. If only two prongs are present on the pitchfork, it wouldn't work as well. Furthermore, the stick must be firmly attached to the prongs: the joiner is very essential to the entire mechanism. Without a strong joiner, the pitchfork would not work properly and would be worthless.

Now that we have the pitchfork and its elements firmly secured in our thoughts, let us look at *how* and *why* the pitchfork works for thesis statements.

Every thesis statement has a simple skeleton. It looks like this:

_____ is _____ because of _____, _____, and _____.

Each blank space represents part of the pitchfork. Look at the following diagram:

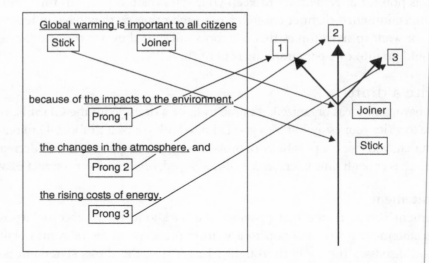

Notice that each prong of the thesis statement is true: it must be for the joiner to work properly. For example:

Global warming is important to all citizens because of the impacts to the environment.

This statement is true, so prong 1 is correct.

Global warming is important to all citizens because of the changes in the atmosphere.

This statement is true, so prong 2 is correct.

Global warming is important to all citizens because of the rising costs of energy.

This statement is true, so prong 3 is also correct.

Having correct, working prongs is essential to writing a good thesis statement. Otherwise, the statement won't make any sense and the rest of the essay will suffer. Look at the example below:

Dogs are the best pets because they are affectionate, loyal, and vicious.

Let's review the prongs to see if the thesis is correct:

Dogs are the best pets because they are affectionate.

This statement could be considered true by the author.

Dogs are the best pets because they are loyal.

This statement could be considered true by the author.

Dogs are the best pets because they are vicious.

This statement, though the author might consider it to be true, does not work in this thesis. A vicious dog is the opposite of an affectionate one (prong 1), so using "vicious" as the third prong creates a contradiction—a problem—in the thesis.

In addition to ensuring that all the prongs are true, you must clearly distinguish between each prong. If two of the prongs are too similar, there will not be enough or equal information for each prong. For example, look at the statement below:

Dogs are the best pets because they are affectionate, loyal, and loving.

Notice that prongs 1 and 3 are very similar. Distinguishing between "affectionate" and "loving" would be difficult for the writer. The essay would be too focused on the "affectionate and loving" part about dogs, and it would make the thesis sound trivial.

In conclusion, the thesis statement is the integral part of your essay. Look over your thesis statement quickly to make sure that all of the pieces of the statement work well together and can stand alone if read only with the joiner. In addition, being careful to develop three distinct prongs will lead to a strong, balanced thesis.

Step 3: Edit/Review

Here is an example of a "Teen Life" essay, using the key items in the brainstorming activity:

There are many important things about living life as a teenager. Some people think it's hard to be a teenager and some other people think that they want to go back to being a teenager because it's their "glory years". Either way, the most important elements of teen life are school, relationships, and entertainment.

There is no doubt that school makes up a big part of the life of a teenager. Sports teams take up a lot of time with practice and games. During and after-school clubs can take up a lot of time too. Finally, working on homework and going to school events can make the life of a teenager very busy. All of these school items can take up time.

Though school events can take up a lot of time, working on relationships can be stressful and time-consuming as well. Teenagers must maintain good relationships with their teachers so they can communicate well with other. The same goes for parental relationships: communication is key to having a healthy parent/child relationship, especially during the difficult teen years. Finally, friend relationships can be the most rewarding, stressful, and timeconsuming for all teenagers. Many of these relationships will last for several years, making these friendships an important part of the teenager's life span and deserving of the care they are given. All of these relationships help to shape the life of a teenager.

Along with friends, entertainment is a very part of a teenager's life. Cell phones and computers make communication a fun and necessary aspect of every teenager's social circle. Many teenagers get interested in music and loyally follow their favorite bands through high school and beyond. Finally, shopping for clothing, accessories, makeup and sports equipment are a great way to socialize and learn about money for a teenager. Teenage entertainment is certainly time-consuming and very different from the lives of their parents.

In conclusion, teenagers have a fast-paced, fun and stress-filled life. Whether its shopping for clothes, working out for the big game, or doing homework on the computer, teenagers are busy workers, trying to make their way through life.

This essay would more than likely receive a 4 on the writing rubric because it is well organized, but there is the possibility that the person grading this essay could give it a 3 because of the missing word, misspellings, weak thesis and topic/conclusion sentences, and word choice.

After you write your essay, you may be thinking, "Whew! I'm done! All I need to do now is turn it in to the proctor, and I'm finished!" But wait! Many students skip over the Edit/Review section of the writing process, and in doing so, lose many points over silly errors.

Here are the steps to effectively edit your essay:

1. Reread your essay carefully. Say the words in your head slowly. Try to pretend that you have never read or heard about this subject before this day. Are all the thoughts clear?

2. Look carefully for skipped words. The brain can sometimes skip over prepositions and articles; words like "of," "if," and "the" are commonly left out of papers.

3. Look carefully at your spelling, paying special attention to homonyms. Common misspelled homonyms are "their" (the possessive), "there" (the noun), and "they're" (a contraction for "they are"). Others include "to" (the preposition), "too" (the adverb), and "two" (the number). If there are other words in your essay that you aren't sure about, err on the side of caution and pick a better word that you can absolutely spell correctly. "Definitely" is not "defiantly": this is a completely different word! Finally, remember that this is an essay, not an email or text message. "You" is not "U," "I" is not "i," and "love" is not "luv."

4. Look at sentence structure. Are all of your sentences indeed sentences? Do they all have a subject and a verb and are one complete thought? If you think some of your sentences are too long and wordy, then break them down into easier to understand statements. Do you have a mix of sentences? Having too many simple sentences will make your essay sound elementary, while having too many compound/complex sentences will make your essay cumbersome and wordy.

5. Look carefully at your punctuation. Is there a period or other end punctuation at the end of every sentence? Are all your commas in the right place?

6. Did you include a topic sentence and end the essay with the conclusion sentence? Remember, topic sentences lead the paragraph and describe what the paragraph is about to the reader. Additionally, conclusion sentences tie up the paragraph, and they let the reader know that the paragraph is indeed complete. Topic and conclusion sentences are the cornerstones to any good written piece, so look your essay over carefully.

7. Think carefully about your choice of words. Did you repeat one word too often? If so, think about synonyms that would fit instead. Did you use simple descriptive words like "good," "bad," "happy," "big," "ok," "stuff," and "things." These words do not tell the reader anything specific; rather, choose words that effectively show your reader *your* complete thought. For example, if you said, "The food was ok at the restaurant," you may have meant any of the following:

   - The food was not hot.
   - The food was appetizing, but not as tasty as the dinner you had last night.
   - The food was too cold.
   - The food wasn't seasoned to your taste.
   - The food came to the table late.

   Do you see how many options there are in the word "ok"?

8. Lastly, look over your subject-verb agreement. Do your verbs match your subject in number and tense? Is the verb tense the same all the way through the essay?

Once you have carefully reviewed your essay, make any corrections and changes neatly. Neatness is an important aspect to any written selection. If the reader has a difficult time getting through the essay because it is messy, it can create a bit of a bias in the reader for content. However, if you remember these steps, you can turn in your essay with confidence.

Let's work each of the above steps and see how it changes the original essay.

Step 1: Reread for clarity

Step 2: Skipped words

Step 3: Spelling/homonyms

There are many important things about living life as a teenager. Some people think it's hard to be a teenager and some other people think that they want to go back to being a teenager because it's their "glory years". Either way, the most important elements of teen life are school, relationships, and entertainment.

> **Step 1:** What does "glory years" mean? Maybe I should change that to "the best years of their lives."

There is no doubt that school makes up a big part of the life of a teenager. Sports teams take up a lot of time with practice and games. During and after-school clubs can take up a lot of time too. Finally, working on homework and going to school events can make the life of a teenager very busy. All of these school items can take up time.

Though school events can take up a lot of time, working on relationships can be stressful and time-consuming as well. Teenagers must maintain good relationships with their teachers so they can communicate well with other. The same goes for parental relationships: communication is key to having a healthy parent/child relationship, especially during the difficult teen years. Finally, friend relationships can be the most rewarding, stressful, and time-consuming for all teenagers. Many of these relationships will last for several years, making these friendships an important part of the teenager's life span and deserving of the care they are given. All of these relationships help to shape the life of a teenager.

> **Step 2:** I skipped a word in the second line of paragraph 3!

Along with friends, entertainment is a very part of a teenager's life. Cell phones and computers make communication a fun and necessary aspect of every teenager's social circle. Many teenagers get interested in music and loyally follow their favorite bands through high school and beyond. Finally, shopping for clothing, accessories, makeup and sports equipment are a great way to socialize and learn about money for a teenager. Teenage entertainment is certainly time-consuming and very different from the lives of their parents.

> **Step 2:** I skipped a word in the first line of paragraph 4!

In conclusion, teenagers have a fast-paced, fun and stress-filled life. Whether its shopping for clothes, working out for the big game, or doing homework on the computer, teenagers are busy workers, trying to make their way through life.

> **Step 3:** "its" should be "it's" or "it is."

> **Step 1:** "Fun" and "stress-filled". . . does that really work? Maybe I should choose two words with more in common.

Now that we have applied the first three steps, we can see that there needs to be a few minor changes to the essay. Here is what the essay could possibly look like, with the changes underlined:

> There are many important things about living life as a teenager. Some people think it's hard to be a teenager and some other people think that they want to go back to being a teenager because it was <u>the best years of their lives</u>. Either way, the most important elements of teen life are school, relationships, and entertainment.
>
> There is no doubt that school makes up a big part of the life of a teenager. Sports teams take up a lot of time with practice and games. During and after-school clubs can take up a lot of time too. Finally, working on homework and going to school events can make the life of a teenager very busy. All of these school items can take up time.
>
> Though school events can take up a lot of time, working on relationships can be stressful and time-consuming as well. Teenagers must maintain good relationships with their teachers so they can communicate well with <u>each other</u>. The same goes for parental relationships: communication is key to having a healthy parent/child relationship, especially during the difficult teen years. Finally, friend relationships can be the most rewarding, stressful, and time-consuming for all teenagers. Many of these relationships will last for several years, making these friendships an important part of the teenager's life span and deserving of the care they are given. All of these relationships help to shape the life of a teenager.
>
> Along with friends, entertainment is a very <u>important</u> part of a teenager's life. Cell phones and computers make communication a fun and necessary aspect of every teenager's social circle. Many teenagers get interested in music and loyally follow their favorite bands through high school and beyond. Finally, shopping for clothing, accessories, makeup and sports equipment are a great way to socialize and learn about money for a teenager. Teenage entertainment is certainly time-consuming and very different from the lives of their parents.
>
> In conclusion, teenagers have a fast-paced, <u>interesting</u> and <u>stress-filled</u> life. Whether it is shopping for clothes, working out for the big game, or doing homework on the computer, teenagers are busy workers, trying to make their way through life.

Now, let's apply the next three steps:

Step 4: Sentence structure
Step 5: Punctuation
Step 6: Topic and conclusion sentence

> There are many important things about living life as a teenager. <u>Some people think it's hard to be a teenager and some other people think that they want to go back to being a teenager because it's the best years of their lives. Either way, the most important elements of teen life are school, relationships, and entertainment</u>.

Step 4: The second sentence is a little wordy. I should condense it or break it into two sentences.

Step 6: My thesis statement is good, but if I add some adjectives to it, it could be great!

There is no doubt that school makes up a big part of the life of a teenager. Sports teams take up a lot of time with practice and games. During and after-school clubs can take up a lot of time too. Finally, working on homework and going to school events can make the life of a teenager very busy. All of these school items can take up time.

Though school events can take up a lot of time, working on relationships can be stressful and time-consuming as well. Teenagers must maintain good relationships with their teachers so they can communicate well with each other. The same goes for parental relationships: communication is key to having a healthy parent/child relationship, especially during the difficult teen years. Finally, friend relationships can be the most rewarding, stressful, and time-consuming for all teenagers. Many of these relationships will last for several years, making these friendships an important part of the teenager's life span and deserving of the care they are given. All of these relationships help to shape the life of a teenager.

Along with friends, entertainment is a very important part of a teenager's life. Cell phones and computers make communication a fun and necessary aspect of every teenager's social circle. Many teenagers get interested in music and loyally follow their favorite bands through high school and beyond. Finally, shopping for clothing, accessories, makeup and sports equipment are a great way to socialize and learn about money for a teenager. Teenage entertainment is certainly time-consuming and very different from the lives of their parents.

In conclusion, teenagers have a fast-paced, interesting and stress-filled life. Whether it is shopping for clothes, working out for the big game, or doing homework on the computer, teenagers are busy workers, trying to make their way through life.

> Step 6: My conclusion sentences in paragraphs 2 and 3 could be better.

> Step 5: A comma is missing after "makeup" in the 4th paragraph. These are items in a list.

> Step 5: A comma is missing after "interesting" in the last paragraph. These are items in a list.

Now, let's take a look at the applied changes:

There are many important things about living life as a teenager. Some people think it's hard to be a teenager while others think their teenage years were the best years of their lives. Either way, the most important elements of teen life are dealing with school expectations, navigating relationships, and enjoying entertainment.

There is no doubt that school makes up a big part of the life of a teenager. Sports teams take up a lot of time with practice and games. During and after-school clubs can take up a lot of time too. Finally, working on homework and going to school events can make the life of a teenager very busy. Though school expectations are very important, they are a time-consuming part of a teenager's life.

Though school events can take up a lot of time, working on relationships can be stressful and time-consuming as well. Teenagers must maintain good relationships with their teachers so they can communicate well with each other. The same goes for parental relationships: communication is key to having a healthy parent/child relationship, especially during the difficult teen years. Finally, friend relationships can be the most rewarding, stressful, and time-consuming for all teenagers. Many of these relationships will last for several years, making these friendships an important part of the teenager's life span and deserving of the care they are given. <u>Navigating through relationships is difficult but a fundamental part of a teenager's life.</u>

Along with friends, entertainment is a very important part of a teenager's life. Cell phones and computers make communication a fun and necessary aspect of every teenager's social circle. Many teenagers get interested in music and loyally follow their favorite bands through high school and beyond. Finally, shopping for clothing, accessories, <u>makeup</u>, and sports equipment are a great way to socialize and learn about money for a teenager. Teenage entertainment is certainly time-consuming and very different from the lives of their parents.

In conclusion, teenagers have a fast-paced, <u>interesting</u>, and stress-filled life. Whether it is shopping for clothes, working out for the big game, or doing homework on the computer, teenagers are busy workers, trying to make their way through life.

It's looking better! But now we have to apply the last two steps:

Step 7: Word choice
Step 8: Subject/verb agreement

In this essay, Step 8 is complete. There are no errors with subject/verb agreement.

For Step 7, quickly scan your paper for repetitive words. In this essay, there are several words that are used over and over again. When this happens at home, we can turn to a thesaurus. However, when testing, you have to call upon your vocabulary knowledge to change some of the repetitive words. Be careful, though, because you must be sure you know the meaning of the words you use in your essay!

Next, look at the "simple" words. This essay uses "important," "difficult," and "a lot" often. Are there superior words that would make the reader understand your point better? Let's look at the essay with the words "important," "difficult," and "a lot" underlined.

There are many <u>important</u> things about living life as a teenager. Some people think it's hard to be a teenager while others think their teenage years were the best years of their lives. Either way, the most <u>important</u> elements of teen life are dealing with school expectations, navigating relationships, and enjoying entertainment.

There is no doubt that school makes up a big part of the life of a teenager. Sports teams take up <u>a lot</u> of time with practice and games. During and after-school clubs can take up <u>a lot</u> of time too. Finally, working on homework and going to school events can make the life of a teenager very busy. Though school expectations are very <u>important</u>, they are a big part of a teenager's life.

Though school events can take up <u>a lot</u> of time, working on relationships can be stressful as well. Teenagers must maintain good relationships with their teachers so they can communicate well with each other. The same goes for parental relationships: communication is key to having a healthy parent/child relationship, especially during the <u>difficult</u> teen years. Finally, friend relationships can be the most rewarding, stressful, and time-consuming for all teenagers. Many of these relationships will last for several years, making these friendships an <u>important</u> part of the teenager's life span and deserving of the care they are given. Navigating through relationships is <u>difficult</u> but a fundamental part of a teenager's life.

Along with friends, entertainment is a very important part of a teenager's life. Cell phones and computers make communication a fun and necessary aspect of every teenager's social circle. Many teenagers get interested in music and loyally follow their favorite bands through high school and beyond. Finally, shopping for clothing, accessories, makeup, and sports equipment are a great way to socialize and learn about money for a teenager. Teenage entertainment is certainly time-consuming and very different from the lives of their parents.

In conclusion, teenagers have a fast-paced, interesting, and stress-filled life. Whether it is shopping for clothes, working out for the big game, or doing homework on the computer, teenagers are busy workers, trying to make their way through life.

The word "important" is used several times in this selection: way too many to be considered appropriate for such a short essay. "A lot" was used only three times, but it was used too close together. "Difficult" is used only twice, but it also is used closely together. Anytime there are two or more words placed so close together in an essay, it "sounds" repetitive to the reader. It is a good choice to change one of them if possible.

Words like "important" lose…ahem…importance when they are used too many times. How does the reader know what is *really* important over something that isn't *really* important at all?

The best way to prepare for word choice is to study your vocabulary. Read often. Create word banks (lists of synonyms) to help you prepare for written tests. For example, a word bank for "important" could include these terms:

Significant
Vital
Imperative
Essential
Critical
Chief
Main
Principal

Finally, what about "things" in the first sentence and "hard" in the second sentence? These words are too simple for this type of essay. Like "important," something that is "hard" for one person, may be easy for another. It is better to change these simple words to words that are more descriptive and relevant to the essay.

Let's change some of the dull, lifeless words in the essay to make the details really pop. Remember: you don't need to change all of the words.

There are many significant elements to living life as a teenager. Some people think it's awkward to be a teenager while others think their teenage years were the best years of their lives. Either way, the most important elements of teen life are dealing with school expectations, navigating relationships, and enjoying entertainment.

There is no doubt that school makes up a <u>considerable</u> part of the life of a teenager. Sports teams take up <u>copious amounts</u> of time with practice and games. During and after-school clubs can take up <u>plenty</u> of time too. Finally, working on homework and going to school events can make the life of a teenager very busy. Though school expectations are <u>vital</u>, they are a time-consuming part of a teenager's life.

Though school events can take up a <u>significant amount</u> of time, working on relationships can be stressful and time-consuming as well. Teenagers must maintain <u>fruitful</u> relationships with their teachers so they can communicate well with each other. The same goes for parental relationships: communication is key to having a healthy parent/child relationship, especially during the <u>trying</u> teen years. Finally, friend relationships can be the most rewarding, stressful, and time-consuming for all teenagers. Many of these relationships will last for several years, making these friendships an <u>essential</u> part of the teenager's life span and deserving of the care they are given. Navigating through relationships is <u>difficult</u> but a fundamental part of a teenager's life.

Along with friends, entertainment is a key part of a teenager's life. Cell phones and computers make communication a fun and necessary aspect of every teenager's social circle. Many teenagers get interested in music and loyally follow their favorite bands through high school and beyond. Finally, shopping for clothing, accessories, makeup, and sports equipment are a great way to socialize and learn about money for a teenager. Teenage entertainment is certainly time-consuming and very different from the lives of their parents.

In conclusion, teenagers have a fast-paced, interesting, and stress-filled life. Whether it is shopping for clothes, working out for the big game, or doing homework on the computer, teenagers are busy workers, trying to make their way through life.

Now isn't that better? The reader can understand what is truly important in the essay, and the details are defined and interesting. You were able to take out "very" twice because the word replacing the "simple" word was so much better.

If you decided to write a draft of your essay before writing your final draft, you would now take the time to rewrite your essay on the necessary paper given to you by your proctor. Be careful to use your best handwriting and don't skip any words! Reread your essay one last time just to be sure. If you do make an error, draw a single line through it and continue. Do not scribble on your paper! You may tear it, and it looks messy.

Though editing may be time-consuming at first, once you practice, the process will become second nature. **For all your hard work in this essay, this essay would be a 5 or even a 6 on the Writing Standards Rubric!**

Step 4: Publish

Now that your essay is finished, you can "publish" it. Since this essay is for a test, "publish" means that since you have thoroughly edited your essay for errors, it is time to turn it in to the proctor once your writing time is complete. Your readers are seeing your very best work. You can be confident that your hard work will show in the quality of your final draft. Congratulations!

Language

What Is the Language Subtest Like?

The language subtest of the CHSPE, which includes both the language mechanics and language expression sections, has 48 multiple-choice questions as well as the writing task discussed in the previous section. The multiple-choice questions cover the following topics:

Language Mechanics
>   **Capitalization:** distinguish correct capitalization
>   **Usage:** identify correctly applied grammar
>   **Punctuation:** distinguish correct punctuation

Language Expression
>   **Sentence structure:** distinguish between clearly written sentences and sentences that contain errors in expression or construction
>   **Prewriting:** plan, organize, and improve writing samples
>   **Content and organization:** determine appropriate editing of short paragraphs

Language Mechanics

Capitalization

Most of us remember the capitalization grammar lessons in elementary school. We were told a set of rules, given many examples, asked to copy down several exercises, and asked to memorize them. However, in the age of texting, email, and computer codes, it is easy to fall out of practice when it comes to capitalization. Take a few minutes to review the following rules and then try the practice test questions.

Rules of Capitalization

1. Capitalize the first word in a sentence:

    The dog loves to listen to the guitar.

2. Capitalize the first word in a direct quote:

    Berta said, "He asked you not to go on the bicycle trip in May."

3. Capitalize the personal pronoun "I" in every instance:

    I enjoy walking in the vineyard at sunset, but Harold thinks I like to walk in the park instead.

4. Capitalize holiday names, days of the week, and months of the year, but not the seasons (except when used in a title):

> In the winter of December 2015, Christmas falls on a Tuesday.
>
> The Westminster Boys' Choir Spring Concert will start at 7:00 p.m.

5. Capitalize the names of cities, towns, counties, states, countries, and nationalities and languages:

> She lives in Corte Madera, California.
>
> Finland has a majority of Finnish and French peoples.

6. Capitalize the names of organizations and buildings:

> The lecture was in Wilsey Hall on the Arizona State University campus.

7. Capitalize people's names, and capitalize family relationship titles when used before a name and in direct address:

> Aunt Jan lives in town, but my other aunts live in the country.
>
> I bought Dad a Father's Day gift, but Jason did not get his dad anything this year.
>
> I do hope you can come, Uncle.

8. Capitalize the names of religions, God, specific religious figures, and holy texts. However, do not capitalize the word "god" if it is used as a generalization:

> Julie is a Christian.
>
> She believes in God and reads the Bible.
>
> They studied the Greek god Apollo.
>
> Michael is a Buddhist, and his favorite goddess is White Tara.

9. Capitalize professional and courtesy titles when used before a name but not when they follow a name:

> Dr. Klaus is the psychiatrist of Mrs. Fogerty, the mayor of Smithville.

10. Capitalize "north," "south," "east," and "west" when used in official names such as those for states or regions. They are lowercase when referring to compass directions:

> The northern section of North Carolina is actually very mountainous.
>
> The people in the South are considered very friendly.

11. Capitalize certain historical periods:

> The Great Depression was an important era in U.S. history.

12. Capitalize the names of sports teams, political groups and their members, social and civic groups, racial groups, and all acronyms:

> The NRA does not support PETA.
>
> The San Francisco Giants are a favorite team in California.
>
> The Democrats and the Republicans rarely agree on an issue.
>
> ABC and NBC have the best shows on television.

Practice questions on capitalization

DIRECTIONS: Each sentence contains an underlined section. Read the sentence and determine whether the underlined section is correct or needs a correction. If the underlined section needs a correction, select the answer that corrects the mistake. If you find no mistake, choose **(D)**, *Correct as is.*

We visited <u>Sacramento, California, on our summer trip</u>.

(A) sacramento, California, on our summer trip

(B) Sacramento, california, on our summer trip

(C) sacramento, california, on our summer trip

(D) Correct as is.

Correct answer: **(D)**

Both city and state names must be capitalized, as stated in rule number 5 in the "Rules for Capitalization" in this chapter. Choices **(A)**, **(B)**, and **(C)** all violate this rule. The sentence is correct as is.

The man took his son to <u>the Smithsonian National Air and Space museum</u>.

(A) the Smithsonian National Air And Space Museum

(B) the Smithsonian National Air and Space Museum

(C) The Smithsonian National Air and Space Museum

(D) Correct as is.

Correct answer: **(B)**

Choice **(B)** is correct because all the essential elements in the name of the museum are capitalized. Choice **(A)** incorrectly capitalizes the "and"; small words such as conjuctions, articles. and prepositions are usually not capitalized in official names or titles. Choice **(C)** incorrectly capitalizes the "the," which is not part of the museum's name.

I live next door to <u>Mr. and mrs. Taylor</u>.

(A) Mr. and Mrs. Taylor

(B) mr. and mrs. Taylor

(C) Mr. and Mrs. taylor

(D) Correct as is.

Correct answer: **(A)**

Choice A correctly capitalizes both courtesy titles, "Mr." and "Mrs." Choice **(B)** violates this rule, and choice **(C)** violates rule 7: personal names are capitalized.

> Sheila and i went to Australia for our winter vacation.
> **(A)** sheila and i went to Australia
> **(B)** Sheila and i went to australia
> **(C)** Sheila and I went to Australia
> **(D)** Correct as is.
>
> Correct answer: **(C)**

Choice **(C)** is correct because "Sheila" (a person's name), "I" (personal pronoun), and Australia (a country) are all correctly capitalized. Choice **(A)** violates rules 3 and 7: the personal pronoun "I" is always capitalized as are people's names. Choice **(B)** violates rule 3 as well as rule 5: capitalize country names.

> Saturday's baseball game is between the San Francisco Giants and the Boston Red sox.
> **(A)** The San Francisco Giants and The Boston Red Sox
> **(B)** the San Francisco Giants and the Boston Red Sox
> **(C)** the san francisco giants and the boston red sox
> **(D)** Correct as is.
>
> Correct answer: **(B)**

Choice **(B)** correctly applies rule 12: team names are capitalized. "The" does not need to be capitalized here because it is only a definite article that describes the team. Choice **(A)** incorrectly capitalizes the "the," while choice **(C)** does not capitalize the team names at all, violating rule 12.

> aunt Jan lives in a town that has no movie theater.
> **(A)** Aunt jan lives
> **(B)** aunt jan lives
> **(C)** Aunt Jan lives
> **(D)** Correct as is.
>
> Correct answer: **(C)**

This answer correctly follows rule 7: in this sentence, "aunt" is used as a title before a name and thus is capitalized. In addition, it is the first word in the sentence and so must be capitalized. Both **(A)** and **(B)** violate rule 7.

> William said, "this is the best ice cream I have ever had!"
> **(A)** said, "this is the best ice cream I
> **(B)** said, "This is the best ice cream I
> **(C)** said, "This is the best ice cream i
> **(D)** Correct as is.
>
> Correct answer: **(B)**

Choice **(B)** correctly follows rule 2: "this" is the first word in a direct quote and therefore should be capitalized. Choice **(A)** ignores this rule and is thus incorrect. Choice **(C)** violates rule 3, which dictates that "I" must always be capitalized.

In the <u>fall of November 2013. Thanksgiving falls on a Thursday</u>.
(A) Fall of November 2013. Thanksgiving falls on the Thursday.
(B) fall of november 2013. Thanksgiving falls on the Thursday.
(C) fall of November 2013. Thanksgiving falls on the thursday.
(D) Correct as is.

Correct answer: **(D)**

The sentence is correct as is because it properly applies rule 4: November (a month), Thanksgiving (a holiday), and Tuesday (a day of the week) are all capitalized. "Fall" is not capitalized because season names are lowercase unless part of a title.

The students in the history class studied <u>hinduism and its gods</u>.
(A) Hinduism and its gods.
(B) hinduism and its Gods.
(C) Hinduism and its Gods.
(D) Correct as is.

Correct answer: **(A)**

Choice **(A)** correctly applies rule 8: "Hinduism" is a religion; therefore, it should be capitalized. In addition, "gods" in this sentence is not specific and thus is not capitalized. Both **(B)** and **(C)** violate rule 8.

Punctuation
End punctuation
There are three appropriate punctuation marks for the end of a sentence: periods, exclamation points, and question marks. Each one of these endings is important because they add tone and imply meaning to a statement.

The **period (.)** is the most common sentence ending. It marks the end of a statement so another one can begin after it. Periods are also used to mark the end of some abbreviations:

Michael played cards with his daughter.

Mr. Vietmeier teaches history.

The **exclamation point (!)** marks the end of an emphatic statement. It shows emotion, such as surprise, anger, joy, and so on:

Edward won the lottery on Tuesday! (joy, surprise)

"Happy birthday!" screamed the students. (excitement)

The **question mark (?)** marks the end of a direct question:

How many more minutes until class is over?

Colon and semicolon

The colon and the semicolon are the two most misused punctuation marks. It is important to know the difference between the two. Review the rules to help you distinguish between the two.

A **semicolon** (;) is used to bring together two independent clauses (or sentences) without the use of a conjunction ("and," "but," "or") and show the close relationship between them:

> Pablo wasn't able to stand the conversation for another minute; Annette's words only continued to provoke his anger.

Notice that if you placed a period between the two clauses, the relationship between them would not be as close. The semicolon connects the two statements together in one sentence, strengthening the association.

A **colon** (:) has two rules of use:

1. Use a colon to introduce a quotation, example, statement, or salutation, or to set off parts in a series.

   > Here are the items on the list: nuts, bread, butter, and ham.
   >
   > Mom gave me the following rule: always close the refrigerator.
   >
   > Dear Sir: (the salutation of a business letter)

2. Use a colon to show time relations.

   > The train left the station at 12:10.

Comma

It is very important that you are able to identify and correct comma errors on the CHSPE and in your own writing. A **comma** (,) is used to indicate a slight pause in a sentence, but be careful to realize that the written word and the spoken word are very different. Just because you pause in a particular place when you speak does not necessarily mean that you would insert a comma into the same place if what you said was written down.

The following list outlines the rules for comma use. Refer to it when you have questions.

Rules for Comma Use

1. Use commas to separate items in a series. Be careful to include a comma before the "and." In some textbooks, this is a conflicting rule; however, for this test, you need to include that comma:

   > I brought a pencil, pen, paper, and a pocketknife to the lecture.

2. Use a comma between a date and the year. This is one of the easiest rules because you use it all the time:

   > I went to the mall on January 4, 2001.

3. Use a comma between the city and the state. This is another easy one:

> I live in Phoenix, Arizona.

Note that when the city-state combination is used midsentence, the state should also be followed by a comma:

> I lived in Phoenix, Arizona, for ten years.

4. Use a comma after the salutation of a nonbusiness letter, and after the closing in all letters:

> Dear Aunt Jan, . . . Sincerely,

5. Use a comma after introductory words or phrases at the beginning of a sentence:

> For example, this is a correct sentence. Sometimes, people do not get these rules right. However, most people try hard. In conclusion, you should make an effort.

6. Use a comma after a positive or negative affirmation in a sentence:

> Yes, sometimes I am perplexed by repetitive questions.
>
> No, I do not eat squid often.

7. Use a comma after a dependent clause when the dependent clause precedes an independent clause. This rule is a bit more difficult. Remember: a **dependent clause** has a subject and a verb but cannot stand alone as a sentence; it does not express a complete thought. An **independent clause** has a subject and a verb and expresses a complete thought, so it can stand alone:

> When I went to the store, I walked my dog.
>
> Because I go to yoga on Fridays, John must take out the trash.

Warning: Be careful to recognize which clause is an independent clause and which one is dependent. This comma rule applies only when the dependent clause comes before the independent clause. Look at this example:

> Because I love popcorn, I go to the movies often.

"Because I love popcorn" is the dependent clause, and "I go to the movies often" is the independent clause. If the clauses are switched around, no comma is needed:

> I go to the movies often because I love popcorn.

8. Use a comma to separate two or more independent clauses joined by a conjunction:

> I ate ham, and I ate cheese.

In this example, two complete thoughts—"I ate ham" and "I ate cheese"—are joined by the conjunction "and." Be careful not to get confused by conjunctions, however. Look at this example:

> I ate ham and cheese.

This simplified version of the previous example has only one subject and one verb, so it does not require a comma before the conjunction.

9. Use a comma to set off a nonrestrictive clause. A **nonrestrictive clause** adds additional information about something in the sentence but does not restrict (or limit) the meaning of the sentence and can thus be removed without loss of meaning. Nonrestrictive clauses usually begin with "which" or "who":

> The kitchen clock, which my mother had given me last Christmas, ticked loudly from its place on the wall.

"Which my mother had given me last Christmas" can be removed from the sentence without loss of meaning. Note that **restrictive clauses**, which usually begin with "that" or "who," do not take a comma because they are essential to the meaning of the sentence:

> The clock that I received last Christmas is broken.

"That I received last Christmas" restricts the meaning of the sentence to a specific clock.

10. Use a comma to set off an appositive. An **appositive** is a word or phrase that briefly describes something else in the sentence. Like nonrestrictive clauses, appositives can be removed from the sentence without any loss of meaning:

> Andy, my best friend, has a hard time being away from work.

If you removed "my best friend," the sentence would still make sense, but it would not be as descriptive.

11. Use a comma to set off quotations. This is another easy one, but many people do not use commas appropriately here. Be careful to watch where you put them:

> "We went over that hill," said John. Mary answered, "Then we went to dinner." "We had lots of fun," added John, "but there were so many people."

12. Use a comma following an introductory prepositional phrase that modifies the verb but does not directly precede it. This one can be tricky:

> On the table, the candle burned brightly.
> On the table burned the candle.

In both sentences, the prepositional phrase "on the table" acts as an adverb modifying the verb: it answers the question "Where did the candle burn?" However, in the first sentence, the phrase is also an introductory phrase that is somewhat removed from the verb it modifies and therefore requires the comma. In the second example, the phrase immediately precedes the word it modifies and therefore does not need a comma.

Practice questions on punctuation

DIRECTIONS: As with the practice questions for capitilization, these questions contain an underlined section that may or may not need a correction. If the underlined section needs a correction, select the answer that corrects the mistake. If you find no mistake, choose **(D)**, *Correct as is.*

The garden was full of <u>peas, tomatoes, corn, zucchini, and, carrots</u>.
(A) peas tomatoes corn zucchini and carrots
(B) peas, tomatoes, corn, zucchini, and carrots
(C) peas: tomatoes: corn: zucchini: and, carrots
(D) Correct as is.

Correct answer: **(B)**

This question addresses comma rule 1: a comma precedes the "and" in a series of items.

She is riding to Chicago in <u>Uncle Pete's and Aunt Lucy's</u> car.
(A) Uncle Petes' and Aunt Lucys'
(B) Uncle Pete and Aunt Lucy's
(C) Uncle Petes and Aunt Lucys
(D) Correct as is.

Correct answer: **(B)**

When two nouns are acting as a unit, that is, they have joint ownership, the second noun takes the possessive. In this case Uncle Pete and Aunt Lucy own the car together, and therefore only "Aunt Lucy" takes the possessive.

<u>"That's right," "We have finally received the package we have been waiting for,"</u> said Peter.
(A) "That's right. We have finally received the package we have been waiting for,"
(B) "That's right," "We have finally received the package we have been waiting for"
(C) "That's right, "We have finally received the package we have been waiting for,"
(D) Correct as is.

Correct answer: **(A)**

This question addresses rules for both commas and quotation marks. Because there is a single speaker, Peter, the closing quotation marks and comma after the first sentence are incorrect. The first sentence of the quote should simply end in a period, and then the quote continues to the next sentence. A comma and closing quotation marks should precede the speaker attribution, "said Peter."

Suzanne swam in the first <u>race; Amy</u> swam in the second.
(A) race, Amy
(B) race Amy
(C) race; and Amy
(D) Correct as is.

Correct answer: **(D)**

The sentence correctly uses a semicolon to connect two independent clauses without a conjunction.

During the holiday trip, you will visit the following <u>countries, Greece, Italy, Croatia, Bulgaria, and Spain</u>.
(A) countries Greece, Italy, Croatia, Bulgaria and Spain
(B) countries; Greece, Italy, Croatia, Bulgaria and Spain
(C) countries: Greece, Italy, Croatia, Bulgaria, and Spain
(D) Correct as is.

Correct answer: **(C)**

Choice **(C)** correctly uses a colon to introduce a series and includes the comma before the "and."

<u>George the tallest boy on the team likes</u> basketball best.
(A) George: the tallest boy on the team, likes
(B) George the tallest boy on the team, likes
(C) George, the tallest boy on the team, likes
(D) Correct as is.

Correct answer: **(C)**

Choice **(C)** correctly uses commas to set off the apositive "the tallest boy on the team."

Molly drinks tea in the <u>morning, because</u> coffee is too strong for her.
(A) because coffee
(B) morning; because
(C) morning: because
(D) Correct as is.

Correct answer: **(A)**

This sentence consists of a independent clause, "Molly drinks tea in the morning," followed by a dependent clause, "because coffee is too strong for her," so no comma is needed. **(A)** A comma is needed only when the dependent clause precedes the independent clause (rule 7).

Mark's birth date <u>is March 5 1971 and he wants</u> to celebrate at Chug Pub this year.
(A) is March 5, 1971 and he wants
(B) is March 5 1971, and he wants
(C) is March 5, 1971, and he wants
(D) Correct as is.

Correct answer: **(C)**

Choice **(C)** correctly applies comma rules 2 and 8. When given the month, day, and year, a comma follows the day, and a comma must be used to separate two or more independent clauses joined by a conjunction.

Usage

Parts of speech

Learning the parts of speech is an essential skill for any student. Knowing the differences among nouns, verbs, adjectives, adverbs, conjunctions, and prepositions will help you with your written work and your conversational abilities.

The good news is that you have been learning grammar for your whole life. Even before you went to school, you started speaking simple, one-syllable nouns and verbs. Then you graduated to more complicated words, and sentences were formed almost overnight. Much of the following will be a review—take the time to look over the following examples!

Nouns

Nouns are persons, places, things, and ideas. The first three are **concrete nouns**, in other words, things you can touch: a park bench, a tree, your friend, and even Alabama. The nouns are boldface in the following sentence:

Suzanne typed the **letter** with a new **typewriter** at her **home** in **Phoenix**.

Ideas are **abstract nouns**; you cannot see or touch them, but they affect people, places, and things. Only idea nouns are boldface in the following sentence:

Love is a great gift.
Freedom is an integral part of American culture.

In addition to concrete and abstract classifications, nouns are also either common or proper. **Common nouns** are not capitalized. **Proper nouns**, which include the names of people, places, organizations, and so on (see "Capitalization" earlier in this chapter), are capitalized. The following example demonstrates common and proper nouns:

Mr. Bailey yelled at Samantha during study hall.
proper   proper   common

The following chart illustrates the classification of nouns:

Noun	Common/Proper	Concrete/Abstract
computer	Common	Concrete
Abigail	Proper	Concrete
freedom	Common	Abstract

Pronouns

Pronouns are replacements for nouns. They can function as nouns in the sentence. Some will function as possessive adjectives, but those will be listed later in the section on adjectives.

Pronouns that act like nouns are

I, me, myself
you, yourself, yourselves
he, him, himself
she, her, herself
it, itself
we, us, ourselves
they, them, themselves

Pronouns help to cut repetitive words and make sentences flow. Take a look at the following sentence, first without pronouns and then with:

Deb regularly takes Deb's son Evan to the park. Deb feeds Evan hot dogs. Evan loves Deb. Deb loves Evan.

With pronouns:

Deb regularly takes her son Evan to the park. She feeds him hot dogs. Evan loves her, and she loves him.

Though this example is somewhat rudimentary, you can see the difference pronouns can make in a sentence.

Adjectives

Adjectives describe nouns. They are the color and style of everything you read. These words paint the pictures in your mind as you read through a piece of fiction or create mood in a non-fiction news article. Adjectives describe colors, sizes, smells, tastes, moods, and more. Let's look at the following sentence:

Bradley ate fruit from a bowl.

Though this is a sentence, it is not a very descriptive one. What kind of fruit did Bradley eat? Was it tasty? What did it smell like? Was it a big or small piece of fruit? And what about the bowl?

If you picture the sentence in your mind, Bradley could look like anyone. Maybe he looks like your Uncle Bob or the boy who sits next to you at lunch. What piece of fruit do you see? A banana? An apple? What about a kiwi or a mango? The point is that we do not know anything specific about Bradley, the fruit, or the bowl because no other information has been given to the reader. Let's look at the next sentence:

Bradley ate the luscious, red fruit from the hand-painted, ceramic bowl.

The added adjectives give us a much better view of the fruit and the bowl. Now we can see the luscious, red fruit. Is it a Washington apple, large and crisp, or is it a gala apple, small and hard and temptingly sweet? We don't know, but we can guess that it is an apple. The bowl has been given a shape and a texture. Your mind, reading "hand-painted" and "ceramic," searches through all the hand-painted and ceramic bowls you have seen in your life and it gives you those images. The sentence may not be completely descriptive, but it gives us a better, more complete picture.

Adjectives can also be possessives. A possessive is a word that shows ownership:

Emma's clothes are not dry yet.

We learned that "Emma," or any person, is a concrete noun, so how can "Emma" now be an adjective? "Emma's" actually describes the clothes. It tells whose clothes are not dry yet. Therefore, "Emma's" modifies "clothes," making it an adjective. To make this rule clearer, think about the word "kitchen," which usually acts as a noun:

The kitchen was remodeled last year.

However, what about this sentence:

The kitchen chair broke yesterday.

In this sentence, "kitchen" is describing the chair. "Kitchen" is acting as an adjective.

Verbs and verb tenses

Verbs are action words; they tell what the subject of a sentence is doing or they describe the subject's state of being ("to be").

Verb tense is an indication of time. The two "simple" tenses—and the ones that are the most commonly used while speaking and writing—are present tense ("she types") and past tense ("she typed"). There are several other tense types; but for our purposes, we will review the following six tenses, which are the ones covered on the CHSPE:

Present: Describes an action or state that is happening now

Past: Describes an action or state that occurred at a particular time in the past

Future: Describes an action or state that is to occur at a future time

Present perfect: Describes an action or state that is now complete or continues up to the present; formed by using "have" or "has" with the past participle (past-tense form) of the verb

Past perfect: Describes an action or state that occurred before some other past action or state; formed by using "had" with the past participle of the verb

Future perfect: Describes an action or state that is expected to be completed before some other action or state; formed by using "will have" with the past participle of the verb

The following chart illustrates the six verb tenses using some sample verbs:

Verb	Present	Past	Future	Present Perfect	Past Perfect	Future Perfect
Walk	She walks.	She walked	She will walk.	She has walked.	She had walked.	She will have walked.
Dress	He dresses.	He dressed	He will dress.	He has dressed.	He had dressed.	He will have dressed.
Clean	She cleans.	She cleaned.	She will clean.	She has cleaned.	She had cleaned.	She will have cleaned.
Play	She plays.	She played.	She will play.	She has played.	She had played.	She will have played.

Notice that the simple future and all the perfect tenses have helping or auxiliary verbs. The most common auxiliary verbs are

be
can, could
do, did
has, have, had
must
ought
shall, should
will, would

Notice also that in the perfect tenses, the auxiliary verb "have" changes tense, while the main verb stays the same, that is, it uses the past participle form of the verb.

The most common problem students have with verb tenses occurs because some verbs are irregular. This means that they change form when moved from one tense to the other. The following chart illustrates the effect of tense on some sample irregular verbs:

Verb	Present	Past	Future	Present Perfect	Past Perfect	Future Perfect
Eat	She eats.	She ate.	She will eat.	She has eaten.	She had eaten.	She will have eaten.
Sleep	She sleeps.	She slept.	She will sleep.	She has slept.	She had slept.	She will have slept.

Verb	Present	Past	Future	Present Perfect	Past Perfect	Future Perfect
Run	He runs.	He ran.	He will run.	He has run.	He had run.	He will have run.
Bring	He brings.	He brought.	He will bring.	He has brought.	He had brought.	He will have brought.
Is	He is.	He was.	He will be.	He has been.	He had been.	He will have been.

Let's look at a few more sentences written in the six main tenses:

1. She walks to the store on Saturdays. (simple present)
2. He walked with her to keep her company. (simple past)
3. They will walk to the store together. (simple future)
4. She has walked to the store every day this week. (present perfect)
5. He had walked every day to keep in shape, but he still gained weight. (past perfect)
6. She will have walked 100 miles by June. (future perfect)

Notice the difference between simple past and past perfect. In sentence 2, "he walked" shows that he simply walked sometime in the past. In sentence 5, "he had walked" shows that his walking took place before he gained weight.

Progressive tenses Progressive tenses use the auxiliary verb "to be" and add an *-ing* ending to the main verb in the verb phrase. There are three types:

Present progressive: Describes an ongoing action that is happening while the statement is being written

Past progressive: Describes an action that was ongoing when some other past action occurred

Future progressive: Describes an action that will be ongoing sometime in the future

Take a look at the chart for some examples:

Verb	Present Progressive	Past Progressive	Future Progressive
Eat	She is eating.	She was eating.	She will be eating.
Write	She is writing.	She was writing.	She will be writing.
Go	She is going.	She was going.	She will be going.

Notice that only the auxiliary verb changes tense, while the main verb just gets an -*ing* ending.

Here are a few more examples of progressive verb forms in sentences:

1. Bonnie is enjoying her dinner of steak and potatoes. (present progressive)
2. The man was swimming his laps when the sea lion interrupted him. (past progressive)
3. The bicyclists on the road will be riding uphill for most of the afternoon. (future progressive)

Be careful when using progressive tenses in your writing assignments, especially the essay for the CHSPE. Improper use of progressive tenses can make the rest of your verbs appear "off." Stick to the simple or perfect tenses whenever you can to make the most of your written work.

Prepositions

The English language contains about 150 prepositions. Yet this is a very small number when you think of the thousands of other words (nouns, verbs, etc.) in our language. Prepositions are important words. We use individual prepositions more frequently than other individual words. In fact, the prepositions "of," "to," and "in" are among the 10 most frequently used words in English. Here is a short list of 70 of the more common one-word prepositions. Many of these prepositions have more than one meaning. Please refer to a dictionary for precise meaning and usage:

aboard	considering	per
about	despite	plus
above	during	regarding
across	except	round
after	excepting	save
against	excluding	since
along	following	than
amid	for	through
among	from	to
around	in	toward, towards
as	inside	under
at	into	underneath
before	like	unlike
behind	minus	until
below	near	up
beneath	of	upon
beside	off	versus
besides	on	via
between	onto	with
beyond	opposite	within
but	outside	without
by	over	
concerning	past	

Prepositional phrases Prepositional phrases give direction and detail to sentences. They can act as adverbs, modifying the verb, or as adjectives, modifying a noun. They are easy to pick out once you know the formula: a prepositional phrase must begin with a preposition, and it must end with a noun. Look at this example:

After the game, the team ate pizza.

"After" is the preposition, and "game" is the noun. The entire phrase "after the game" is the prepositional phrase modifying the verb "ate": it answers the question "When did they eat?"

A single sentence can include several prepositional phrases, and sometimes they back up to each other. Just remember to find the first noun after the preposition (be careful because some nouns function like adjectives), and you will know where one phrase ends and the next one begins. Look at this expample:

The horse walked around the red barn, under the leafy tree, and behind the tractor.

This sentence has three prepositional phrases: "around the red barn," "under the leafy tree," and "behind the tractor." Each of the phrases acts as an adverb modifying "walk" (the phrases answer the question "where?"). Notice that there are commas separating the phrases because they are in a series. However, take a look at this example:

In the book on the shelf, you will find my name.

You don't need a comma between prepositional phrases in cases where the second prepositional phrase modifies the noun in the first. In this sentence, "on the shelf" acts as an adjective modifying the noun "book," which is the object of the first preposition, "in the book." Here, you don't need a comma.

Practice questions on verb tenses

DIRECTIONS: Each sentence contains an underlined section. Read the sentence and determine whether the underlined section is correct or needs a correction. If the underlined section needs a correction, select the answer that corrects the mistake. If you find no mistake, choose **(D)**, *Correct as is.*

When the boys returned from the camping trip, <u>they have learned</u> to build a fire, roast marshmallows, and pitch a tent.

(A) they had learned

(B) they has learned

(C) they have been learning

(D) Correct as is.

Correct answer: **(A)**

Choice **(A)** correctly uses past perfect tense. The boys' learning of camp skills occurred before another past action, their return home.

Yesterday I went to the store <u>to buy some fruits and vegetables</u> for the picnic.
- **(A)** to buys some fruits and vegetables
- **(B)** to bought some fruits and vegetables
- **(C)** to buying some fruits and vegetables
- **(D)** Correct as is.

Correct answer: **(D)**

This sentence uses the infinitive "to be." Infinitives always take this form: the present participle (simple present-tense form of the verb) preceded by "to."

By the end of the year, the company <u>will have produce</u> two million shoes.
- **(A)** would have produce
- **(B)** will have produced
- **(C)** will have produces
- **(D)** Correct as is.

Correct answer: **(B)**

This sentence calls for the future perfect tense, which describes a future action that is expected to be completed prior to some other action. In this case, the two million shoes will be produced before the year ends. Future perfect tense is formed using "will have" and the past participle of the verb; thus, choice **(B)** is correct.

Before the movie started, he <u>bought some popcorn, purchased a drink, and goes</u> to the restroom.
- **(A)** buys some popcorn, purchased a drink, and goes
- **(B)** bought some popcorn, purchases a drink, and goes
- **(C)** bought some popcorn, purchased a drink, and went
- **(D)** Correct as is.

Correct answer: **(C)**

Remember that all of the verbs in a sentence must be in the same tense for the sentence to be grammatically correct. There are four verbs in this sentence: "started" (past tense), "bought" (past tense), "purchased" (past tense), and "goes" (present tense). In sentences like these, you must make all the verbs agree with each other. Choice **(C)** changes "goes" to the past tense, "went," thus creating the needed agreement with the other verbs.

The <u>students buy</u> pencils, books, pens, and paper for yesterday's language class.
- **(A)** students buying
- **(B)** students bought
- **(C)** students will buy
- **(D)** Correct as is.

Correct answer: **(B)**

Be careful to read through the whole sentence because otherwise you may miss key words! In this sentence, "yesterday" tells you what verb tense makes sense in the sentence. "Yesterday" places this sentence in the past, so the verb must be past tense.

Language Expressions

Sentence structure

There are four types of sentences: simple, compound, complex, and compound-complex.

Simple sentences contain only one independent clause:

Ann went to the store.

"Ann" is the subject; "went" is the verb. There is only one clause.

Compound sentences contain two or more independent clauses joined by a conjunction ("and," "but," or "or"):

Ann went to the store, and Larry stayed home.

Ann went to the store, Larry stayed home, and I ate all the cookies.

In the first example, "Ann" is the subject of the verb "went," and "Larry" is the subject of the verb "stayed." The two clauses are joined by the conjunction "and," which is preceded by a comma. The second example adds a third independent clause, in which "I" is the subject and "ate" is the verb. Each of the clauses could stand alone as a sentence; each expresses a complete thought.

Complex sentences have at least one independent clause and one dependent clause:

If I went to the store, Larry would stay home.

Larry went to the store because I wanted to stay home.

In the first example, "If I went to the store" is a dependent clause. It cannot stand by itself because it does not express a complete thought. (If you were to put a period after this clause, it would be a fragment.) Because this is a dependent clause, it needs the independent clause "Larry would stay home" to make it a complete sentence. In the second example, "Larry went to the store" is the independent clause. It is followed by the dependent clause "because I wanted to stay home."

Compound-complex sentences are a combination of compound and complex sentences. These sentences must have one or more dependent clauses and two or more independent clauses. These sentences are generally very long and complicated. It is very important to pay attention to punctuation rules when you write these sentence or analyze them for errors. Here are some examples:

Because it is sunny outside, the game time will be at 4:00 p.m., and the party will be at 7:00 p.m.

The school day was longer than expected, but the students stayed engaged because the spring carnival would begin right after classes.

Although Annabelle likes to travel, she couldn't ride on the boat to Finland because she had a bad cold, and her headache would not go away.

The first example has two independent clauses ("the game time will be at 4:00 p.m." and "the party will be at 7:00 p.m.") and one dependent clause ("because it is sunny outside").

The second sentence has two independent clauses ("the school day was longer than expected" and "the students stayed engaged") and one dependent clause ("because the spring carnival would begin right after classes").

The third sample sentence has two independent clauses ("she couldn't ride on the boat to Finland" and "her headache would not go away") and two dependent clauses ("Although Annabelle likes to travel" and "because she had a bad cold").

Practice questions on sentence structure

DIRECTIONS: Identify each type of sentence.

Eli and his friends skied and drank hot chocolate all weekend.
(A) Simple
(B) Compound
(C) Complex
(D) Compound-complex

Correct answer: **(A)**

Though a simple sentence may have more than one subject and more than one verb, it is still one complete thought. "Eli" and "friends" together are the subject of the one sentence, while the verbs "skied" and "drank" are the actions of the compound subject.

Because there are two events this weekend, the wedding planner had to revise her schedule to accommodate all the guests.
(A) Simple
(B) Compound
(C) Complex
(D) Compound-complex

Correct answer: **(C)**

This sentence has one dependent clause ("because there are two events this weekend") and one independent clause ("the wedding planner had to revise her schedule to accommodate all the guests"). Therefore, according to the rules, this sentence is complex.

Test preparation can be tedious, but the end results are usually very rewarding.
(A) Simple
(B) Compound
(C) Complex
(D) Compound-complex

Correct answer: **(B)**

This sentence has two independent clauses: "test preparation can be tedious" and "the end results are usually very rewarding." They are each complete thoughts, with separate subjects and verbs. This is a compound sentence.

The mail carrier delivers several flyers to me every week, and though I asked the post office to stop my junk mail, I continue to get deliveries.

(A) Simple

(B) Compound

(C) Complex

(D) Compound-complex

Correct answer: **(D)**

This sentence has two independent clauses and one dependent clause. The independent clauses are "the mail carrier delivers several flyers to me every week" and "I continue to get deliveries." The dependent clause is "though I asked the post office to stop my junk mail." This is a compound-complex sentence.

Latin roots

Many of today's common words were formed from Latin words. The following is a basic list of Latin roots, prefixes, and suffixes. Having a working knowledge of a few roots, prefixes, and suffixes can really aid you in identifying the meaning of vocabulary words that may be unfamiliar to you. This list was compiled from the following website: *http://www.infoplease.com*.

Latin Root	Basic Meaning	Example Words
-dict-	to say	contradict, dictate, diction, edict, predict
-duc-	to lead, bring, take	deduce, produce, reduce
-gress-	to walk	digress, progress, transgress
-ject-	to throw	eject, inject, interject, project, reject, subject
-pel-	to drive	compel, dispel, impel, repel
-pend-	to hang	append, depend, impend, pendant, pendulum
-port-	to carry	comport, deport, export, import, report, support
-scrib-, -script-	to write	describe, description, prescribe, prescription, subscribe, subscription, transcribe, transcription
-tract-	to pull, drag, draw	attract, contract, detract, extract, protract, retract, traction
-vert-	to turn	convert, divert, invert, revert

Latin Prefix	Basic Meaning	Example Words
co-	together	coauthor, coedit, coheir
de-	away, off; generally indicates reversal or removal in English	deactivate, debone, defrost, decompress, deplane
dis-	not, not any	disbelief, discomfort, discredit, disrepair, disrespect
inter-	between, among	international, interfaith, intertwine, intercellular, interject
non-	not	nonmetallic, nonresident, nonviolence, nonskid, nonstop
omni-	all-seeing, all-doing, in all ways or places	omnipresent, omnivore
post-	after	postdate, postwar, postnasal, postnatal
pre-	before	preconceive, preexist, premeditate, predispose, prepossess, prepay
re-	again; back, backward	rearrange, rebuild, recall, remake, rerun, rewrite
sub-	under	submarine, subsoil, subway, subhuman, substandard
trans-	across, beyond, through	transatlantic, transpolar

Latin Suffix	Basic Meaning	Example Words
-able, -ible	forms adjectives; means "capable or worthy of"	likable, flexible
-ation	forms nouns from verbs	creation, civilization, automation, speculation, information
-fy, -ify	forms verbs; means "to make or cause to become"	purify, acidify, humidify

Latin Suffix	Basic Meaning	Example Words
-ment	forms nouns from verbs	entertainment, amazement, statement, banishment
-ty, -ity	forms nouns from adjectives	subtlety, certainty, cruelty, frailty, loyalty, royalty, eccentricity, electricity, peculiarity, similarity, technicality

Tricky words

The following words are often used incorrectly. This guide details the proper use for each.

Affect and effect

"Affect" has several meanings. It can mean to influence someone or something to an action or a feeling, and it is most commonly used as a verb:

The humidity affected her hair.

The bee sting negatively affected her health.

It can also mean to act in a different way than is usual:

The actress's affect was too dramatic.

"Effect" is not as complicated. Most of the time, it means the result of something done, and it is most commonly used as a noun:

The helium had an effect on her voice.

The wine had a negative effect on her conversation skills.

An easy way to remember the difference between the two is to remember this simple sentence:

The arrow affected the aardvark. The effect was eye-popping.

The trick is to notice that "arrow" and "affected" both begin with "a." The arrow "affects"; "affects" is used as a verb. Second, "eye-popping" and "effect" both begin with "e." The word "eye" on its own is a noun, and "effect" is a noun, too.

Are and our

"Are" is a verb. It is the simple plural present tense of the infinitive "to be," a state-of-being verb. "Are" is used with a plural subject and with the pronoun "you":

Donnie and Marie are here in the building!

Do you think the boys are the ones the police want in the lineup?

You are the first person I asked.

"Our" is the first-person plural possessive pronoun. Because it shows possession, it is a possessive adjective:

Our book is on the table; yours is on the desk.

Though she and I looked for our bag of groceries, we were unable to find them.

Bring and take

"Bring" indicates the action is directed toward you:

I bring my lunch with me to school.

"Take" indicates the action is directed away from you:

Take this with you when you leave.

Lay and lie

"Lay" is an action performed by a being to something else. It means to put something down or place on a table. It is a transitive verb: it needs a complement (a direct object) to complete the thought:

I lay the clothes on the bed.

"I" is the subject, and "lay" is the verb. "Lay" needs the direct object "clothes" to make a complete thought.

"Lie" is an action performed by a being to itself. It means to recline or repose. The subject of the sentence performs it. It is an intransitive verb: it needs no complement (direct object) to complete the sentence:

I lie on the bed.

"I" is the subject, and "lie" is the verb.

Remember this phrase to help you remember the definitions of "lie" and "lay": you'll lay an egg on the ground if you don't lie down!

However, using "lay" and "lie" gets more complicated when the verbs are conjugated. Look at the following chart:

	Simple			Perfect		
	Present	**Past**	**Future**	**Present**	**Past**	**Future**
Lay	I lay the book on the shelf.	I laid the book there yesterday.	I will lay the book on the teacher's desk when she asks for it.	I have laid the tools there.	I had laid the tools there even before you asked me to.	By the time the class arrives, I will have laid the tools out for them.
Lie	I lie on the bed.	Yesterday, I lay on the bed.	Tomorrow, I will lie there again.	I have lain on the bed all day.	I had lain on the bed for hours.	I will have lain for two weeks.

Less and fewer

"Less" is used for amounts that cannot be counted:

> Because of the drought, there was less water in the reservoir than the public works department had expected.

"Fewer" is used for quantities that can be counted:

> There are fewer apples in the fruit bowl today than yesterday.

Principal and principle

A "principal" is a person who oversees a school or organization. You may remember the popular phrase in school: "You have a **pal** in your princi**pal**."

> "Principles" are morals or character traits that a person believes to be true:
> He lives his life by a set of Hindu principles.

Their, there, and they're

To distinguish among these three synonyms, you must know what part of speech each is.

"Their" is the third-person plural possessive pronoun. It indicates that more than one person owns something:

> Uncle John and Aunt Mary drove their car to Niagara Falls.

"There" is a noun. It describes a place or a moment in time:

> I want to go there with you someday.
>
> Are you there?

The last form, "they're," is a combination of two words, a contraction of "they are." For "they're" to be correct in the sentence, you must be able to substitute "they are" in its place and still have the sentence make sense.

> They're coming with us today.
>
> I don't know if you noticed, but they're the only ones still dancing.

To, too, and two

Each of these words has a particular use. Once distinguished, they are easy to remember.

"To" is a preposition; prepositions introduce prepositional phrases. These phrases give extra information to the reader to define and/or clarify a statement:

> She goes.
>
> She goes to the store. (clarifies where she went)

"To" is also used to introduce an infinitive. An infinitive is the most basic form of the verb: it consists of "to" and the present participle of a verb:

> to live
>
> to sing

When asked to conjugate verbs (show the tenses), you will always be given the verbs in infinitive form:

	Conjugation of "to Live" and "to Sing"					
	Singular			**Plural**		
Infinitive	**Present**	**Past**	**Future**	**Present**	**Past**	**Future**
To live	I live.	She lived.	He will live.	We live.	They lived.	They will live.
To sing	I sing.	She sang.	He will sing.	We sing.	They sang.	They will sing.

"Too" is an adverb meaning "very," "to an excessive degree," or "also." Adverbs modify verbs, adjectives, and other adverbs:

I want to go, too! (describes "want")

There are too many cooks in the kitchen! (describes "many")

"Two" is a number. "Two" can be used as an adjective or a noun, but it always represents a real or implied number of people, places, or things:

I only have room for two. (used as noun)

There are two chairs at that desk. (used as adjective modifying "chairs")

Your and you're

Similar to "their" and "they're," "your" and "you're" are two words that sound the same but have very different meanings.

"Your" is a possessive pronoun, just like "their" and "our." It shows the possession of something by "you":

Even though you said this is your bicycle, I really think it is mine.

You really took your time in the store!

"You're" is a contraction, just like "they're." It is the combination of the two words "you are." If you can replace "you're" in the sentence with "you are," you know "you're" is correct:

You're very quiet today.

Do you think you're going to the party on Saturday?

"Your" and "you're" are probably the most commonly misused tricky words. If you can commit these to memory, it is unlikely that you will make similar errors with "their" and "they're."

MATHEMATICS
REVIEW

Mathematics Review

The mathematics section has 50 multiple-choice questions that assess content in the following areas: number sense and operations; patterns, relationships, and algebra; data, statistics, and probability; and geometry and measurement. The questions also assess the mathematical processes of communication and representation, estimation, mathematical connections, and reasoning and problem solving. The skills and processes assessed are reviewed here.

Math Basics
Reading Numbers

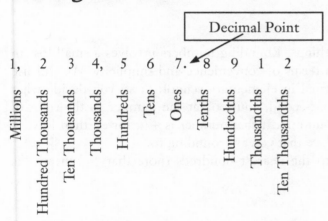

When reading numbers, the decimal point serves as reference point for determining the value of a number. Each decimal place has a different value depending upon its distance from the decimal point. Decimal places to the right of the decimal point become increasingly small, while decimal places to the left of the decimal point became increasingly large.

Examples of How to Read Numbers

2,376,921: two million, three hundred seventy-six thousand, nine hundred twenty-one
  570,845: five hundred seventy thousand, eight hundred forty-five
   64,780: sixty-four thousand, seven hundred eighty
    3,642: three thousand, six hundred forty-two
      463: four hundred sixty-three
       75: seventy-five

9: nine

.6: six tenths

2.5: two and five tenths

52.7: fifty-two and seven tenths

745.3: seven hundred forty-five and three tenths

3,451.2: three thousand, four hundred fifty-one and two tenths

.15: fifteen hundredths

2.74: two and seventy-four hundredths

38.66: thirty eight and sixty-six hundredths

494.79: four hundred ninety-four and seventy-nine hundredths

7,901.84: seven thousand nine hundred one and eighty-four hundredths

.925: nine hundred twenty-five thousandths

8.321: eight and three hundred twenty-one thousandths

27.209: twenty-seven and two hundred nine thousandths

.1812: one thousand eight hundred twelve ten thousandths

7.2397: seven and two thousand three hundred ninety-seven ten thousandths

54.1886: fifty-four and one thousand eight hundred eighty-six ten thousandths

105.2647: One hundred five and two thousand six hundred forty-seven ten thousandths

Rounding Numbers

Numbers are rounded in order to simplify things. Rounding numbers involves a small loss in terms of accuracy but often a bigger gain in terms of convenience and simplicity. We will use the basic rules for rounding that we all learned in elementary school. First, you decide what decimal place that you want to round off to. Second, you look at the number to the right of it. If that number is 5 or higher, then you round up. If that number is 4 or lower, then leave it alone. Last, drop all numbers less than the place that you are rounding to.

The following numbers are rounded to the nearest hundreds (note that "≈" means "is approximately equal to"):

$6,539 \approx 6,500$

$1,250 \approx 1,300$

$75,372 \approx 75,400$

$5,124 \approx 5,100$

$105,666 \approx 105,700$

$845 \approx 800$

The following numbers are rounded to the nearest tens:

$287 \approx 290$

$3,298 \approx 3,300$

$124 \approx 120$

$845 \approx 850$

$1,952 \approx 1,950$

$27,231 \approx 27,230$

$946 \approx 950$

$2,474 \approx 2,470$

The following numbers are rounded to the nearest ones:

$16.1 \approx 16$

$731.43 \approx 731$

$275.6 \approx 276$

$8.9 \approx 9$

$98.5 \approx 99$

$11.4 \approx 11$

$16.75 \approx 17$

$103.1 \approx 103$

$841.55 \approx 842$

$63.49 \approx 63$

The following numbers are rounded to the nearest tenths:

$5.85 \approx 5.9$

$27.35 \approx 27.4$

$4.915 \approx 4.9$

$13.77 \approx 13.8$

$16.67 \approx 16.7$

$127.89 \approx 127.9$

$84.53 \approx 84.5$

$38.571 \approx 38.6$

The following numbers are rounded to the nearest hundredths:

$1.395 \approx 1.40$

$7.359 \approx 7.36$

$2.461 \approx 2.46$

$6.555 \approx 6.56$

$56.1167 \approx 56.12$

$11.895 \approx 11.90$

$110.258 \approx 110.26$

$27.564 \approx 27.56$

$8.9577 \approx 8.96$

$70.896 \approx 70.90$

The following numbers are rounded to the nearest thousandths:

$27.6581 \approx 27.658$

$165.7006 \approx 165.701$

$1.9825 \approx 1.983$

$13.5785 \approx 13.579$

$275.8996 \approx 275.900$

$.9573 \approx .957$

$70.13968 \approx 70.140$

$235.7893 \approx 235.789$

Fractions

Fractions allow us to represent a part of something. The top part of a fraction is called the **numerator**, and the bottom part of a fraction is called the **denominator**.

Addition of fractions

To add two fractions together, you first need to find the **lowest common denominator**. A common denominator is a number that both denominators can divide evenly into. For example,

$$\frac{1}{2} + \frac{1}{5} = \frac{5 \times 1}{5 \times 2} + \frac{2 \times 1}{2 \times 5} = \frac{5}{10} + \frac{2}{10} = \frac{7}{10}$$

The common denominator will be 10 because both of the denominators, 2 and 5, can divide evenly into it. First, multiply the top and bottom of the first fraction by 5. Then, multiply the top and bottom of the second fraction by 2. This gives both fractions a common denominator of 10. Last, add the numerators of the two fractions together to get the answer, $\frac{7}{10}$.

Examples

$$\frac{3}{15} + \frac{2}{5} = \frac{3}{15} + \frac{3 \times 2}{3 \times 5} = \frac{3}{15} + \frac{6}{15} = \frac{9}{15} \quad or \quad \frac{3}{5}$$

$$\frac{1}{4} + \frac{2}{3} = \frac{3 \times 1}{3 \times 4} + \frac{4 \times 2}{4 \times 3} = \frac{3}{12} + \frac{8}{12} = \frac{11}{12}$$

$$\frac{5}{9} + \frac{4}{7} = \frac{7 \times 5}{7 \times 9} + \frac{9 \times 4}{9 \times 7} = \frac{35}{63} + \frac{36}{63} = \frac{71}{63} \quad or \quad 1\frac{8}{63}$$

$$\frac{1}{3} + \frac{1}{2} = \frac{2 \times 1}{2 \times 3} + \frac{3 \times 1}{3 \times 2} = \frac{2}{6} + \frac{3}{6} = \frac{5}{6}$$

$$\frac{1}{12} + \frac{3}{8} = \frac{2 \times 1}{2 \times 12} + \frac{3 \times 3}{3 \times 8} = \frac{2}{24} + \frac{9}{24} = \frac{11}{24}$$

$$1\frac{3}{5} + 2\frac{5}{6} = \frac{8}{5} + \frac{17}{6} = \frac{6 \times 8}{6 \times 5} + \frac{5 \times 17}{5 \times 6} = \frac{48}{30} + \frac{85}{30} = \frac{133}{30} \quad or \quad 4\frac{13}{30}$$

Instead of finding a common denominator, you can turn a fraction into a decimal by dividing the top number by the bottom number. Do this to both fractions, then add.

Examples (All calculations are rounded off to the hundredths.)

$$\frac{1}{4} + \frac{2}{3} = .25 + .67 = .92$$

$$\frac{5}{9} + \frac{4}{7} = .56 + .57 = 1.13$$

$$\frac{1}{3} + \frac{1}{2} = .33 + .5 = .83$$

$$\frac{1}{12} + \frac{3}{8} = .08 + .38 = .46$$

$$1\frac{3}{5} + 2\frac{5}{6} = 1.6 + 2.83 = 4.43$$

$$\frac{2}{7} + \frac{1}{5} = .29 + .2 = .49$$

$$\frac{1}{14} + \frac{7}{8} = .07 + .88 = .95$$

$$\frac{35}{30} + \frac{2}{6} = 1.17 + .33 = 1.5$$

$$4\frac{4}{5} + 3\frac{3}{4} = 4.8 + 3.75 = 8.55$$

Subtraction of fractions

As with addition of fractions, you need to find the lowest common denominator to subtract fractions.

Examples

$$\frac{2}{5} - \frac{3}{15} = \frac{3 \times 2}{3 \times 5} - \frac{3}{15} = \frac{6}{15} - \frac{3}{15} = \frac{3}{15} = \frac{1}{5}$$

$$\frac{2}{3} - \frac{1}{4} = \frac{4 \times 2}{4 \times 3} - \frac{3 \times 1}{3 \times 4} = \frac{8}{12} - \frac{3}{12} = \frac{5}{12}$$

$$\frac{1}{2} - \frac{1}{3} = \frac{3 \times 1}{3 \times 2} - \frac{2 \times 1}{2 \times 3} = \frac{3}{6} - \frac{2}{6} = \frac{1}{6}$$

$$\frac{3}{8} - \frac{1}{12} = \frac{3 \times 3}{3 \times 8} - \frac{2 \times 1}{2 \times 12} = \frac{9}{24} - \frac{2}{24} = \frac{7}{24}$$

$$2\frac{5}{6} - 1\frac{4}{5} = \frac{17}{6} - \frac{9}{5} = \frac{5 \times 17}{5 \times 6} - \frac{6 \times 9}{6 \times 5} = \frac{85}{30} - \frac{54}{30} = \frac{31}{30} \text{ or } 1\frac{1}{30}$$

$$\frac{1}{3} - \frac{1}{4} = \frac{4 \times 1}{4 \times 3} - \frac{3 \times 1}{3 \times 4} = \frac{4}{12} - \frac{3}{12} = \frac{1}{12}$$

$$\frac{3}{7} - \frac{2}{6} = \frac{6 \times 3}{6 \times 7} - \frac{7 \times 2}{7 \times 6} = \frac{18}{42} - \frac{14}{42} = \frac{4}{42} = \frac{2}{21}$$

$$\frac{4}{5} - \frac{1}{2} = \frac{2 \times 4}{2 \times 5} - \frac{5 \times 1}{5 \times 2} = \frac{8}{10} - \frac{5}{10} = \frac{3}{10}$$

$$3\frac{3}{4} - 1\frac{3}{5} = \frac{15}{4} - \frac{8}{5} = \frac{5 \times 15}{5 \times 4} - \frac{4 \times 8}{4 \times 5} = \frac{75}{20} - \frac{32}{20} = \frac{43}{20} \text{ or } 2\frac{3}{20}$$

You can also turn a fraction into a decimal by dividing the top number by the bottom number. Do this to both fractions, then subtract.

Examples (All calculations are rounded off to the hundredths.)

$$\frac{1}{2} - \frac{1}{3} = .5 - .33 = .17$$

$$\frac{5}{7} - \frac{5}{8} = .71 - .63 = .08$$

$$\frac{7}{8} - \frac{1}{4} = .88 - .25 = .63$$

$$\frac{2}{9} - \frac{1}{6} = .22 - .17 = .05$$

$$\frac{4}{5} - \frac{2}{3} = .8 - .67 = .13$$

$$\frac{5}{6} - \frac{2}{7} = .83 - .29 = .54$$

$$\frac{8}{10} - \frac{3}{5} = .8 - .6 = .2$$

$$\frac{7}{8} - \frac{1}{8} = .88 - .13 = .75$$

$$2\frac{1}{2} - \frac{3}{4} = 2.5 - .75 = 1.75$$

Multiplication of fractions

When multiplying fractions, multiply the top number by the top number, and the bottom number by the bottom number.

Examples (All calculations are rounded off to the hundredths.)

$$\frac{3}{4} \times \frac{2}{5} = \frac{3 \times 2}{4 \times 5} = \frac{6}{20} = .3$$

$$\frac{4}{7} \times \frac{1}{2} = \frac{4 \times 1}{7 \times 2} = \frac{4}{14} = .29$$

$$\frac{5}{21} \times \frac{7}{9} = \frac{5 \times 7}{21 \times 9} = \frac{35}{189} = .19$$

$$\frac{1}{12} \times \frac{3}{4} = \frac{1 \times 3}{12 \times 4} = \frac{3}{48} = .06$$

$$\frac{3}{7} \times \frac{6}{8} = \frac{3 \times 6}{7 \times 8} = \frac{18}{56} = .32$$

$$\frac{7}{9} \times \frac{2}{3} = \frac{7 \times 2}{9 \times 3} = \frac{14}{27} = .52$$

$$\frac{3}{8} \times \frac{4}{6} = \frac{3 \times 4}{8 \times 6} = \frac{12}{48} = .25$$

$$\frac{2}{5} \times \frac{9}{2} = \frac{2 \times 9}{5 \times 2} = \frac{18}{10} = 1.8$$

$$\frac{10}{3} \times \frac{3}{5} = \frac{10 \times 3}{3 \times 5} = \frac{30}{15} = 2.0$$

Division of fractions

To divide fractions, you multiply the first fraction by the **reciprocal** of the second fraction. In other words, multiply the first fraction by the second fraction turned upside down.

Examples (All calculations are rounded off to the hundredths.)

$$\frac{1}{4} \div \frac{1}{3} = \frac{1}{4} \times \frac{3}{1} = \frac{3}{4} = .75$$

$$\frac{5}{9} \div \frac{2}{7} = \frac{5}{9} \times \frac{7}{2} = \frac{35}{18} = 1.94$$

$$\frac{3}{14} \div \frac{9}{20} = \frac{3}{14} \times \frac{20}{9} = \frac{60}{126} = .48$$

$$\frac{5}{8} \div \frac{1}{4} = \frac{5}{8} \times \frac{4}{1} = \frac{20}{8} = 2.5$$

$$\frac{11}{17} \div \frac{2}{3} = \frac{11}{17} \times \frac{3}{2} = \frac{33}{34} = .97$$

$$\frac{1}{2} \div \frac{1}{4} = \frac{1}{2} \times \frac{4}{1} = \frac{4}{2} = 2$$

$$\frac{13}{16} \div \frac{2}{3} = \frac{13}{16} \times \frac{3}{2} = \frac{39}{32} = 1.22$$

$$\frac{6}{10} \div \frac{6}{15} = \frac{6}{10} \times \frac{15}{6} = \frac{90}{60} = 1.5$$

$$\frac{4}{5} \div \frac{9}{12} = \frac{4}{5} \times \frac{12}{9} = \frac{48}{45} = 1.07$$

Decimals

Decimals are numbers that use **base ten**. As we have seen, fractions can be turned into decimal numbers. Decimal numbers can be added, subtracted, multiplied, and divided.

When adding or subtracting decimal numbers without a calculator, make sure to keep the decimal points of the two numbers aligned. When multiplying or dividing decimal numbers, also be careful about the placement of the decimal point in the answer. The decimal point serves as a reference point for a number so that you can determine its value. Numbers to the right of the decimal point have a value less than 1, while numbers to the left of the decimal point have a value of 1 or greater.

Examples

73.0	6.9	1.33	96.14
+ .8	+ .3	+2.29	+ .34
73.8	7.2	3.62	96.48

53.0	2.2	2.52	89.58
− .7	− .5	− .23	−87.53
52.3	1.7	2.29	2.05

When multiplying or dividing decimal numbers, it is important to put the decimal point in the right place. When multiplying decimals, you move the decimal point of the answer, from right to left, the number of decimal spaces represented in the two numbers. When dividing decimals, you move the decimal point of the denominator to the right and then move the decimal point of the numerator the same number of decimal places to the right. Then divide.

2	17	3.16	17.72
× .4	× .2	× .72	× .63
.8	3.4	2.2752	11.1636

.94	32	2.177	38.6288
÷.1	÷ .4	÷ .35	÷ .56
9.4	80.0	6.22	68.98

Practice questions

A platinum diamond ring has a center stone in it that weighs .875 carats. Several small diamonds that together weigh .375 carats surround the center stone. What is the total carat weight of the diamonds in this ring?

$.875 + .375 = 1.25$ carats

A wood planer is a machine used to shave the edge off a piece of wood. You start with a piece of wood that is 10 in. thick and pass it through the planer that is set for .125 of an inch. How thick is this piece of wood now?

$10.0 - .125 = 9.875$ in

If 1 inch equals 2.54 cm, then how many centimeters does 35 inches equal?

$35 \times 2.54 = 88.9$ cm

There are 28.35 grams in an ounce; how many ounces are there in 567 grams?

$567 \div 28.35 = 20$ ounces

A metal supply company sells a wide selection of aluminum sheet metal. Their thinnest sheet is .025 in. Their thickest sheet is .1875 in. What is the difference in inches between their thickest and their thinnest aluminum sheet metal?

$.1875 - .025 = .1625$ in

If one kilogram equals 2.2 pounds, then how many pounds does 24.5 kilograms weigh?

$24.5 \times 2.2 = 53.9$ pounds

It takes 1.75 square yards of cotton fabric to make a pillowcase. If you have 30 square yards of fabric, then how many pillowcases can you make?

$30 \div 1.75 = 17.14$ or 17 pillowcases

The rainfall for a four-day period in inches was .8, .06, .25, and 1.05. What is the total rainfall for these four days?

$.8 + .06 + .25 + 1.05 = 2.16$ in

A cake recipe calls for $3\frac{1}{2}$ cups of flour. How many cups of flour are needed to make seven cakes?

$3.5 \times 7 = 24.5$ cups

Athletic shoes normally sell for \$40.75, but they are on sale for \$27.95. How much is the savings?

$\$40.75 - \$27.95 = \$12.80$

Percentages

Percentages refer to the number of times out of 100 that something occurs. Percentages can be used to express the proportions of ingredients in a recipe, the proportion of people favoring a particular political candidate, or the likelihood that it will rain tomorrow. A percentage can be obtained from a fraction.

A percentage tells us how a part of something relates to a whole in terms of size, quantity, or likelihood. A percentage can be calculated by counting how many items in a set are similar, and then dividing this count by the total number of items.

First, a fraction is turned into decimal form by dividing the top number by the bottom number. Then, this decimal number is turned into a percentage by moving the decimal point two places to the right and then adding a percentage sign.

Examples

$$\frac{1}{4} = .25 = 25\%$$

$$\frac{2}{3} \approx .67 = 67\%$$

$$\frac{2}{5} = .40 = 40\%$$

$$\frac{7}{6} \approx 1.17 = 117\%$$

$$\frac{3}{4} = .75 = 75\%$$

$$\frac{1}{8} = .125 = 12.5\%$$

$$\frac{2}{25} = .08 = 8\%$$

$$\frac{3}{5} = .6 = 60\%$$

Practice questions

A small desert town located in the Southwest receives little rain. Last year, it rained only 11 out of the 365 days. In this town, what percent of the days did it rain last year? Round to the nearest percent.

$11 \div 365 \approx .03$

It rained 3% of the days.

On a cruise ship, passengers have their choice between a standard stateroom and a deluxe stateroom. There are 242 standard staterooms and 96 deluxe. What percent of the staterooms are deluxe? Round the answer to the nearest percent.

$242 + 96 = 338$ total staterooms

$96 \div 338 \approx .28$

So 28% of the staterooms are deluxe rooms.

The enrollment statistics at one state college shows that out of 10,400 students enrolled, 5,460 are women. What percentage of the students are women? Also, what percentage are men? Round the answers to the nearest tenth of a percent.

$5,460 \div 10,400 = .525$, so 52.5% of the students are women.
$100\% - 52.5\% = 47.5\%$, so 47.5% are men.

A mayoral candidate wants to know how well she is doing in her election campaign. So she conducts a survey. Out of 2,000 eligible voters surveyed, 1,260 said that they plan to vote for her in the upcoming election. What percent of the vote is this?

$1,260 \div 2,000 = .63$

The candidate has 63% of the vote.

In a recent survey of 8,000 coffee drinkers, 960 of them preferred decaffeinated coffee to regular coffee. What percent of coffee drinkers prefer decaffeinated?

$960 \div 8,000 = .12$

Of the coffee drinkers surveyed, 12% prefer decaffeinated.

A high school has a total enrollment of 2,130 students. Of these students, 1,491 own a cell phone. What percent of the students at this high school own a cell phone?

$1,491 \div 2,130 = .7$

In this high school, 70% of the students own a cell phone.

One throw of two fair dice produces 36 equally likely outcomes. There are six ways to roll a 7. What percent of the rolls is a 7 expected?

$6 \div 36 \approx .17$

So 17% of the time a 7 is expected.

A cell phone company is having a sale. A phone that normally sells for $160 is on sale for $120. What is the percent savings?

$160 - 120 = 40$

$40 \div 160 = .25$, or a 25% savings

A television commercial advertising chewing gum claims that four out of five dentists surveyed recommend a particular brand of gum to their patients who chew gum. What percent of the surveyed dentists recommend this gum?

$4 \div 5 = .8$, meaning that 80% of the dentists recommend the gum.

Nine games into the season, a college basketball player has taken 55 shots and made 38 of them. What is this player's shooting percentage?

$38 \div 55 \approx .69$, so the player has shot the ball successfully 69% of the time.

A professional football team had 50,000 fans attend their game last week. This week, 60,000 fans attended their game. What is the percent increase in attendance from last week to this week?

$60,000 - 50,000 = 10,000$

$10,000 \div 50,000 \approx .2 = 20\%$ increase in attendance

A venture capitalist invested $500,000 into a business endeavor that paid back all of the investment plus a profit of $80,000. What is the percent profit from this deal?

$80,000 \div 500,000 = .16 = 16\%$ profit

In order to calculate the percentage of a given quantity, you first have to convert the percentage into decimal form. A percentage is converted into decimal form by dividing it by 100. A simple way to divide by 100 is to move the decimal point two places to the left:

$75\% = .75$

After converting the percentage into decimal form, the second step is to multiply the given quantity by your decimal number. For example, 75% of 30 would be approximately 23:

$30 \times .75 = 22.5 \approx 23$

The following section has several examples for calculating the percentage of a given amount.

Practice questions

A businesswoman has a meal at a nice restaurant. She likes to tip 20% when the service is excellent. How much money will she tip on a $35 meal?

$35 \times .2 = 7$

The woman would leave a $7 tip.

A money market account pays 1.93% annual interest. If you put $10,000 in this account for one year, how much interest will you earn?

$1.93\% = .0193$

$10,000 \times .0193 = 193$
You would earn $193 interest.

A small tropical country exports 35% of its bananas. This country consumes a total of 685,000 pounds of bananas each year. How many pounds of bananas does this country export each year?

$685,000 \times .35 = 239,750$
The country exports 239,750 pounds of bananas annually.

A horse rancher has land located in the Great Plains region, where she owns 1,200 horses. She has different breeds of horses, but her favorite is the mustang; 65% of her horses are mustangs. How many mustangs does the rancher own?

$1,200 \times .65 = 780$
The rancher owns 780 mustangs.

In one suburban city, 42% of the people are homeowners. This city has a population of 90,000 people. How many homeowners are there in this city?

$90,000 \times .42 = 37,800$
There are 37,800 homeowners in the city.

At one college, 70% of the students who own computers own a laptop computer. If 1,840 students at this college own computers, how many students own laptop computers?

$1,840 \times .7 = 1,288$
Of the computer-owning students, 1,288 own laptops.

At one freshwater lake, 38% of the fish are largemouth bass. If there are 20,500 fish in this lake, how many are largemouth bass?

$20,500 \times .38 = 7,790$
The lake is home to 7,790 largemouth bass.

A traveler likes to tip 15% on taxi car rides. If the taxi fare amounts to $28, how much money should the traveler tip?

$28 \times .15 = 4.2$
The traveler should tip $4.20.

A math competency exam was administered to 1,375 students; 84% of the students passed the math exam. How many students passed this test?

$1,375 \times .84 = 1,155$
On this math exam, 1,155 students passed.

In a recent survey, 57% of the respondents reported owning a dog. If 300 people responded to this survey, how many were dog owners?

$300 \times .57 = 171$
Of the people who responded to the survey, 171 were dog owners.

A liquid vanilla extract used for baking is 40% alcohol by volume. How many quarts of alcohol are there in 12 quarts of this vanilla extract?

$12 \times .4 = 4.8$
In 12 quarts of the extract, there are 4.8 quarts of alcohol.

The sales tax at one restaurant is .08. One customer has a bill for food that comes to $24.50. How much is the sales tax on this amount?

$24.5 \times .08 = 1.96$, so the tax is $1.96.

Math Symbols

Parentheses ( ) and brackets [ ] are grouping symbols that mean, "Do this first." If there are parentheses inside a bracket, then do what is inside the parentheses first. You must work from the inside out. When a number is next to a parentheses or brackets, this means multiply. When two parentheses or two brackets are next to each other, this also means multiply.

Examples

$3(5) = 3 \times 5 = 15$

$(11)(2) = 11 \times 2 = 22$

$-2(10 + 20) = -2(30) = -60$

$15(9 - 4) = 15(5) = 75$

$7(12 \div 2) = 7(6) = 42$

$5(10 - 1) = 5(9) = 45$

$(4 \times 8)\, 3 = (32)\, 3 = 96$

$4[9] = 36$

$8[9 + 4] = 8[13] = 104$

$2[8 - (2 \times 3)] = 2[8 - 6] = 2[2] = 4$

$3[8 \times 4] = 3[32] = 96$

$[5 + 1][10 - 2] = [6][8] = 48$

$[9][7] = 63$

$3[10 + 2] = 3[12] = 36$

Order of Operations

When a mathematical expression does not have grouping symbols like parentheses or brackets, you must follow the order of operations rule. This rule tells you to do power and roots first, multiplication and division second, and addition and subtraction third. Further, these operations are done from left to right.

Examples

$2 + 10 \times 3 = 2 + (10 \times 3) = 2 + 30 = 32$

$9 - 60 \div 4 = 9 - (60 \div 4) = 9 - 15 = -6$

$18 - 4 \times 2 = 18 - (4 \times 2) = 18 - 8 = 10$

$7 \times 3^2 = 7 \times 9 = 63$

$12 \div 4 + 2 \times 5 = (12 \div 4) + (2 \times 5) = 3 + 10 = 13$

$7 - 4 \times 2 = 7 - 8 = -1$

$5 \times 9 - 2 = 45 - 2 = 43$

$5 + 24 \times 2 = 5 + 48 = 53$

$10 - \sqrt{81} - 3 = 10 - 9 - 3 = -2$

$3 \times 6 + 2^3 = 18 + 8 = 26$

$30 - 5 \times 4 = 30 - 20 = 10$

$12 \times \sqrt{25} - 16 \times 2 = 12 \times 5 - 16 \times 2 = 60 - 32 = 28$

$4^2 \times 4 + 2 = 16 \times 4 + 2 = 64 + 2 = 66$

$2 + 63 \div 7 = 2 + 9 = 11$

$19 - 8 \times 2 = 19 - 16 = 3$

Factorial

In mathematics, the factorial of a number, which is represented by an exclamation point (!) following the number, is the product of all positive integers less than or equal to it. For example, 4! is read "4 factorial." To calculate the factorial of a number, multiply the number by one less than that number; then multiply the resulting product by the next lower number, and repeat this process until you have multiplied by 1. The product of these numbers is the given number's factorial value. The factorial value of 4, for example, is 24:

$4! = 4 \times 3 \times 2 \times 1 = 24$

A special case is 0!, which is equal to 1.

Examples

$0! = 1$
$1! = 1$
$2! = 2 \times 1 = 2$
$3! = 3 \times 2 \times 1 = 6$
$4! = 4 \times 3 \times 2 \times 1 = 24$
$5! = 5 \times 4 \times 3 \times 2 \times 1 = 120$
$6! = 6 \times 5 \times 4 \times 3 \times 2 \times 1 = 720$
$7! = 7 \times 6 \times 5 \times 4 \times 3 \times 2 \times 1 = 5,040$
$8! = 8 \times 7 \times 6 \times 5 \times 4 \times 3 \times 2 \times 1 = 40,320$
$9! = 9 \times 8 \times 7 \times 6 \times 5 \times 4 \times 3 \times 2 \times 1 = 362,880$
$10! = 10 \times 9 \times 8 \times 7 \times 6 \times 5 \times 4 \times 3 \times 2 \times 1 = 3,628,800$
$11! = 11 \times 10 \times 9 \times 8 \times 7 \times 6 \times 5 \times 4 \times 3 \times 2 \times 1 = 39,916,800$
$12! = 12 \times 11 \times 10 \times 9 \times 8 \times 7 \times 6 \times 5 \times 4 \times 3 \times 2 \times 1 = 479,001,600$

Evaluating factorial expressions
Fractions

$$\frac{3!}{4!} = \frac{6}{24} = \frac{1}{4} \quad \text{or} \quad .25$$

$$\frac{8!}{5!} = \frac{40,320}{120} = 336$$

$$\frac{9!}{7!} = \frac{362,880}{5,040} = 72$$

$$\frac{3!}{5!} = \frac{6}{120} = \frac{1}{20} \quad \text{or} \quad .05$$

$$\frac{6!}{0!} = \frac{720}{1} = 720$$

Multiplication

$(3!)(2!) = 6 \times 2 = 12$
$5![5!] = 120 \times 120 = 14,400$
$2[6!] = 2 \times 720 = 1,440$
$4!(20) = 24 \times 20 = 480$
$(6)(7!) = 6 \times 5,040 = 30,240$
$(5!)10 = 120 \times 10 = 1,200$

[8!][3!] = 40,320 × 6 = 241,920
[4!][5!] = 24 × 120 = 2,880
25(7!) = 25 × 5,040 = 126,000

Addition

5! + 2! = 120 + 2 = 122
8! + 4! = 40,320 + 24 = 40,344
4! + 1! = 24 + 1 = 25
3! + 3! = 6 + 6 = 12
1! + 0! = 1 + 1 = 2
9! + 6! = 362,880 + 720 = 363,600
10! + 7! = 3,628,800 + 5,040 = 3,633,840

Subtraction

(9 − 6)! = 3! = 6
(6 − 1)! = 5! = 120
(7 − 5)! = 2! = 2
(9 − 8)! = 1! = 1
(5 − 1)! = 4! = 24
(8 − 8)! = 0! = 1
(14 − 7)! = 7! = 5,040

Division

$$\frac{5!}{3! \times 2!} = \frac{120}{6 \times 2} = \frac{120}{12} = 10$$

$$\frac{7!}{2! \times 4!} = \frac{5,040}{2 \times 24} = \frac{5,040}{48} = 105$$

$$\frac{4!}{3! \times 3!} = \frac{24}{6 \times 6} = \frac{24}{36} = \frac{2}{3} \approx .67$$

Scientific Notation

The purpose of scientific notation is to use only a few numbers to represent a larger number.

Converting a number in decimal form to scientific notation

A few basic steps can be used to convert a decimal number, greater than 1, into scientific notation:

1. Move the decimal point to the left until it stops right before the last digit.
2. Count how many decimal places you moved the decimal point.
3. Multiply your new number by 10 raised to the power of the number of places the decimal point was moved.

Examples

$50 = 5\underset{\smile}{0} = 5.0 \times 10$

$45 = 4\underset{\smile}{5} = 4.5 \times 10$

$900 = 9\underset{\smile\smile}{00} = 9.0 \times 10^2$

$7,000 = 7\underset{\smile\smile\smile}{000} = 7.0 \times 10^3$

$10,574 = 1\underset{\smile\smile\smile\smile}{0574} = 1.0574 \times 10^4$

$1,500,000 = 1\underset{\smile\smile\smile\smile\smile\smile}{500000} = 1.5 \times 10^6$

A few basic steps can be used to convert a decimal number, less than 1, into scientific notation:

1. Move the decimal point to the right until it stops right after the first nonzero digit.
2. Count how many decimal places you moved the decimal point.
3. Multiply your new number by 10 raised to the negative power of the number of places the decimal point was moved.

Examples

$.2 = .\underset{\smile}{2} = 2.0 \times 10^{-1}$

$.06 = .\underset{\smile\smile}{06} = 6.0 \times 10^{-2}$

$.0087 = .\underset{\smile\smile\smile}{0087} = 8.7 \times 10^{-3}$

$.000421 = .\underset{\smile\smile\smile\smile}{000421} = 4.21 \times 10^{-4}$

$.0000684 = .\underset{\smile\smile\smile\smile\smile}{0000684} = 6.84 \times 10^{-5}$

$.000005 = .\underset{\smile\smile\smile\smile\smile\smile}{000005} = 5.0 \times 10^{-6}$

$.00000018 = .\underset{\smile\smile\smile\smile\smile\smile\smile}{00000018} = 1.8 \times 10^{-7}$

A few basic steps can be used to convert a number in scientific notation into a decimal number. If the exponent on the 10 is positive, then use the following steps:

1. Whatever the value of the exponent, move the decimal point that many places to the right.
2. Add zeros in the open places.

Examples

$8.0 \times 10 = 8.0 = 80$

$1.5 \times 10^2 = 1.5 = 150$

$3.125 \times 10^3 = 3.125 = 3,125$

$6.0 \times 10^4 = 6.0 = 60,000$

$7.92 \times 10^5 = 7.92 = 792,000$

$9.2166 \times 10^6 = 9.2166 = 9,216,600$

$2.75 \times 10^7 = 2.75 = 27,500,000$

To convert a number in scientific notation into a decimal number when the exponent on the 10 is negative, use these steps:

1. Whatever the value of the exponent, move the decimal point that many places to the left.
2. Add zeros in the open places.

Examples

$9.0 \times 10^{-1} = 9.0 = .9$

$6.25 \times 10^{-2} = 6.25 = .0625$

$7.1 \times 10^{-3} = 7.1 = .0071$

$8.18 \times 10^{-4} = 8.18 = .000818$

$4.0 \times 10^{-5} = 4.0 = .00004$

$1.0 \times 10^{-6} = 1.0 = .000001$

$2.5 \times 10^{-7} = 2.5 = .00000025$

$1.35 \times 10^{-8} = 1.35 = .0000000135$

Estimation

Estimation is the process of coming up with an answer that is close to an exact answer. The advantage of estimation is that it saves you time. Estimates are obtained by rounding off numbers and then performing simple calculations.

Practice questions

Jim is having a pizza party for 11 of his close friends. He wants to serve each guest a mini-pizza. Mini-pizzas cost $6.79 each. Estimate the total cost.

The cost of each mini-pizza, $6.79, rounds up to $7, while the number of pizzas rounds down to 10. Now multiply:

$10 \times \$7 = \$70$

Note: The actual cost of the pizzas is $74.69.

The average annual rainfall in the state of California is 17.28 in. The average annual rainfall in the state of Ohio is 37.77 in. Estimate how many more inches of rain falls in Ohio compared to California.

Ohio's rainfall rounds to 38 in, and California's to 17 in, leaving you with the following equation:

$38 - 17 = 21$ in

Note: The actual measurement is 20.49 in.

The population of San Francisco, California, is 764,976 people. The population of Sacramento, California, is 460,242 people. Estimate the combined population of the two cities.

Rounded to the nearest ten thousand, San Franciso's population is 760,000, and Sacramento's is 460,000, so

$760,000 + 460,000 = 1,220,000$ people

Note: The actual count is 1,225,218 people.

The average high temperature for the city of San Diego, California, is 71.3 degrees Fahrenheit. The average high temperature for the city of Seattle, Washington, is 44.75 degrees Fahrenheit. Estimate the difference between these two temperatures.

$71 - 45 = 26$ degrees

Note: The actual temperature difference is 26.55 degrees.

In 2006, the population of California was 36,121,296 people. During that same period, the population for the state of Texas was 23,367,534 people. Estimate how many more people lived in California than in Texas during this time.

$36,000,000 - 23,000,000 = 13,000,000$ people

Note: The actual number of people is 12,753,762.

A real estate developer wants to divide a 157-acre piece of land into 8 equal lots. Estimate the size of each lot.

$160 \div 8 = 20$ acres

Note: The actual number of acres per lot is 19.625.

A publisher is putting together a book using paper that is .0048 of an inch thick. The book needs to be 468 pages long. Not counting the front and back cover, estimate how thick this book will be.

.005 × 500 = 2.5 in.

Note: The actual thickness in inches will be 2.2464.

A woodshop project for building a jewelry box requires the use of 31 finishing nails. If each of 28 students in a class decides to build a jewelry box, estimate the number of nails needed.

30 × 30 = 900 nails

Note: The actual number of nails needed is 868.

The annual average snowfall for the city of Denver, Colorado, is 60.3 in. The annual average snowfall of the city of New York is 28.6 in. Estimate how much more snow Denver gets compared to New York.

60 − 29 = 31 in.

Note: The actual difference is 31.7 in.

The average weight of apples from one particular apple farm is .5625 pounds. Estimate the weight of a case of apples if there are 24 apples in a case.

.6 × 24 = 14.4 pounds

Note: The actual weight of a case would be closer to 13.5 pounds.

A gallon of paint covers 250 sq. ft. Estimate how many gallons are needed to cover an area of 2,455 sq. ft.

2,500 ÷ 250 = 10

Note: The actual amount of paint needed is 9.82 gallons.

A certain dress fabric sells for $7.75 per square yard. Estimate how much six yards of this fabric will cost.

$8.00 × 6 = $48.00

Note: The actual cost of the yardage is $46.50.

A sporting goods store sells skateboards for $45. The sales tax is 8.25%. Estimate how much the sales tax would be on a skateboard.

.08 × $45.00 = $3.60

Note: The actual sales tax is $3.71.

A manufacturer makes one gauge of sheet metal that is .0747 in. thick. One order requires packing a stack of 25 sheets. Estimate the total thickness of this order.

25 × .07 = 1.75 in.

Note: The actual thickness would be 1.8675 in.

A northern California fishing lake called Clear Lake has a surface area of 43,785 acres. A southern California fishing lake called Lake Casitas has a surface area of 2,700 acres. Estimate the combined surface area of these lakes.

$$44,000 + 3,000 = 47,000$$

Note: The actual area is 46,485 acres.

Exponents and Roots

Exponents

An exponent on a number means raise the number to a power. Exponents are used to show repeated multiplication. There are two parts to a power: the base and the exponent:

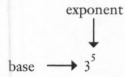

This expression is read as "three to the fifth power." When we raise a base to an exponent of 2, we use the term "squared." For example, 4^2 is read as "4 squared."

Positive exponents

The value of powers with positive exponents can be calculated by multiplying the base times itself as many times as the exponent.

Examples

$2^2 = 2 \times 2 = 4$
$2^3 = 2 \times 2 \times 2 = 8$
$2^4 = 2 \times 2 \times 2 \times 2 = 16$
$2^5 = 2 \times 2 \times 2 \times 2 \times 2 = 32$
$2^6 = 2 \times 2 \times 2 \times 2 \times 2 \times 2 = 64$
$2^7 = 2 \times 2 \times 2 \times 2 \times 2 \times 2 \times 2 = 128$
$2^8 = 2 \times 2 \times 2 \times 2 \times 2 \times 2 \times 2 \times 2 = 256$

$3^2 = 3 \times 3 = 9$
$3^3 = 3 \times 3 \times 3 = 27$
$3^4 = 3 \times 3 \times 3 \times 3 = 81$
$3^5 = 3 \times 3 \times 3 \times 3 \times 3 = 243$
$3^6 = 3 \times 3 \times 3 \times 3 \times 3 \times 3 = 729$
$3^7 = 3 \times 3 \times 3 \times 3 \times 3 \times 3 \times 3 = 2,187$
$3^8 = 3 \times 3 \times 3 \times 3 \times 3 \times 3 \times 3 \times 3 = 6,561$

$8^2 = 8 \times 8 = 64$ $4^3 = 4 \times 4 \times 4 = 64$
$5^2 = 5 \times 5 = 25$ $4^5 = 4 \times 4 \times 4 \times 4 \times 4 = 1,024$
$6^4 = 6 \times 6 \times 6 \times 6 = 1,296$ $3^5 = 3 \times 3 \times 3 \times 3 \times 3 = 243$

$$5^6 = 5 \times 5 \times 5 \times 5 \times 5 \times 5 = 15,625$$
$$4^7 = 4 \times 4 \times 4 \times 4 \times 4 \times 4 \times 4 = 16,384$$
$$7^8 = 7 \times 7 \times 7 \times 7 \times 7 \times 7 \times 7 \times 7 = 5,764,801$$

Negative exponents

A negative exponent means a reciprocal. A reciprocal of a number is 1 divided by that number. Notice that when a number with a negative exponent goes from the numerator to the denominator, the exponent turns positive. To determine the value of a power with a negative exponent, first invert the number; that is, create a fraction with the power as the denominator and 1 as the numerator. This is the reciprocal. Then change the sign on the exponent to positive. Last, multiply this fraction by itself the number of times indicated by the exponent.

Examples

$$2^{-2} = \frac{2^{-2}}{1} = \frac{1}{2^2} = \frac{1}{2} \times \frac{1}{2} = \frac{1}{4}$$

$$2^{-3} = \frac{2^{-3}}{1} = \frac{1}{2^3} = \frac{1}{2} \times \frac{1}{2} \times \frac{1}{2} = \frac{1}{8}$$

$$3^{-2} = \frac{3^{-2}}{1} = \frac{1}{3^2} = \frac{1}{3} \times \frac{1}{3} = \frac{1}{9}$$

$$5^{-2} = \frac{5^{-2}}{1} = \frac{1}{5^2} = \frac{1}{5} \times \frac{1}{5} = \frac{1}{25}$$

$$4^{-4} = \frac{4^{-4}}{1} = \frac{1}{4^4} = \frac{1}{4} \times \frac{1}{4} \times \frac{1}{4} \times \frac{1}{4} = \frac{1}{2}$$

Roots

Roots are the opposites of exponents. Exponents answer the question, "What number would you get if you multiplied a number times itself so many times?" Roots answer the question, "What number times itself, so many times, will give you the number that you have?"

The following expression is read as "the *nth* root of *a* is a number *b*":

root ⟶ $\sqrt[n]{a} = b$

↑
radical symbol

When the root of a radical expression is 2, then we call this the square root of a number. The 2 is usually not written, as in the following:

$$\sqrt{25} = 5$$

This is read, "The square root of 25 equals 5." This is because $5 \times 5 = 25$.

When the root of a radical expression is 3, then we call this the cube root of a number, as in the following example:

$\sqrt[3]{27} = 3$

This is read, "The cube root of 27 equals 3." This is because $3 \times 3 \times 3 = 27$.

When the root of a radical expression is 4, then we call this the 4th root of a number, for example:

$\sqrt[4]{16} = 2$

This is read, "The fourth root of 16 equals 2." This is because $2 \times 2 \times 2 \times 2 = 16$.

Examples

$\sqrt{64} = 8$ This is read, "The square root of 64 equals 8." This is because $8 \times 8 = 64$.

$\sqrt{100} = 10$ This is read, "The square root of 100 equals 10." This is because $10 \times 10 = 100$.

$\sqrt[3]{8} = 2$ This is read, "The cube root of 8 equals 2." This is because $2 \times 2 \times 2 = 8$.

$\sqrt[3]{64} = 4$ This is read, "The cube root of 64 equals 4." This is because $4 \times 4 \times 4 = 64$.

$\sqrt[3]{8} = 2$ This is read, "The cube root of 8 equals 2." This is because $2 \times 2 \times 2 = 8$.

$\sqrt[4]{625} = 5$ This is read, "The fourth root of 625 equals 5." This is because $5 \times 5 \times 5 \times 5 = 625$.

$\sqrt[3]{216} = 6$ This is read, "The cube root of 216 equals 6." This is because $6 \times 6 \times 6 = 216$.

$\sqrt[5]{243} = 3$ This is read, "The fifth root of 243 equals 3." This is because $3 \times 3 \times 3 \times 3 \times 3 = 243$.

$\sqrt{400} = 20$ This is read, "The square root of 400 equals 20." This is because $20 \times 20 = 400$.

Not all radical expressions equal whole numbers. It is possible to have decimal answers to radical equations such as square roots. These calculations are done with a calculator.

Examples (rounded to the nearest hundredth)

$\sqrt{30} = 5.48$

$\sqrt{8} = 2.83$

$\sqrt{125} = 11.18$

A number squared and the square root of a number are opposites. If you take a number and square it, then take the square root of that number, you will have the number that you started with.

Examples

$5^2 = 25$ and $\sqrt{25} = 5$

$7^2 = 49$ and $\sqrt{49} = 7$

$9^2 = 81$ and $\sqrt{81} = 9$

$10^2 = 100$ and $\sqrt{100} = 10$

Absolute Value

On the number line, the number 0 serves as a reference point. Negative numbers are to the left of 0. They represent smaller and smaller values the farther left you go. Positive numbers are to the right of 0. They represent larger and larger values the farther right you go.

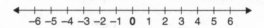

The absolute value of a number means how far a number is from 0 on the number line. The absolute value is never negative. The absolute value shows how far from 0 the number lies and not in which direction.

The symbol for the absolute value of a number has two bars that look like this: | |. For example, "the absolute value of 4 is equal to" is written like this:

$|4| =$

The answer is $|4| = 4$.

Another example, "the absolute value of -4 is equal to" is written like this:

$|-4| =$

The answer is $|-4| = 4$.

On the number line, the absolute value of 4 and -4 looks like this:

Remember that with absolute values, it is the distance from 0 that matters.

Examples

$|6| = 6$
$|0| = 0$
$|-2| = 2$
$|12| = 12$
$|4| = 4$
$|-4| = 4$
$|-7| = 7$
$|9| = 9$

$|20| = 20$
$|-5| = 5$
$|-16| = 16$
$|-3| = 3$
$|-6| = 6$
$|10| = 10$
$|11| = 11$
$|-1| = 1$

The negative of an absolute value

Sometimes it is necessary to simplify an absolute value that has a negative sign in front of it. In that case, first take the absolute value of the number inside the absolute value bars. Then apply the negative.

Examples

$-|5| = -(5) = -5$
$-|-5| = -(5) = -5$
$-|-2| = -(2) = -2$

Ratios and Proportions

Ratios

A ratio expresses a comparison of two quantities by division. There are several ways to express a ratio: using the word "to" between the numbers being compared, using a colon between the numbers, or using a fraction:

$2 \text{ to } 3 = 2{:}3 = \dfrac{2}{3}$

or

$1 \text{ to } 4 = 1{:}4 = \dfrac{1}{4}$

Ratios are helpful because they allow us to compare the quantities of two groups.

Practice questions

In one classroom, there were 5 boys and 15 girls. What is the ratio of boys to girls?

The ratio is 5 boys to 15 girls. In lowest terms, this is 1 to 3:

$\dfrac{5 \text{ boys}}{15 \text{ girls}} = \dfrac{1 \text{ boy}}{3 \text{ girls}}$

In another classroom, there were 8 boys and 12 girls. What is the ratio of the number of boys to the total number of students?

The ratio is 8 boys to 20 students. In this problem, it was necessary to add the number of boys and girls together to get the total. In lowest terms, the ratio is 2 to 5:

$$\frac{8 \text{ boys}}{20 \text{ total}} = \frac{2 \text{ boys}}{5 \text{ total}}$$

An antique marble collector has 50 marbles: 15 of them are yellow, 10 are red, and 25 are blue. What is the ratio of yellow marbles to blue marbles?

The ratio is 15 yellows to 25 blues. In lowest terms, this is 3 to 5:

$$\frac{15 \text{ yellow}}{25 \text{ blue}} = \frac{3 \text{ yellow}}{5 \text{ blue}}$$

In the same marble collection as used in the previous question—15 of the marbles are yellow, 10 are red, and 25 are blue—what is the ratio of yellow marbles to red marbles?

The ratio is 15 yellows to 10 reds. In lowest terms, this is 3 to 2:

$$\frac{15 \text{ yellow}}{10 \text{ red}} = \frac{3 \text{ yellow}}{2 \text{ red}}$$

In the same marble collection as the previous question, in which 15 marbles are yellow, 10 are red, and 25 are blue, what is the ratio of yellow marbles to total marbles?

Now set up the ratio: 15 yellows to 50 total marbles. In lowest terms, this is 3 to 10:

$$\frac{15 \text{ yellow}}{50 \text{ total}} = \frac{3 \text{ yellow}}{10 \text{ total}}$$

Proportions

A proportion is a way of comparing two ratios in fraction form. In a proportion, the two ratios are equal to one another. For example, $\frac{9}{12} = \frac{15}{20}$ is read, "The ratio of 9 to 12 equals the ratio of 15 to 20."

Determining if two ratios form a proportion

Two ratios form a proportion if their cross products are equal. A cross product is obtained by multiplying the numerator of each fraction by the denominator of the other fraction.

Examples

$$\frac{3}{6} = \frac{9}{18} \qquad \frac{18 \times 3}{6} \diagdown \frac{6 \times 9}{18} \qquad 54 = 54$$

The cross products are equal, so the ratios form a proportion.

$$\frac{15}{21} = \frac{2}{3} \qquad \frac{3 \times 15}{21} \diagdown \frac{21 \times 2}{3} \qquad 45 \neq 42$$

The cross products are not equal, so the ratios do not form a proportion.

$$\frac{5}{40} = \frac{2}{16} \quad \frac{16 \times 5}{40} \diagdown \frac{40 \times 2}{16} \quad 80 = 80$$

The cross products are equal, so the ratios form a proportion.

Solving a proportion that contains a variable

In math, a variable is a symbol that can take on more than one value. Variables are represented by italicized lowercase letters (x, y, etc.) in italic. When it comes to solving an unknown variable for a proportion, the main task at hand is to isolate the variable, that is, get it by itself. We want to multiply or divide each fraction by the same amount, step by step, until we get the variable by itself equal to its value.

Example

Given the proportion $\frac{x}{9} = \frac{4}{6}$, solve for x.

First, find the cross product of $\frac{x}{9} = \frac{4}{6}$:

$$\frac{x}{9} = \frac{4}{6} = \frac{6 \times x}{9} \diagdown \frac{9 \times 4}{6} = 6x = 36$$

Then divide each side of the equation by the number being multiplied by x, in this case, 6:

$$\frac{6x}{6} = \frac{36}{6} = x = 6$$

Practice questions

Given the proportion $\frac{y}{14} = \frac{4}{7}$, solve for y.

First, find the cross product:

$$\frac{y}{14} = \frac{4}{7} = \frac{7 \times y}{14} \diagdown \frac{14 \times 4}{7} = 7y = 56$$

Then divide each side of the equation by the number being multiplied by y:

$$\frac{7y}{7} = \frac{56}{7} = y = 8$$

Given the proportion $\frac{y}{24} = \frac{5}{30}$, solve for y.

First, find the cross product:

$$\frac{y}{24} = \frac{5}{30} = \frac{30 \times y}{24} \diagdown \frac{24 \times 5}{30} = 30y = 120$$

Then divide each side of the equation by the number being multiplied by y:

$$\frac{30y}{30} = \frac{120}{30} = y = 4$$

Given the proportion $\frac{8}{4} = \frac{32}{x}$, solve for x.

First, find the cross product:

$$\frac{8}{4} = \frac{32}{x} = \frac{x \times 8}{4} \diagdown \frac{4 \times 32}{x} = 8x = 128$$

Then divide each side of the equation by the number being multiplied by x:

$$\frac{8x}{8} = \frac{128}{8} = x = 16$$

Given the proportion $\frac{9}{z} = \frac{6}{20}$, solve for z:

First, find the cross product:

$$\frac{9}{z} = \frac{6}{20} = \frac{20 \times 9}{z} \diagdown \frac{z \times 6}{20} = 180 = 6z$$

Then divide each side of the equation by the number being multiplied by z:

$$\frac{180}{6} = \frac{6z}{6} = z = 30$$

Algebra

Algebra Basics

Positive and negative numbers

Negative numbers are the opposite of positive numbers. Only 0 is neither positive nor negative. Positive and negative numbers can be represented on the number line. Negative numbers are to the left of 0. The farther left you go, the smaller the number becomes. Positive numbers are to the right of 0. The farther right you go, the larger the number becomes. Here is an example of a number line:

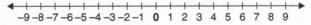

Adding positive and negative numbers

When adding a positive and a negative number, the number line can be used as a tool to find the answer.

Examples

$5 + (-2) = 3$
$8 + (-6) = 2$
$-4 + (2) = -2$
$-1 + (-7) = -8$
$-5 + (10) = 5$
$14 + (-7) = 7$
$-9 + (-9) = -18$
$24 + (-12) = 12$
$6 + (-6) = 0$
$-17 + (13) = -4$
$-2 + (-8) = -10$
$-30 + (11) = -19$
$21 + (-3) = 18$
$42 + (-13) = 29$
$-8 + (3) = -5$
$-25 + (-5) = -30$
$36 + (-23) = 13$
$-50 + (-28) = -78$

Subtracting positive and negative numbers

As with addition, a number line can be used as a tool when subtracting positive and negative numbers.

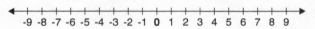

When using the number line to subtract, find the first number on the number line. If the second number is positive, then move that many places to the left to find the answer. If the second number is negative, then move that many places to the right. This is because the opposite of a negative number is a positive number.

When subtracting positive and negative numbers, there are several possibilities. Subtracting a negative number turns the operation into addition, as in the following examples:

$7 - (-3) = 7 + 3 = 10$
$5 - (-12) = 5 + 12 = 17$
$-21 - (-7) = -21 + 7 = -14$
$-8 - (-8) = -8 + 8 = 0$

Subtracting two positive numbers can result in a negative solution. In this case, subtract the smaller number from the larger one and make the aswswer the sign of the larger number. Here are some examples:

$10 - 12 = -2$
$9 - 20 = -11$
$45 - 60 = -15$

When subtracting positive and a negative numbers proceed like this. Think of the first number as the starting point. Next, subtract the next number appropriately.

Examples

$5 - (-2) = 7$ or $5 + 2 = 7$
$8 - (-6) = 14$ or $8 + 6 = 14$
$-4 - (2) = -6$
negative 4 minus 2 equals -6

$-1 - (7) = -8$
negative 1 minus 7 equals -8

$-5 - (10) = -15$
negative 5 minus 10 equals -15

$14 - (-7) = 21$ or $14 + 7 = 21$
$-9 - (-9) = 0$
negative 9 plus 9 equals 0

$-24 - (12) = -36$
negative 24 minus 12 equals -36

$6 - (-6) = 12$ or $6 + 6 = 12$

$-17 - (13) = -30$
negative 17 minus 13 equals -30

$2 - (-8) = 10$ or $2 + 8 = 10$

$-30 - (11) = -41$
negative 30 minus 11 equals -41

$21 - (-3) = 24$ or $21 + 3 = 24$

$-42 - (13) = -55$
negative 42 minus 13 equals -55

$-8 - (3) = -11$
negative 8 minus 3 equals -11

$-25 - (5) = -30$
negative 25 minus 5 equals -30

$36 - (-23) = 59$ or $36 + 23 = 59$

$-50 - (28) = -78$
negative 50 minus 28 equals -78

Multiplying positive and negative numbers

When multiplying positive and negative numbers, first multiply the two numbers and ignore the signs on the numbers. Then choose the correct sign for the answer depending on the signs of the two numbers. Use the rules in the following chart to determine the correct sign.

Rules for Multiplying Positive and Negative Numbers

Rule	Symbol	Example
A positive times a positive is a positive.	$(+)(+) = +$	$2(2) = 4$
A positive times a negative is a negative.	$(+)(-) = -$	$2(-2) = -4$
A negative times a positive is a negative.	$(-)(+) = -$	$-2(2) = -4$
A negative times a negative is a positive.	$(-)(-) = +$	$-2(-2) = 4$

Examples

$-4 \times 3 = -12$

$7(-9) = -63$

$-15(-10) = 150$

$5[-8] = -40$

$-1 \times -12 = 12$

$[36][-2] = -72$

$(-17)(4) = -68$

$-5 \times -5 = 25$

$[-14](-30) = 420$

$-23 \times 5 = -115$

$1(-1) = -1$

$(8)(-7) = -56$

$-6 \times -7 = 42$

$-9[9] = -81$

$(20)(-8) = -160$

$[19](-1) = -19$

$67 \times -5 = -335$

$-3 \times -7 = 21$

$25(-2) = -50$

$-13[4] = -52$

$-4 \times -4 = 16$

Dividing positive and negative numbers

The steps for dividing positive and negative numbers are the same as those for multiplication. First, divide the two numbers and ignore the signs on the numbers. Then choose the correct sign for the answer depending upon the signs of the two numbers. Use the rules in the following chart to determine the sign for the answer.

Rules for Dividing Positive and Negative Numbers

Rule	Symbol	Example
A positive divided by a positive is a positive.	$+ \div + = +$	$6 \div 2 = 3$
A positive divided by a negative is a negative.	$+ \div - = -$	$6 \div -2 = -3$
A negative divided by a positive is a negative.	$- \div + = -$	$-6 \div 2 = -3$
A negative divided by a negative is a positive.	$- \div - = +$	$-6 \div -2 = 3$

Examples

$-12 \div 3 = -4$

$-63 \div 9 = -7$

$150 \div -10 = -15$

$-40 \div -8 = 5$

$12 \div -12 = -1$

$-72 \div -2 = 36$

$-68 \div 4 = -17$

$25 \div -5 = -5$

$420 \div -30 = -14$

$-115 \div 5 = -23$

$1 \div -1 = -1$

$-56 \div -7 = 8$

$$\frac{42}{-6} = -7 \qquad \frac{-81}{-9} = 9 \qquad \frac{-160}{20} = -8$$

$$\frac{25}{-50} = -\frac{1}{2} \qquad \frac{-6}{-36} = \frac{1}{6} \qquad \frac{-8}{24} = -\frac{1}{3}$$

Constants and variables

In mathematics, a constant is a number that does not change. For example, the number 5 is a constant; so is $\sqrt{3}$ and the number π. By contrast, a variable can take on more than one value. Variables are represented by italicized lowercase letters.

Multiplying constants and variables

When a number is immediately next to a variable, it means "multiply the variable by this amount." For example, $3x = 3 \times x$.

When multiplying variables with the same base, add the exponents. Here are some examples:

$$x \times x^2 = x^1 \times x^2 = x \times x \times x = x^3$$

$$x^2 \times x^3 = x \times x \times x \times x \times x = x^5$$

$$y \times y = y^2$$

$$z^5 \times z^3 = z \times z \times z \times z \times z \times z \times z \times z = z^8$$

When multiplying variables with constants, multiply the constant by the constant and the variable by the variable. Here are some examples:

$$x^2 \times 5x^2 = 1 \times 5 \times x \times x \times x \times x = 5x^4$$

$$2y \times 4y^2 = 2 \times 4 \times y \times y \times y = 8y^3$$

$$10z^6 \times 7z = 10 \times 7 \times z \times z \times z \times z \times z \times z \times z = 70z^7$$

$$5a^2 \times 3a^3 = 5 \times 3 \times a \times a \times a \times a \times a = 15a^5$$

When multiplying variables with different bases, simply put the two variables next to each other:

$$x \times y = xy$$

$$x^2 \times y = x^2 y$$

$$y^2 \times z^2 = y^2 z^2$$

$$x^3 \times z^3 = x^3 z^3$$

When multiplying variables with constants and different bases, first multiply the constants, then put like terms (meaning the like variables) together:

$$7x^2 \times 4y = 7 \times 4 \times x \times x \times y = 28x^2 y$$

$$2x \times 4y^2 = 2 \times 4 \times x \times y \times y = 8xy^2$$

$$3z \times 4x^2 = 3 \times 4 \times z \times x \times x = 12zx^2$$

$$x \times 5y^3 = 1 \times 5 \times x \times y \times y \times y = 5xy^3$$

$$9x^4 \times 6y^2 = 9 \times 6 \times x \times x \times x \times x \times y \times y = 54x^4 y^2$$

$$8x^3 \times 8z^2 = 8 \times 8 \times x \times x \times x \times z \times z = 64x^3 z^2$$

$$2x^2 y \times 7x^3 y^2 = 2 \times 7 \times x \times x \times y \times x \times x \times x \times y \times y = 14x^5 y^3$$

When dividing variables, you must have similar bases. First, divide the constants, and then divide the variables by canceling like terms and simplifying:

$$\frac{x^3}{x^2} = \frac{\cancel{x} \times \cancel{x} \times x}{\cancel{x} \times \cancel{x}} = x$$

$$\frac{10z^4}{2z} = \frac{10 \times z \times z \times z \times \cancel{z}}{2 \times \cancel{z}} = 5z^3$$

$$\frac{6x^2}{x^4} = \frac{6 \times \cancel{x} \times \cancel{x}}{\cancel{x} \times \cancel{x} \times x \times x} = \frac{6}{x^2}$$

$$\frac{x^2 y^3}{xy^2} = \frac{\cancel{x} \times x \times \cancel{y} \times \cancel{y} \times y}{\cancel{x} \times \cancel{y} \times \cancel{y}} = xy$$

$$\frac{20xy^2}{5y^2} = \frac{20 \times x \times \cancel{y} \times \cancel{y}}{5 \times \cancel{y} \times \cancel{y}} = 4x$$

$$\frac{x^2}{x^4} = \frac{\cancel{x} \times \cancel{x}}{\cancel{x} \times \cancel{x} \times x \times x} = \frac{1}{x^2}$$

$$\frac{27y^6}{9y^2} = \frac{27 \times \cancel{y} \times \cancel{y} \times y \times y \times y \times y}{9 \times \cancel{y} \times \cancel{y}} = 3y^4$$

$$\frac{48yz^3}{6z^2} = \frac{48 \times y \times \cancel{z} \times \cancel{z} \times z}{6 \times \cancel{z} \times \cancel{z}} = 8yz$$

Slope of a Line

The slope is a measure of the steepness of a line:

Slope $= \dfrac{rise}{run} =$ the amount of change in y, for each one unit change in x.

For example, the equation $y = 2x + 3$ is the equation of a line; the 2 in the equation is the slope. This means that for every one-unit change in x, the y measurement goes up 2 units. The number 3 in this equation is called the y-intercept. The y-intercept is the point where the line crosses the y-axis. The y-intercept is the value of y when x equals 0. The general equation for a line is $y = mx + b$ where m is the slope and b is the y-intercept.

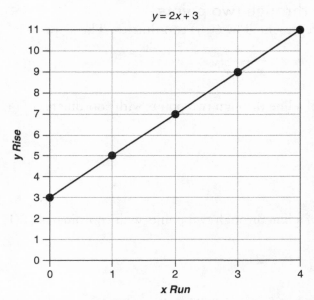

A line graph can show the relationship between two measurements, for example, between the number of music CDs that someone buys and the total cost:

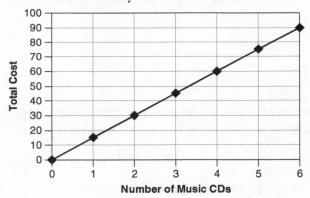

How much would it cost to buy four music CDs?

Find 4 on the axis labeled "Number of Music CDs." Go straight up until you hit the line, and then look left at the axis labeled "Total Cost." The cost is $60.

How much does each CD cost?

The answer to this question is actually the slope of the line. By looking at the graph, we can see that for each one-unit change in number of CDs, the total cost goes up $15. Thus, each CD costs $15.

The slope of a line through two points

A point on a graph is represented by (x, y) coordinates. The slope of a line through two points is given by the formula. $m = \dfrac{y_2 - y_1}{x_2 - x_1}$.

Examples

What is the slope of a line through two points with coordinates of $(4, 2)$ and $(6, 8)$?

$$m = \frac{8 - 2}{6 - 4} = \frac{6}{2} = 3$$

The slope is 3.

What is the slope of a line through two points with coordinates of $(1, 10)$ and $(5, 2)$?

$$m = \frac{2 - 10}{5 - 1} = \frac{-8}{4} = -2$$

The slope is -2.

What is the slope of a line through two points with coordinates of $(5, 6)$ and $(9, 7)$?

$$m = \frac{7 - 6}{9 - 5} = \frac{1}{4}$$

The slope equals $\dfrac{1}{4}$.

There are three different types of slopes: positive slopes, negative slopes, and a zero slope. The slope of a vertical line is undefined because in such a line, both x values are equal. In our slope equation $m = \dfrac{y_2 - y_1}{x_2 - x_1}$, this would make the denominator 0, and we can never divide by 0. Therefore, the slope of a vertical line is undefined.

In a **positive slope**, as the measurement of one variable increases, the measurement on the other variable also increases. The resulting line looks like this:

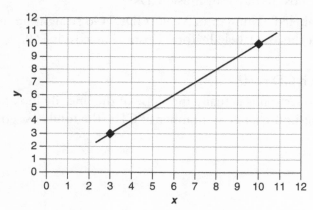

In a **negative slope**, as the measurement of one variable increases, the measurement on the other variable decreases, resulting in the following line:

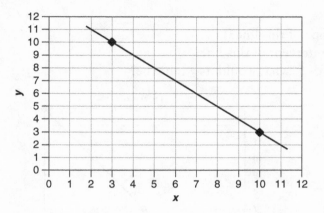

In a **zero slope**, the y measurements stays the same across different x values. The result is a horizontal line:

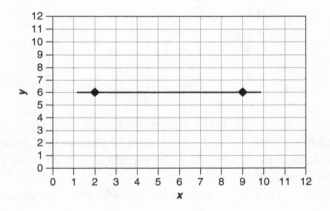

Linear Relationships

As mentioned in the previous section, the general equation for a line is $y = mx + b$ where m is the slope and b is the y-intercept. The slope tells us the steepness of the line. The slope is the amount of change in y for each one unit change in x. The y-intercept is the place where the line crosses the y-axis. Linear relationships define how two variables are related on a straight line. A linear relationship is defined in an equation that includes the slope and the y-intercept.

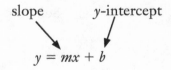

Practice questions

Given the equation and the graph of the line in the chart shown, answer the following questions:

a. What is the slope of this line?
b. What is the y-intercept of this line?
c. For an x value of 5, what would its y value be?

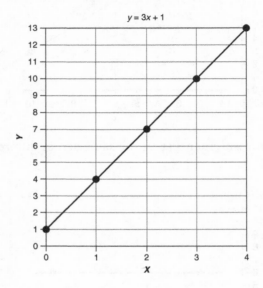

a. The given equation, $y = 3x + 1$, is the equation of a line with slope equal to 3. This means that for every one-unit change in x, the y measurement goes up 3 units.
b. The y-intercept is 1, as indicated by the given equation, $y = 3x + 1$. This is the point where the line crosses the y-axis.
c. Using the equation $y = 3x + 1$, an x value of 5 would give a y value of 16 because $y = 3(5) + 1 = 16$.

Evaluating Expressions

To evaluate an expression means to find its values. First, replace each variable with a number. Then simplify using order of operations.

Example

Evaluate: $2x - 4$ for $x = 10$ Solution: $(2)(10) - 4 = 20 - 4 = 16$

Practice questions

Evaluate: $12 + 3y$ for $y = 5$ Solution: $12 + (3)(5) = 12 + 15 = 27$

Evaluate: $x + 8y$ for $x = 9$ and $y = 4$ Solution: $9 + (8)(4) = 9 + 32 = 41$

Evaluate: $-3a + 2b$ for $a = 7$ and $b = 5$ Solution: $(-3)(7) + (2)(5) = -21 + 10 = -11$

Evaluate: $6(y + z)$ for $y = 4$ and $z = 5$ Solution: $(6)(4 + 5) = (6)(9) = 54$

Evaluate: $a(23 + b)$ for $a = 5$ and $b = 2$ Solution: $(5)(23 + 2) = (5)(25) = 125$

Evaluate: $4x + 3y + 1$ for $x = 9$ and $y = 8$ Solution: $(4)(9) + (3)(8) + 1 = 36 + 24 + 1 = 61$

Evaluate: $-6(m - n)$ for $m = 18$ and $n = 12$ Solution: $(-6)(18 - 12) = (-6)(6) = -36$

Evaluate: $7a + 2b$ for $a = -2$ and $b = 4$ Solution: $(7)(-2) + (2)(4) = -14 + 8 = -6$

Evaluate: $\dfrac{28}{p + q}$ for $p = 6$ and $q = 1$ Solution: $\dfrac{28}{6 + 1} = \dfrac{28}{7} = 4$

Evaluate: $x^2 + x - 1$ for $x = 5$ Solution: $5^2 + 5 - 1 = 25 + 5 - 1 = 29$

Evaluate: $38 - \dfrac{28}{y} + 13$ for $y = 4$ Solution: $38 - \dfrac{28}{4} + 13 = 38 - 7 + 13 = 44$

Evaluate: $a^2 + \dfrac{3b}{12} + 10$ for $a = 9$ and $b = -8$ Solution: $9^2 + \dfrac{(3)(-8)}{12} + 10 = 81 - 2 + 10 = 89$

Quadratic Functions

Quadratic functions are equations where the highest exponent on the input variable is squared. The graph of a quadratic function is a U-shaped curve, and this graph is called a parabola. The opening of the parabola can be facing up or down. Here are some examples of quadratic functions:

$y = x^2 + x$
$y = x^2 + 3x - 5$
$y = 6x^2 - 2x + 1$

Practice questions

Graph the quadratic function $y = \dfrac{1}{2}x^2$.

Using integer values for x between and including -5 to 5 produces the following graph. In order to graph this equation, first list the whole numbers between -5 and 5. Then, plug each of these numbers into the equation as x values and determine their corresponding y values. A table of these paired coordinates is given on the next page.

x	y
−5	12.5
−4	8
−3	4.5
−2	2
−1	.5
0	0
1	.5
2	2
3	4.5
4	8
5	12.5

Next, on graph paper, plot each one of these coordinates as a point on the graph. Last, connect the dots using a smooth curve.

$$y = \frac{1}{2}x^2$$

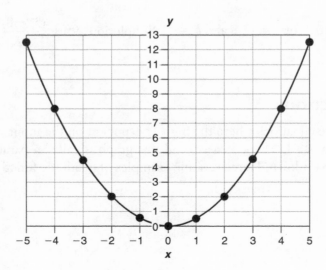

Graphing Inequalities

An inequality is a mathematical statement that contains one of the following symbols:

>, meaning "greater than"
<, meaning "less than"
≥, meaning "greater than or equal to"
≤, meaning "less than or equal to"
≠, meaning "not equal to"

Inequalities can include variables.

The solution for an inequality can be graphed on the number line. A graph with an open dot does not include that point. A graph with a closed dot includes that point.

Examples

$x > 2$

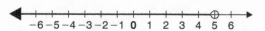

The open dot shows that the point is *not* a part of the solution. The symbol is a greater-than sign, so the area to the right of 2 is darkened.

$a < 5$

The open dot shows that the point is *not* a part of the solution. The symbol is a less-than sign, so the area to the left of 5 is darkened.

$m \geq -4$

The closed dot shows that the point *is* a part of the solution. The symbol is a greater-than-or-equal-to sign, so the area to the right of -4 is darkened.

$y \leq 2$

The closed dot shows that the point *is* a part of the solution. The symbol is a less-than-or-equal-to sign, so the area to the left of 2 is darkened.

$y \leq -2$

The closed dot shows that the point *is* a part of the solution. The symbol is a less-than-or-equal-to sign, so the area to the left of -2 is darkened.

$w < 7$

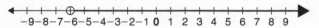

The open dot shows that the point is *not* a part of the solution. The symbol is a less-than sign, so the area to the left of 7 is darkened.

$x > -6$

The open dot shows that the point is *not* a part of the solution. The symbol is a greater-than sign, so the area to the right of -6 is darkened.

$y \geq 3$

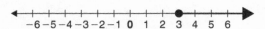

The closed dot shows that the point *is* a part of the solution. The symbol is a greater-than-or-equal-to sign, so the area to the right of 3 is darkened.

$z < -1$

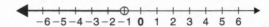

The open dot shows that the point is *not* a part of the solution. The symbol is the less-than sign, so the area to the left of −1 is darkened.

$x \geq 0$

The closed dot shows that the point *is* a part of the solution. The symbol is a greater-than-or-equal-to sign, so the area to the right of 0 is darkened.

Solving Linear Equations

In linear equations, there are two variables. Each variable is to the first power. The graph of a linear equation produces a line. Linear equations can be solved by substituting in a given x value and then solving for y.

Example

Given the equation $y = 5x + 2$, find the solution for $x = 6$.

$y = 5(6) + 2$

$y = 30 + 2$

$y = 32$

Practice questions

Solve for $x = 4$: $y = 2x - 1$

$y = 2(4) - 1$

$y = 8 - 1$

$y = 7$

Solve for $x = -3$: $y = x + 14$

$y = (-3) + 14$

$y = 11$

Solve for $x = 5$: $y = -5x + 5$

$y = -5(5) + 5$

$y = -25 + 5$

$y = -20$

Solve for $x = -2$: $y = -8x + 18$

$y = -8(-2) + 18$

$y = 16 + 18$

$y = 34$

Solve for $x = -1$: $y = 12x + 5$

$y = 12(-1) + 5$

$y = -12 + 5$

$y = -7$

Solve for $x = 8$: $y = \frac{1}{4}x + 7$

$y = \frac{8}{4} + 7$

$y = 2 + 7$

$y = 9$

Solve for $x = 15$: $y = \frac{2}{3}x + 5$

$y = \frac{2(15)}{3} + 5$

$y = \frac{30}{3} + 5$

$y = 10 + 5$

$y = 15$

Solve for $x = 25$: $y = \frac{3}{5}x - 6$

$y = \frac{3(25)}{5} - 6$

$y = \frac{75}{5} - 6$

$y = 15 - 6$

$y = 9$

Solve for $x = -12$: $y = \dfrac{-1}{2}x + 24$

$y = \dfrac{-1(-12)}{2} + 24$

$y = \dfrac{12}{2} + 24$

$y = 6 + 24$

$y = 30$

Solve for $x = 8$: $y = \dfrac{3}{4}x - 5$

$y = \dfrac{3(8)}{4} - 5$

$y = \dfrac{24}{4} - 5$

$y = 6 - 5$

$y = 1$

Sometimes, to find the solution for a linear equation, you must first solve for y. In other words, you must manipulate the equation so that y is by itself on one side of the equals sign. To get the variable y by itself, you must add or subtract equal amounts to both sides of the equation or you must multiply or divide each side by the same number. Think of the equals sign as a teeter-totter: whatever you do to one side, do to the other, and it will stay balanced. Once the equation is set equal to y, you can solve the equation by substituting in the given value and then simplifying.

Example

Given the equation $-x + 2y = 6$, find the solution for an x value of 8.

First, solve for y in the linear equation. Begin by adding x to both sides; this moves the x variable to the opposite side of the equation:

$-x + 2y = 6$
$+ x \ -x + 2y = 6 + x$
$2y = 6 + x$

Then divide both sides of the equation by 2; this isolates the y, thus giving you the value for y:

$\dfrac{2y}{2} = \dfrac{6}{2} + \dfrac{x}{2}$

$y = 3 + \dfrac{x}{2}$

Now you are ready to move on to the second step in solving the linear equation. Substitute the given value of x into the equation and calculate y. In this case, $x = 8$:

$$y = 3 + \frac{x}{2}$$

$$y = 3 + \frac{8}{2}$$

$$y = 3 + 4$$

$$y = 7$$

For the equation $-x + 2y = 6$, if $x = 8$, then $y = 7$.

Solving a System of Linear Equations

A system of two linear equations is actually just two lines. The solution to a system of two linear equations is simply the point at which these two lines intersect.

Example

What is the solution to the following system of linear equations?

$2x + y = 8$
$\ x - y = 1$

This question is really asking, "Given the equations for two different lines, what value of x and y fit both equations?" Solve by substitution. First, solve for x using one of the equations:

$x - y = 1$
$x - y + y = 1 + y$
$x = y + 1$

Then substitute in $(y + 1)$ for x in the other equation, $2x + y = 8$, and solve for y:

$2(y + 1) + y = 8$

$2y + 2 + y = 8$

$3y + 2 = 8$

$3y = 8 - 2$

$3y = 6$

$\dfrac{3y}{3} = \dfrac{6}{3}$

$y = 2$

Next, substitute this y value of 2 into either one of the original equations and solve for x:

$x - y = 1$
$x - 2 = 1$
$x - 2 = 1$
$\quad\ x = 1 + 2$
$\quad\ x = 3$

The solution is $x = 3$ and $y = 2$. In other words, the point $(3, 2)$.

Given the same system of two linear equations, what does the solution look like graphically? The solution from the previous section, $x = 3$ and $y = 2$, means that the two lines intersect at the point $(3, 2)$:

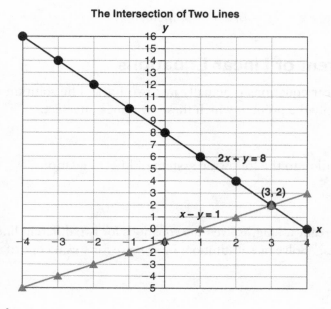

The Intersection of Two Lines

Alternative method

You learn in mathematics that sometimes it is better to work backwards to solve a problem. This is one of those times. Because the CHSPE math section has a multiple-choice format, it is possible to work this type of problem backwards. It works like this: in the same way that you can take a point (x, y) and put it into the equation of a line to see if it is true, you can do this to two equations. When a point is true for both equations, that is the right answer. That point represents the intersection of the two lines. Because you will have four answers to choose from, *try each of the possible points, one at a time, until you find a point that is true for both equations.* That will be the correct answer.

Example

What is the solution to the following system of equations?

$4x + 2y = 20$
$7x - 5y = 1$

(A) $(1, 5)$ **(C)** $(3, 4)$

(B) $(4, 4)$ **(D)** $(6, 2)$

The strategy is to try each answer, one at a time, to see which point makes both of the equations true.

First, try answer choice **(A)**, (1, 5):

$4x + 2y = 4(1) + 2(5) = 4 + 10 = 14$

This is not the answer because it does not match the answer of 24 given in the equation.

Next, try **(B)**, (4, 4):

$4x + 2y = 4(4) + 2(4) = 16 + 8 = 24$

This coordinate is true for the first equation. Now try it in the second equation:

$7x - 5y = 7(4) - 5(4) = 28 - 20 = 8$

This is not the answer because it does not match the answer of 1 given in the equation.

Move on to choice **(C)**, (3, 4):

$4x + 2y = 4(3) + 2(4) = 12 + 8 = 20$
$7x - 5y = 7(3) - 5(4) = 21 - 20 = 1$

Choice **(C)** is the correct answer.

Algebraic Expressions and Equations

Algebra is a language. Speaking algebra involves translating written English into algebraic expressions or equations. "Less than" means subtract. "More than" means add. "Is" means equals. "Of" means times (or to multiply). After reading a word problem once, read it again substituting in the word "equal" for the word "is" and the word "times" for the word "of," and you will know what the equation for the problem should look like. The following chart gives some examples of written expressions translated into algebraic equations.

English Expression	Algebra Translation
Three less than a number	$x - 3$
Half as large as area A	$1/2A$
Five more than twice a number	$2x + 5$
One less than five times a number is 14	$5x - 1 = 14$
25% of a number	$.25x$

Practice questions

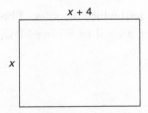

The length of the rectangle above is four units longer than the width. What expression represents the area of the rectangle?

The formula for the area of a rectangle is length $\times$ width. The length of this rectangle is x, and the width is $x + 4$, so the area for this rectangle would be

$x(x + 4) = x^2 + 4x$

Britney went to the county fair and spent a total of $27. She spent $6 on admission, $9 on food, and went on 8 rides. All of the rides were the same price. What was the price of each ride?

Let x equal the number of rides. That means $8x$ is the total cost for the rides. That cost plus the costs for admission ($6) and food ($9) totaled $27. Turn this into an equation, and then solve for the missing value:

$$6 + 9 + 8x = 27$$

$$15 + 8x = 27$$

$$8x = 27 - 15$$

$$8x = 12$$

$$x = \frac{12}{8}$$

$$x = 1.5$$

Each ride cost $1.50.

A train is traveling at a rate of 40 miles per hour. Its destination is 200 miles away. How long will the trip take?

Using the formula distance = rate $\times$ time, set up the equation using the values given:

$d = r \times t$

$200 = 40t$

Now solve for t by getting t by itself. You get t by itself by dividing both sides of the equation by the rate (r), 40:

$$\frac{200}{40} = \frac{\cancel{40}t}{\cancel{40}}$$

$5 = t$

The trip will take five hours.

A marble bag contains both black and white marbles. There are four times as many white marbles than black marbles. There are a total of 30 marbles in the bag. How many black marbles are in the bag?

Let x represent the number of black marbles. The number of white marbles is four times that of black marbles, or in algebraic terms, $4x$. Now set up the equation:

$4x + x = 30$

$5x = 30$

$\dfrac{\cancel{5}x}{\cancel{5}} = \dfrac{30}{5}$

$\quad x = 6$ black marbles

A customer at a restaurant receives a bill for \$13.64. This amount includes a 10% tax. How much did just the food cost?

Let x represent the cost of the food. That means that 10% of x, or $.1x$, is the tax, and the sum of x and $.1x$ is the bill total, \$13.64. Now set up the equation:

$x + .1x = 13.64$

$1.1x = 13.64$

$\dfrac{\cancel{1.1}x}{\cancel{1.1}} = \dfrac{13.64}{\underset{1}{1.1}}$

$\quad x = \$12.40$

The food portion of the bill is \$12.40.

A shopper bought three pairs of pants and a shirt that cost half as much as one pair of pants. The total cost for these clothes was \$210. How much did the shirt cost?

Let x represent the cost of one pair of pants. That means $3x$ is the total cost of the pants and $\dfrac{1}{2}$ of x (or $.5x$) is the cost of the shirt. The sum of these is the total cost, \$210:

$3x + .5x = 210$

$3.5x = 210$

$\dfrac{\cancel{3.5}x}{\cancel{3.5}} = \dfrac{210}{3.5}$

$\quad x = 60$

The cost of one pair of pants is \$60. But the question asks us to find the cost of the shirt. Because the shirt cost half the amount of a pair of pants, the following equation gives the answer:

$\dfrac{1}{2}x = \dfrac{1}{2}(60) = 30$

The cost of the shirt is $30.

A business investment is predicted to pay 8% interest over one year. If an investor wants to make $1,200 in profit, how much does the investor have to invest?

Let x represent the amount of money needed to invest. Remember that 8% converted to a decimal is .08. Now set up the equation:

$$.08(x) = 1,200$$

$$\frac{.08(x)}{.08} = \frac{1,200}{.08}$$

$$x = 15,000$$

The investor needs to invest $15,000.

A new laptop computer sells for $1,650 after a 25% discount. How much did the computer sell for before the discount?

Let x represent the prediscounted price. That means that 25% of x, or $.25x$, is the amount of the discount. The difference between the x and $.25x$, then, is $1,650. (As you do the first step of the equation, remember that x alone is the same as $1x$, so $1x - .25x = .75x$):

$$x - .25(x) = 1,650$$

$$.75(x) = 1,650$$

$$\frac{.75(x)}{.75} = \frac{1,650}{.75}$$

$$x = 2,200$$

The computer cost $2,200 before the discount.

A cell phone company has monthly charges of $30 for the first 1,000 minutes. After the first 1,000 minutes, they charge at the rate of 15¢ for each minute. One customer receives a monthly bill for $63. How many minutes did this cell phone customer talk?

Let x represent the number of minutes talked beyond 1,000. Therefore, 15¢ $\times$ x, or $.15x$, is the cost of those used minutes. Now set up the equation:

$$30 + .15(x) = 63$$

$$-30 + 30 + .15(x) = 63 - 30$$

$$.15(x) = 33$$

$$\frac{.15x}{.15} = \frac{33}{.15}$$

$$x = 220$$

The cell phone customer talked 220 minutes over the 1,000 minutes the $30 paid for. But the question asks for the total number of minutes talked: 1,000 + 220 = 1,220 minutes.

Geometry

Lines

A line is a series of points that extends in two directions without end:

A line segment is a part of a line:

A ray is a part of a line that extends in one direction without end:

An angle is formed by two rays with a common endpoint. The rays are the sides of the angle. The common endpoint is the vertex.

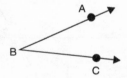

Angles are measured in degrees. A straight line has 180°. When the sum of the measures of two angles equals 180°, the angles are called supplementary. In the following illustration, ∠ABD and ∠DBC are supplementary:

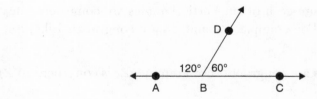

When the sum of the measure of two angles equals 90°, the angles are called complementary. Here, ∠WXZ and ∠ZXY are complementary angles:

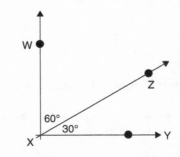

Parallel lines are two lines in the same plane that do not intersect:

A transversal is a line that intersects two other lines at different points. When two parallel lines are intersected by a transversal, then the angles have specific relationships:

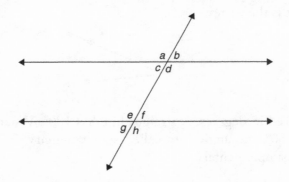

Vertical angles are opposite each other. Vertical angles are congruent, meaning they have equal measurements. For example, ∠a and ∠d are congruent. Likewise, ∠b and ∠c are congruent.

Alternate interior angles are congruent. For example, ∠c is congruent to ∠f. Likewise, ∠d is congruent to ∠e.

Supplementary angles, as mentioned earlier, add to 180°. For example, ∠a + ∠b = 180°. Likewise, ∠g + ∠b = 180°.

Practice questions

In the figure below, if ∠x is equal to 35°, what does ∠y equal?

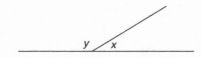

∠x and ∠y are supplementary angles: their measures add up to 180°. To determine the measure of ∠y, simply substract the measure of ∠x from 180:

$180 - 35 = 145°$

In the figure below, if ∠b is equal to 40°, what does ∠a equal?

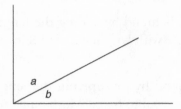

∠a and ∠b are complementary angles: the sum of their measures equals 90°. To find the measure of ∠a, substract the measure of ∠b from 90:

$90 - 40 = 50°$

In the figure below, if ∠p is equal to 55°, what does ∠q equal?

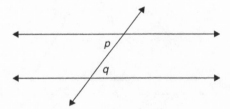

Because ∠p and ∠q are alternate interior angles, they are equal. Therefore, ∠q equals 55°.

Plane Figures

A plane is like a flat sheet of paper with no thickness that stretches out in all directions. Plane figures are two-dimensional figures.

A square is a figure that has four 90° angles and four congruent sides. A 90° angle is called a right angle:

The perimeter of a square is found by adding the length of the four sides together. For example, the perimeter of a square with sides equal to 5 in. would be

$5 + 5 + 5 + 5 = 20$ in

The area of a square is found by multiplying the length of one side times another. For example, the area of a square with sides equal to 5 in. would be

$5 \times 5 = 25$ sq in

A rectangle is a figure that has four 90° angles:

The perimeter of a rectangle is found by adding the length of the four sides together. For example, the perimeter of a rectangle with length equal to 8 in. and width equal to 6 in. would be

$8 + 8 + 6 + 6 = 28$ in

The area of a rectangle is found by multiplying the length times its width. For example, the area of a rectangle with length equal to 8 and width equal to 6 would be

$8 \times 6 = 48$ sq in

A triangle is a three-sided figure. A triangle is measured in terms of its base and height.

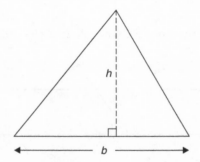

The perimeter of a triangle is the sum of the length of the sides. For example, given a triangle with sides equal to 3, 4, and 5 in., the perimeter would be equal to

$3 + 4 + 5 = 12$ in.

The area of a triangle is calculated using the formula $a = \frac{1}{2}bh$ where a is the area, b is the base, and h is the height. For example, the area of a triangle with base equal to 7 in. and height equal to 8 in. would be calculated as follows:

$$a = \frac{1}{2}bh$$

$$a = \frac{1}{2}(7)(8)$$

$$a = \frac{1}{2} \times 56$$

$$a = 28 \text{ sq in}$$

A right triangle is a triangle that has a right angle. A right angle is equal to 90°. Here are some examples.

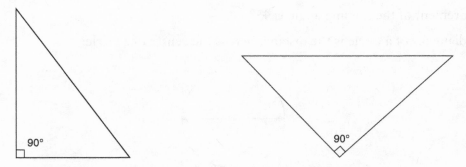

The measurements of the three angles of any triangle, added together, equal 180°:

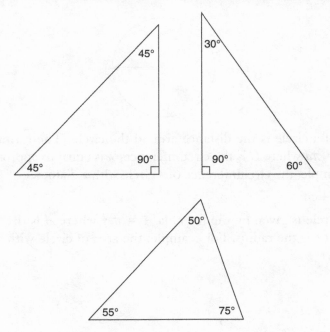

Knowing that the angles of any triangle add to 180° can be useful information. If you know the measurement of any two angles, then you can determine the measurement of the third angle. For example, given the triangle below, what is the measurement of the missing angle?

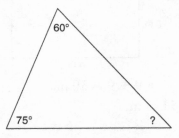

First, add the measures of the two given angles:

60 + 75 = 135

Then subtract this amount from 180:

$180 - 135 = 45$

The measurement of the missing angle is 45°.

The diameter of a circle is the distance across the center of a circle:

The radius of a circle is the distance from the center of the circle to the perimeter:

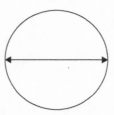

The circumference of a circle is the distance around the circle. The formula for the circumference of a circle is $C = \pi d$ where C is the circumference, π is equal to approximately 3.14, and d is the diameter. For example, the circumference of a circle with a diameter of 10 cm would be

$C = 3.14 \times 10 = 31.4$ cm

The area of a circle is given by the formula $A = \pi r^2$ where A is the area, π is equal to approximately 3.14, and r is the radius. For example, the area of circle with a radius of 5 m would be calculated this way:

$A = 3.14 \times 5^2$
$A = 3.14 \times 25$
$A = 78.5$ sq m

Practice questions

Given the rectangle below, find its perimeter and its area.

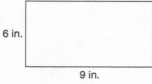

The perimeter is equal to $6 + 6 + 9 + 9 = 30$ in.

The area is equal to $6 \times 9 = 54$ sq in.

The triangle below is measured in feet. Find its area.

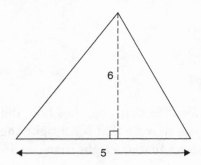

Recall that the formula for the area of a triangle is $a = \dfrac{1}{2}\, bh$. Now plug in the triangle's measurements:

$a = \dfrac{1}{2}\,(5)(6)$

$a = \dfrac{1}{2}\,(30)$

$a = 15$ sq ft

Given the triangle below, find the measurement of the missing angle.

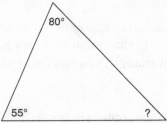

Add the measurements of the two given angles:

$80 + 55 = 135$

Then subtract this amount from 180, which is the total of all three angles:

$180 - 135 = 45$

The measurement of the missing angle is $45°$.

Given a circle with a radius of 3 m, find its circumference and area.

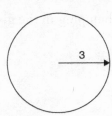

The formula for the circumference of a circle is $C = \pi d$, where d is the diameter. So first calculate the diameter by multiplying the radius, 3 m, by 2: the diameter is 6 m. Now calculate the circumference using the given formula:

$C = 3.14 \times 6$
$C = 18.84$ m

The area is found using the formula A $= \pi r^2$:

$A = 3.14 \times 3^2$
$A = 3.14 \times 9$
$A = 28.26$ sq m

Pythagorean Theorem

The Pythagorean theorem is a formula that describes how the sides of a right triangle relate to one another. A right triangle is a triangle that has a right angle in it. A right angle measures 90°. The Pythagorean theorem states that in a right triangle, $A^2 + B^2 = C^2$:

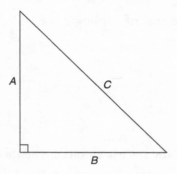

A and B are called legs, and C is called the hypotenuse. The hypotenuse is the side of the triangle that is opposite the right angle. The Pythagorean theorem is useful in the following way: given the length of any two sides of a right triangle, you can figure out the length of the third.

Practice questions

In a right triangle, one leg is 3 in. the other leg is 4 in. What is the length of the hypotenuse?

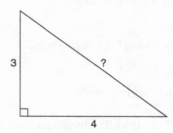

First write down the formula, and then plug in the given measurements of the legs:

$A^2 + B^2 = C^2$
$3^2 + 4^2 = C^2$

Now solve for C:

$3^2 + 4^2 = C^2$
$9 + 16 = C^2$
$25 = C^2$
$\sqrt{25} = \sqrt{C}$
$5 = C$

The hypotenuse is 5 in.

If one leg of a right triangle is 6 in., and the hypotenuse is 10 in., what is the length of the other leg?

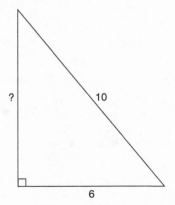

First, write down the equation for the Pythagorean theorem, and then put into the equation whatever information that you are given. The hypotenuse C is equal to 10 and one of the legs, B, is equal to 6:

$A^2 + B^2 = C^2$
$A^2 + 6^2 = 10^2$

Then solve for A:

$$A^2 + 6^2 = 10^2$$
$$A^2 + 36 = 100$$
$$A^2 + 36 - 36 = 100 - 36$$
$$A^2 = 64$$
$$\sqrt{A} = \sqrt{64}$$
$$A = 8$$

The the measurement of leg A is 8 in.

Geometric Transformations

A geometric figure can be transformed by reflecting its image across the x- or the y-axis. For example, the following figure shows a triangle $A'B'C'$ that is the image of triangle ABC that results from reflecting the triangle ABC across the x-axis:

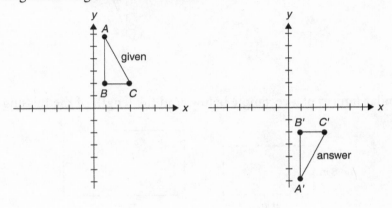

Likewise, the next figure shows a triangle $A'B'C'$ that is the image of triangle ABC that results from reflecting the triangle ABC across the y-axis:

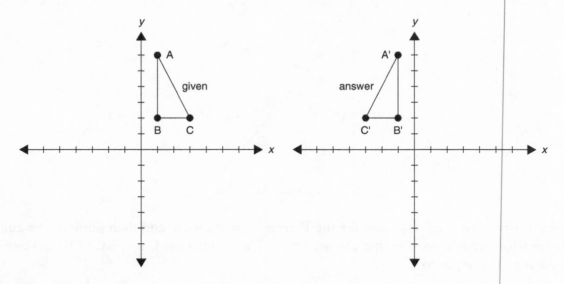

Similar Figures

Similar figures have the same shape but not the same size. They have corresponding angles and corresponding sides. In the following example, triangle ABC is similar to triangle XYZ:

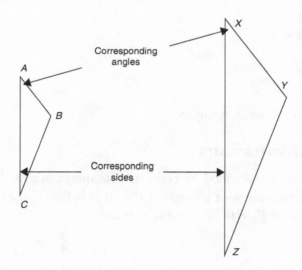

Example

Given the similar figures of a rectangle below, find the length of the missing side.

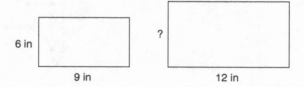

Set this problem up as a proportion. Write a proportion for the corresponding sides. Let x represent the length of the missing side. Then solve for x:

$$\frac{x}{6} = \frac{12}{9}$$

$$x = \frac{12 \times 6}{9}$$

$$x = \frac{72}{9}$$

$$x = 8 \text{ in}$$

Measurement

Scale Drawing

A scale drawing is a drawing that is similar to the actual object or place. A scale drawing is drawn larger or smaller than the actual object or place. All scale drawings have a scale that tells you how the distance in the drawing relates to the actual object or place. This scale is in the form of a ratio.

Example

Each unit of measurement on the following graph represents 1 foot. A flowerbed is drawn the shape of a rectangle with the measurements of 3 ft by 4 ft:

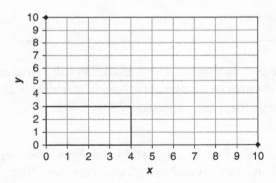

Calculate the perimeter and the area of this rectangle.

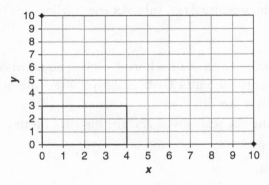

The perimeter is equal to $4 + 4 + 3 + 3 = 14$ ft. And the area equals $4 \times 3 = 12$ sq. ft.

Practice questions

The drawing shown below is a scaled drawing of a soccer field in which 1 centimeter (cm) = 10 m. Find the area of the Penalty Area in square meters.

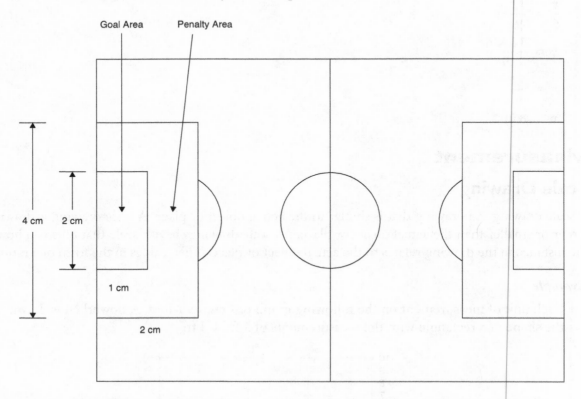

First, calculate the large area that includes both the Penalty Area and the Goal Area. Remember that the formula for the area of a rectangle is length × width. In this case, the length, 4 cm, represents 40 m, and the width, 2 cm, represents 20 m:

$40 \times 20 = 800$

The combined area of the Penalty Area and Goal Area is 800 sq. m.

Second, calculate the area of the Goal Area; 2 cm represents 20 m, and 1 cm represents 10 m:

$20 \times 10 = 200$ sq m

Last, in order to find the Penalty Area, subtract the smaller area from the larger area:

$800 - 200 = 600$ sq m

A map of California is drawn to scale where 1 inch is equal to 60 miles. On this map, the distance from Sacramento to Santa Cruz is 2.5 in. Find the actual distance from Sacramento to Santa Cruz in miles.

Write a proportion using the scale given and the distance on the map:

$$\frac{\text{map scale (inches)}}{\text{actual (miles)}} \rightarrow \frac{1}{60} = \frac{2.5}{x}$$

Then cross multiply and solve for x:

$$\frac{1}{60} = \frac{2.5}{x}$$

$$x \times 1 = 2.5 \times 60$$

$$x = 150$$

The distance from Sacramento to Santa Cruz is 150 miles.

A map of California is drawn to scale where 1 inch is equal to 80 miles. On this map, the distance from Los Angeles to Berkeley is 4.75 in. Find the actual distance from Los Angeles to Berkeley in miles.

Write a proportion using the scale given and the distance on the map:

$$\frac{\text{map scale (inches)}}{\text{actual (miles)}} \rightarrow \frac{1}{80} = \frac{4.75}{x}$$

Then cross multiply and solve for x:

$$\frac{1}{80} = \frac{4.75}{x}$$

$$x \times 1 = 4.75 \times 80$$

$$x = 380$$

The distance from Los Angeles to Berkeley is 380 miles.

Perimeter

The perimeter is the distance around a figure. As discussed in the section on plane figures, the perimeter of a figure equals the sum of the lengths of all of its sides. For example, in the following square, each side is 6 in, so the perimeter would be $6 + 6 + 6 + 6 = 24$ in. or 6×4 since all sides are equal:

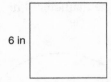

6 in

Likewise, the perimeter of the following rectangle would be $7 + 7 + 10 + 10 = 34$ cm or $(2 \times 7) + (2 \times 10)$ since opposite sides are equal:

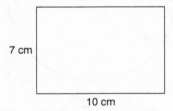

7 cm

10 cm

The perimeter of a triangle is found by adding together the lengths of the three sides. For example, the following triangle-shaped yard has sides that measure 10 m, 8 m, and 7 m, and thus has a perimeter of 25 m:

10 + 8 + 7 = 25

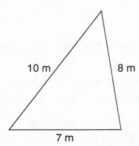

Even in a complex figure, the perimeter is found by adding together the lengths of the sides:

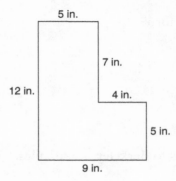

Perimeter = 12 + 5 + 7 + 4 + 5 + 9 = 42 in.

Circumference

The circumference of a circle is the distance around the circle. As discussed in the section about plane figures, the formula for the circumference of a circle is $C = \pi d$ where C is the circumference, π is equal to approximately 3.14, and d is the diameter. The diameter of a circle is the distance across the center of a circle:

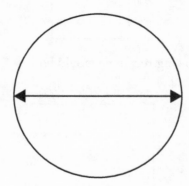

If the diameter in the figure above was 7 cm, the circumference would be calculated as follows:

$C = \pi d$
$C = 3.14 \times 7$
$C = 21.98$ cm

The radius of a circle is the distance from the center of the circle to the side of the circle. The diameter is equal to two times the radius:

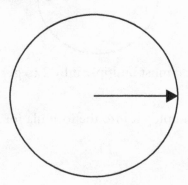

Practice questions

Given a circle with a diameter of 100 m, find its circumference.

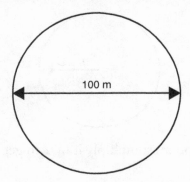

$C = \pi d$
$C = 3.14 \times 100$
$C = 314$ m

Given a circle with a diameter of 9 in., find its circumference.

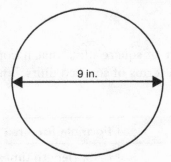

$C = \pi d$
$C = 3.14 \times 9$
$C = 28.26$ in

Given a circle with a radius of 6 in. find its circumference.

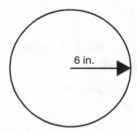

Because the radius is given, you must multiply it by 2 to get the diameter:

$6 \times 2 = 12$

Now take the diameter, 12, and plug it into the formula for circumference of a circle:

$C = \pi d$
$C = 3.14 \times 12$
$C = 37.68$ in

Given a circle with a radius of 15 cm, find its circumference.

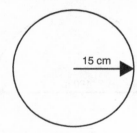

Because the radius is given, you must multiply it by 2 to get the diameter:

$15 \times 2 = 30$

Now insert the diameter into the formula:

$C = \pi d$
$C = 3.14 \times 30$
$C = 94.2$ cm

Area

The area of a figure is the number of square units that it contains. Area is a two-dimensional measurement and it is expressed in terms of squared units. The following chart lists the formulae for areas of different figures.

Figure	Formula for Area	
Square and rectangle	$l \times w$ (length times width)	
Triangle	$\frac{1}{2} bh \left(\frac{1}{2} \text{ base times height} \right)$	
Circle	πr^2 (3.14 times the square of the radius)	

Practice questions

Given the square below, find its area.

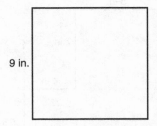

9 × 9 = 81 sq in

What is the area of the following rectangle?

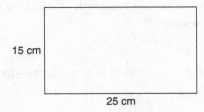

25 × 15 = 375 sq cm

Given a triangle with a base of 6 in and a height of 4 in, determine its area.

area = $\frac{1}{2}$ *bh*

area = $\frac{1}{2}$ (6)(4) = 12 sq in

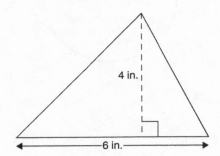

Given the complex figure below, determine its area.

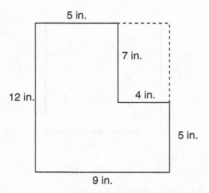

First, imagine that the figure is one big rectangle. Calculate the area of this rectangle by multiplying its length by its width:

$9 \times 12 = 108$ sq in

Second, calculate the area of the space that is actually missing from this rectangle:

$4 \times 7 = 28$ sq in

Last, subtract the smaller area from the larger area to get the area of the figure:

$108 - 28 = 80$ sq in

Given a circle with a radius of 5 m, find its area.

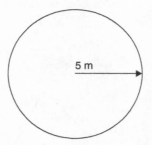

$A = \pi r^2$
$A = 3.14 \times 5^2$
$A = 3.14 \times 25$
$A = 78.5$

The area equals 78.5 sq. m.

Given a circle with a radius of 4 in., find its area.

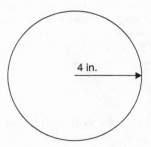

$A = \pi r^2$
$A = 3.14 \times 4^2$
$A = 3.14 \times 16$
$A = 50.24$

The area equals 50.24 sq. in.

Given a circle with a radius of 12 cm, find its area.

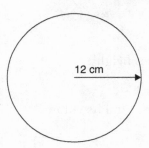

$A = \pi r^2$
$A = 3.14 \times 12^2$
$A = 3.14 \times 144$
$A = 452.16$

The area equals 452.16 sq. cm.

Volume

The volume of a three-dimensional figure is the number of cubic units that it holds. Length is a one-dimensional measurement. Area is a two-dimensional measurement. Volume is a three-dimensional measurement. The following chart gives the formulas for finding the volume of different three-dimensional figures.

Figure	Formula for Volume	
Box or cube	$l \times w \times h$ (length times width times height)	
Cylinder	r^2h (3.14 times the square of the radius times the height)	

Practice questions

The box below is measured in feet. Find the volume of this box.

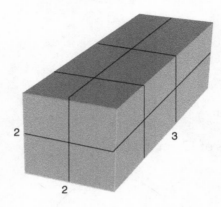

Multiply length times width times height:

$3 \times 2 \times 2 = 12$ cu ft

The box below is measured in inches. Find its volume.

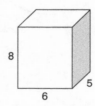

Multiply the lengths of the sides:

$8 \times 6 \times 5 = 48 \times 5 = 240$ cu in

The cylinder below is measured in inches. It has a radius of 3 and a height of 10. Find its volume.

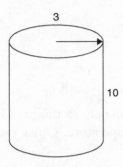

Recall that the formula for the volume of a cylinder is $\pi r^2 h$, where π is approximately 3.14, r is the radius, and h is the height. Using the given dimensions, the equation for the volume of the given cyclinder would look like this:

$V = (3.14)(3^2)(10)$
$V = (3.14)(9)(10)$
$V = (28.26)(10)$
$V = 282.6$ cu in

The cylinder below is measured in centimeters. It has a radius of 4 and a height of 3. Find its volume.

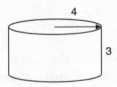

$V = \pi r^2 h$
$V = (3.14)(4^2)(3)$
$V = (3.14)(16)(3)$
$V = (50.24)(3)$
$V = 150.72$ cu cm

The cylinder below is measured in yards. It has a radius of 6 and a height of 15. Find its volume.

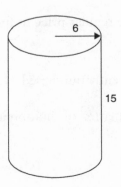

$V = \pi r^2 h$

$V = (3.14)(6^2)(15)$

$V = (3.14)(36)(15)$

$V = (113.04)(15)$

$V = 1{,}695.6$ cu yd

Measurement Problems

Measurement is the act of assigning numbers to things. There are many types of measurements, ranging from distance to weight to temperature. Other examples of measurements include time, money, volume, area, degree, and rate.

Practice questions

A car is traveling at the rate of 50 miles per hour. How many minutes will it take to travel 255 miles?

Start with the formula for distance:

distance = rate × time

Convert the formula for distance into the formula for time by dividing distance by rate:

distance/rate = time

Now plug in the given values for distance and rate and solve for time:

$\dfrac{255}{50} = $ time

$5.1 = $ time

The car would take 5.1 hours to travel the given distance, but the question asks for the number of minutes. Convert these hours into minutes by multiplying by 60:

60 × 5.1 = 306

The trip would take 306 minutes.

Music CDs are regularly $20 each. But this week only, they are on sale for 15% off. How much is the sale price?

First, find out how much money is saved by multiplying the discount, in decimal form, times the regular price:

.15 × $20 = $3 savings

Then subtract this savings from the regular price to find the sale price:

$20 − $3 = $17 sale price

An industrial painting company recently purchased 215 gallons of paint at $9.45 per gallon. What was the total cost?

Finding the total cost is simply a matter of multiplying the total amount purchased times the price per gallon:

215 × $9.45 = $2,031.75

A freeway commuter drives 44 miles back and forth to work each day, 5 days a week for 50 weeks a year. How many miles a year does this commuter drive back and forth to work? First, calculate how many miles the commuter drives each week:

44 miles $\times$ 5 days = 220 miles per week

Then multiply the miles per week by the number of weeks the commuter drives yearly to calculate the total miles driven per year:

220 $\times$ 50 = 11,000 miles

Thirty-six people share a community garden. The garden covers an area of 12,960 sq. ft. If each person were to receive the same size plot, how many square feet would it be? This is a simple division problem: divide the total area of the garden by the number of people who are to receive a plot:

12,960 $\div$ 36 = 360

Each person would receive a plot of 360 sq. ft.

A worker earns $42,000 a year doing skilled labor. How much does this worker earn each month? To calculate the monthly wage, divide the yearly salary by the number of months worked:

42,000 $\div$ 12 = $3,500 per month

Golf is a serious game, and so is the cost of the equipment. One popular set of golf clubs sells for $250. What is the total cost if the sales tax is 4%? The sales tax percentage, 4%, in decimal form is .04. To find the amount of tax on the golf clubs, multiply the cost of the clubs by the tax:

$250 $\times$ .04 = $10

Now add the tax to the price of the clubs to find the total cost:

$250 + $10 = $260

Bright-Lights Electronics sells a new television for $395. What is the total cost if the sales tax is 7%? As in the previous problem, first convert the sales tax percentage to a decimal: 7% in decimal form is .07. Next, multiply the cost of the television set by this tax rate:

$395 $\times$ .07 = $27.65

Add the amount of tax to the television price to arrive at the final cost:

$395 + $27.65 = $422.65

One night at a comfortable hotel costs a traveler $85.60 plus tax. What is the total price if the tax is 5.6%? Follow the steps as in the previous two problems. First, convert 5.6% to decimal form: .056. Then multiply the tax by the room rate:

.056 $\times$ $85.60 = $4.79 (rounded to the nearest hundredth)

Finally, add the room rate to the the tax to arrive at the total price for the room:
$85.60 + $4.79 = $90.39

At a sporting goods store, a man sees a pair of sunglasses that looks just right. The sunglasses sell for $42. What is the total price if the tax is 6.5%?
6.5% = .065
.065 × $42 = $2.73
$42 + $2.73 = $44.73
The total price of the sunglasses is $44.73.

An industrial supply company gives nonprofit organizations a 12% discount. How much would a $1,500 order cost after the discount?
12% = .12
The discount = .12 × $1,500 = $180
The discounted price = $1,500 − $180 = $1,320

A restaurant gives senior citizens a 20% discount on meals. How much would an $8.50 meal cost a senior citizen?
20% = .20
The discount = .20 × $8.50 = $1.70
The discounted price = $8.50 − $1.70 = $6.80

A business conference gives a 5% discount to all registrants who pay in advance. The regular price is $320. How much is the discounted price?
5% = .05
The discount = .05 × $320 = $16
The discounted price = $320 − $16 = $304

Downtown Clothing Store sells dress shirts for $36. If you buy two shirts, then you get the second one for $\frac{1}{4}$ off. How much do two shirts cost?

$\frac{1}{4}$ = .25

The discount = .25 × $36 = $9

Calculate the cost of the second shirt by deducting the discount from the original price:

$36 − $9 = $27

To arrive at the final cost for two shirts, add the price of the first shirt to the discounted price of the second shirt:

$36 + $27 = $63

A Celsius temperature (C) can be converted to a Fahrenheit temperature (F) using the formula $F = \dfrac{9}{5}C + 32$.

A traveler from the United States is visiting another country where they use the Celsius temperature scale. The temperature on the thermometer reads 25° Celsius. How many degrees Fahrenheit is this?

$F = \dfrac{9}{5}(25) + 32$

$F = \dfrac{225}{5} + 32$

$45 + 32 = 77°$ Fahrenheit

Fahrenheit temperature can be converted to a Celsius temperature using the formula $C = \dfrac{5}{9}(F - 32)$.

A traveler visiting the United States comes from a foreign country that uses the Celsius temperature scale. The temperature on the thermometer reads 86° Fahrenheit. How many degrees Celsius is this?

$C = \dfrac{5}{9}(86 - 32)$

$C = \dfrac{5}{9}(54)$

$\dfrac{270}{9} = 30°$ Celsius

How many ounces are there in $4\dfrac{3}{4}$ pounds?

There are 16 ounces in a pound, and $4\dfrac{3}{4}$ in decimal form is 4.75. Now multiply:

$4.75 \times 16 = 76$ ounces

Estimating Measurements

As discussed in the Math Basics section of this chapter, estimation is the process of arriving at an answer that is close to an exact answer. The advantage of estimation is that it saves you time. Estimates are obtained by rounding off numbers and then performing simple calculations.

Practice questions

Sherry is having a birthday party for 21 of her close friends. She wants to serve each guest an ice cream sundae. Ice cream sundaes cost $1.79 each. Estimate the total cost.

The number of Sherry's friends rounds down to 20, while the cost of each sundae rounds up to $2. Now multiply:

20 × $2 = $40

Note: The actual cost of the sundaes is $37.59.

The average annual rainfall in the state of Kansas is 28.61 in. The average annual rainfall in the state of New Mexico is 8.91 in. Estimate how many more inches of rainfall they get in Kansas compared to New Mexico.

Kansas's rainfall rounds up to 29 in, and New Mexico's rounds up to 9. Now substract:

29 − 9 = 20 in

Note: The actual measurement is 19.7 in.

The population of San Diego, California, is 1,266,731 people. The population of San Jose, California, is 939,899 people. Estimate the combined population of the two cities.

San Diego's population rounds to 1,300,000; San Jose's to 900,000. Now add:

1,300,000 + 900,000 = 2,200,000 people

Note: The actual count is 2,206,630 people.

A wood bookshelf requires the use of 32 screws. If each of 18 students in a class decided to build this bookshelf, estimate the number of screws needed.

The number of screws per bookshelf rounds to 30; the number of students building bookshelves rounds to 20. Now multiply:

30 × 20 = 600 screws

Note: The actual number of screws needed is 576.

The annual average snowfall for the city of Seattle, Washington, is 7.3 in. The annual average snowfall for the city of Fairbanks, Alaska, is 67.9 in. Estimate how much more snow Fairbanks gets compared to Seattle.

68 − 7 = 61 in.

Note: The actual difference is 60.6 in.

The average weight of an orange from one particular orange orchard is .622 pounds. Estimate the weight of a sack of oranges if there are 20 oranges in a sack.

.6 × 20 = 12 pounds

Note: The actual weight would be 12.44 pounds.

A gallon of liquid fertilizer covers 125 sq. ft. Estimate how many gallons are needed to cover an area of 3,475 sq. ft.

3,500 ÷ 125 = 28 gallons

Note: The actual amount is 27.8 gallons.

Graphing

A graph is a picture of a set of numbers. A graph displays a set of numbers so that patterns can be seen. Graphs allow you to communicate information in an understandable manner. It has been said that "a picture is worth a thousand words." Likewise, "a graph is worth a thousand numbers."

Sometimes, before a set of numbers is graphed, it is put into a special format called a **frequency distribution**. A frequency distribution is two columns of numbers. The first column has scores in it, and the second column has frequencies. Graphing a frequency distribution of scores allows you to see how frequently particular scores or groups of scores occurred relative to the others.

The exact method for creating a frequency distribution depends on the range of the scores. If the scores have a narrow range of values, then list this range from the minimum score to the maximum score. Put this list in a column labeled "Scores." Then count the frequency of each score and enter these numbers into a column labeled "Frequency." If the scores have a wide range of values, a different method is used. In this situation, the scores must be broken down into class intervals. Between 8 and 20 intervals are sufficient. These class intervals are listed in a column labeled "Class Intervals." Then count the frequency of scores in each interval and enter these numbers in a column labeled "Frequency."

Frequency Histograms

A frequency histogram is a graph of a frequency distribution. As explained in the previous section, a frequency distribution breaks a set of numbers into intervals and counts how many numbers fall in each interval.

Examples

Take a look at the following set of 20 scores:

   7, 4, 8, 7, 9, 5, 4, 8, 6, 2, 2, 9, 5, 7, 4, 5, 7, 3, 6, 4

Because this is a small range of scores, the frequency of the scores can be counted. So the frequency distribution for this range of scores looks like this:

Scores	Frequency
9	2
8	2
7	4
6	2
5	3
4	4
3	1
2	2

Now we can use this frequency distribution to draw a frequency histogram:

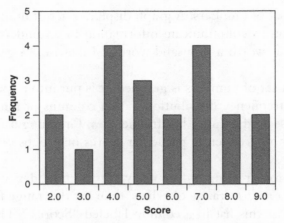

Let's try another example, this time with a range of 100 scores. Because the range of these scores is large, we need to use class intervals to divide the scores into groups. Let's make each class interval five scores wide. In addition to the frequency distribution, which only includes the class intervals and the frequency counts, we'll also include the midpoint of each class interval. We'll use these midpoints on the axis labeled "Score" on the histogram:

Class Interval	Frequency	Midpoint
96–100	25	98
91–95	28	93
86–90	14	88
81–85	11	83
76–80	9	78
71–75	5	73
66–70	7	68
61–65	1	63

This frequency distribution results in the following frequency histogram:

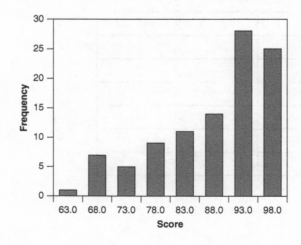

The frequency histogram below represents 500 scores. The average for this set of scores is 50:

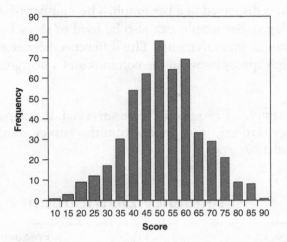

The frequency histogram below represents 1,000 scores. The average for this set of scores is 100:

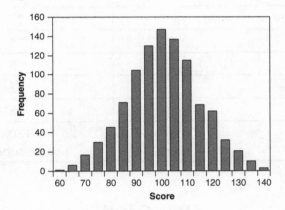

Our final frequency histogram example, shown below, illustrates the results of a pop math quiz in a class of 30 high school students. From this graph we can see that 5 students earned a score of 5. We can also see the most frequently occurring score is 7:

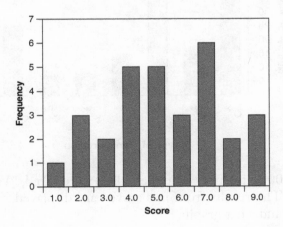

Bar Graph

Nominal categories are best displayed in a bar graph. The number of members in each category can be counted and displayed. Bar graphs can also be used to show how these nominal categories are related on continuous measurements. The difference between a bar graph and a histogram is that a bar graph has spaces between the columns and a histogram does not.

Examples

In a metropolitan city, a sample of 150 people were surveyed. Participants were asked, "What is your main mode of transportation?" The results from this survey are displayed in the form of a frequency distribution and a bar graph:

Frequency Distribution

Category	Frequency
Car	40
Bus	20
Subway	35
Taxi	15
Walk	8
Bicycle	7
Train	25
	150 people surveyed

Bar Graph

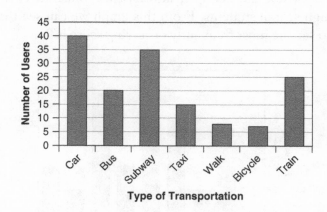

In another survey, 200 elementary school children were asked, "What is your favorite subject in school?" The results from this survey are displayed in the form of a frequency distribution and a bar graph:

Frequency Distribution

Category	Frequency
English	30
History	24
Math	36
Science	32
Art	44
Physical Education (P.E.)	34
	200 children surveyed

Bar Graph

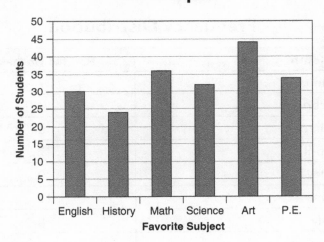

Companies are often interested in comparing their sales figures with their competitors. In one area of the country, five supply companies control the sales of wood and hardware. The total sales last year for these companies are listed in the following frequency distribution and then charted on a bar graph:

Frequency Distribution

Company	Sales Last Year
Company A	$1,200,000
Company B	$4,400,000
Company C	$3,200,000
Company D	$3,200,000
Company E	$2,800,000

Bar Graph

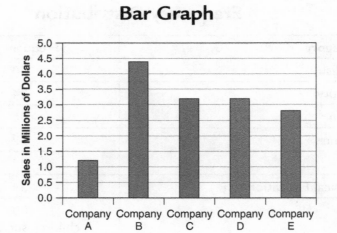

Greenville gets a good bit of rain. The average number of inches of rainfall for each month is displayed in the following frequency distribution and then in a bar graph:

Frequency Distribution

Month	Rainfall (inches)
January	7
February	4
March	5
April	7
May	9
June	10
July	8
August	6
September	9
October	10
November	11
December	10

Bar Graph

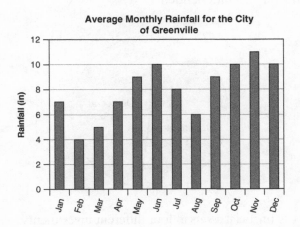

Pie Chart

While the frequencies for a set of nominal categories are displayed with a bar graph, the *relative* frequencies are displayed using a pie chart. In essence, a pie chart compares parts of a whole. In a pie chart, all of the percentages add up to 100%.

Examples

The enrollment figures at one public college reveals that 52% of the student body are female while 48% are male. These enrollment figures are easily displayed in a pie chart:

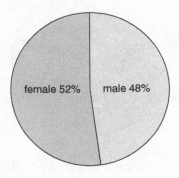

Outside a movie theater, an exit-survey taker asked the moviegoers, "Would you recommend this movie to a friend?" Of the respondents, 62% said yes while 38% said no:

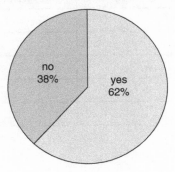

A political poll of voters in one area found that 48% of the voters are Democrat, 35% are Republican, and 17% are independent:

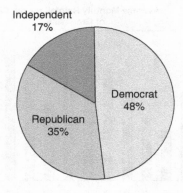

A small company has its financial assets in four different investments:

Investment	Percent of Assets
Stocks	20
Bonds	20
Cash	45
Mutual funds	15

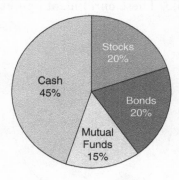

The percentage of students earning each grade in a high school geometry class is displayed in the following table and then on a pie chart:

Grade	Percent of Class
A	20
B	25
C	30
D	15
F	10

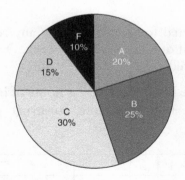

Residents of one city were surveyed to collect demographic information. The results from this survey gives a breakdown according to race.

Race	Percent of City
White	31
Black	14
Asian	23
Hispanic	27
Other	5

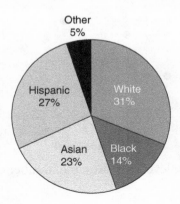

Scatter Plot

A scatter plot is a graph that shows the relationship between two variables. A scatter plot is just a set of (x, y) coordinates. Each coordinate is a point on the graph. The x value represents a measurement on one variable, while the y value represents a measurement on another variable. Remember that a variable is just a measurement that can take on more than one value. A scatter plot is useful because in one picture, you can see if there appears to be a relationship between two variables.

Examples

A research study was conducted to see if there was any relationship between grade level in school and the amount of homework each week. One student from each grade level 1 through 12 was surveyed.

Given: Variable *x* is the grade level. Variable *y* is hours of homework each week.
Task: Using the data in the following table, construct a scatter plot and describe the relationship.

x	Grade level	1	2	3	4	5	6	7	8	9	10	11	12
y	Hours of homework	2	3	3	6	4	10	7	10	12	9	14	15

You can think of these two variables as one set of (*x*, *y*) coordinates on a graph. Remember that a coordinate is just a point. Graph the following points: (1, 2), (2, 3), (3, 3), (4, 6), (5, 4), (6, 10), (7, 7), (8, 10), (9, 12), (10, 9), (11, 14), and (12, 15):

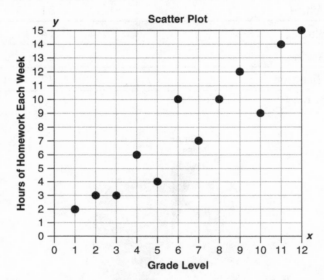

This graph shows that, as grade level increases, the number of homework hours tends to increase.

A research study was conducted to see if there was any relationship between math skill and art skill. A sample of 12 people agreed to participate in the study. Each person took two tests. One was an art test. The other was a math test.

Given: Variable *x* is the math test score. Variable *y* is the art test score.
Task: Using the data in the following table, construct a scatter plot and describe the relationship between the two variables.

x	Math test score	1	2	3	3	4	5	6	7	7	8	9	10
y	Art test score	11	9	7	9	6	9	6	7	4	3	5	2

You can think of these two variables as one set of (*x*, *y*) coordinates on a graph. Remember that a coordinate is just a point. Graph the following points: (1, 11), (2, 9), (3, 7), (3, 9), (4, 6), (5, 9), (6, 6), (7, 7), (7, 4), (8, 3), (9, 5), and (10, 2):

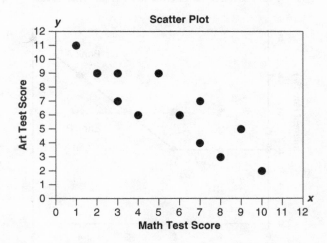

This graph shows that as math skill increases, art skill tends to decrease.

Line Graph

A line graph is a way of showing how two measurements are related. A line can also be used to show how something changes over time. When creating a line graph where time is one of the measurements, time should be displayed on the *x*-axis, which is the horizontal axis.

Examples

The average temperature for the city of Appleton was recorded for five consecutive days. Using these temperatures, a line graph was created to show changes in temperature over time:

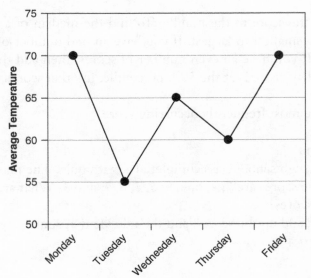

The following graph shows the interest rate paid by two different banks on a savings account. The interest rate depends on the amount of the balance.

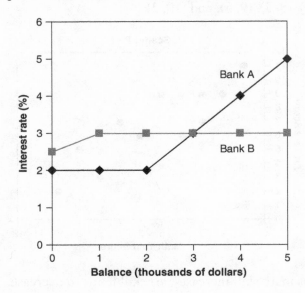

Statistics

Averages

Averages tell us what is usual, normal, and to be expected. They are measurements of central tendency. Averages take into consideration all of the numbers in a data set. There are three types of averages. They are the mean, median, and mode.

The **mean** is the average score. The mean is what we typically think of as the average. To calculate the mean of a set of scores, add up all of the scores and then divide by the number of scores.

The **median** is the score in the middle. To find the median of a given data set, first rank order the scores from smallest to largest. If you have an odd number of scores, then the middle score is the median. If you have an even number of scores, then add the two middle scores and divide by 2. The median score is at the 50th percentile; in other words, it is higher than 50% of all the scores.

The **mode** is the most frequently occurring score.

Practice questions

Ten students in a high school class completed a math quiz. The maximum number of points possible is 10. The scores are 7, 4, 6, 4, 9, 5, 7, 8, 7, and 3. What are the mean, median, and mode of the test scores?

To find the mean, add up the scores, and then divide that sum by 10, the number of scores:

$$7 + 4 + 6 + 4 + 9 + 5 + 7 + 8 + 7 + 3 = 60$$

$$\text{mean} = \frac{60}{10} = 6$$

The mean score is 6.

For the median, first rank order the scores from smallest to largest:

{3, 4, 4, 5, 6, 7, 7, 7, 8, 9}

Because there is an even number of scores, the median is between the two middle scores, which are 6 and 7. So find the mean of these two middle numbers:

$$\text{median} = \frac{6+7}{2} = \frac{13}{2} = 6.5$$

The median is 6.5.

Last, the mode: The mode is 7 because it occurs more often than any other score.

The number of runs scored by a baseball team was recorded for an eight-game period:

Scores: {3, 2, 5, 6, 2, 2, 1, 3}

What are the mean, median, and mode of the runs scored?

For the mean, add up the scores, and then divide by the total number of scores, in this case 8:

3 + 2 + 5 + 6 + 2 + 2 + 1 + 3 = 24

$$\text{mean} = \frac{24}{8} = 3$$

To find the median, first rank order the scores from smallest to largest:

{1, 2, 2, 2, 3, 3, 5, 6}

Because there is an even number of scores, the median is between the two middle scores, 2 and 3. Calculate the mean of these two scores to find the median:

$$\text{median} = \frac{2+3}{2} = \frac{5}{2} = 2.5$$

Last, the mode is 2 because that is the score that occurs more often than any other score.

In a survey on foot size, nine elementary high school boys had their feet measured:

Sizes: {7, 6, 6, 10, 5, 7, 6, 9, 7}

Find the mean, median, and mode of foot size for this group of boys.

For the mean, add up the foot sizes, and then divide by the total number of foot sizes:

7 + 6 + 6 + 10 + 5 + 7 + 6 + 9 + 7 = 63

$$\text{mean} = \frac{63}{9} = 7$$

The mean foot size is 7.

To find the median, first rank order the scores from smallest to largest:

{5, 6, 6, 6, 7, 7, 7, 9, 10}

Because there is an odd number of scores, the median is the score in the middle: 7.

Last, the mode: In this data set, there are two modes, 6 and 7, because they both appear most often.

Employees at a manufacturing company took a job-satisfaction survey. The scores were 3, 4, 6, 7, 2, 7, 4, 8, 5, 9, 4, and 1. Low scores indicate low job satisfaction, and high scores indicate high job satisfaction. What are the mean, median, and mode of the survey scores?

To calculate the mean, add up the scores, and then divide by the total number of scores:

$3 + 4 + 6 + 7 + 2 + 7 + 4 + 8 + 5 + 9 + 4 + 1 = 60$

$$\text{mean} = \frac{60}{12} = 5$$

The mean job satisfaction score is 5.

To find the median, first rank order the scores from smallest to largest:

$\{1, 2, 3, 4, 4, 4, 5, 6, 7, 7, 8, 9\}$

Because there is an even number of scores, the median is between the two middle scores, 4 and 5. The mean of these two scores is the median:

$$\text{median} = \frac{4 + 5}{2} = \frac{9}{2} = 4.5$$

Finally, the mode is 4 because it occurs more often than any other score.

A basketball team had a contest to see how many baskets each team member could make during a two-minute period. The 11 team members scored as follows:

Scores: $\{7, 10, 9, 5, 7, 6, 8, 7, 9, 10, 8\}$

Find the mean, median, and mode of the scores.

To calculate the mean, add up the scores, and then divide by the total number of scores:

$7 + 10 + 9 + 5 + 7 + 6 + 8 + 7 + 9 + 10 + 8 = 86$

$$\text{mean} = \frac{86}{11} = 7.82 \text{ (rounded to the nearest hundredth)}$$

To find the median, first rank order the scores from smallest to largest:

$\{5, 6, 7, 7, 7, 8, 8, 9, 9, 10, 10\}$

Because there is an odd number of scores, the median is the score in the middle: 8.

Finally, the mode is 7 because it occurs more often than any other score.

The yearly rainfall totals for a particular county in the Midwest was recorded for five consecutive years. The yearly rainfall amounts are listed in the following table. What was the average yearly rainfall?

Year	Rainfall (inches)
1	19
2	28
3	22
4	35
5	23

Add up the rainfall measurements, and then divide by the number of years:

$19 + 28 + 22 + 35 + 23 = 127$

$$\frac{127}{5} = 25.4$$

The average yearly rainfall was 25.4 in.

A crate full of 50 large apples weighs 26.5 pounds, which converts to 424 ounces. What is the average weight of the apples in this crate, in ounces?

In this case, the sum of all the items you are averaging is already done for you: 424 is the weight of all 50 apples. Now you simply divide by the number of apples to find the average weight per apple:

$$\frac{424}{50} = 8.48 \text{ ounces}$$

Last year, one particular family spent a total of $871.80 on telephone bills. What is the average monthly bill?

As in the previous question, this question supplies the sum of the items you are averaging: $871.80. Simply divide the sum by the number of months in a year to find the monthly average:

$$\frac{871.80}{12} = \$72.65$$

One aluminum-recycling center processes tons of aluminum each month. The table displays the amount of aluminum processed for a six-month period. What is the average amount recycled per month?

Month	Tons Recycled
1	18,000
2	28,000
3	41,000
4	24,000
5	34,000
6	23,000
Total	168,000

Divide the total amount recycled by the number of months to arrive at the average amount recycled per month:

$$\frac{168,000}{6} = 28,000 \text{ tons}$$

At a recent college track and field event, eight women athletes ran the 100-m dash. The total time for all eight athletes was 97.12 s. What was the average time for this race?

$$\frac{97.12}{8} = 12.14 \text{ seconds}$$

The annual income of one particular independent contractor varies depending upon how good business is that year. Using the earnings for the last four years listed below, calculate his average income per year.

Year	Income
1	$51,000
2	$47,000
3	$53,000
4	$42,000

The sum of the contractor's income over the last four years is $193,000. Divide that by 4 to arrive at his yearly average:

$$\frac{193,000}{4} = \$48,250$$

Variability

When describing a set of numbers, it is important to know a measure of variability. Variability refers to the spread of the scores. Variability is concerned with the question, "Are the scores clustered close together, or are they spread far apart?" The **range** is a measure of variability. The range is simply the highest score minus the lowest score. The range is a single number, and although it does convey the spread of a set of scores, its use is limited.

A frequency distribution is one way to look at the variability in a set of scores. For example, the frequency distribution in the following graph shows the frequencies of 1,000 scores (N is the symbol for sample size). The mean score for this distribution is 100. Notice how far the scores are spread from this mean of 100 on the graph, and compare it with the two graphs that follow:

Population 1

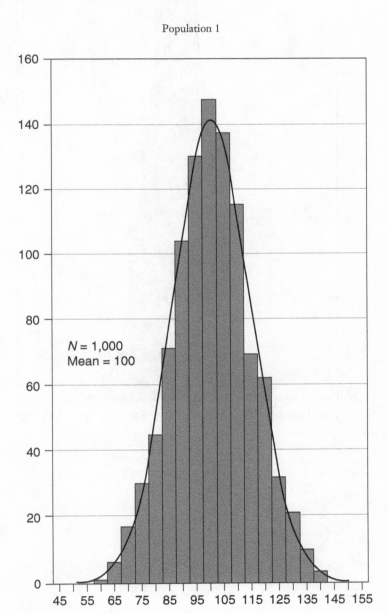

The population of scores in the next graph has the same size and the same mean as the distribution before it. This distribution is also similar in shape. The only difference is that it has less variability in its scores. Notice that the scores are not spread so far apart from the mean compared with the previous distribution:

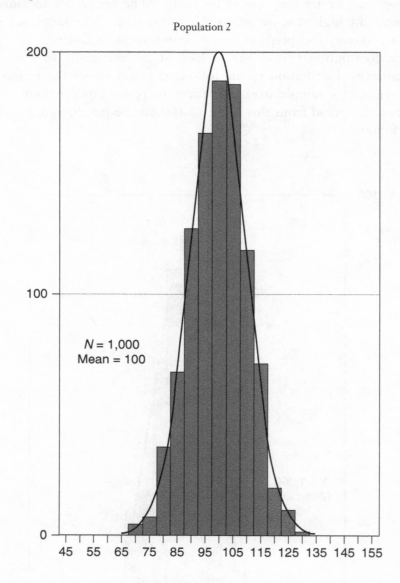

Population 2

The population of scores in this final graph has the same size and the same mean as the distribution before it. This distribution is also similar in shape. The only difference is that it has greater variability in its scores. Notice that the scores are spread farther apart from the mean compared with the previous distribution:

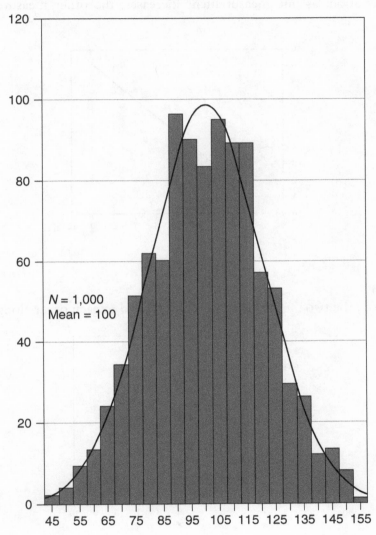

Population 3

Correlation

Correlation is a statistical technique that tells you if two measurements go together along a straight line. A scatter plot is one way of looking at correlation. There are three different types of correlation:

Positive Correlation

In a positive correlation, as one measurement increases, the other measurement also tends to increase.

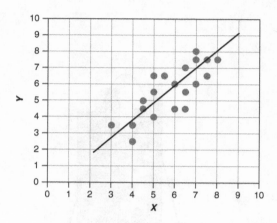

Zero Correlation

In a zero correlation, the two measurements are not related to each other along a straight line.

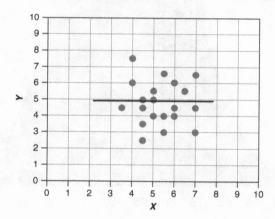

Negative Correlation

In a negative correlation, as one measurement increases, the other measurement tends to decrease.

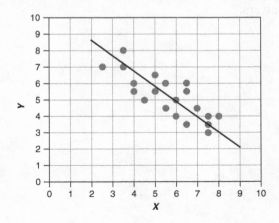

Permutation

The term "permutations" refers to the number of ways a set of elements can be arranged, when order is important.

When we are interested in the number of ways that a set of elements can be ordered, and we include all of the elements, $n!$ gives us the answer. (Recall that the exclamation point is the sign for "factorial.") For example, if we wanted to find out how many different ways we could order three people standing in line, we would set up the following equation:

$3! = 3 \times 2 \times 1 = 6$

So there are six ways to order the line of three people.

Let's say we wanted to find out how many different ways we could order five playing cards:

$5! = 5 \times 4 \times 3 \times 2 \times 1 = 120$

There are 120 ways to order the five cards.

Let's say we wanted to find out how many different ways we could order eight shirts in a clothes closet:

$8! = 8 \times 7 \times 6 \times 5 \times 4 \times 3 \times 2 \times 1 = 40,320$

There are 40,320 ways to arrange the shirts in the closet.

When we are interested in the number of ways a subset can be selected from a set of elements, *and order matters*, the number of permutations is represented by $P(n, r)$, where n is the total number of elements and r is the number of elements to be selected. The formula for permutations is

$$P(n,r) = \frac{n!}{(n - r)!}.$$

Practice questions

Determine how many different ways you can arrange four books on a shelf out of seven books, where order matters.

$$P(n,r) = \frac{n!}{(n-r)!}$$

$$P(7,4) = \frac{7!}{(7-4)!}$$

$$P(7,4) = \frac{7!}{3!}$$

$$P(7,4) = \frac{5,040}{6}$$

$$P(7,4) = 840$$

Determine the number of permutations of 10 elements when we are selecting 3 of them.

$$P(n,r) = \frac{n!}{(n-r)!}$$

$$P(10,3) = \frac{10!}{(10-3)!}$$

$$P(10,3) = \frac{10!}{7!}$$

$$P(10,3) = \frac{3,628,800}{5,040}$$

$$P(10,3) = 720$$

Combinations

Combinations refer to the number of ways a set of elements can be arranged when order is *not* important.

When we are interested in the number of ways a subset can be selected from a set of elements and order *does not* matter, the number of combinations is represented by **C(n, k)** where *n* is the total number of elements and *k* is the number of elements to be selected. The formula for combinations is

$$_nC_k = \frac{n!}{k!(n-k)!}$$

Practice questions

Determine how many different ways you can make a pizza choosing three items out of five items.

$$_nC_k = \frac{n!}{k!(n-k)!}$$

$$_5C_3 = \frac{5!}{3!(5-3)!}$$

$$_5C_3 = \frac{5!}{3!(2!)}$$

$$_5C_3 = \frac{120}{6(2)}$$

$$_5C_3 = \frac{120}{12} = 10$$

Determine how many different ways you can choose five movies out of a collection of eight.

$$_nC_k = \frac{n!}{k!(n-k)!}$$

$$_8C_5 = \frac{8!}{5!(8-5)!}$$

$$_8C_5 = \frac{8!}{5!(3!)}$$

$$_8C_5 = \frac{40,320}{120(6)}$$

$$_8C_5 = \frac{40,320}{720} = 56$$

Determine how many different ways you can choose four coins out of a collection of six.

$$_nC_k = \frac{n!}{k!(n-k)!}$$

$$_6C_4 = \frac{6!}{4!(6-4)!}$$

$$_6C_4 = \frac{6!}{4!(2!)}$$

$$_6C_4 = \frac{720}{24(2)}$$

$$_6C_4 = \frac{720}{48} = 15$$

Probability

Probability Theory

A probability is a number between 0 and 1 that allows us to talk about chance, likelihood, and uncertainty. If an outcome or event has a probability of 0, it never happens. If an outcome or event has a probability of 1, it always happens. If an outcome or event has a probability of .5 or 50%, it happens about one-half of the time. The probability of an event is represented by p:

$$0 \le p \le 1$$

In probability theory, the collection of all possible outcomes from an experiment is called a sample space. A sample space is expressed as two huge brackets with all of the possible outcomes listed inside. For example, if the experiment is to flip a coin and observe the outcome, the two equally likely possible outcomes are heads (H) and tails (T). The sample space looks like this:

[H, T]

Probabilities have complementary relationships. The probability of event E happening plus the probability of that event *not* happening is equal to 1:

$$P(E) + P(\overline{E}) = 1$$

One derivation of this equation is read, "The probability of event E happening is equal to one minus the probability of event E *not* happening":

$$P(E) = 1 - P(\overline{E})$$

The other derivation of this equation is read, "The probability of event E not happening is equal to one minus the probability of event E happening":

$$P(\overline{E}) = 1 - P(E)$$

Examples

An experiment is to flip a fair coin once. There are two possible outcomes from this experiment. The sample space looks like this:

[H, T]

Each outcome is equally likely. Each outcome has a $\frac{1}{2}$ chance of happening. This fraction of $\frac{1}{2}$ can be expressed as the decimal number .5 or as the percentage 50%.

An experiment is to throw one fair die to see what number it rolls. There are six possible outcomes from this experiment. The sample space looks like this:

Each outcome has a $\frac{1}{6}$ chance of happening. If we list a set of all possible outcomes from an experiment next to a list of their corresponding probabilities, this is called a probability distribution. For example, in the case of rolling one fair die, the probability distribution looks like this:

Outcome	1	2	3	4	5	6
Probability	$\frac{1}{6}$	$\frac{1}{6}$	$\frac{1}{6}$	$\frac{1}{6}$	$\frac{1}{6}$	$\frac{1}{6}$

One important characteristic of a probability distribution is that the sum of all the probabilities equals 1.0 or 100%.

Random chance

A probability is an average. Averages are never predictive for single events (unless they are 0 or 1). The reason that you cannot accurately predict if a fair coin will land heads or tails on any single flip, even though you know that $p = .5$, is because of random chance. Random chance is a powerful, invisible force that permeates the universe and has a hand in all events. Random chance is the unknowable effects on the outcome of every experiment. A big part of statistics is calculating the probability of getting particular experimental results due to chance.

Compound Events

Compound events are when two events occur at the same time.

Examples

If the experimenter were to flip two fair coins, or one fair coin twice (same thing), the sample space would look like this:

{HH, HT, TH, TT}

The probability of any single outcome is one chance in four or $\frac{1}{4}$ or .25 or 25%.

The first step in using probability theory is to generate a sample space, then count the total number of different possible outcomes from the experiment. The second step is to assign probabilities to each outcome. For example, in the sample space {H, T}, the probability of H or T equals $\frac{1}{2}$ or .5 or 50%.

Let's look at another example: if the experimenter were to throw two fair dice to see what the sum looks like, there are 36 different possible outcomes. The sample space looks like this:

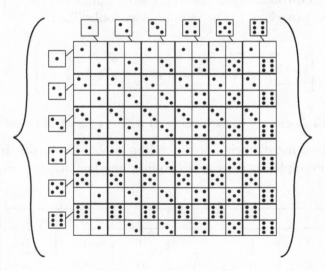

If a sample space is a list of all possible outcomes, then a selected collection of outcomes is called an event. An event is a subset of a sample space. For example, let's say that we define an event *A* as occurring when the two dice added together equals 7. Looking at the 36 different outcomes, we can count six different ways that *A* can happen.

The next step is to add up the probabilities that define that event. In the dice example, the probability of each single outcome is equal to $\frac{1}{36}$. Because there are six ways to roll a 7, the probability of the event of rolling a 7 is equal to

$$\frac{1}{36} + \frac{1}{36} + \frac{1}{36} + \frac{1}{36} + \frac{1}{36} + \frac{1}{36} = \frac{6}{36} = \frac{1}{6}$$

The fraction $\frac{1}{6}$ is equal to about .167 or about 17%. Thus, we can say that there is a 17% chance that the roll of two fair dice will result in a total score of 7.

A probability distribution can be created when you list a set of mutually exclusive (nonoverlapping) events alongside their corresponding probabilities. For example, in the case of throwing two fair dice, the probability distribution relating events with their corresponding probabilities looks like this:

Event	2	3	4	5	6	7	8	9	10	11	12
Probability	$\frac{1}{36}$	$\frac{2}{36}$	$\frac{3}{36}$	$\frac{4}{36}$	$\frac{5}{36}$	$\frac{6}{36}$	$\frac{5}{36}$	$\frac{4}{36}$	$\frac{3}{36}$	$\frac{2}{36}$	$\frac{1}{36}$

Now this is where a probability comes from. For an experiment that produces equally likely outcomes, count the total number of possible outcomes that favor the event that you are interested in, then divide that number by the total number of all possible outcomes. A probability is a ratio. The probability of event E occurring can be represented by the following formula:

$$P(E) = \frac{\text{total number of outcomes that favor the event}}{\text{total number of all possible outcomes}}$$

A common confusion that students encounter when calculating the probability of an event is the question of which number should divide which number. The answer is simple: divide the smaller number by the larger number. For example, for the event defined as rolling a 7, there are 6 possible outcomes that meet this criterion out of a total of 36 possible outcomes. Therefore, the probability of rolling a 7 is 6 divided by 36 or $\frac{1}{6}$, which equals about .167 or about 17%. In other words, over the long run, approximately 17 times out of 100 you can expect to roll the number 7 on one throw of two fair dice.

Consider one more example: if the experiment is to flip a coin and throw a die, these two events are independent because the outcome of the coin in no way affects the outcome of the die. The sample space would look like this:

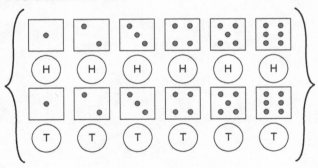

There are 12 different possible outcomes. The coin and the die are independent from each other because the probability of getting, say, heads and 4 is equal to the probability of getting heads, which is $\frac{1}{2}$ times the probability of getting 4, which is $\frac{1}{6}$:

$$\frac{1}{2} \times \frac{1}{6} = \frac{1}{12}$$

Two events are independent if they do not cause or influence each other.

Nature, however, occasionally creates some illusions contrary to the law of independence. For example, if you flip a coin 10 times and get 10 tails straight in a row, what do you think the probability is that the next flip is a head? The answer is 50%. But doesn't it seem that it should be more than that; after all, isn't a head just bound to come up by chance soon to even things out? Yes, eventually, but not necessarily on the next flip. The coin does not remember that it just came up tails 10 times and that now it is time to land heads in order to satisfy the law of large numbers.

Frequently, people erroneously attribute predictive power to single events, rather than to averages over the long run. For example, when you flip a fair coin, the probability of getting heads or tails is $\frac{1}{2}$ or .5 or 50%. Knowing this does not allow you to predict what will appear on the next coin flip. Probabilities claim only that after a lot of flips, on the average, the probability of getting a head or tail is equal to .5.

PRACTICE TEST 1

Both Practice Tests are also on CD in our special interactive CHSPE TestWare®. We recommend that you first take these tests on computer for the added benefits of timed testing conditions, automatic scoring and diagnostic feedback.

PRACTICE TEST 1
ENGLISH-LANGUAGE ARTS SECTION

Language Subtest

DIRECTIONS: Look at the underlined words in each sentence. You may see a mistake in punctuation, capitalization, or word usage. If you spot a mistake in the underlined section of a sentence, select the answer that corrects the mistake. If you find no mistake, choose **(D)**, *Correct as is*.

1. The horse wagged <u>its'</u> tail.
   - **(A)** it is
   - **(B)** its
   - **(C)** it's
   - **(D)** Correct as is.

2. No one has a blue car except <u>me</u>.
   - **(A)** I
   - **(B)** they
   - **(C)** she
   - **(D)** Correct as is.

3. Joe ordered a copy of the new <u>book he has wants</u> for his birthday next month.
   - **(A)** book he wanted
   - **(B)** book he will want
   - **(C)** book himself wanted
   - **(D)** Correct as is.

4. <u>The game was almost over she was tired</u>.
   - **(A)** The game was almost over; she was tired.
   - **(B)** The game was almost over she, was tired.
   - **(C)** The game was almost over: she was tired.
   - **(D)** Correct as is.

5. Jordan is <u>the taller student</u> in the whole class.
   - **(A)** the tall student
   - **(B)** the taller students
   - **(C)** the tallest student
   - **(D)** Correct as is.

GO TO NEXT PAGE ➡

6. When I finish chopping the vegetables, <u>I will cook the shrimp</u>.
   - **(A)** I will have cook the shrimp.
   - **(B)** I am cooking the shrimp.
   - **(C)** I cooked the shrimp.
   - **(D)** Correct as is.

7. Jason <u>and me</u> have the most baseball cards.
   - **(A)** and I
   - **(B)** and mine
   - **(C)** and myself
   - **(D)** Correct as is.

8. <u>To goes walking</u> in the woods is a wonderful thing.
   - **(A)** To going walking
   - **(B)** To go walking
   - **(C)** To walking
   - **(D)** Correct as is.

9. <u>The boy said I will get the car and wash it</u>.
   - **(A)** The boy said "I will get the car and wash it."
   - **(B)** The boy said, "I will get the car and wash it".
   - **(C)** The boy said, "I will get the car and wash it."
   - **(D)** Correct as is.

10. They brought <u>they're</u> equipment on the camping trip.
   - **(A)** their
   - **(B)** there are
   - **(C)** there
   - **(D)** Correct as is.

11. People need to <u>be more carefuller</u> when they ride their bikes.
   - **(A)** be carefuller
   - **(B)** be more careful
   - **(C)** being more careful
   - **(D)** Correct as is.

12. The wooden box holds <u>lesser</u> candles than the silver box.
   - **(A)** least
   - **(B)** fewest
   - **(C)** fewer
   - **(D)** Correct as is.

13. <u>The Empire state building</u> is a famous monument.
   - **(A)** The empire state building
   - **(B)** The Empire State Building
   - **(C)** The Empire State building
   - **(D)** Correct as is.

14. Most people today regularly <u>recycles</u> plastic and glass.
   - **(A)** can recycle
   - **(B)** are recycles
   - **(C)** recycle
   - **(D)** Correct as is.

15. I purchased some <u>potatoes, corn, oranges grapes and bread at the market</u>.
   - **(A)** potatoes, corn, oranges, grapes, and, bread at the market.
   - **(B)** potatoes corn oranges grapes and bread at the market.
   - **(C)** potatoes, corn, oranges, grapes, and bread at the market.
   - **(D)** Correct as is.

GO TO NEXT PAGE

16. "Okay, Robert." "You can let the guests in now," said his mom.

   (A) "Okay, Robert." You can let the guests in now," said his mom.

   (B) "Okay, Robert. You can let the guests in now", said his mom.

   (C) "Okay, Robert. You can let the guests in now," said his mom.

   (D) Correct as is.

17. When we get to the top of the hill, we are set up the tent.

   (A) we can

   (B) we had been

   (C) we did

   (D) Correct as is.

18. The Golden gate bridge is a very popular landmark.

   (A) The golden gate bridge

   (B) The Golden Gate bridge

   (C) The Golden Gate Bridge

   (D) Correct as is.

19. The show, predicted to be a hit.

   (A) The show was predicted to be a hit.

   (B) The show, predict to be a hit.

   (C) The show to be predicted, to be a hit.

   (D) Correct as is.

20. During the lesson, the teacher writing on the board.

   (A) written on

   (B) writing on

   (C) wrote on

   (D) Correct as is.

21. The guitarist in the band was playing his instrument very loudly.

   (A) was play

   (B) will playing

   (C) was played

   (D) Correct as is.

22. Dolphins are known to be very curiosity.

   (A) curiousness

   (B) curiouser

   (C) curious

   (D) Correct as is.

23. The grocery store is known for his fine produce.

   (A) it's

   (B) its

   (C) her

   (D) Correct as is.

24. The cow was grazed in the meadow.

   (A) was grazing

   (B) grazing

   (C) is graze

   (D) Correct as is.

25. Yesterday, the carpenter need the tape measure for the project.

   (A) will need

   (B) needed

   (C) is needing

   (D) Correct as is.

26. There are four apples that are placing in the bowl.

   (A) place

   (B) to be placing

   (C) placed

   (D) Correct as is.

27. I didn't know where I was going to.

   (A) I didn't know where I was going.

   (B) I didn't know where to I was going.

   (C) I didn't know to where I was going.

   (D) Correct as is.

GO TO NEXT PAGE

28. After he baked the cake, he <u>frosts</u> the top layer.
    (A) did frosted
    (B) would frost
    (C) frosted
    (D) Correct as is.

29. The <u>smaller</u> of the four girls was named Missy.
    (A) smallest
    (B) most small
    (C) more smaller
    (D) Correct as is.

30. <u>Whenever I go</u> to the record store, I buy a new album.
    (A) When I went
    (B) Whenever I went
    (C) Whenever I did go
    (D) Correct as is.

31. <u>Some flowers arranging in the vase smell very sweet</u>.
    (A) In the vase smelling sweet, are some arranging flowers.
    (B) Some flowers arranged in the vase smell very sweet.
    (C) In the vase are arranged flowers, smell very sweet.
    (D) Correct as is.

32. <u>"driving on this road is challenging." Said Bobby</u>.
    (A) "Driving on this road is challenging," said Bobby.
    (B) "Driving on this road is challenging said Bobby".
    (C) Driving on this road is challenging "said Bobby."
    (D) Correct as is.

33. <u>The food critic gives the restaurant a glowing review in the article yesterday</u>.
    (A) The food critic giving the restaurant a glowing review in the article yesterday.
    (B) The food critic gave the restaurant a glowing review in the article yesterday.
    (C) The food critic will give the restaurant a glowing review in the article yesterday.
    (D) Correct as is.

34. <u>He and me</u> will clean up the mess.
    (A) Him and I
    (B) He and myself
    (C) He and I
    (D) Correct as is.

35. We will visit <u>the grand canyon</u> this summer.
    (A) The Grand Canyon
    (B) the Grand Canyon
    (C) the grand Canyon
    (D) Correct as is.

36. <u>I will ride my bike; she will ride the bus</u>.
    (A) I will ride my bike she will ride the bus.
    (B) I will ride my bike, she will ride the bus.
    (C) I will ride my bike; She will ride the bus.
    (D) Correct as is.

GO TO NEXT PAGE ➡

DIRECTIONS: Refer to the passage to answer the next set of questions.

1   The first reason why Jonathan's life is bad is he can't think for them self's. They are told what to do and they do it. They are like sheep, and just go along with everyone else. They don't try to brake away even when they know what they are doing is bad or inconsequential. They are to scares to be the only person that is not following the rest of the people. They are to scared to

5   be their own person. Also they are told the way to live. They don't have decisions they are told how to do every thing. They don't have decisions to make about their life: what they want to do and what they want to say. There life's depend on what the media and what other people say. This is how they live.

37. Which part of line 1 is incorrect?

The first reason why Jonathan's life is bad is he can't think for them self's.

(A) The first reason

(B) Jonathan's life

(C) he can't think

(D) for them self's.

38. Which word in lines 2–3 is misspelled?

They are like sheep, and just go along with everyone else. They don't try to brake away even when they know what they are doing is bad or inconsequential.

(A) sheep

(B) everyone

(C) brake

(D) inconsequential

39. Which part of lines 3–4 is incorrect?

They are to scares to be the only person that is not following the rest of the people.

(A) to scares

(B) the only person

(C) not following

(D) rest of the people

40. What is a better way to write lines 4–5?

They are to scared to be their own person. Also they are told the way to live.

(A) They are too scared to be their own persons, and they are told the way to live.

(B) They are too scared to be his own person, and he is told the way to live.

(C) He scares his own person; he is told the way to live.

(D) Scared to be their own persons, and he is told the way to live.

41. What is the best way to rewrite lines 5–6?

They don't have decisions they are told how to do every thing.

(A) They don't have decisions, they are told how to do everything.

(B) They don't have decisions — they are told how to do everything.

(C) They don't have decisions; they are told how to do everything.

(D) They don't have decisions = they are told how to do everything.

42. What is the best way to rewrite line 7?

There life's depend on what the media and what other people say.

(A) There lives depend on what the media and what other people say.

(B) Their lives depend on what the media and what other people say.

(C) They're lives depend on what the media and what other people say.

(D) They are living depend on what the media and what other people say.

GO TO NEXT PAGE ➡

> **DIRECTIONS:** Refer to the passage to answer the next set of questions.

1　　Many teachers across the United States is concerned about decreasing pay and benefits as well as numerous school closures. Sports stars and Hollywood actors consistently make huge salaries, while teachers, who cared and educated the children of America, are given salaries that are difficult, if not impossible, for comfortable survival. Jamie Oaks, a teacher in Delaware, stated
5　　"My administrators regularly get substantial raises while I only get the cost of living percentage every year." Consistent, new teachers have to supplement their income with a second job. Coupling with late nights of grading and updating curriculum, many burn out quickly and move on to other lines of work. Peter Portman, a teacher in Kansas who left his teach position after 22 years, said, "I had to support my family any way I could. It was a tough decision, but I have to
10　　be their for them."

43. What is the error in lines 1–2?

<u>Many teachers across the United States</u> <u>is</u> <u>concerned</u> <u>about decreasing pay</u> and benefits as <u>well as numerous school closures</u>.

(A) Many teachers across the United States

(B) Is concerned

(C) about decreasing pay

(D) well as numerous school closures

44. What is the error in lines 2–4?

Sports stars and <u>Hollywood actors</u> consistently make huge salaries, while teachers, <u>who cared and educated the children</u> of America, <u>are given salaries</u> that <u>are difficult, if not impossible, for comfortable survival</u>.

(A) Hollywood actors

(B) who cared and educated the children

(C) are given salaries

(D) are difficult, if not impossible, for comfortable survival

45. What is the error in lines 4–6?

Jamie Oaks, <u>a teacher in Delaware,</u> <u>stated</u> "<u>My</u> administrators regularly <u>get substantial raises</u> while I only get the cost of living percentage <u>every year.</u>"

(A) a teacher in Delaware

(B) stated "My

(C) get substantial raises

(D) every year."

46. What is the error in line 6?

<u>Consistent,</u> <u>new teachers</u> have to <u>supplement</u> their income <u>with a second job</u>.

(A) Consistent

(B) new teachers

(C) supplement

(D) with a second job

47. What is the error in lines 6–8?

<u>Coupling with late nights</u> of grading and <u>updating curriculum</u>, many <u>burn out quickly</u> and <u>move on to other lines of work</u>.

(A) Coupling with late nights

(B) updating curriculum

(C) burn out quickly

(D) move on to other lines of work

48. What is the error in lines 8–9?

<u>Peter Portman,</u> a teacher in Kansas who left his <u>teach position</u> after 22 years, <u>said, "I</u> had to <u>support my family any way</u> I could.

(A) Peter Portman,

(B) teach position

(C) said, "I had

(D) support my family any way

GO TO NEXT PAGE ➡

PRACTICE TEST 1
ENGLISH-LANGUAGE ARTS SECTION
Writing Task

DIRECTIONS: Carefully read the writing task and review the "Writer's Checklist" below. You must be specific and explain your reasons for your opinion.

Writing Topic
There are many people who support the idea of a year-round school year with longer, dispersed breaks throughout the year and a shorter summer. What are your feelings about year-round schooling?

Writer's Checklist
The following "Writer's Checklist" (© 2008 by NCS Pearson, Inc.) will be provided with the CHSPE writing task.

- Did I write about the topic?
- Did I express my ideas in complete sentences?
- Did I give enough details to explain or support my ideas?
- Did I include only those details that are about my topic?
- Did I write my ideas in an order that is clear for the reader to follow?
- Did I write a topic sentence for each paragraph?
- Did I use a capital letter at the beginning of each sentence and for all other words that should be capitalized?
- Did I use the correct punctuation at the end of each sentence and within each sentence?
- Did I spell words correctly?
- Did I print or write clearly?

GO TO NEXT PAGE ➡

PRACTICE TEST 1
ENGLISH-LANGUAGE ARTS SECTION
Reading Subtest

DIRECTIONS: Select the word or group of words that has the same, or nearly the same, meaning as the word that is in **boldface**.

1. **Abrasive** most nearly means
   (A) smooth; glassy.
   (B) unkempt.
   (C) rough; coarse; harsh.
   (D) ill; sick; unhealthy.

2. **Bilk** most nearly means
   (A) cheat; defraud.
   (B) allow.
   (C) negotiate; arbitrate.
   (D) sulk.

3. **Covert** most nearly means
   (A) to persuade.
   (B) hidden; undercover.
   (C) to enlist.
   (D) elegant; classy.

4. **Engender** most nearly means
   (A) cause.
   (B) differentiate.
   (C) harm.
   (D) discuss.

5. **Hangar** most nearly means
   (A) yacht.
   (B) storage area for a plane.
   (C) holder for clothes.
   (D) sewing machine.

6. **Knotty** most nearly means
   (A) disobedient; unruly.
   (B) sticky.
   (C) impudent.
   (D) complex; difficult to solve.

7. **Nuance** most nearly means
   (A) spiritual dance.
   (B) relative.
   (C) something subtle.
   (D) inaudible.

8. **Plagiarism** most nearly means
   (A) taking credit for someone else's writing or ideas.
   (B) an ancient Greek tradition.
   (C) the study of rocks and minerals.
   (D) believing in more than one religion.

GO TO NEXT PAGE

9. **Renown** most nearly means
   (A) odd.
   (B) quiet.
   (C) fame.
   (D) ownership.

10. **Tangent** most nearly means
   (A) small citrus fruit.
   (B) going off the main subject.
   (C) belonging to a group.
   (D) open-air market.

11. **Caricature** most likely means
   (A) interesting.
   (B) boring.
   (C) a serious work of literature.
   (D) a cartoon.

12. **Cynicism** most likely means
   (A) quiet.
   (B) to be a leader.
   (C) self-interested.
   (D) giving to others.

13. **Ingenious** most likely means
   (A) dull or boring.
   (B) stylish.
   (C) quaint.
   (D) inventive.

14. **Binge** most likely means
   (A) to hold back.
   (B) to indulge.
   (C) to give to others.
   (D) to bring help.

15. **Exile** most nearly means
   (A) run away.
   (B) come forward.
   (C) forced to leave.
   (D) move to a new place.

16. **Regime** most nearly means
   (A) a government.
   (B) a class.
   (C) one person.
   (D) a business.

17. **Furlough** most nearly means
   (A) absence from work.
   (B) finding a new job.
   (C) sitting to dinner.
   (D) going to visit friends.

18. **Rein** most nearly means
   (A) to give to someone else.
   (B) to watch television.
   (C) to keep under control.
   (D) to become lost.

19. **Sanction** most nearly means
   (A) to break the law.
   (B) permission.
   (C) to be idle.
   (D) loiter.

20. **Trauma** most nearly means
   (A) injury.
   (B) help.
   (C) recording.
   (D) supply.

GO TO NEXT PAGE ➡

DIRECTIONS: In each of the sentences below, the word in **boldface** may be unfamiliar to you. Use the other words in the sentence to help you decide what the word in **boldface** means.

21. Because of the lack of ratings, the television show went on **hiatus** until further notice.
    (A) A break
    (B) Continuation
    (C) An island
    (D) A higher payroll

22. The **pliancy** of the wax made the candle melt very fast.
    (A) Flexibility
    (B) Stiff
    (C) Steady
    (D) Harmfulness

23. Pansy's **tirade** left the room a total mess.
    (A) Tantrum
    (B) Fight
    (C) Scream
    (D) Sobs

24. The detail in the Venetian lace was quite **intricate** which made it very expensive.
    (A) Simplicity
    (B) Complex
    (C) Compound
    (D) Elementary

25. The **gyration** of the amusement park ride made Emily sick to her stomach.
    (A) Spinning
    (B) Rolling
    (C) Rocking
    (D) Falling

26. "Do you think that Emile reached his **quota** today?" asked Jonathon.
    (A) Score
    (B) Required amount
    (C) Deadline
    (D) Home

27. The man was very **ambivalent** about which candidate to pick.
    (A) Excited
    (B) Undecided
    (C) Calm
    (D) Hungry

28. Joe was considered by many to be a **cantankerous**, old man who was not very well-liked.
    (A) bad-tempered
    (B) funny
    (C) curious
    (D) friendly

29. "How do you think she felt about that **derogatory** comment?" asked Billy.
    (A) pleasant
    (B) suspicious
    (C) spicy
    (D) uncomplimentary

30. Paella is a fabulous dish that **exemplifies** the country of Spain.
    (A) irritates
    (B) serves as a good example
    (C) creates a disturbance
    (D) denigrates

GO TO NEXT PAGE

DIRECTIONS: Refer to the passage below to answer the following questions.

Excerpt from *How to Speak and Write Correctly*
by Joseph Devlin (1871–1934)

There are upwards of 200,000 words in the recent editions of the large dictionaries, but the one-hundredth part of this number will suffice for all your wants. Of course you may think not, and you may not be content to call things by their common names; you may be ambitious to show superiority over others and display your learning or, rather, your pedantry and lack of learning. For instance, you may not want to call a spade a spade. You may prefer to call it a spatulous device for abrading the surface of the soil. Better, however, to stick to the old familiar, simple name that your grandfather called it. It has stood the test of time, and old friends are always good friends.

To use a big word or a foreign word when a small one and a familiar one will answer the same purpose, is a sign of ignorance. Great scholars and writers and polite speakers use simple words.

To go back to the number necessary for all purposes of conversation, correspondence, and writing, which is 2,000, we find that a great many people who pass in society as being polished, refined, and educated use less, for they know less. The greatest scholar alive hasn't more than four thousand different words at his command, and he never has occasion to use half the number.

31. Why would someone use complex words over simple words?
    (A) To show imagination
    (B) To act superior
    (C) To be purposefully gracious
    (D) To be worldly and graceful in polite society

32. How many words does the author think are "sufficient for all your wants"?
    (A) 2,000
    (B) 20,000
    (C) 100,000
    (D) 200,000

33. What is the best meaning of "pedantry"?
    (A) Lack of imagination
    (B) Great imagination
    (C) Intelligence
    (D) Degree

34. Why does the author think that it's better to use simple language over complex words?
    (A) So the uneducated can understand better.
    (B) It takes less time.
    (C) It is a sign of ignorance to use big words when a simple word works just as well.
    (D) It shows lack of imagination.

35. At the end of paragraph 1, the author says that "old friends are always good friends." What are "friends" in this passage?
    (A) People known for a long time
    (B) Words
    (C) Clothing
    (D) Garden tools

GO TO NEXT PAGE ➡

> **DIRECTIONS:** Refer to the text below to answer the following questions.

Chocolate-Dipped Apples

Ingredients

$\frac{2}{3}$ cup white chocolate chips

1 teaspoon ground cinnamon

2 cups apple slices

$\frac{3}{4}$ cup semisweet chocolate chips

Directions

1. In a microwave, melt the white chocolate chips in a microwave-safe glass or ceramic bowl in 30-second intervals, stirring after each melting, for 3 minutes. Do not overheat or chocolate will scorch. Stir in the cinnamon. Spread the mixture thinly on wax paper into a 9-inch square, then place onto a baking sheet. Freeze until hard, about 5 minutes. Remove from the freezer and crush the white chocolate into small pieces and place into a bowl.

2. Melt the semisweet chocolate chips in a microwave-safe glass or ceramic bowl in 30-second intervals, stirring after each melting, for 3 minutes. Do not overheat or chocolate will scorch. Skewer each apple slice with a fork. Dip the apple into the semisweet chocolate, wiping off excess, then dip the apple into the white chocolate pieces. Carefully remove the fork and place the chocolate dipped apple slices onto a plate covered with wax paper. Refrigerate until hard, about 45 minutes.

36. How many times would you have to stir the white chocolate when melting it in the microwave?
    - (A) 2
    - (B) 3
    - (C) 4
    - (D) 6

37. If the chocolate is overheated, it will
    - (A) burn.
    - (B) melt.
    - (C) evaporate.
    - (D) harden.

38. "Skewer" means to
    - (A) fix.
    - (B) sharpen.

- (C) poke through.
- (D) mold.

39. The greatest single ingredient is
    - (A) apples.
    - (B) white chocolate.
    - (C) semi-sweet chocolate.
    - (D) cinnamon.

40. Why do the chocolate-dipped apple slices have to harden?
    - (A) They taste better that way
    - (B) So the chocolate doesn't slide off
    - (C) So they melt in your mouth better
    - (D) It makes the apples taste sweeter

GO TO NEXT PAGE ➡

DIRECTIONS: Refer to the text below to answer the following questions.

Basic Warranty for Lifeguard Umbrellas

Warranty

Umbrella Source products are guaranteed to be free from defects in original material and workmanship. This guarantee includes the following:

- Frame
- Crank (if applicable)
- Tilt mechanism (if applicable)
- Housing (if applicable)
- Rib Cleats
- Valance Clamps
- Cap

This guarantee does not cover the following:

- Product failure caused by unreasonable use, misuse, or neglect
- Acts of nature (e.g., wind/storm damage)

If a defect in original material or workmanship does occur during the warranty period, Lifeguard Umbrellas will, at its discretion, repair or replace the product at no charge. We must have photos of the damaged item, as well as photos of the box the damaged item was shipped in. Please email us pictures no larger than 300k in file size. Size 4 × 6 photos can also be mailed to us if you are unable to email them.

Source: *http://www.lifeguardumbrellas.com*

41. This warranty does not cover which of the following?
    - (A) Cap
    - (B) Pleat
    - (C) Acts of nature
    - (D) Housing

42. An "act of nature" could be defined as
    - (A) a tornado.
    - (B) closing the umbrella.
    - (C) opening the umbrella.
    - (D) putting the umbrella in the car.

43. What is the proof of damage they request in the warranty?
    - (A) Written documentation
    - (B) Photos

    - (C) A piece of the umbrella in an envelope
    - (D) The shipping number

44. Which of the following items would be the top of the umbrella?
    - (A) Crank
    - (B) Handle
    - (C) Shank
    - (D) Valance

45. What is a good example of "unreasonable misuse"?
    - (A) Using the umbrella in a rainstorm
    - (B) Using the umbrella as a sunshade on a warm day
    - (C) Using the umbrella during a monsoon
    - (D) Keeping the umbrella at work

GO TO NEXT PAGE

DIRECTIONS: Refer to the poem below to answer the following questions.

Stopping by Woods on a Snowy Evening
by Robert Frost (1874–1963)

1   Whose woods these are I think I know.
His house is in the village though;
He will not see me stopping here
To watch his woods fill up with snow.

5   My little horse must think it queer
To stop without a farmhouse near
Between the woods and frozen lake
The darkest evening of the year.
He gives his harness bells a shake

10   To ask if there is some mistake.
The only other sound's the sweep
Of easy wind and downy flake.

The woods are lovely, dark, and deep.
But I have promises to keep,
15   And miles to go before I sleep.
And miles to go before I sleep.

46. Who is the speaker of the poem?
  (A) The author
  (B) Farmer who owns the woods
  (C) Horse
  (D) An unknown villager

47. What does "queer" mean in line 5?
  (A) Dangerous
  (B) Quiet
  (C) Alarming
  (D) Unusual

48. What "mistake" does the horse ask of the speaker?
  (A) Why he hasn't eaten
  (B) Why they are stopping in the snow
  (C) Why they are out so late
  (D) Why they haven't galloped

49. What is the tone of this poem?
  (A) Frantic
  (B) Dangerous
  (C) Peaceful and quiet
  (D) Silent

50. What element of figurative language is in line 11?
  (A) Metaphor
  (B) Simile
  (C) Irony
  (D) Alliteration

GO TO NEXT PAGE ➡

DIRECTIONS: Refer to the passage below to answer the following questions.

Excerpt from *Alice in Wonderland*
by Lewis Carroll (1831–1898)

At the beginning of this seemingly simple fairy tale, Alice, bored by her sister's reading aloud, chases after a rabbit she spies wearing a jacket and carrying a pocket-watch. Intrigued, she follows him and finds herself in a surreal adventure.

Alice was beginning to get very tired of sitting by her sister on the bank, and of having nothing to do: once or twice she had peeped into the book her sister was reading, but it had no pictures or conversations in it, "and what is the use of a book," thought Alice, "without pictures or conversations?"

So she was considering in her own mind (as well as she could, for the hot day made her feel very sleepy and stupid) whether the pleasure of making a daisy-chain would be worth the trouble of getting up and picking the daisies, when suddenly a White Rabbit with pink eyes ran close by her.

There was nothing so very remarkable in that; nor did Alice think it so very much out of the way to hear the Rabbit say to itself, "Oh dear! Oh dear! I shall be too late!" (when she thought it over afterwards, it occurred to her that she ought to have wondered at this, but at the time it all seemed quite natural); but when the Rabbit actually took a watch out of its waistcoat-pocket, and looked at it, and then hurried on, Alice started to her feet, for it flashed across her mind that she had never before seen a rabbit with either a waistcoat-pocket, or a watch to take out of it, and burning with curiosity, she ran across the field after it, and was just in time to see it pop down a large rabbit-hole under the hedge.

In another moment down went Alice after it, never once considering how in the world she was to get out again.

51. From the information given in paragraph 1, what word would best describe Alice?

(A) Bored

(B) Cryptic

(C) Cold

(D) Sloppy

52. Why does Alice see the White Rabbit in paragraph 2?

(A) She is having hallucinations.

(B) She is going insane from boredom.

(C) She is dreaming.

(D) She is writing a story.

53. Which answer *best* describes the White Rabbit?

(A) He is wearing a wrist-watch and hat.

(B) He talks and is wearing a hat.

(C) He is wearing a hat and a wrist-watch.

(D) He talks and wears clothing.

54. Why doesn't Alice think that seeing the White Rabbit talk is unusual?

(A) All the rabbits that Alice sees talk to her.

(B) Because he is skipping at the same time.

(C) Because she is dreaming.

(D) Because he is running across the field.

GO TO NEXT PAGE

DIRECTIONS: Refer to the passage below to answer the following questions.

Excerpt from *Myths of the Norsemen*
by H. A. Guerber (1859–1929)

Some editing was done to this text to make it more readable for students.

The Creation of Man

1   Although the gods had from the beginning designed Midgard, what is known as "Earth," as the abode of man, there were at first no human beings to inhabit it. One day Odin, Vili, and Ve, according to some authorities, started out together and walked along the seashore, where they found two trees, the ash, Ask, and the elm, Embla, hewn into rude semblances of the human

5   form. The gods gazed at first upon the inanimate wood in silent wonder; then, perceiving the use it could be put to, Odin gave these logs souls, Vili bestowed motion and senses, and Vi contributed blood and blooming complexions.

     Thus endowed with speech and thought, and with power to love and to hope and to work, and with life and death, the newly created man and woman were left to rule Midgard at will.

10   They gradually peopled it with their descendants, while the gods, remembering they had called them into life, took a special interest in all they did, watched over them, and often gave them their aid and protection.

55. In line 4, the word "hewn is most likely to mean?

(A) Wet

(B) Dry

(C) Sandy

(D) Carved

56. Who are Odin, Vili, and Ve?

(A) Humans

(B) Pre-humans

(C) Animals

(D) Gods

57. What items didn't Odin, Vili, and Ve give to the new humans?

(A) Love

(B) Hatred

(C) Hope

(D) Ability to work

58. The gods treat the humans like

(A) their children.

(B) their pets.

(C) their enemies.

(D) their teachers.

GO TO NEXT PAGE ➡

DIRECTIONS: Refer to the following chart to answer the questions below.

Faculty and student familiarity with the below information will help to prevent many violations of academic integrity. However, for faculty members who suspect academic dishonesty among their students, and for students who find themselves *charged* with academic dishonesty, the following flow-chart lays out the official College Academic Integrity procedure.

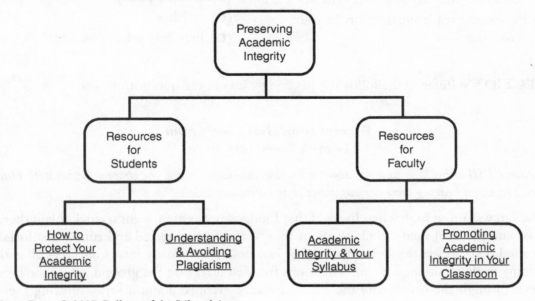

Source: Penn State, © 2007 College of the Liberal Arts

59. The words "academic integrity" most likely mean

(A) everything in school stays the same.

(B) schools reach for the highest limits possible.

(C) students should be honest in their studies.

(D) teachers should grade students quickly.

60. In preserving academic integrity, how many resource groups does this flow chart supply to the readers?

(A) 2

(B) 3

(C) 4

(D) 5

61. What option should faculty refer to when charged with academic dishonesty?

(A) Understanding and avoiding plagiarism

(B) Promoting academic integrity and how to protect it

(C) Protecting academic integrity and plagiarism

(D) Promoting academic integrity in the classroom

62. According to the flow chart, students should understand and avoid which element of academic dishonesty?

(A) The syllabus

(B) Resources

(C) Plagiarism

(D) Preservation

GO TO NEXT PAGE

63. If a faculty member thought that a student was worried about being accused of cheating on a test, which is the best area the teacher should refer the student?

(A) How to protect your academic integrity

(B) Understanding and avoiding plagiarism

(C) Academic integrity and your syllabus

(D) Promoting academic integrity in your classroom

64. If a student was concerned that a teacher misrepresented his/her class or that the class materials or books were not correctly stated, the student would be the most concerned about the teacher's

(A) classroom experience.

(B) grading policy.

(C) syllabus.

(D) literature selections.

DIRECTIONS: Refer to the following passage to answer the questions below.

Excerpt from *Huckleberry Finn*
by Mark Twain (1835–1910)

From Chapter VIII of his famous novel about a boy and an escaped slave, the chapter begins with Huck sleeping under a tree and hearing some curious noises in the distance.

The sun was up so high when I waked that I judged it was after eight o'clock. I laid there in the grass and the cool shade thinking about things, and feeling rested and ruther comfortable and satisfied. I could see the sun out at one or two holes, but mostly it was big trees all about, and gloomy in there amongst them. There was freckled places on the ground where the light sifted
5   down through the leaves, and the freckled places swapped about a little, showing there was a little breeze up there. A couple of squirrels set on a limb and jabbered at me very friendly.

I was powerful lazy and comfortable—didn't want to get up and cook breakfast. Well, I was dozing off again when I thinks I hears a deep sound of "boom!" away up the river. I rouses up, and rests on my elbow and listens; pretty soon I hears it again. I hopped up, and went and
10   looked out at a hole in the leaves, and I see a bunch of smoke laying on the water a long ways up—about abreast the ferry. And there was the ferryboat full of people floating along down. I knowed what was the matter now. "Boom!" I see the white smoke squirt out of the ferryboat's side. You see, they was firing cannon over the water, trying to make my carcass come to the top.

65. What is the setting most like in the selection?

(A) Rocky and hard

(B) Green and cool

(C) Desert and hot

(D) Snowy and cold

66. What does the word "jabbered" in line 6 best mean?

(A) Whispered

(B) Cried

(C) Talked

(D) Defined

67. In the selection, the author purposefully misspells words such as "ruther" in line 2 and "knowed" in line 12. What is this an example of in writing?

(A) Characterization

(B) Metaphor

(C) Personification

(D) Irony

GO TO NEXT PAGE

68. In line 4, the text says that "there was freckled places on the ground." What would best represent the word "freckled"?

(A) Skin with spots on it

(B) A lamppost

(C) Moonlight on the ground

(D) Sunshine shining through the leaves

69. The word "boom" in lines 8 and 12 is an example of

(A) Irony.

(B) Voice.

(C) Onomatopoeia.

(D) Hyperbole.

70. What could best explain why the people on the ferryboat want to make Huck's "carcass" rise to the top of the water?

(A) They think he is dead and want to recover his body.

(B) They think he stole some money, hid it in the water, and hope to see it float.

(C) They think that his pet dog was drowned in the river.

(D) They think that his hidden boat will come to the surface once they fire cannons over it.

71. What word would best describe Huck's mood?

(A) Pensive

(B) Overwhelmed

(C) Relaxed

(D) Scared

DIRECTIONS: Refer to the following recipe to answer the questions below.

Deviled Eggs

Ingredients

- 6 hard-boiled eggs
- 2 tablespoons minced sweet onion
- 2 teaspoons sweet pickle relish, minced
- 2 tablespoons mayonnaise
- 2 teaspoons creamed horseradish sauce (found in deli section)
- 2 teaspoons yellow mustard
- Salt to taste
- Garnishes: paprika, olives, chives, parsley, and/or pimento

Directions

1. Slice hard-boiled eggs in half lengthwise. Remove egg yolks to a bowl, and set egg whites aside.
2. Mash the egg yolks until crumbly. Add sweet onion, pickle relish, mayonnaise, creamed horseradish sauce, mustard, and salt to taste. Mix until well-combined.
3. Pipe or spoon into egg white halves. Garnish with paprika, olives, chives, parsley, and/or pimento. Chill before serving. Makes 12 servings.

GO TO NEXT PAGE

72. If people ate two servings of the above recipe, how many eggs would they eat?

    (A) ½ an egg

    (B) 1 egg

    (C) 1 and ½ eggs

    (D) 2 eggs

73. Why should the eggs be hardboiled?

    (A) So the yolks will be runny

    (B) So the egg white will be runny

    (C) So the yolks will be firm

    (D) So they are easier to handle

74. The word "garnish" best means

    (A) essentials.

    (B) decoration.

    (C) important.

    (D) core ingredient.

75. Why should the horseradish be creamed instead of whole horseradish?

    (A) Creamed tastes better

    (B) Creamed is cheaper

    (C) Creamed is easier to find in the market

    (D) Creamed would blend easier

76. What does the phrase "salt to taste" best mean?

    (A) Taste the salt first

    (B) Salt is tasty

    (C) Salt as preferred by the chef

    (D) Salt as the author prefers

77. Why are the eggs the first ingredient on the list?

    (A) They are the most important.

    (B) They are the least important.

    (C) They are used first.

    (D) It doesn't matter that they are listed first.

DIRECTIONS: Refer to the following text to answer the questions below.

Sonnet 130
by William Shakespeare (1564–1616)

My mistress' eyes are nothing like the sun,
Coral is far more red, than her lips red,
If snow be white, why then her breasts are dun:
If hairs be wires, black wires grow on her head:
5   I have seen roses damasked, red and white,
But no such roses see I in her cheeks,
And in some perfumes is there more delight,
Than in the breath that from my mistress reeks.
I love to hear her speak, yet well I know,
10   That music hath a far more pleasing sound:
I grant I never saw a goddess go,
My mistress when she walks treads on the ground.
And yet by heaven I think my love as rare,
As any she belied with false compare.

GO TO NEXT PAGE

78. The best word to describe the woman in the sonnet is
(A) ugly.
(B) unhappy.
(C) beautiful.
(D) scared.

79. In line 3, the word "dun" mostly likely means
(A) white.
(B) dirty.
(C) red.
(D) bruised.

80. In line 4, Shakespeare writes, "If hairs be wires, black wires grow on her head." The element of figurative used in this line is
(A) simile.
(B) metaphor.
(C) personification.
(D) hyperbole.

81. In the last line, the word "belied" most likely means
(A) misrepresented.
(B) same.
(C) blushed.
(D) believed.

82. What is the best meaning of "with false compare" in the last line?
(A) Contradictions
(B) Truths
(C) Ridiculous comparisons
(D) Special

83. In line 13, the word "rare" most likely means
(A) special.
(B) underdone.
(C) coarsely made.
(D) finished.

84. In line 6, Shakespeare writes, "But no such roses see I in her cheeks." What word best describes "roses."
(A) Flowers
(B) Blush
(C) Rash
(D) Sunburn

GO TO NEXT PAGE ➡

PRACTICE TEST 1
MATHEMATICS SECTION

1. Evaluate: 7.9×10^2

(A) .079　　　　(C) 790

(B) 79　　　　　(D) 7,900

2. Simplify: $\dfrac{2!}{3!}$

(A) $\dfrac{1}{3}$　　　　(C) $\dfrac{1}{4}$

(B) .67　　　　(D) 9

3. A businesswoman takes a taxi ride. She likes to tip 20% when the service is excellent. How much money will she tip on a $30 fare?

(A) $4.50　　　(C) $6.75

(B) $6.00　　　(D) $7.00

4. A bag contains 4 black marbles and 16 white marbles. What is the ratio of the number of black marbles to the total number of marbles?

(A) 1:2　　　　(C) 1:4

(B) 2:3　　　　(D) 1:5

5. Which of the following points lies on the line expressed by the equation $4x - 2y = 10$?

(A) (1, 4)　　　(C) (3, 1)

(B) (2, 3)　　　(D) (6, 1)

6. The points (1, 1), (1, 4), (4, 1), (4, 4) are the vertices of a polygon. What type of polygon is formed by these points?

(A) Triangle　　　(C) Parallelogram

(B) Square　　　　(D) Trapezoid

7. Simplify: $\dfrac{42x^4 y^6}{6xy^2}$

(A) $7x^3 y$　　　　(C) $7x^3 y^4$

(B) $7xy^6$　　　　(D) $7xy^6$

8. What is the next number in this sequence: 100, 90, 95, 85, 90, 80, _____?

(A) 75　　　　(C) 85

(B) 80　　　　(D) 90

9. Baseball caps regularly cost $32. They are on sale for 25% off. What is the sale price of the baseball caps?

(A) $24　　　　(C) $28

(B) $26　　　　(D) $30

GO TO NEXT PAGE ➡

10. What is the slope of the line below?

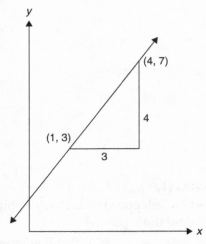

(A) $-\dfrac{3}{4}$ (C) $\dfrac{3}{4}$

(B) $\dfrac{4}{3}$ (D) $-\dfrac{4}{3}$

11. The fraction $\dfrac{6}{18}$ is equal to which value?

(A) $\dfrac{1}{3}$ (C) $\dfrac{3}{6}$

(B) .38   (D) .25

12. Estimate: 185×312

(A) 600   (C) 60,000

(B) 6,000   (D) 600,000

13. What is the equation of the line shown on the graph?

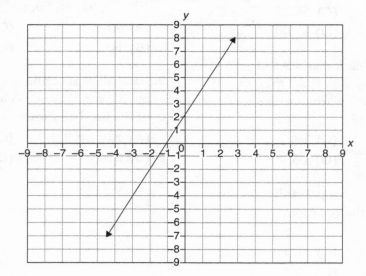

(A) $y = 2x + 2$ (C) $y = \dfrac{1}{2}x - 2$

(B) $y = 2x - 2$ (D) $y = \dfrac{1}{2}x + 2$

GO TO NEXT PAGE ➡

14. If $x = 6$ and $y = 9$, then $\dfrac{xy - 6}{3} + 4 =$

(A) 8   (C) 17
(B) 10   (D) 20

15. What is the absolute value of -5?

(A) $-\dfrac{1}{5}$ (C) $\dfrac{1}{5}$

(B) 5   (D) -5

16. Five cards are shown: a heart, a diamond, a moon, a sun, and a lightning bolt. If you randomly select a single card, what is the probability that it is *not* a heart?

(A) .75   (C) .85
(B) .80   (D) .90

17. Green Taxi Company used the data in the following table to support its claim, "We have one-fifth the number of customer complaints that Blue Taxi Company has." Why is this claim misleading?

Taxi Company	Customer Complaints	Months in Business
Blue Taxi	100	25
Green Taxi	20	4

(A) On the average, Blue Taxi has more complaints.

(B) The claim should say "one-fourth" of the number of complaints.

(C) The claim should say "one-tenth" of the number of complaints.

(D) On the average, Green Taxi has more complaints *per month*.

18. How many different ways can you order 4 books on a shelf where order matters?

(A) 6   (C) 24
(B) 12   (D) 36

GO TO NEXT PAGE ➡

19. Solve for x: $5x + 2 = 6$

(A) $\dfrac{1}{4}$ (C) $\dfrac{2}{3}$

(B) $\dfrac{1}{2}$ (D) $\dfrac{4}{5}$

20. What is the solution set to the following system of equations?

$$y = \begin{cases} 5x - 3 \\ 4x \end{cases}$$

(A) $(2, 7)$ (C) $(4, 17)$

(B) $(3, 12)$ (D) $(5, 22)$

21. Given the following similar figures of a rectangle, find the length of the missing side.

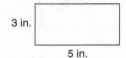

3 in.

5 in.   ?   20 in.

(A) 6 inches   (C) 10 inches
(B) 9 inches   (D) 12 inches

22. What is the slope of a line containing the points $(1, 8)$ and $(10, 2)$?

(A) -3 (C) $\dfrac{2}{3}$

(B) $\dfrac{-2}{3}$ (D) 3

23. Evaluate:

$$2a^2 + \frac{5b}{2} - 8 \quad \text{for} \quad a = -4 \quad \text{and} \quad b = 2$$

(A) -12 (C) 29
(B) 5 (D) 32

24. Solve for x: $\dfrac{x}{6} + 9 = 13$

(A) 24 (C) 36
(B) 32 (D) 42

25. The graph shows the relationship between the number of CDs purchased and the total cost. What is the price of each CD?

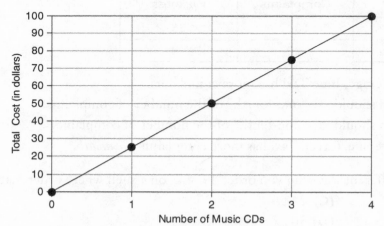

(A) $20.00   (C) $27.50
(B) $25.00   (D) $30.00

GO TO NEXT PAGE ➡

26. What expression does the following graph represnt?

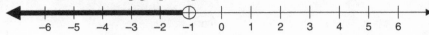

(A) $x > -1$ (C) $x < -1$

(B) $x \geq -1$ (D) $x \leq -1$

27. Write the following as an algebraic expression:

Eight more than five times a number

(A) $8x$ (C) $8x + 5$

(B) $8(5x)$ (D) $5x + 8$

28. The following chart shows the English test scores of three students. What was Paul's average score?

	Test 1	Test 2	Test 3	Test 4
Peter	10	7	5	4
Paul	3	6	9	10
Mary	9	8	10	5

(A) 7   (C) 9

(B) 8   (D) 10

29. A fair coin is flipped three times. What is the probability of getting three heads?

(A) $\dfrac{1}{2}$ (C) $\dfrac{1}{8}$

(B) $\dfrac{1}{4}$ (D) $\dfrac{1}{16}$

30. Which is the graph of the equation $y = x$?

(A)

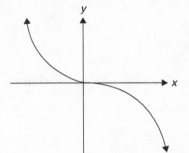

(B)

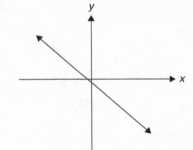

(C)

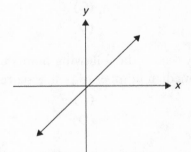

(D)

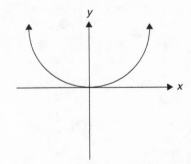

GO TO NEXT PAGE

31. Given the following triangle, what is the measurement of the missing angle?

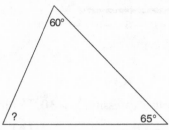

(A) 30°   (C) 55°
(B) 45°   (D) 60°

32. What is the value of *x* in the triangle shown?

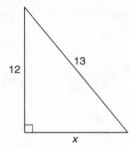

(A) 3   (C) 5
(B) 4   (D) 6

33. A purse contains four different coins. How many different combinations of two coins can you choose, where order does *not* matter?

(A) 3   (C) 6
(B) 4   (D) 9

34. Tiffany scored the following points in her high school basketball games: 8, 2, 5, 9, 0, 4, 7. What is her median number of points scored?

(A) 2   (C) 7
(B) 5   (D) 9

35. A die has six sides. What is the probability of rolling a 3, 4, or 5 in one throw of a fair die?

(A) $\dfrac{1}{6}$ (C) $\dfrac{1}{2}$

(B) $\dfrac{1}{3}$ (D) $\dfrac{2}{3}$

GO TO NEXT PAGE ➡

36. On one roll of two fair dice, what is the probability that they equal 12?

(A) $\dfrac{1}{36}$ (C) $\dfrac{1}{12}$

(B) $\dfrac{1}{24}$ (D) $\dfrac{1}{6}$

37. In the figure, l_1 is parallel to l_2. If $\angle q$ is equal to 60°, what does $\angle p$ equal?

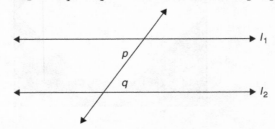

(A) 30°   (C) 60°
(B) 40°   (D) 120°

38. The scaled drawing of a volleyball court shown below is drawn using the scale 1 centimeter is equal to 2 meters. What is the area of the volleyball court in square meters?

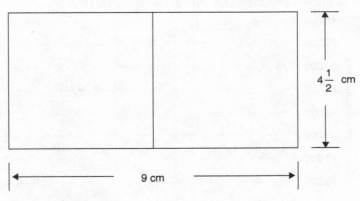

(A) 40.5   (C) 162
(B) 81   (D) 205

GO TO NEXT PAGE

39. What is the area of the *unshaded* region in the figure shown?

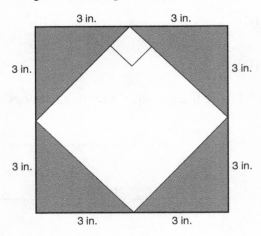

(A) 4.5 in²   (C) 18 in²

(B) 9 in²   (D) 32 in²

40. The following graph shows the number of apples produced by a grower in Washington for the years 1995, 1997, and 1999. Based on the data in the graph, which of the following was the most probable number of apples produced by this grower in 2001?

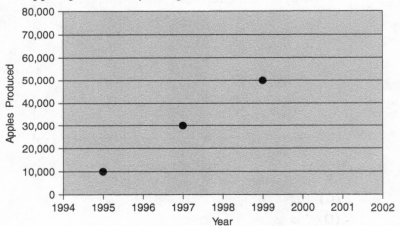

(A) 50,000   (C) 70,000

(B) 60,000   (D) 80,000

GO TO NEXT PAGE ➡

41. Which of the following ΔA'B'C' is the image of triangle ABC that results from reflecting the triangle ABC across the *x*-axis?

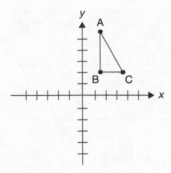

(A)

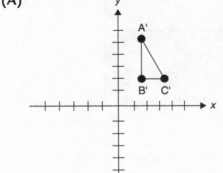

(C)

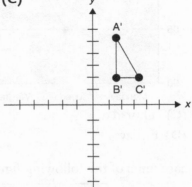

(B)

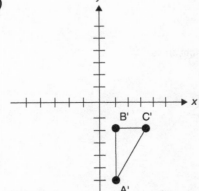

(D)

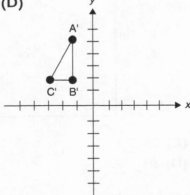

GO TO NEXT PAGE ➡

42. The following graph represents the high temperature for five days of the week. Which day had the smallest change in temperature from that of the previous day?

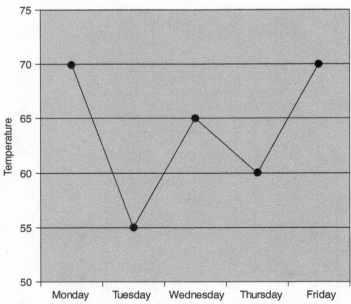

(A) Tuesday   (C) Thursday

(B) Wednesday   (D) Friday

43. What is the area in square units of the following figure?

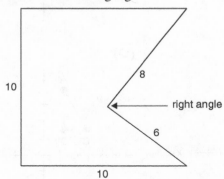

(A) 48   (C) 76

(B) 72   (D) 80

44. In a certain class, the number of boys, b, is equal to three times the number of girls, g. Which of the following equations expresses this relationship?

(A) $3 \times b = g$ (C) $g \times b = 3$

(B) $3 \times b = g \times b$ (D) $3 \times g = b$

45. Simplify: $20 + 9 \div 3$

(A) 23   (C) 26

(B) 7   (D) 9

GO TO NEXT PAGE ➡

46. A rectangular duck pond is on a square lot. The rest of the lot is a flower garden. In the scaled drawing below, each unit represents 10 feet. How many square feet is the flower garden?

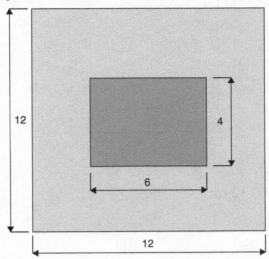

(A) 7,200   (C) 12,000

(B) 8,500   (D) 14,400

47. Approximately how many inches is the circumference of the following circle?

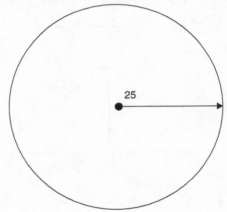

(A) 27   (C) 225

(B) 160   (D) 1,875

GO TO NEXT PAGE ➡

48. What is the length of the missing side in the following right triangle?

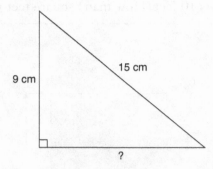

(A) 6 cm   (C) 9 cm

(B) 8 cm   (D) 12 cm

49. What is $\dfrac{\text{the area of } A}{\text{the area of } B}$?

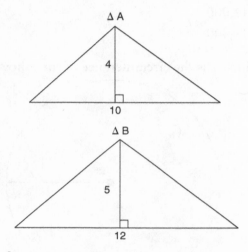

(A) $\dfrac{1}{8}$ (C) $\dfrac{2}{3}$

(B) $\dfrac{1}{4}$ (D) $\dfrac{4}{5}$

GO TO NEXT PAGE ➡

50. Given the similar figures of a rectangle below, find the length of the missing side.

4 feet

5 feet

?

10 feet

(A) 8 feet   (C) 10 feet

(B) 9 feet   (D) 11 feet

STOP

Practice Test 1 Answer Key

Question Number	Correct Answer
ENGLISH-LANGUAGE ARTS SECTION: LANGUAGE SUBTEST	
1.	(B)
2.	(A)
3.	(B)
4.	(A)
5.	(C)
6.	(D)
7.	(A)
8.	(B)
9.	(C)
10.	(A)
11.	(B)
12.	(C)
13.	(B)
14.	(C)
15.	(C)
16.	(C)
17.	(A)
18.	(C)
19.	(A)
20.	(C)

Question Number	Correct Answer
21.	(D)
22.	(C)
23.	(B)
24.	(A)
25.	(B)
26.	(C)
27.	(A)
28.	(C)
29.	(A)
30.	(D)
31.	(B)
32.	(A)
33.	(B)
34.	(C)
35.	(B)
36.	(D)
37.	(D)
38.	(C)
39.	(A)
40.	(A)
41.	(C)
42.	(B)
43.	(B)
44.	(B)
45.	(B)
46.	(A)
47.	(A)
48.	(B)
ENGLISH-LANGUAGE ARTS SECTION: READING SUBTEST	
1.	(C)
2.	(A)
3.	(B)
4.	(A)
5.	(B)

Question Number	Correct Answer
6.	(D)
7.	(C)
8.	(A)
9.	(C)
10.	(B)
11.	(D)
12.	(C)
13.	(D)
14.	(B)
15.	(C)
16.	(A)
17.	(A)
18.	(C)
19.	(B)
20.	(A)
21.	(A)
22.	(A)
23.	(A)
24.	(B)
25.	(A)
26.	(B)
27.	(B)
28.	(A)
29.	(D)
30.	(B)
31.	(B)
32.	(A)
33.	(A)
34.	(C)
35.	(B)
36.	(D)
37.	(A)
38.	(C)
39.	(A)
40.	(B)

Question Number	Correct Answer
41.	(C)
42.	(A)
43.	(B)
44.	(D)
45.	(C)
46.	(A)
47.	(D)
48.	(B)
49.	(C)
50.	(D)
51.	(A)
52.	(C)
53.	(D)
54.	(C)
55.	(D)
56.	(D)
57.	(B)
58.	(A)
59.	(C)
60.	(A)
61.	(D)
62.	(C)
63.	(A)
64.	(C)
65.	(B)
66.	(C)
67.	(A)
68.	(D)
69.	(C)
70.	(A)
71.	(C)
72.	(B)
73.	(C)
74.	(B)
75.	(D)
76.	(C)

Question Number	Correct Answer
77.	(C)
78.	(A)
79.	(B)
80.	(B)
81.	(A)
82.	(C)
83.	(A)
84.	(B)
MATHEMATICS SECTION	
1.	(C)
2.	(A)
3.	(B)
4.	(D)
5.	(C)
6.	(B)
7.	(C)
8.	(C)
9.	(A)
10.	(B)
11.	(A)
12.	(C)
13.	(A)
14.	(D)
15.	(B)
16.	(B)
17.	(D)
18.	(C)
19.	(D)
20.	(B)
21.	(D)
22.	(B)
23.	(C)
24.	(A)
25.	(B)
26.	(C)
27.	(D)

PRACTICE TEST 1 ANSWER KEY

Question Number	Correct Answer
28.	(A)
29.	(C)
30.	(C)
31.	(C)
32.	(C)
33.	(C)
34.	(B)
35.	(C)
36.	(A)
37.	(C)
38.	(C)
39.	(C)
40.	(C)
41.	(B)
42.	(C)
43.	(C)
44.	(D)
45.	(A)
46.	(C)
47.	(B)
48.	(D)
49.	(C)
50.	(A)

PRACTICE TEST 1 DETAILED EXPLANATIONS

PRACTICE TEST 1 DETAILED EXPLANATIONS
ENGLISH-LANGUAGE ARTS SECTION
Language Subtest

1. **(B)** its

   In this case "its" is the correct answer because "it" is the horse and it "possesses" a tail. Therefore, the answer must be in the possessive, which is "its." Don't be confused with "it's"! "It's" is a contraction for "it is."

2. **(A)** I

   "I" is the best answer because the rest of the sentence is implied to the reader. For example, "No one has a blue car except I" implies the finish word "*do.*" So the entire sentence is actually "No one has a blue car except I *do.*" Because "I" is the only correct pronoun as a first person singular subject (the subject of "do"), it is the only correct answer.

3. **(B)** book he will want

   This sentence has two verbs: "has" and "wants." Because this is incorrect, the next step is to look at the tense of the sentence. "Joe ordered a book for his birthday next month" shows the reader that Joe's birthday hasn't arrived yet; therefore, the future tense verb is the best choice.

4. **(A)** The game was almost over; she was tired.

   Knowledge of semicolons and colons is important for this sentence. The given sentence is a run-on: two complete thoughts shoved together without correct punctuation. A semicolon can act as a conjunction, and there is no capitalization of the next word after the semi-colon. **(B)** inserts a random comma in the middle of the sentence, between the subject and the verb. Finally, **(C)** capitalizes "she," which is incorrect form.

5. **(C)** the tallest student

   In this sentence, the information "the whole class" is important to choosing the correct answer. The comparative form (when comparing only two things) uses an "-er" ending. For example "This glass is bigger than that one," the superlative form compares one thing to many and has the "-est" ending. In the given sentence, Jordan is compared to more than one person. Therefore, he is the "tallest," not the "taller," student.

6. **(D)** Correct as is.
   This sentence is correct because the tense matches the verb used in the sentence. The first phrase, "when I finish chopping the vegetables," shows something that is happening now. The second part of the sentence, "I will cook the shrimp," shows what will happen in the future after the present task is completed. The other examples show verb inaccuracies.

7. **(A)** and I
   (A) is correct because "I" is the only first-person, singular pronoun that can be used as part of a subject. If you get confused, take out the other subject (Jason in this sentence) and just read through the answers. It sounds correct to say, "I have the most baseball cards," while it sounds odd to say, "Mine have the best baseball cards" or "Myself have the best baseball cards" or "Me have the best baseball cards."

8. **(B)** To go walking
   Though this isn't the best-constructed sentence, you will see examples like this one on the test. The infinitive "to go" is a verb phrase and should not be confused with the active verb "go." Recognizing that "to go" is an infinitive is important because infinitives are always written with the present tense singular form of a verb with "to" in front of it. Infinitives are considered the core element of any verb. Examples of infinitives are "to eat," "to swim," "to sing," "to be," and "to write." The entire phrase is considered one part of speech. We know this is an infinitive because you could remove it from the sentence and it would still make sense. The sentence "Walking in the woods is a wonderful thing" is a complete thought. It has a subject and a verb; therefore, "goes" isn't an essential part to the sentence. Knowing this information, the words "to goes" doesn't make sense. The correct choice could only be "to go."

9. **(C)** The boy said, "I will get the car and wash it."
   The comma always goes after the verb and before the quotation marks when a sentence is set up in this way. The end punctuation goes inside the last quotation mark to finish the complete thought.

10. **(A)** their
    "They're" is a contraction for "they are," which would not make sense in this sentence. "There are" and "there" are not the correct answers because "there" is not the correct pronoun as it is not a possessive.

11. **(B)** be more careful
    "Carefuller" is not a word so this sentence is incorrect. If you chose **(C)**, the infinitive would be "to being"; we know that is not correct since infinitives can only take one form (see answer 8). Finally, because "careful" is more than one syllable, it is incorrect to add the "-er" ending to it. Instead, add "more" for comparative and "most" for the superlative.

12. **(C)** fewer
    This answer can be a little tricky. "Lesser" means "not as important as something else." It does not mean less in number. "Least" is incorrect because it is the superlative form of "less than" and only two items are compared in this sentence. "Fewer," in this case, is the correct answer.

13. **(B)** The Empire State Building
    All of the words must be capitalized in this example because "Empire State Building" is one proper noun. "The" is at the beginning of the sentence, so we know that has to be capitalized.

14. **(C)** recycle
    Subject-verb agreement questions are peppered throughout the test. In this example, "people" is the subject. "People" is plural; therefore, it takes a plural verb. In this case, "recycle" is the only correct choice.

15. **(C)** potatoes, corn, oranges, grapes, and bread at the market
    Comma placement is tested in this sentence. Anytime there is a list, be sure to add a comma after all the separate items *and* include a comma before the last "and" in the list. **(A)** includes a comma *after* the last "and" which is incorrect.

16. **(C)** "Okay, Robert. You can let the guests in now," said his mom.
    Anytime there is more that one quote together, you only need one set of quotation marks. Having each sentence separated by quotation marks indicates a change in speaker, so if the same speaker is making a statement, only one set is needed to be correct. Remember, when a sentence is presented with the quote(s) first, add the comma before the last quotation mark, keeping the following verb in lowercase.

17. **(A)** we can
    "Are" is the wrong verb for this sentence. Choices **(B)** and **(C)** imply time in the past. "Can" is the only correct choice.

18. **(C)** The Golden Gate Bridge
    All of the words must be capitalized in this example because "Golden Gate Bridge" is one proper noun. "The" is at the beginning of the sentence, so we know that has to be capitalized.

19. **(A)** The show was predicted to be a hit.
    The given "sentence" isn't a sentence at all. There is only a subject (show), but there is no verb as "predicted" is not in the correct form. The comma breaks this into two fragments. A helping verb must be added to "predicted" for the sentence to make sense, and the comma must be removed.

20. **(C)** wrote on
    The given "sentence" isn't a sentence at all. There is only a subject (teacher), but there is no verb as "writing" is not in the correct form. The comma breaks this into two fragments. "Writing" must be in a different tense, specifically the simple present tense. Therefore, **(C)** is the only correct choice.

21. (D) Correct as is.

This sentence is correct because there is correct subject-verb agreement and the verb tense is correct in the sentence. The other choices do not present correct tense: "was play" and "will playing" are not correct verb forms and "was played" is not in the correct tense for this sentence.

22. (C) curious

"Curiosity" is an abstract noun. "Are known" is a linking verb. Linking verbs are unusual because they describe the "state-of-being." Verbs that apply to the five senses are generally linking verbs. Predicate adjectives are descriptive words that complement the subject. The best way to see if they fit is to flip around the subject and the predicate adjective to see if it could work as a sentence.

For example:

She is hot.

Hot is she.

Though the second sentence is unlikely, it does work as a complete thought. Predicate nominatives are nouns that follow state-of-being verbs. They cannot be switched around. For example:

Michael is a teacher.

Teacher is a Michael.

This, obviously, does not work.

So, in this sentence, "to know" is a linking verb ("are known" in this sentence). "Curiosity" doesn't work because if you flipped it around, it wouldn't make sense:

Curiosity are known to be dolphins.

Therefore, you know that it must have an adjective: "curious."

23. (B) its

Pronoun agreement is tested in this question. The grocery store is a thing; consequently, the correct pronoun would be "it." Because it is a possessive pronoun in this sentence, "its" is the correct choice. Remember that "it's" is a contraction for "it is" and would not make sense in this sentence.

24. (A) was grazing

This question tests simple verb tense. Because "cow" is the subject, the correct past tense verb here would be "was grazing." This verb shows an action that was happening yesterday. The other choices either need helping verbs **(B)** or are completely incorrect **(C)**.

25. (B) needed

This question tests simple verb tense. Because "carpenter" is the subject, the correct past tense verb here would be "needed." This verb shows an action that was happening in the past because the word "yesterday" begins the sentence, thus setting the tense.

26. (C) placed

The given "sentence" isn't a sentence at all. There is only a subject (apples), but there is no verb as "are placing" is not in the correct form. "Are placing" must be in a different tense, specifically past plural tense. Therefore, **(C)** is the only correct choice.

27. **(A)** I didn't know where I was going.

It is grammatically incorrect (though commonly used) to end a sentence with a preposition, specifically when the "to" is acting like an adverb. It is correct to either leave the "to" off the sentence or create a prepositional phrase to finish the sentence.

28. **(C)** frosted

In this sentence, the prepositional phrase at the beginning gives a clue that the action in the main part of the sentence will happen after the beginning part. Therefore, the best choice is the past tense verb "frosted." **(A)** is completely incorrect and isn't a valid choice because "did frost" would be correct, but still would not fit in this sentence. **(B)** is in the future tense, which also does not fit the given statement.

29. **(A)** smallest

In this sentence, the information "four girls" is important to choosing the correct answer. The comparative form (when comparing only two things) uses an "-er" ending. For example, "This glass is bigger than that one." The superlative form compares one thing to many and has the "-est" ending. In the given sentence, Missy is compared to more than one person. Therefore, she is the "smallest," not the "smaller," girl.

30. **(D)** Correct as is.

This sentence can be a bit tricky. "Whenever" is a word that tells time and in this sentence the single subject "I" takes the singular present tense verb "go." In the second part of the sentence, we see that there is another subject ("I") and another verb ("buy"). These are also singular and in the present tense. Therefore, the other choices are incorrect because "went" in **(A)** is past tense. In **(B)**, "went" is past tense, and in **(C)**, "did go" is also in past tense (and it has an unneeded helping verb).

31. **(B)** Some flowers arranged in the vase smell very sweet.

"Arranging in the vase" is incorrect because "arranging" is acting like a verb; therefore, it would need to have a helping verb in front of it to make sense. Though all of the choices aren't perfect, **(B)** is the best choice because there is correct subject/verb agreement and correct verb tense in the sentence, making it understandable.

32. **(A)** "Driving on this road is challenging," said Bobby.

When a sentence is presented with the quote(s) first, add the comma before the last quotation mark, keeping the following verb in lowercase.

33. **(B)** The food critic gave the restaurant a glowing review in the article yesterday.

"Gives" is the problem in this sentence. The subject of the sentence is "critic." Since "critic" is singular, the verb must be singular as well, but the sentence is in past tense. "Gives" is singular present tense, while "gave" is singular past tense. Be careful to read through the entire sentence to make your selection, as "yesterday" was the last word and could have been easily overlooked.

34. **(C)** He and I
    (C) is correct because "I" is the only first-person, singular pronoun that can be used as part of a subject. If you get confused, take out or use the other subject by itself ("he" in this sentence) and just read through the answers. It sounds correct to say, "I will clean up the mess" and "He will clean up the mess," while it sounds odd to say, "Him will clean up the mess," "Myself will clean up the mess," and "Me will clean up the mess."

35. **(B)** the Grand Canyon
    All of the words must be capitalized in this example because "Grand Canyon" is one proper noun. "The" is not at the beginning of the sentence; therefore, it is not capitalized.

36. **(D)** Correct as is.
    Semicolons are tested in this question. Remember that semicolons can be used in place of a conjunction and the sentence will still make sense. In **(A)**, there is no punctuation, which creates a run-on sentence. In **(B)**, there is only a comma, which creates a comma splice, a type of run-on sentence. In **(C)**, there is a semicolon, but "she" is capitalized, making the choice incorrect.

37. **(D)** for them self's
    The correct way to make this word plural is to spell it "themselves." The other parts of the sentence are grammatically correct.

38. **(C)** brake
    "Brake" in this sentence is spelled in its other form, meaning to stop. The correct form in this sentence is "break," meaning to separate.

39. **(A)** to scares
    Both words in this phrase are incorrect for the sentence. "To" is spelled in prepositional form. The correct form should be "too," meaning "more than wanted or needed." Additionally, "scares" in this sentence should be "scared." The helping verb "are" takes the past tense form of the verb. You wouldn't write "are scares"; it doesn't make sense.

40. **(A)** They are too scared to be their own persons, and they are told the way to live.
    In this example, you have to blend the two sentences together and fix any errors you see along the way. **(A)** is the best choice because the "too" is fixed, and there is a conjunction and a comma separating the two independent clauses, making the sentence grammatically correct. **(B)** may look to be a good choice, but the pronouns are mismatched: "they" is plural, while "he" is singular. **(C)** does not use the correct verb tense for the singular subject "he." **(D)** has an added conjunction where one is not needed, making the sentence grammatically incorrect.

41. **(C)** They don't have decisions; they are told how to do everything.
    The given example is a run-on sentence, with two sentences together with no separating punctuation. Since a semicolon can act like a conjunction and a comma, **(C)** is the best choice. Just inserting a comma, like in example **(A)**, creates a comma splice, a different type of run-on sentence. In **(D)**, the "=" sign is obviously incorrect. This symbol is only used in mathematics or note taking. In **(B)**, a dash is used to separate the clauses. A dash is used like a super comma; it is used to set off information as if it were in a set of parentheses.

42. **(B)** Their lives depend on what the media and what other people say.
In this sentence, the only error is the use of "their." "Their" is a possessive adjective and is the correct choice for this sentence. The example uses "there," which is a pronoun that means a place. In **(C)**, "they're" is a contraction for "they are," which would not make sense in the rest of the sentence. Choice **(D)** exhibits this inaccuracy as well.

43. **(B)** Is concerned
This type of sentence is commonly used in testing. The subject is "teachers," which is plural so it would have to have a plural verb. "Is concerned" is singular. The other elements of the sentence are correct.

44. **(B)** who cared and educated children
This is a tricky sentence. The beginning part of the sentence talks about sports stars and actors and then it switches to what teachers do for children. The verbs, therefore, should be the same tense because they are occurring at the same time. "Make" is present tense and "cared" and "educated" are past tense. For the sentence to be correct, "cared" and "educated" would need to be in the present tense.

45. **(B)** stated "My
In this sentence, for the above answer to be correct, there would need to be a comma between "stated" and "My." All of the other answers are grammatically correct.

46. **(A)** Consistent
"Consistent" is an adjective. In this sentence, "consistent" is modifying the verb, i.e., *how often* the teachers have to supplement their incomes. Adverbs modify verbs, so the correct form for this sentence would be "consistently." All of the other choices are correct.

47. **(A)** Coupling with late nights
"Coupling," though not often used, is a gerund, or a word that looks like a verb and acts like a noun. In this sentence, a noun doesn't fit in this position. It is not a subject or an object in the sentence. The correct form is "coupled."

48. **(B)** teach position
"Teach" is a verb. It cannot be used as an adjective, like it is in the sentence. "Teaching" is the adjectival form of "teach" and would be the correct form for the sentence. The other answers are grammatically correct.

PRACTICE TEST 1 DETAILED EXPLANATIONS
ENGLISH-LANGUAGE ARTS SECTION
Writing Task

The following is an example of a well-written response to the essay question. This essay would receive a 6 on the Writing Rubric.

When most students think about the beginning of a long school year, there is always one light at the end of the tunnel: summer vacation. After months of difficult homework assignments and never-ending projects, summer gives students the chance to unwind and relax before starting a new school year. Additionally, summer gives students the chance to work summer jobs, earning valuable funds and gaining life experience for the future. Also, summer vacation allows students to travel to various countries and across the United States to do volunteer work and explore other high schools and colleges. All in all, summer vacation is essential for student growth because it affords time to relax after a stressful year, work summer jobs, and travel across the United States and the world.

June, July, and August give students enough time to fully unwind and relax after a stressful year in school. With increased academic expectations and the competitive high school and college application process, many students welcome the opportunity to just simply do nothing. This "recharging" is a fruitful labor as students can approach the next school year rested and ready to work. Everyone, most of all students, needs the chance to rest.

Summer jobs allow students to explore different types of work environments and learn from these new settings. Many companies would not hire a student if there were only a short period of time the student was available to work; rather, most business owners prefer to hire workers who will stay at their jobs for a long period of time. Additionally, many students work at sleep-away camps: most of these camps have month to six-week programs. Finally, lots of students need the summer to earn money for college or high school tuition or outside clubs. Taking this time away from students would make a huge difference to the quality of their high school and college careers.

Lastly, many students use the three months of summer to travel. Volunteer work, wandering the United States, visiting family, and exploring new countries are all important aspects of healthy character development, and having enough time to fully explore and socialize is a building block to one's identity. Indeed, isn't it imperative that the students of today spend time outside their regular communities to learn more about the United States and the world? Is that possible to do in two weeks?

Chopping up summer vacation into smaller vacations may at first appear to be a bright idea, but after analyzing the positives and negatives, one can see that a full vacation is key to balancing out the heavy workload of the school year. Additionally, having the time to learn a new skill, earn funds, travel to a foreign country, volunteer, and visit family is an important aspect of the growing process. Without a doubt, the three-month summer vacation is a traditional opportunity that is rewarding for all students.

PRACTICE TEST 1 DETAILED EXPLANATIONS
ENGLISH-LANGUAGE ARTS SECTION

Reading Subtest

1. **(C)** rough; coarse; harsh

2. **(A)** cheat; defraud

3. **(B)** hidden; undercover

4. **(A)** cause

5. **(B)** storage area for a plane

6. **(D)** complex; difficult to solve

7. **(C)** something subtle

8. **(A)** taking credit for someone else's writing or ideas

9. **(C)** fame

10. **(B)** going off the main subject

11. **(D)** a cartoon

12. **(C)** self-interested

13. **(D)** inventive

14. **(B)** to indulge

15. **(C)** forced to leave

16. **(A)** a government

17. **(A)** absence from work

18. **(C)** to keep under control

19. **(B)** permission

20. **(A)** injury

21. **(A)** a break

22. **(A)** flexibility

23. **(A)** tantrum

24. **(B)** complex

25. **(A)** spinning

26. **(B)** Required amount

27. **(B)** Undecided

28. **(A)** bad-tempered

29. **(D)** uncomplimentary

30. **(B)** serves as a good example

31. **(B)** To act superior
    The author says in line 4 that the only reason why someone would try to speak in big words would be "to show superiority over others." The others answers are directly opposite of this statement.

32. **(A)** 2,000
    The author says that "one-hundredth" of 200,000 words are sufficient for most people. Be careful of numbers! Your eyes may have gone directly to 200,000 because that is the first number in the text.

33. **(A)** Lack of imagination
    In this question, you have to infer what the author means. "Pedantry" is a word used often, and when this happens in questions, you must look at how the word is used in context. The phrase reads "your pedantry and lack of learning." Therefore, lack of imagination is the best answer.

34. **(C)** It is a sign of ignorance to use big words when a simple word works just as well.
    This is a main idea question. The author wants you to realize through his text that using big words isn't really needed when the same, simple words that have been used for decades do the job just fine. He uses the example of a spade to make his point in the piece.

35. **(B)** Words
    This is a metaphor. He is comparing words to friends, and simple words are like old friends; they stick around for a long time and are easily dependable.

36. **(D)** 6
    This is a numbers question. If you have to stir something every 30 seconds for 3 minutes, you would stir it 6 times, or twice a minute times 3 minutes.

37. **(A)** burn
    They use the word "scorch," which means to burn or scald. "Melt" is not strong enough to be a synonym for "scorch."

38. **(C)** poke through
    The author says to "skewer each apple slice with a fork." A fork would poke through the apple. The other choices would not make sense. Use visualization to help you with these types of questions.

39. **(A)** apples

Look at the proportions of the ingredients. The recipe calls for 2 cups of apple slices, while everything else is much less than 2 cups.

40. **(B)** So the chocolate doesn't slide off

This is a logic question. Melted chocolate would be hard to handle on an apple slice if you wanted to eat it with your hands. Putting them in the refrigerator to harden makes them an easier and less messy snack.

41. **(C)** Acts of nature

The warranty is divided into what is covered and what is not covered. "Acts of nature" are in the "not covered" section while the others are in the "covered" section.

42. **(A)** a tornado

In looking at all the choices, a tornado is much more severe than opening, closing, or putting the umbrella in the car. Since the warranty says that "acts of nature" are not covered, we can infer that a tornado would not be covered.

43. **(B)** Photos

The bottom of the warranty states that photos of the umbrella and the box are required for repair.

44. **(D)** Valance

Even if you didn't know the meaning of the word "valance," you could definitely remove some of the answers that you know aren't correct, like "handle" and "crank."

45. **(C)** Using the umbrella during a monsoon

(A) and **(B)** are common uses for an umbrella, and in **(D)**, the user is just keeping it at work, which isn't a stressful environment. Using the umbrella during a monsoon, however, wouldn't be the best decision, and it would probably destroy the umbrella.

46. **(A)** The author

Even if you didn't know that it was the author speaking, you could rule out **(B)** (the farmer who owns the woods) because the speaker says he isn't there. The horse doesn't talk and appears as a separate entity. For **(D)**, there is no unknown villager talked about, so this would not be a good choice.

47. **(D)** Unusual

In line 5, the speaker thinks his horse must think that stopping in the woods on a cold night with no barn nearby is "queer." If you tried each word choice and inferred what you could from the poem, "unusual" is the best choice.

48. **(B)** Why they are stopping in the snow

The horse is perplexed; stopping in the snow without a house or barn nearby is unusual. The other choices don't make sense in context to the lines in the poem.

49. **(C)** Peaceful and quiet

The quiet surroundings and steady beat of the poem give this poem a peaceful, quiet rhythm. The last two lines, especially, are almost like a lullaby: quiet and tranquil. "Silent" is not a good choice because the author talks about the sound of the snow and the jingle of the harness.

50. **(D)** Alliteration

The "s" sound in "sound's sweep" is alliteration. This sound embodies the sound of snow and wind, that quiet, almost whispery coldness.

51. **(A)** Bored

Alice looks over her sister's shoulder while she's reading, and she can't understand why the book doesn't have pictures in it. She is tired of sitting next to her sister, and she hasn't anything to keep herself occupied. She's bored.

52. **(C)** She is dreaming.

In the second line of paragraph 2, the author says that Alice is feeling "sleepy" and "stupid," and, because she doesn't want to get up to pick flowers, she is feeling somewhat lazy on the hot day. The best guess is that she's dreaming: after all, she sees a rabbit wearing clothes and a pocket watch!

53. **(D)** He talks and wears clothing.

The author describes the White Rabbit as wearing a pocket-watch (waist-coat watch) and talking. He does not mention a hat in this excerpt.

54. **(C)** Because she is dreaming.

When a person dreams, usually strange things can happen and it seems normal. The other answers do not make sense for this question. If all rabbits talked to Alice, then she wouldn't be curious to follow this rabbit.

55. **(D)** Carved

If you replaced the word choices in the sentence, "carved" is the only choice that would work in the context of the sentence.

56. **(D)** gods

In the text, it says in the first line that the gods had no humans for the Earth. Therefore, they were the only beings in existence, except for plant life.

57. **(B)** Hatred

The text says, in paragraph 2, that the gods gave humans love, hope, and the ability to work, along with life and death. "Hatred" is not mentioned.

58. **(A)** their children

Because the gods "took a special interest in all they did, watched over them, and often gave them their aid and protection," they act like parents to the new humans. Though some people may think that **(B)** could be a correct answer, because the text includes "remembering they had called them into life," choosing "children" is the best choice.

59. **(C)** students should be honest in their studies

Integrity means to be honest/honorable.

60. **(A)** 2

In the flow chart, under "Preserving Academic Integrity," there are two Resource options: Resources for Students and Resources for Faculty.

61. (D) Promoting academic integrity in the classroom
The only complete option given is **(D)**. The other choices are combinations of the other sections.

62. (C) Plagiarism
The other options are from the Faculty and above sections, not from the Resource for Students.

63. (A) How to protect your academic integrity
(B) may have been a close second choice, but plagiarism is when a person copies the writing of someone else without giving proper credit to the author. The "Protecting Academic Integrity" option covers all forms of cheating, including tests.

64. (C) syllabus
The syllabus is a document each teacher gives to students at the beginning of the year. It outlines the class and classroom procedures, gives information on materials and supplies, and states office hours.

65. (B) Green and cool
The selection states in lines 1–2 that he "laid there in the grass and the cool shade thinking about things."

66. (C) Talked
Though squirrels can't "talk" like humans, they are "talking" to him in a "friendly" way.

67. (A) Characterization
Here, Twain writes Huck with a particular "voice." We read his words as he would actually say them out loud, adding to his character. Choice **(C)** may have tricked you, but remember that personification is giving human characteristics to something not human.

68. (D) Sunshine shining through the leaves
In this text, the sunlight shines through the leaves, making light spots on the ground.

69. (C) onomatopoeia
Onomatopoeia is when words are spelled like they sound. "Boom" is an example, as well as "Shh."

70. (A) They think he is dead and want to recover his body.
In this question, you would have to know the definition of "carcass" to make the best choice. "Carcass" is defined as a dead form; in this case, the selection says "his carcass," making it his dead body.

71. (C) relaxed
He says in the first line of the second paragraph that he is "powerful lazy and comfortable." He also sleeps late and feels "rested, ruther comfortable, and satisfied."

72. (B) 1 egg
The recipe says that each egg should be sliced in half, making 12 half eggs. There are 12 servings, meaning that 1 serving is half an egg. Therefore, if the person had two servings, he/she would eat 1 egg.

73. (C) So the yolks will be firm
The yolks need to be firm because further in the recipe, it states that the yolks are "mashed until crumbly." They would have to be firm and hard to become crumbly when mashed.

74. (B) decoration
"Garnish" means to adorn, decorate, or artistically add to something. The garnishes in the recipe are not needed to be successful; rather, they are for beautification only.

75. (D) Creamed would blend easier
The recipe asks for creamed horseradish because it is being added to other thick elements such as the mayo. Whole horseradish is a root and looks something like whole ginger or a gnarled tree root.

76. (C) Salt as preferred by the chef
This phrase is used often in recipes. It is because some people like their meals saltier than others; therefore, if no particular amount of salt is given, the chef can salt the product as much or as little as he/she prefers.

77. (C) They are used first.
The eggs are important, but to say they are the most important doesn't make sense. To have deviled eggs, the recipe needs ALL the items. Items on the recipe list are almost always listed in order of use. Therefore, the eggs are listed first.

78. (A) ugly
Shakespeare's famous sonnet declares his mistress's lack of beauty, thus making fun of love sonnets.

79. (B) dirty
Because the sonnet is all contradictions, he says that snow is white, but her breasts are "dun." Therefore, her breasts are not white but dirty.

80. (B) metaphor
Hairs are compared to wires, but the words "like" or "as" are not used in the comparison, making the comparison a metaphor.

81. (A) misrepresented
"Belie" means to contradict or misrepresent. In this case, he doesn't want his mistress misrepresented by "flowery" metaphors and similes.

82. (C) Ridiculous comparisons
Shakespeare's sonnet is a total contradiction to the flowery love sonnets at the time. He is saying that his sonnet represents "truth"—that though his woman isn't the most beautiful, what he says about her is true, and he loves her just the same.

83. (A) special
His love, in this case, is special to him, and it is rare like a gem.

84. (B) Blush
Roses, in this selection, mean flushed, or rosy, cheeks.

PRACTICE TEST 1 DETAILED EXPLANATIONS
MATHEMATICS SECTION

1. **(C)** This is scientific notation. Because the exponent is a 2, move the decimal point two places to the right and add zeros in the open spaces. The answer is 790.

2. **(A)** This is a factorial (!) problem. Multiply the given number by one less than that number; then multiply the resulting product by the next lower number, and repeat this process until you have multiplied by 1:

$$\frac{2!}{3!} = \frac{2 \times 1}{3 \times 2 \times 1} = \frac{1}{3}$$

3. **(B)** This is a simple percentage problem. Remember that 20% = .2:

$30(.2) = \$6.00$

4. **(D)** The total number of marbles is 20: 16 white marbles + 4 black marbles = 20 marbles. So the ratio of black marbles to all marbles is 4:20, which in simplest form is 1:5.

5. **(C)** Substitute each answer into the equation until you find a point that makes the equation true. $4(3) - 2(1) = 10$ is true. So the answer is (3, 1).

6. **(B)** Plot the points on an x, y graph. Then connect the nearest points. The figure created is a square.

7. **(C)** First, simplify the constants by dividing 42 by 6. Then simplify the x and y variables by subtracting the exponents on each:

$$\frac{42x^4 y^6}{6xy^2} = 7x^3 y^4$$

8. **(C)** The pattern is to subtract 10 from one number and then add 5 to the next number. The last number is 80, which was arrived at by subtracting 10, so add 5:

$80 + 5 = 85$

9. **(A)** First, calculate the discount, and then subtract this from the regular price:

$32(.25) = 8$

$32 - 8 = 24$

The sale price for the cap is $24.

10. **(B)** The formula for slope is rise over run, or $\dfrac{y_1 - y_2}{x_1 - x_2}$, so plug in the given points—(1, 3) and (4, 7)—and evaluate:

$$\frac{3 - 7}{1 - 4} = \frac{-4}{-3}$$

The negative signs cancel each other out, so the slope is $\dfrac{4}{3}$.

11. **(A)** $\dfrac{6}{18} = \dfrac{1}{3}$

12. **(C)** First round the numbers and then multiply:

$$200 \times 300 = 60,000$$

13. **(A)** The important parts in the equation of a line are the slope and the y-intercept. Remember that the general equation for a line is $y = mx + b$, where m is the slope and b is the y-intercept. Looking at the graph, you can see that the line intersects the y-axis at 2, so that gives you one part of the equation: $y = mx + 2$. Now, again looking at the graph, choose two points on the line and use the formula of rise over run, $\dfrac{y_1 - y_2}{x_1 - x_2}$, to find the slope. We'll use the points (1, 4) and (0, 2):

$$\frac{4 - 2}{1 - 0} = \frac{2}{1} = 2$$

The slope of this line is 2. The y-intercept is 2. Therefore, the correct equation is $y = 2x + 2$.

14. **(D)** $\dfrac{xy - 6}{3} + 4 = \dfrac{(6)(9) - 6}{3} + 4 = 20$

15. **(B)** The absolute value of a number, other than 0, is positive. The absolute value of -5 is 5.

16. **(B)** There are five possible outcomes, and four of them satisfy the question. So the probability of not getting a heart is $\dfrac{4}{5}$, or in decimal form, .80.

17. **(D)** The number of complaints is not as important as the average number of complaints. This is because an average takes into consideration how long a company has been in business. Blue Taxi has $\dfrac{100}{25}$ or an average of 4 complaints per month. However, Green Taxi has $\dfrac{20}{4}$ or an average of 5 complaints per month. Therefore, on average, Green Taxi has more complaints per month. It is misleading for a company to say that they receive fewer complaints than another company when they have not been in business as long.

18. **(C)** This is asking for the number of permutations of four things from a set of four things. The answer is 4!:

$$4! = 4 \times 3 \times 2 \times 1 = 24$$

19. (D)

$$5x + 2 = 6$$
$$5x = 6 - 2$$
$$5x = 4$$
$$\frac{5x}{5} = \frac{4}{5}$$
$$x = \frac{4}{5}$$

20. (B) Solving a system of linear equations involves finding the point at which two lines intersect. One approach to this problem is to substitute each answer, one at time, into the two formulas given. The correct answer is the one that makes both of the equations true. In this case, the point (3, 12) makes both equations true:

$$y = 5x - 3$$
$$12 = 5(3) - 3$$
$$12 = 15 - 3$$
$$y = 4x$$
$$12 = 4(3)$$

21. (D) Set this problem up as a proportion. Write a proportion for the corresponding sides. Let x represent the length of the missing side. Then solve for x:

$$\frac{x}{3} = \frac{20}{5}$$
$$x = \frac{20 \times 3}{5}$$
$$x = 12 \text{ inches}$$

22. (B) Use the formula for the slope of a line through two points:

$$m = \frac{y_2 - y_1}{x_2 - x_1}$$

$$m = \frac{2 - 8}{10 - 1} = \frac{-6}{9} = \frac{-2}{3}$$

The slope is equal to $\frac{-2}{3}$.

23. (C) Substitute the values given into the expression and simplify:

$$2a^2 + \frac{5b}{2} - 8 = 2(-4)^2 + \frac{5(2)}{2} - 8 = 32 + 5 - 8 = 29$$

24. **(A)**

$$\frac{x}{6} + 9 = 13$$

$$\frac{x}{6} + 9 - 9 = 13 - 9$$

$$\frac{x}{6} = 4$$

$$6 \times \frac{x}{6} = 4 \times 6$$

$$x = 24$$

25. **(B)** The price of each CD is actually the slope of the line. The slope is rise over run. For each CD purchased, the cost goes up $25.

26. **(C)** The arrow is pointing in the less-than direction and it has an open circle. This number line represents less than -1 or, in symbol form, $x < -1$.

27. **(D)** The words "eight more than five times a number" can be turned into an expression. The part "eight more" means to add 8. "Five times a number" means to multiply by 5. Let x represent the number. The correct expression is $5x + 8$.

28. **(A)** The average score for Paul is calculated by adding his four test scores and then dividing by 4:

$$3 + 6 + 9 + 10 = 28$$

$$\frac{28}{4} = 7$$

29. **(C)** There are eight different possible outcomes that can result from flipping a fair coin three times. Only one of these includes three heads. So the probability of getting three heads is $\frac{1}{8}$.

30. **(C)** An equation of the form $y = x$ will produce a line with a slope of positive 1 and a y-intercept of 0.

31. **(C)** The sum of the angles of a triangle must total 180°. To find the missing value, first add the two known measurements together and then subtract from 180:

$$60 + 65 = 125$$

$$180 - 125 = 55°$$

32. **(C)** Solve using the Pythagorean theorem, $a^2 + b^2 = c^2$; remember that c represents the hypotenuse, the side opposite the right angle:

$$a^2 + b^2 = c^2$$

$$12^2 + b^2 = 13^2$$

$$144 + b^2 = 169$$

$$144 - 144 + b^2 = 169 - 144$$

$$b^2 = 25$$

$$b = \sqrt{25} = 5$$

33. **(C)** Use the formula for the combination of four different things taken two at a time:

$$_nC_k = \frac{n!}{k!(n-k)!}$$

$$_4C_2 = \frac{4!}{2!(4-2)!}$$

$$_4C_2 = \frac{4!}{2!(2!)}$$

$$_4C_2 = \frac{24}{2(2)}$$

$$_4C_2 = \frac{24}{4} = 6$$

34. **(B)** To find the median score, the scores must be first ordered from smallest to largest:

0, 2, 4, 5, 7, 8, 9

The median score is the one in the middle. In this case, it is 5.

35. **(C)** There are six possible and equally likely outcomes from rolling one fair die. Rolling a 3, 4, or 5 would cover three out of the six possibilities. Therefore, the probability of rolling a 3, 4, or 5 would be $\frac{3}{6}$ or $\frac{1}{2}$.

36. **(A)** There are 36 possible outcomes from throwing two dice. There is only one way to throw a 12. Therefore, the probability is $\frac{1}{36}$.

37. **(C)** In the figure, $\angle q$ is equal to $\angle p$ because they are alternate interior angles of parallel lines. Therefore, $\angle p$ is equal to 60°.

38. **(C)** In the scaled drawing, length is equal to 9 centimeters and width is equal to 4.5 centimeters. The scale is "1 centimeter is equal to 2 meters." So multiply the given measurements by 2 to find the dimensions in meters:

length = 9 × 2 = 18 meters

width = 4.5 × 2 = 9 meters

Last, to find area, multiply length times width:

18 × 9 = 162

The answer is 162 square meters.

39. **(C)** The shaded region is made up of four separate triangles. Calculate the area of one triangle using the formula $\frac{1}{2}bh$ (one-half the base times the height). In the present problem, the base is 3 and the height is 3:

$$\frac{1}{2}(3)(3) = \frac{1}{2}(9) = 4.5$$

This is the area of one triangle. Because there are four triangles in the shaded region, multiply this area by 4:

4.5(4) = 18

Next, calculate the area of the big square. Each side is 6 inches (3 inches + 3 inches), and the formula for the area of a square is length times width:

6(6) = 36

Last, subtract the area of the shaded triangles from the area of the big square to get the area of the unshaded region:

36 − 18 = 18

The answer is 18 square inches.

40. **(C)** The pattern that this data suggest is a straight line. If this imaginary line were extended up, it would predict a value of 70,000 for the year 2001.

41. **(B)** Find the side of the figure closest to the x-axis and measure the distance of this side from the x-axis. A reflection of the figure will put this side the same distance from the x-axis, but on the other side of the axis. Also, notice the point labeled "A." A reflection of this point across the x-axis will also be the same distance from the x-axis, but on the other side.

42. **(C)** The smallest change in temperature from the previous day can be determined by looking for the shortest line segment on the graph. The shortest line segment extends from Wednesday to Thursday, indicating that Thursday experienced the smallest temperature change from that of the previous day.

43. **(C)** Imagine that this figure is a square with a triangle missing. First, calculate the area of the missing triangle:

$$\frac{1}{2}hb = \frac{1}{2}(8)(6) = \frac{1}{2}48 = 4$$

Then calculate the area of the imaginary square:

10 × 10 = 100

Last, subtract the area of the triangle from the square:

100 − 24 = 76

44. **(D)** The written expression "the number of boys, b, is equal to three times the number of girls, g" can be written as $3 \times g = b$.

45. **(A)** The rule called order of operations tells us to do multiplication and division before addition and subtraction. Therefore, $20 + 9 \div 3 = 20 + 3 = 23$.

46. **(C)** First, calculate the area of the duck pond. Remember that each unit is equal to 10 feet, so the length of the duck pond is 4 × 10, or 40 feet, and its width is 6 × 10, or 60 feet:

Area = 40 × 60 = 2,400 square feet

Next, calculate the area of the whole lot:

120 × 120 = 14,400 square feet

Last, subtract the area for the duck pond from that of the whole lot to find the area of the flower garden:

14,400 − 2,400 = 12,000 square feet

47. **(B)** To find the circumference of a circle, use the formula $2\pi r$. Pi (π) can be rounded to 3.14:

$2\pi r$

$2(3.14)(25) = 157$

The circumference is *approximately* equal to 160 inches.

48. **(D)** Solve using the Pythagorean theorem:

$$a^2 + b^2 = c^2$$
$$a^2 + 9^2 = 15^2$$
$$a^2 + 81 = 225$$
$$a^2 + 81 - 81 = 225 - 81$$
$$a^2 = 144$$
$$a = \sqrt{144}$$
$$a = 12$$

49. **(C)** The formula for the area of a triangle is $\frac{1}{2}bh$, where b equals the base and h equals the height. First, find the area of each triangle:

Area of triangle A $= \frac{1}{2}(4)(10) = 20$

Area of triangle B $= \frac{1}{2}(5)(12) = 30$

Now, divide the area of triangle A by the area of triangle B, and put this fraction into lowest terms:

$$\frac{20}{30} = \frac{2}{3}$$

50. **(A)** Set up this problem as a proportion. Write a proportion for the corresponding sides. Let x represent the length of the missing side, and then solve for x:

$$\frac{x}{4} = \frac{10}{5}$$
$$5x = 10 \times 4$$
$$x = \frac{10 \times 4}{5}$$
$$x = 8 \text{ feet}$$

PRACTICE TEST 2

Both Practice Tests are also on CD in our special interactive CHSPE TestWare®. We recommend that you first take these tests on computer for the added benefits of timed testing conditions, automatic scoring and diagnostic feedback.

PRACTICE TEST 2
ENGLISH-LANGUAGE ARTS SECTION
Language Subtest

DIRECTIONS: Look at the underlined words in each sentence. You may see a mistake in punctuation, capitalization, or word usage. If you spot a mistake in the underlined section of a sentence, select the answer that corrects the mistake. If you find no mistake, choose **(D)**, *Correct as is*.

1. The man <u>had boughten</u> a new suit for the wedding.
   - **(A)** has boughten
   - **(B)** had bought
   - **(C)** has buying
   - **(D)** Correct as is.

2. <u>Their</u> once was a woman who owned 22 cats.
   - **(A)** There is
   - **(B)** They're
   - **(C)** There
   - **(D)** Correct as is.

3. The house on the corner <u>is sold</u> for $230,000.
   - **(A)** was sold
   - **(B)** was selled
   - **(C)** selled
   - **(D)** Correct as is.

4. Yesterday <u>is</u> the last day of summer school.
   - **(A)** isn't
   - **(B)** were
   - **(C)** was
   - **(D)** Correct as is.

5. The only person who has a dog is <u>I</u>.
   - **(A)** myself
   - **(B)** me
   - **(C)** mine
   - **(D)** Correct as is.

6. The train <u>pulled</u> out of the station at nine o'clock on May 5 of last year.
   - **(A)** pulls
   - **(B)** pulled
   - **(C)** pulling
   - **(D)** Correct as is.

GO TO NEXT PAGE ➡

315

7. The frog hopped on <u>it's</u> legs into the river.
   - **(A)** its
   - **(B)** its'
   - **(C)** their
   - **(D)** Correct as is.

8. Most holidays <u>are spent</u> with family and friends.
   - **(A)** is spent
   - **(B)** spent
   - **(C)** spending
   - **(D)** Correct as is.

9. <u>Me and my family went</u> on vacation to Hawaii.
   - **(A)** My family and me went
   - **(B)** My family and I went
   - **(C)** Me and my family goes
   - **(D)** Correct as is.

10. <u>"Hey, what is that!" said Donny.</u>
    - **(A)** "Hey, what is that," said Donny?
    - **(B)** Hey what is that said Donny.
    - **(C)** "Hey, what is that?" said Donny.
    - **(D)** Correct as is.

11. The science lab had <u>test-tubes, beakers, chemicals, and burners.</u>
    - **(A)** test-tubes beakers chemicals and burners.
    - **(B)** test-tubes; beakers; chemicals; and burners.
    - **(C)** test tubes: beakers, chemicals, and burners.
    - **(D)** Correct as is.

12. The soccer star played for the following <u>teams Arsenal Bayern-Munich Juventus and Benfica.</u>
    - **(A)** teams: Arsenal Bayern-Munich Juventus and Benfica.
    - **(B)** teams; Arsenal, Bayern-Munich, Juventus, and Benfica.
    - **(C)** teams: Arsenal, Bayern-Munich, Juventus, and Benfica.
    - **(D)** Correct as is.

13. After the parade, the boy <u>goes</u> to the candy shop.
    - **(A)** go
    - **(B)** went
    - **(C)** was gone
    - **(D)** Correct as is.

14. Hippos are considered to be one of the <u>dangerouser</u> animals of all in Africa.
    - **(A)** dangerest
    - **(B)** more dangerous
    - **(C)** most dangerous
    - **(D)** Correct as is.

15. The captain of the ship put on <u>it's</u> hat.
    - **(A)** its
    - **(B)** his
    - **(C)** their
    - **(D)** Correct as is.

16. Oranges <u>belongs in</u> the citrus family of foods.
    - **(A)** belongs to
    - **(B)** belong to
    - **(C)** belonging in
    - **(D)** Correct as is.

GO TO NEXT PAGE

17. Water is <u>importanter</u> than food for survival.
    (A) more important
    (B) most important
    (C) importanest
    (D) Correct as is.

18. Paula cried out, <u>where is my history book!</u>
    (A) "where is my history book?"
    (B) "Where is my history book"?
    (C) "Where is my history book?"
    (D) Correct as is.

19. The plate <u>isn't not</u> on the table.
    (A) isnt not
    (B) is not not
    (C) isn't
    (D) Correct as is.

20. Cookies were <u>brought from home; cake</u> was bought at the store.
    (A) brought from home, cake
    (B) brought from home; Cake
    (C) brought; from home cake
    (D) Correct as is.

21. Luigi practiced his guitar every day because <u>he wanting</u> to get better.
    (A) he did want
    (B) he wanted
    (C) he want
    (D) Correct as is.

22. The bus driver <u>yelled You kids need to be quiet!</u>
    (A) yelled, You kids need to be quiet!
    (B) yelled "You kids need to be quiet!"
    (C) yelled, "You kids need to be quiet!"
    (D) Correct as is.

23. <u>They're is</u> a wonderful movie on television tonight.
    (A) Their is
    (B) There is
    (C) There are
    (D) Correct as is.

24. Jordan bought some <u>candy an apple and a bottle of water.</u>
    (A) candy an apple, and a bottle of water.
    (B) candy, an apple, and a bottle of water.
    (C) candy, an apple, and, a bottle of water.
    (D) Correct as is

25. The computer <u>repaired</u> by the technician.
    (A) was repaired
    (B) repairing
    (C) were repaired
    (D) Correct as is.

26. Tommy has <u>two go</u> on a job interview at three o'clock.
    (A) to go
    (B) too go
    (C) to goes
    (D) Correct as is.

27. The travelers <u>completed</u> the arduous expedition on time.
    (A) will be completed
    (B) are completed
    (C) were completed
    (D) Correct as is.

28. Vegetables <u>are an important</u> parts of a healthy diet.
    (A) is an important
    (B) are important
    (C) has important
    (D) Correct as is.

GO TO NEXT PAGE

PRACTICE TEST 2

29. The letter was mailed to <u>chicago illinois.</u>
    (A) Chicago; Illinois.
    (B) Chicago Illinois.
    (C) Chicago, Illinois.
    (D) Correct as is.

30. <u>Some people is</u> late to arrive at a party.
    (A) Some peoples is
    (B) Some people are
    (C) Somes people are
    (D) Correct as is.

31. Paintings by Picasso are considered <u>to be value</u> by art collectors.
    (A) to being valuable
    (B) to have valued
    (C) to be valuable
    (D) Correct as is.

32. Many genres of music are <u>popular: Jazz being</u> one of the most well known.
    (A) popular; Jazz are
    (B) popular, Jazz be
    (C) popular, but Jazz is
    (D) Correct as is.

33. Duke <u>Ellington a famous music composer wrote</u> that song.
    (A) Ellington, a famous music composer wrote
    (B) Ellington, a famous music composer, wrote
    (C) Ellington, a famous music, composer wrote
    (D) Correct as is.

34. The poster was part of <u>are</u> presentation.
    (A) hour
    (B) ours
    (C) our
    (D) Correct as is.

35. The <u>panda who was named Billy was</u>
    (A) panda; who was named Billy, was
    (B) panda, who was named Billy, was
    (C) panda, which was named Billy, was
    (D) Correct as is.

36. <u>michigan is a state that has many lakes.</u>
    (A) Michigan is a state that has many lakes.
    (B) michigan, is a state that has many lakes.
    (C) Michigan is a state, that has, many lakes.
    (D) Correct as is.

37. Charles Dickens wrote the book <u>the tale of two cities.</u>
    (A) Charles Dickens wrote the book <u>The tale of two Cities.</u>
    (B) Charles Dickens wrote the book <u>The Tale of Two Cities.</u>
    (C) Charles Dickens wrote the book <u>the Tale of two Cities.</u>
    (D) Correct as is.

38. <u>Me and Lisa</u> are best friends.
    (A) I and Lisa
    (B) Lisa and I
    (C) Me and her
    (D) Correct as is.

39. My sandwich had <u>pickles cheese mustard and onions</u> on it.
    (A) pickles; cheese; mustard; and onions
    (B) pickles: cheese mustard and onions
    (C) pickles, cheese, mustard, and onions
    (D) Correct as is.

40. <u>He gave herself</u> a haircut to save money.
    (A) He gave himself
    (B) He gave myself
    (C) I gave himself
    (D) Correct as is.

GO TO NEXT PAGE

41. <u>"What do you call it?" asked Bernie.</u>
   - **(A)** What do you call it asked Bernie.
   - **(B)** What do you call it. Asked Bernie.
   - **(C)** "What do you call it"? asked Bernie.
   - **(D)** Correct as is.

42. <u>Walk is</u> the best exercise for people who have bad knees.
   - **(A)** Walk are
   - **(B)** Walking is
   - **(C)** Walkings are
   - **(D)** Correct as is.

DIRECTIONS: Refer to the passage below to answer the following questions.

Excerpt from MARS
by Percival Lowell

1   Once in about every fifteen years a startling visitant makes his appearance upon our midnight skies — a great red star that rises at sunset through the haze about the eastern horizon, and then, mounting higher with the deepening night, blazes forth against the dark background of space with a splendor that outshines Sirius and rivals the giant Jupiter himself. Startling for its size, the
5   stranger looks the more fateful for being a fiery red. Small wonder that by many folk it is taken for a portent certainly no one who had not followed in their courses what the Greeks so picturesquely called "the wanderers" would recognize in the apparition. An orderly member of our own solar family. Nevertheless, one of the wanderers it is, for that star is the planet Mars…

43. The author gives Mars a gender. What is it?
   - **(A)** Male
   - **(B)** Female
   - **(C)** Neither male nor female
   - **(D)** Both male and female

44. In line 2, the author calls Jupiter "<u>a great red star.</u>" What correction should be made to this underlined section?
   - **(A)** a great, red star
   - **(B)** a great red, star
   - **(C)** a great, red, star
   - **(D)** Correct as is

45. How can the following sentence be written better?
   Startling for its size, the stranger looks the more fateful for being a fiery red.
   - **(A)** The stranger startling for its size, looks the more fateful for being fiery red.
   - **(B)** For being more fiery red, the stranger, startling for its size, looks the more fateful for being a fiery red.
   - **(C)** The stranger looks the more fateful startling for its size and for being fiery red.
   - **(D)** Fiery red, the startling sized stranger looks the more fateful.

GO TO NEXT PAGE ➡

46. In the following sentences, there are errors in punctuation. Which is the correct sentence?

... certainly no one who had not followed in their courses what the Greeks so picturesquely called "the wanderers" would recognize in the apparition. An orderly member of our own solar family.

(A) ... certainly no one who had not followed in their courses what the Greeks so picturesquely called "the wanderers" would recognize in the apparition. An orderly member of our own solar family.

(B) ... certainly, no one who had not followed in their courses what the Greeks so picturesquely called "the wanderers" would recognize in the apparition an orderly member of our own solar family.

(C) ... certainly no one who had not followed in their courses what the Greeks so picturesquely called "the wanderers" would recognize in the apparition. An orderly member of our own solar family.

(D) ... certainly, no one who had not followed in their courses what the Greeks so picturesquely called "the wanderers" would recognize, in the apparition an orderly member of our own solar family.

47. How can the underlined words in the sentences below include better detail?

Small wonder that by many folk it is taken for a portent certainly <u>no one who had not followed in their courses</u> what the Greeks so picturesquely called "the wanderers" would recognize in the apparition. An orderly member of our own solar family.

(A) no one who had not followed in their courses

(B) no one who had not followed in them courses

(C) no one who had not followed in his/her courses

(D) no one who had not followed in those courses

48. How can the underlined words in the sentence below be written better?

Once in about every fifteen years <u>a startling visitant</u> makes his appearance upon our midnight skies....

(A) a startled visitant

(B) a startled visitor

(C) a start visitor

(D) Correct as is.

GO TO NEXT PAGE ➡

PRACTICE TEST 2
ENGLISH-LANGUAGE ARTS SECTION

Writing Task

DIRECTIONS: Carefully read the writing task and review the "Writer's Checklist" below. You must be specific and explain your reasons for your opinion.

Writing Topic
Since a person must be 18 years old to vote, should the drinking age be lowered to 18 as well? Be sure to explain your answer with specific examples.

Writer's Checklist
The following "Writer's Checklist" (© 2008 by NCS Pearson, Inc.) will be provided with the CHSPE writing task.

- Did I write about the topic?
- Did I express my ideas in complete sentences?
- Did I give enough details to explain or support my ideas?
- Did I include only those details that are about my topic?
- Did I write my ideas in an order that is clear for the reader to follow?
- Did I write a topic sentence for each paragraph?
- Did I use a capital letter at the beginning of each sentence and for all other words that should be capitalized?
- Did I use the correct punctuation at the end of each sentence and within each sentence?
- Did I spell words correctly?
- Did I print or write clearly?

PRACTICE TEST 2
ENGLISH-LANGUAGE ARTS SECTION
Reading Subtest

DIRECTIONS: Refer to the charts below to answer the following questions.

Associate Membership Fees

- I hereby apply for **Associate Membership** in the Institute of Juggling Arts.

Please enclose the appropriate amount for the month in which you apply. This covers your entrance fee and first-year dues.

• Jan.: $610	• April: $346	• July: $150	• Oct.: $100
• Feb.: $522	• May: $258	• Aug.: $135	• Nov.: $90
• Mar.: $434	• June: $170	• Sept.: $125	• Dec.: $80

Annual renewals will become due each January 1. Dues are currently $700.

Nonresident Associate Membership Fees

- I hereby apply for **Nonresident Associate Membership** in the Institute of Juggling Arts.

Please enclose the appropriate amount for the month in which you apply. This covers your entrance fee and first-year dues.

• Jan.: $725	• April: $593	• July: $461	• Oct.: $329
• Feb.: $681	• May: $549	• Aug.: $417	• Nov.: $285
• Mar.: $637	• June: $505	• Sept. $373	• Dec.: $241

Annual renewals are due January 1. Dues for NONRESIDENTS are $900.

GO TO NEXT PAGE ➡

1. "Dues" are listed for both resident and non-resident applicants. "Dues" most likely means
   - (A) that something is ready to be completed.
   - (B) member fees.
   - (C) member uniforms.
   - (D) member hotel rates.

2. For Associate Members, which is the most cost effective month to apply for membership?
   - (A) January
   - (B) February
   - (C) March
   - (D) April

3. What is the best reason that non-resident rates are more expensive than resident rates?
   - (A) Residents will come more often.
   - (B) Non-residents will come more often.
   - (C) Residents will not come as often.
   - (D) Non-residents will not come as often.

4. The name of the organization is The Institute for the Juggling Arts. What is the best meaning for "Arts"?
   - (A) Skills
   - (B) Music
   - (C) Drawing
   - (D) Painting

DIRECTIONS: Refer to the poem below to answer the following questions.

Excerpt from "The Raven"
by Edgar Allan Poe (1809–1849)

This famous poem tells the tale of a man alone in his bedroom who, one sleepless night, has a strange visitor: a raven. Only the first and second stanzas are given here: there are eighteen in all.

1   Once upon a midnight dreary, while I pondered, weak and weary,
      Over many a quaint and curious volume of forgotten lore,
      While I nodded, nearly napping, suddenly there came a tapping,
      As of some one gently rapping, rapping at my chamber door.
5   "'Tis some visitor," I muttered, "tapping at my chamber door—
      Only this, and nothing more."

      Ah, distinctly I remember it was in the bleak December,
      And each separate dying ember wrought its ghost upon the floor.
      Eagerly I wished the morrow:—vainly I had sought to borrow
10   From my books surcease of sorrow—sorrow for the lost "Lenore—
      For the rare and radiant maiden whom the angels name Lenore—
      Nameless here for evermore.

GO TO NEXT PAGE ➡

5. The rhyme scheme of this poem is
   (A) abcabc.
   (B) aabbcc.
   (C) abcbbb.
   (D) abbcaa.

6. The tone of this selection can best be described as
   (A) creepy.
   (B) cheerful.
   (C) irritated.
   (D) arrogant.

7. An unusual element about this poem is that it has
   (A) internal rhyme.
   (B) allegory.
   (C) metaphorical meaning.
   (D) personification.

8. In the following line, what literary element is most obviously represented by the underlined words?
   While I <u>nodded, nearly napping</u>, suddenly there came a tapping
   (A) Assonance
   (B) Simile
   (C) Alliteration
   (D) Metaphor

9. In the following line, what is the most obvious meaning of the underlined words?
   Over many a <u>quaint and curious volume of forgotten lore</u>
   (A) A large, new book of fanciful tales
   (B) A small, unusual old book of historical legends
   (C) A large, old book of historical legends
   (D) A small, unusual new book of fanciful tales

DIRECTIONS: Refer to the following chart to answer the questions below.

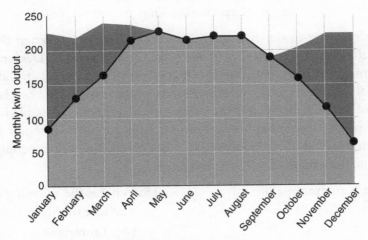

● Your gas/oil boiler producing your hot water

● Northstar Energy solar panels producing your FREE hot water

GO TO NEXT PAGE ➡

10. Which month does the your gas or oil boiler create the most hot water?

   (A) October

   (B) November

   (C) January

   (D) March

11. In which month do the solar panels create the most heat?

   (A) March

   (B) April

   (C) May

   (D) October

12. In the above chart, why is solar energy higher in May, July, and August than in March and April?

   (A) People use less energy in those months so they put out their panels more.

   (B) People use less energy in those months so the panels have more unused energy in reserve.

   (C) It is sunnier in those months so the panels can gather more energy.

   (D) People use more energy indoors because of the weather.

13. What is the best reason to explain the monthly kilowatt output being higher in the winter and early spring months?

   (A) People begin to use air conditioning in those months.

   (B) Heat is not used more in those months.

   (C) Gas and oil are used more for hot water in those months.

   (D) May is the coldest month of the year.

DIRECTIONS: Refer to the following passage to answer the questions below.

Excerpt from "I Have a Dream"
by Dr. Martin Luther King, Jr. (1929–1968)

In a sense we've come to our nation's capital to cash a check. When the architects of our republic wrote the magnificent words of the Constitution and the Declaration of Independence, they were signing a promissory note to which every American was to fall heir. This note was a promise that all men, yes, black men as well as white men, would be guaranteed the "unalienable Rights" of "Life, Liberty and the pursuit of Happiness." It is obvious today that America has defaulted on this promissory note, insofar as her citizens of color are concerned. Instead of honoring this sacred obligation, America has given the Negro people a bad check, a check which has come back marked "insufficient funds."

14. This entire text is an example of

   (A) simile.

   (B) metaphor.

   (C) personification.

   (D) onomatopoeia.

15. What is the meaning of "architects" in the first line of the text?

   (A) Librarians

   (B) Creators

   (C) Bankers

   (D) Policemen

GO TO NEXT PAGE ➡

16. What is the meaning of the underlined words in the following sentence?

When the architects of our republic wrote the magnificent words of the Constitution and the Declaration of Independence, <u>they were signing a promissory note to which every American was to fall heir.</u>

(A) The writers of the document wrote secrets that only their ancestors could understand.

(B) The bankers in charge of this document would inherit a lot of tax funds.

(C) The creators of the document signed a sort of promise to the American people.

(D) The policemen would enforce the secret laws to protect the American people.

17. What is the best meaning of the word "inalienable"?

(A) Not able to be given away

(B) Taken from one person to another

(C) A place where no foreigners are welcome

(D) Outer space

18. What is the meaning of the underlined words in the following sentence?

Instead of honoring this <u>sacred obligation</u>, America has given the Negro people a bad check, a check which has come back marked "insufficient funds."

(A) unimportant event

(B) worthy duty

(C) holy act

(D) afraid chore

19. What is the meaning of the underlined words in the following sentence, in context with the other information of the piece?

Instead of honoring this sacred obligation, <u>America has given the Negro people a bad check</u>, a check which has come back marked "insufficient funds."

(A) The bank gave African-American people illegal checks.

(B) The government has not given African-American people the same opportunities as white people.

(C) Bad checks are only given by Americans.

(D) America gives away bad checks.

20. Which is the best answer that describes the main idea of this text?

(A) African-American people have not been given what has been promised them by the American government.

(B) African-American people write bad checks.

(C) African-American people have not kept their promise to their "sacred obligation."

(D) People are like checks: some are good, while others come back "insufficient funds."

GO TO NEXT PAGE ➡

DIRECTIONS: Refer to the following chart to answer the questions below.

The Chester Oaks Country Club
Golf Membership Options

	Champion	Challenger	Warrior	Blocker	Banker	Basic
Membership donation	$10,000	$5,000	$2,500	$1,000	$500	$250
One-year club membership	Yes	Yes	Yes	Yes	Yes	Yes
Box of 3 golf balls and club tees	Yes	Yes	Yes	Yes	Yes	No
Club T-shirt	Yes	Yes	Yes	Yes	Yes	No
Hours of private coaching	10	8	6	2	2	0
Tournament fees	Yes	Yes	Yes	Yes	No	No
Club jacket	Yes	Yes	Yes	Yes	No	No
Dining room dinners	25	15	10	0	0	0

21. If a person had $3000 and did not want private coaching, which of the following would be the best option?
    (A) Champion
    (B) Challenger
    (C) Warrior
    (D) Blocker

22. Which membership gives the most options included in the member donation?
    (A) Champion
    (B) Warrior
    (C) Banker
    (D) Basic

23. Which membership has the least amount of private coaching hours?
    (A) Basic
    (B) Banker
    (C) Challenger
    (D) Champion

24. Which three memberships have dining room options?
    (A) Basic, Challenger, Banker
    (B) Warrior, Blocker, Banker
    (C) Champion, Challenger, Warrior
    (D) Challenger, Warrior, Blocker

DIRECTIONS: Refer to the following passage to answer the questions on the next page.

1   In the United States, there are many who feel that America's youth should be protected from certain texts that may corrupt, confuse, and/or manipulate the minds of students. There are others who believe that the same texts can inspire, intrigue, and motivate students who normally would not read a book for enjoyment. There are teachers and librarians who advocate, and openly fight for, the use
5   of controversial, censored literature because such texts promote animated discussion and dialogue, and the texts also can encourage the student to think on more abstract levels because they have to

GO TO NEXT PAGE

interpret the content for themselves. Even though there are moral and ethical standards on both sides of censorship debates, where does the actual right of academic freedom for teachers amalgam-
10 ate? How should teachers, librarians, and administrators choose books for the classroom, and, like in past history, should the administration of a school be able to overrule a teacher's choice because of controversy over a text? Lastly, who should be able to create these defined axioms?

25. What are the "more abstract levels" discussed in line 7?

(A) simple suggestions

(B) touchable results

(C) complicated ideas

(D) insane theories

26. In lines 8-9, the word "amalgamate" is most likely to mean

(A) combine.

(B) separate.

(C) administer.

(D) scale.

27. What is the position of the writer in this piece?

(A) A promoter of censored literature

(B) A promoter of uncensored literature

(C) Someone who thinks that reading should be heavily monitored

(D) Someone who believes that only librarians should choose books

28. In the last line, the word "axioms" is most likely to mean

(A) parameters.

(B) truths.

(C) demands.

(D) suggestions.

DIRECTIONS: Refer to the passage to answer the questions on the next page.

The Birds, the Beasts, and the Bat
From Aesop's Fables by Aesop (620 BCE–563 BCE)

The Birds and the Beasts declared war against each other. No compromise was possible, and so they went at it tooth and claw. It is said the quarrel grew out of the persecution the race of Geese suffered at the teeth of the Fox family. The Beasts, too, had cause for fight. The Eagle was constantly pouncing on the Hare, and the Owl dined daily on Mice.

It was a terrible battle. Many a Hare and many a Mouse died. Chickens and Geese fell by the score—and the victor always stopped for a feast.

Now the Bat family had not openly joined either side. They were a very politic race. So when they saw the Birds getting the better of it, they were Birds for all there was in it. But when the tide of battle turned, they immediately sided with the Beasts.

When the battle was over, the conduct of the Bats was discussed at the peace conference. Such deceit was unpardonable, and Birds and Beasts made common cause to drive out the Bats. And since then the Bat family hides in dark towers and deserted ruins, flying out only in the night.

The deceitful have no friends.

GO TO NEXT PAGE ➡

29. What was the cause of the original fight between the Geese and the Foxes?

(A) Land boundaries

(B) Food

(C) Prejudice

(D) Water safety

30. A "victor" would be defined as

(A) the winner.

(B) the loser.

(C) an owl.

(D) a referee.

31. Why would the Bats not join the fight?

(A) They didn't care about the outcome.

(B) Too many of their friends and family had died.

(C) They are both beast and bird, so they used both sides to their advantage.

(D) They simply weren't around.

32. After the battle was over, whose fate was discussed amongst the animals?

(A) Foxes

(B) Owls

(C) Geese

(D) Bats

33. According to the fable, why do bats only come out at night?

(A) They are not wanted by the other animals.

(B) They prefer to live in caves.

(C) The other animals punished them, removing them from daylight "society."

(D) There is more food available at night.

34. The last line is "the deceitful have no friends." This would best be described as

(A) a summary.

(B) a moral.

(C) irony.

(D) characterization.

DIRECTIONS: Refer to the following passage to answer the questions on the next page.

Excerpt from *A Midsummer Night's Dream*
by William Shakespeare (1564–1616)

1
More strange than true: I never may believe
These antique fables, nor these fairy toys.
Lovers and madmen have such seething brains,
Such shaping fantasies, that apprehend
5
More than cool reason ever comprehends.
The lunatic, the lover and the poet
Are of imagination all compact:
One sees more devils than vast hell can hold,
That is, the madman: the lover, all as frantic,
10
Sees Helen's beauty in a brow of Egypt:
The poet's eye, in fine frenzy rolling,

GO TO NEXT PAGE ➡

Doth glance from heaven to earth, from earth to heaven;
And as imagination bodies forth
The forms of things unknown, the poet's pen
15   Turns them to shapes and gives to airy nothing
A local habitation and a name.
Such tricks hath strong imagination,
That if it would but apprehend some joy,
It comprehends some bringer of that joy;
20   Or in the night, imagining some fear,
How easy is a bush supposed a bear!

35. In lines 6–7, Shakespeare writes, "The lunatic, the lover and the poet/Are of imagination all compact." These lines are best defined as

(A) lovers and madmen are narrow-minded.

(B) lovers and madmen have small imaginations.

(C) lovers and madmen have different dreams.

(D) lovers and madmen have similar minds.

36. The meaning of lines 13–16 could best be defined as

(A) poets can write poems about dreams and fantasies.

(B) poets are insane.

(C) poets write about realistic things.

(D) madmen believe they are poets.

37. The meaning of lines 20–21 could best be defined as

(A) if you fear them, bears can come in the night.

(B) shadows can seem real with an active imagination.

(C) bears can hide in bushes.

(D) bushes can hide bears.

38. What does the word "seething" in line 3 most likely mean?

(A) Angry

(B) Sad

(C) Insane

(D) Happiness

39. The lunatic, the lover, and the poet are

(A) compared.

(B) contradicted.

(C) explained.

(D) encouraged.

40. In line 11, the word "frenzy" most likely means

(A) drunkenness.

(B) scared.

(C) paralyzing.

(D) ecstasy.

GO TO NEXT PAGE ➡

DIRECTIONS: Refer to the following bar graph to answer the questions below.

Coffee Drinkers

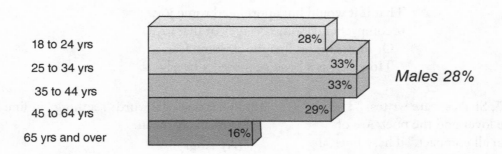

18 to 24 yrs — 28%
25 to 34 yrs — 33%
35 to 44 yrs — 33%
45 to 64 yrs — 29%
65 yrs and over — 16%

Males 28%

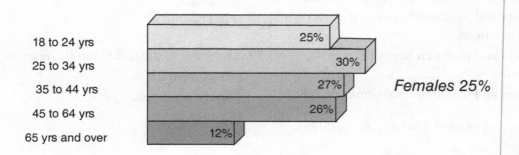

18 to 24 yrs — 25%
25 to 34 yrs — 30%
35 to 44 yrs — 27%
45 to 64 yrs — 26%
65 yrs and over — 12%

Females 25%

41. The male and female percentages on the right (Males 28% and Females 25%) most likely refer to the

(A) percentage of 25-year-old males who drink more than two cups of coffee daily.

(B) percentage of 30-year-old females who drink more than two cups of coffee daily.

(C) average percentage who drink more than two cups of coffee daily.

(D) average percentage who don't drink more than two cups of coffee daily.

42. What is the percentage of males aged 45–64 who drink more than two cups of coffee daily?

(A) 29%

(B) 33%

(C) 28%

(D) 26%

43. Of females who drink more than two cups of coffee daily, 30% are aged

(A) 65 and over

(B) 18–24

(C) 25–34

(D) 45–64

GO TO NEXT PAGE ➡

44. Which answer is the best assumption based on the above data?

(A) Men's coffee consumption will increase after age 65.

(B) Coffee consumption decreases in men and women after 65 because of health issues.

(C) Men drink more coffee than women at age 35 because coffee is more readily available to men.

(D) Men and women in their early 20s drink more coffee because they are uneducated.

45. A man who is 35 and drinks more than two cups of coffee daily is part of what percentage?

(A) 30%

(B) 31%

(C) 32%

(D) 33%

46. Why do more men than women drink coffee?

(A) Men are able to drink more coffee because they don't get sick as often.

(B) Women don't have as much money as men to buy coffee.

(C) Women are not educated about coffee consumption.

(D) There is not enough information given to make a prediction.

DIRECTIONS: Refer to the following passage to answer the questions on the next page.

Excerpt from *The Yellow Wallpaper*
by Charlotte Gilman (1860–1935)

The Yellow Wallpaper is a short story told in the first person. The main character is a young woman who has been taken to the country to "rest"; for what reason, the reader does not know. This selection describes her room in the house.

1   It is a big, airy room, the whole floor nearly, with windows that look all ways, and air and sunshine galore. It was nursery first and then playroom and gymnasium, I should judge; for the windows are barred for little children, and there are rings and things in the walls.

         The paint and paper look as if a boys' school had used it. It is stripped off—the paper—in
5   great patches all around the head of my bed, about as far as I can reach, and in a great place on the other side of the room low down. I never saw a worse paper in my life.

         One of those sprawling flamboyant patterns committing every artistic sin.

         It is dull enough to confuse the eye in following, pronounced enough to constantly irritate and provoke study, and when you follow the lame uncertain curves for a little distance they
10   suddenly commit suicide—plunge off at outrageous angles, destroy themselves in unheard of contradictions.

         The color is repellent, almost revolting; a smoldering unclean yellow, strangely faded by the slow-turning sunlight.

         It is a dull yet lurid orange in some places, a sickly sulphur tint in others.
15   No wonder the children hated it! I should hate it myself if I had to live in this room long.

GO TO NEXT PAGE

47. In line 4, Gilman says that the room looks as "if a boys' school used it." This most likely means
    (A) it was neat and sunny.
    (B) it was on the ground floor.
    (C) it was somewhat torn up by abuse.
    (D) it was stifling with small windows.

48. What does the word "flamboyant" mean in line 7?
    (A) Flashy
    (B) Modest
    (C) Sedate
    (D) Average

49. What would best describe an "artistic sin"?
    (A) A creative crime
    (B) A satisfactory photograph
    (C) A tastefully decorated room
    (D) A hospital room

50. What element of figurative language is line 7?
    (A) Personification
    (B) Metaphor
    (C) Irony
    (D) Hyperbole

51. How is "lame" best defined in line 9?
    (A) Handicapped
    (B) Limping
    (C) Flimsy
    (D) Stupid

52. What element of figurative language is "when you follow the lame uncertain curves for a little distance they suddenly commit suicide"?
    (A) Onomatopoeia
    (B) Simile
    (C) Characterization
    (D) Personification

53. Which would define the character of the wallpaper described in lines 12–13?
    (A) Wonderful
    (B) An acceptable selection
    (C) Boring
    (D) Horrific

54. On line 14, what is the best definition for "lurid"?
    (A) Garish
    (B) Insipid
    (C) Pastel
    (D) Sparkly

GO TO NEXT PAGE ➡

DIRECTIONS: Select the word or group of words that has the same, or nearly the same, meaning as the word that is in **boldface**.

55. **Copyright** is most likely to mean
   (A) right to publish a textual work.
   (B) rights to photocopy.
   (C) giving credit to authors.
   (D) free to the public.

56. **Solemn** is most likely to mean
   (A) oath.
   (B) serious.
   (C) characterized.
   (D) friendly.

57. **Daft** is most likely to mean
   (A) crazy.
   (B) important.
   (C) affectionate.
   (D) angry.

58. **Befuddled** is most likely to mean
   (A) clear.
   (B) unclear.
   (C) special.
   (D) sweet.

59. **Sublime** is most likely to mean
   (A) beauty.
   (B) behavior.
   (C) admiration.
   (D) inspiring.

60. **Probity** is most likely to mean
   (A) decency.
   (B) accurate.
   (C) beginning.
   (D) rocky.

61. **Augur** is most likely to mean
   (A) predict.
   (B) bedraggled.
   (C) sloppy.
   (D) disguised.

62. **Gaunt** is most likely to mean
   (A) heavy.
   (B) fullness.
   (C) skinny.
   (D) fit.

63. **Beguile** is most likely to mean
   (A) charm.
   (B) arrogant.
   (C) loud.
   (D) smile.

64. **Rustic** is most likely to mean
   (A) modern.
   (B) slick.
   (C) cool.
   (D) crude.

65. **Piety** is most likely to mean
   (A) happy.
   (B) holy.
   (C) creative.
   (D) sickly.

GO TO NEXT PAGE ➡

DIRECTIONS: In each of the sentences below, the word in **boldface** may be unfamiliar to you. Use the other words in the sentence to help you decide what the word in **boldface** means.

66. The mouse was **conditioned** to drink from the water bottle when the scientist rang the bell.
    (A) circumstances.
    (B) factors.
    (C) influenced.
    (D) swimming.

67. The **crux** of the problem will be difficult to solve.
    (A) side.
    (B) center.
    (C) underneath.
    (D) top.

68. The **outcrop** of coral is considered to be a national treasure.
    (A) occurrences.
    (B) rows.
    (C) garden.
    (D) formation.

69. The computer system had **manifest** problems that required several hours of service.
    (A) obvious.
    (B) display.
    (C) shows.
    (D) ailment.

70. The **scar** in the land needed to be filled with rocks and dirt.
    (A) hill.
    (B) mountain.
    (C) gutter.
    (D) trench.

71. Mitchell **gesticulated** to the waitress when he could not pronounce the name of the dish.
    (A) screamed.
    (B) cried.
    (C) gestured.
    (D) spoke softly.

72. The **lodgments** were not quite what Alexandra and Louis expected, but they decided to stay anyway.
    (A) housing.
    (B) holes.
    (C) tents.
    (D) caves.

73. In the moonlight, the water had an **efflorescence** that was beautiful and mystifying.
    (A) dryness.
    (B) sparkling quality.
    (C) misty.
    (D) unusual.

74. Though the show was on **hiatus**, the channel continued to show reruns.
    (A) nightly.
    (B) weekly.
    (C) vacation.
    (D) in the morning.

GO TO NEXT PAGE ➡

75. The students had to **adapt** to their new surroundings because the school underwent extensive renovations over the summer.
    (A) familiarize.
    (B) postpone.
    (C) skip.
    (D) saunter.

76. Due to his **impecunious** situation, the man had to sell his yacht.
    (A) having no money.
    (B) having extreme wealth.
    (C) having bad taste.
    (D) having no religion.

77. The new interior of the opera house was covered with **ornate** tapestries.
    (A) peaceful.
    (B) tumultuous.
    (C) highly decorated.
    (D) extremely intelligent.

78. After 15 minutes of silent meditation her mind felt **lucid**.
    (A) melancholy.
    (B) worried.
    (C) clear.
    (D) fashionable.

79. After six hours, the woman finally led the other eight campers up to the edge of the **precipice**.
    (A) large tractor.
    (B) building.
    (C) hurricane.
    (D) steep slope.

80. The living room in the large mansion was **capacious** and comfortable.
    (A) spacious.
    (B) cramped.
    (C) hideous.
    (D) old.

81. The woman received an alarming notice from school about her son and his **truancy**.
    (A) award for good behavior.
    (B) absences without permission.
    (C) certificate of outstanding achievement.
    (D) dictionary of synonyms.

82. I was unaware that the networks would be hosting several **soirees** to launch the new television show.
    (A) party.
    (B) broadcast.
    (C) lunch.
    (D) awards.

83. The storm clouds were a **harbinger** of the coming hurricane.
    (A) welcome.
    (B) foreshadowing.
    (C) ending.
    (D) retelling.

84. The **patrimony** of the dog is unknown.
    (A) hair.
    (B) size.
    (C) ancestry.
    (D) weight.

GO TO NEXT PAGE ➡

PRACTICE TEST 2
MATHEMATICS SECTION

1. Evaluate: 5.8×10^4
   - (A) .00058
   - (B) .0058
   - (C) 5,800
   - (D) 58,000

2. Simplify: $\dfrac{5!}{3!}$
   - (A) 6
   - (B) 12
   - (C) 20
   - (D) 60

3. A businesswoman has a meal at a nice restaurant. She likes to tip 25% when the service is excellent. How much money will she tip on a $28 meal?
   - (A) $4.50
   - (B) $6.00
   - (C) $6.75
   - (D) $7.00

4. A jar contains 10 blue jelly beans and 25 jelly beans of other colors. What is the ratio of the number of blue jelly beans to the total number of jelly beans?
   - (A) 1:3
   - (B) 2:3
   - (C) 2:5
   - (D) 2:7

5. Which of the following points lies on the line expressed by the equation $-3x + 7y = 5$?
   - (A) (2, 2)
   - (B) (10, 5)
   - (C) (2, 5)
   - (D) (5, 10)

6. The points (2, 2), (5, 6), (8, 1) are the vertices of a polygon. What type of polygon is formed by these points?
   - (A) Triangle
   - (B) Square
   - (C) Parallelogram
   - (D) Trapezoid

7. Simplify: $\dfrac{64x^4 y^7}{8xy^3}$
   - (A) $8x^3y$
   - (B) $8xy^6$
   - (C) $8x^3y^4$
   - (D) $8xy^2$

8. What is the next number in this sequence: 2, 3, 5, 9, 17, ___?
   - (A) 29
   - (B) 33
   - (C) 41
   - (D) 43

9. Sports jerseys cost $36. They are on sale for 30% off. What is the sale price of the jerseys?
   - (A) $22.10
   - (B) $24.60
   - (C) $25.20
   - (D) $27.00

GO TO NEXT PAGE ➡

10. What is the slope of the line below?

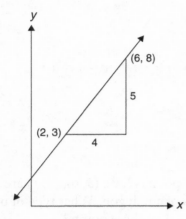

(A) $-\dfrac{4}{5}$ (C) $\dfrac{4}{5}$

(B) $\dfrac{5}{4}$ (D) $-\dfrac{5}{4}$

11. Simplify: $\dfrac{8}{48}$

(A) $\dfrac{1}{3}$ (C) $\dfrac{1}{6}$

(B) .38   (D) .25

12. Estimate: 312×420

(A) 1,200   (C) 120,000

(B) 12,000   (D) 1,200,000

13. What is the equation of the line shown on the graph?

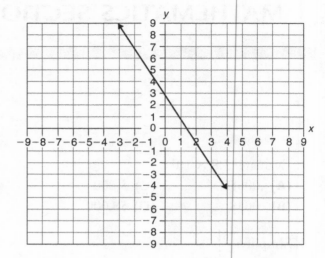

(A) $y = 2x + 3$ (C) $y = -2x + 3$

(B) $y = 2x - 3$ (D) $y = -2x - 3$

14. If $x = 9$ and $y = 8$, then $\dfrac{xy \div 4}{6} + 10 =$

(A) 12   (C) 17

(B) 13   (D) 20

15. What is the absolute value of -2?

(A) $-\dfrac{1}{2}$ (C) $\dfrac{1}{2}$

(B) 2   (D) -2

16. Five cards are shown: a heart, a diamond, a moon, a sun, and a lightning bolt. If you randomly select a single card, what is the probability of getting a heart or a sun?

(A) .40   (C) .70

(B) .65   (D) .85

GO TO NEXT PAGE ➡

17. The following graph shows the interest rates paid by Bank A and Bank B on a savings account. The interest rate depends upon the amount of the balance. For what balance amounts does Bank A pay a higher interest rate than Bank B?

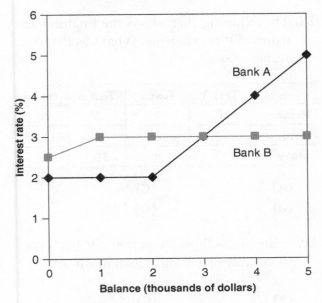

(A) $3,000 only

(B) Less than $3,000

(C) More than $3,000

(D) All amounts

18. How many different ways can you order five books on a shelf where order matters?

(A) 12   (C) 60

(B) 24   (D) 120

19. Solve for x: $10x - 5 = 3$

(A) $\dfrac{1}{4}$ (C) $\dfrac{2}{3}$

(B) $\dfrac{1}{2}$ (D) $\dfrac{4}{5}$

20. What is the solution set to the following system of equations?

$$\begin{cases} y = 3x - 8 \\ y = 2x \end{cases}$$

(A) $(2, 4)$ (C) $(8, 16)$

(B) $(3, 6)$ (D) $(5, 22)$

21. Given the following similar figures of a rectangle, find the length of the missing side.

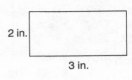
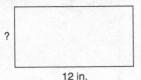

(A) 6 in.   (C) 9 in.

(B) 8 in.   (D) 10 in.

22. What is the slope of a line through the points $(4, 5)$ and $(6, 13)$?

(A) -4 (C) $\dfrac{3}{4}$

(B) $-\dfrac{3}{4}$ (D) 4

23. Evaluate: $4a^3 + \dfrac{b}{3} - 5$ for $a = 2 \quad b = 21$

(A) -12 (C) 29

(B) 5 (D) 34

24. Solve for x: $\dfrac{x}{5} - 7 = 8$

(A) 5 (C) 75

(B) 15 (D) 82

GO TO NEXT PAGE ➡

25. The graph shows the relationship between variable X and variable Y. Which trend does this graph support?

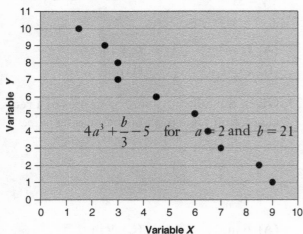

(A) As variable X increases, variable Y tends to decrease.

(B) As variable X increases, variable Y tends to increase.

(C) As variable X decreases, variable Y tends to decrease.

(D) Variable X and variable Y are unrelated.

26. What expression does the following graph represent?

```
←—+——+——●——+——+——+——+——+——+——+——+——+——+——→
 -6 -5 -4 -3 -2 -1  0  1  2  3  4  5  6
```

(A) $x > -4$ (C) $x < -4$

(B) $x \geq -4$ (D) $x \leq -4$

27. Write the following as an algebraic expression:

Ten less than four times a number

(A) $4x - 10$ (C) $10(x - 4)$

(B) $4(10x)$ (D) $10x - 4$

28. The following chart shows the English test scores of three students. What was Peter's average score?

	Test 1	Test 2	Test 3	Test 4
Peter	10	7	5	6
Paul	3	6	9	10
Mary	9	8	10	5

(A) 7   (C) 9

(B) 8   (D) 10

29. A fair coin is flipped two times. What is the probability of getting at least one head?

(A) $\dfrac{1}{4}$ (C) $\dfrac{2}{3}$

(B) $\dfrac{1}{3}$ (D) $\dfrac{3}{4}$

GO TO NEXT PAGE ➡

30. Which of the following is the graph of the equation $y = -x$?

(A)

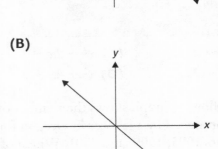

(B)

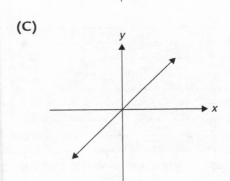

(C)

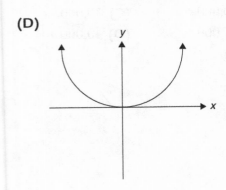

(D)

31. Given the following triangle, what is the measurement of the missing angle?

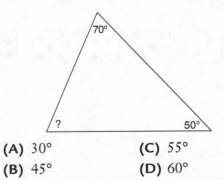

(A) 30°	**(C)** 55°
(B) 45°	**(D)** 60°

32. What is the value of x in the triangle shown?

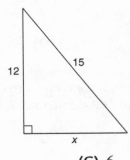

(A) 3	**(C)** 6
(B) 4	**(D)** 9

33. A purse contains five different coins. How many different combinations of three coins can you choose where order does *not* matter?

(A) 4	**(C)** 9
(B) 6	**(D)** 10

34. Jimmy scored the following points in his high school basketball games: 6, 2, 4, 2, 8, 0, 9. What is his median number of points scored?

(A) 2	**(C)** 5
(B) 4	**(D)** 9

GO TO NEXT PAGE ➡

35. A die has six sides. What is the probability of rolling a 2 or a 6 in one throw of a fair die ?

   (A) $\dfrac{1}{6}$ (C) $\dfrac{1}{2}$

   (B) $\dfrac{1}{3}$ (D) $\dfrac{2}{3}$

36. On one roll of two fair dice, what is the probability that they equal 2?

   (A) $\dfrac{1}{36}$ (C) $\dfrac{1}{12}$

   (B) $\dfrac{1}{24}$ (D) $\dfrac{1}{6}$

37. In the figure, if $\angle q$ is equal to 65°, what does $\angle l$ equal? Assume lines l_1 and l_2 are parallel.

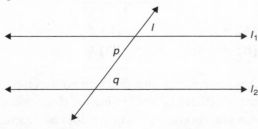

   (A) 25°   (C) 65°

   (B) 35°   (D) 115°

38. What is the volume in cubic inches of the box shown?

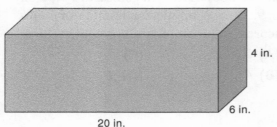

   (A) 480   (C) 800

   (B) 720   (D) 880

39. The length of the rectangle is two units longer than the width. Which expression represents the area of the rectangle?

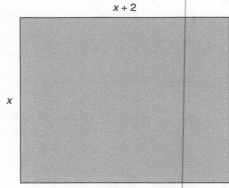

   (A) $x^2 + 2$ (C) $x^2 + 2x + 2$

   (B) $x^2 + 2x$ (D) $x^2 + 4x + 8$

40. The following graph shows the number of pears produced by a grower in Oregon for the years 1995, 1999, and 2001. Which of the following was the most probable number of pears produced by this grower in 1997?

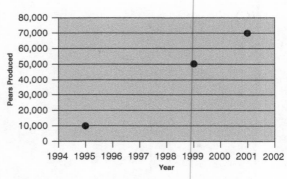

   (A) 20,000   (C) 30,000

   (B) 25,000   (D) 40,000

GO TO NEXT PAGE ➡

41. Which of the following ΔA'B'C' is the image of ΔABC that results from reflecting the ΔABC across the *y*-axis?

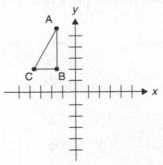

(C)

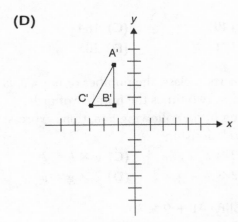

(A)

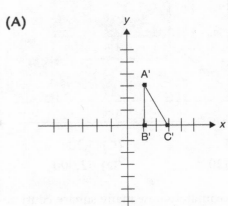

(D)

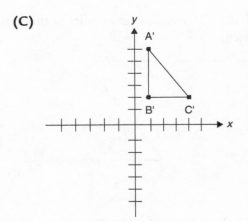

(B)

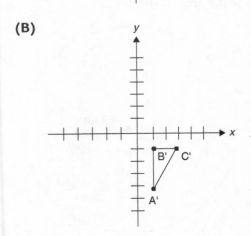

42. The graph shows the average monthly rainfall for the city of Stuckeyville. Which month has the fourth highest average monthly rainfall?

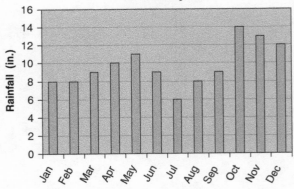

(A) November   **(C)** May

(B) April   **(D)** December

GO TO NEXT PAGE

43. What is the area in square units of the figure shown?

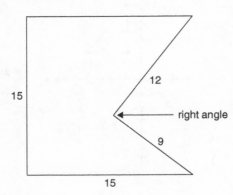

(A) 149   (C) 184

(B) 171   (D) 205

44. In a certain class, the number of boys, b, is equal to two times the number of girls, g. Which of the following equations expresses this relationship?

(A) $2 \times b = g$ (C) $g \times b = 2$

(B) $2 \times b = g \times b$ (D) $2 \times g = b$

45. Simplify: $41 + 9 \times 3$

(A) 51   (C) 73

(B) 68   (D) 150

46. A rectangular fish pond is on a square lot. The rest of the lot is a flower garden. In the following scaled drawing, each unit represents 10 feet. How many square feet is the flower garden?

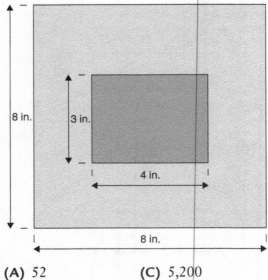

(A) 52   (C) 5,200

(B) 520   (D) 52,000

47. Approximately how many square centimeters is the area of the circle?

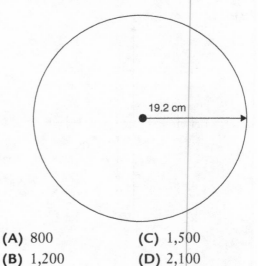

(A) 800   (C) 1,500

(B) 1,200   (D) 2,100

GO TO NEXT PAGE ➡

48. What is the length of the missing side in the following right triangle?

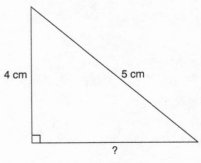

(A) 3 cm   (C) 5 cm

(B) 4 cm   (D) 6 cm

49. What is the value of $\dfrac{\text{Area of } \Delta A}{\text{Area of } \Delta B}$?

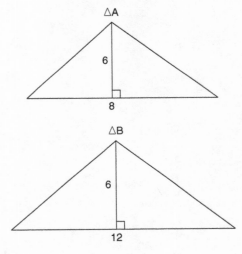

(A) $\dfrac{1}{4}$ (C) $\dfrac{2}{3}$

(B) $\dfrac{1}{3}$ (D) $\dfrac{4}{5}$

50. Given the similar figures of a rectangle below, find the length of the missing side.

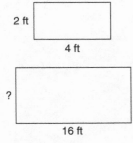

(A) 8 feet   (C) 10 feet

(B) 9 feet   (D) 11 feet

STOP

Practice Test 2 Answer Key

Question Number	Correct Answer
ENGLISH-LANGUAGE ARTS SECTION: **LANGUAGE SUBTEST**	
1.	(B)
2.	(C)
3.	(A)
4.	(C)
5.	(D)
6.	(B)
7.	(A)
8.	(D)
9.	(B)
10.	(C)
11.	(D)
12.	(C)
13.	(B)
14.	(C)
15.	(B)
16.	(B)
17.	(A)
18.	(C)
19.	(C)
20.	(D)

Question Number	Correct Answer
21.	(B)
22.	(C)
23.	(B)
24.	(B)
25.	(A)
26.	(A)
27.	(D)
28.	(B)
29.	(C)
30.	(B)
31.	(C)
32.	(C)
33.	(B)
34.	(C)
35.	(B)
36.	(A)
37.	(B)
38.	(B)
39.	(C)
40.	(A)
41.	(D)
42.	(B)
43.	(A)
44.	(D)
45.	(D)
46.	(B)
47.	(C)
48.	(B)
ENGLISH-LANGUAGE ARTS SECTION: READING SUBTEST	
1.	(B)
2.	(A)
3.	(D)
4.	(A)
5.	(C)

Question Number	Correct Answer
6.	(A)
7.	(A)
8.	(C)
9.	(B)
10.	(D)
11.	(C)
12.	(C)
13.	(C)
14.	(B)
15.	(B)
16.	(C)
17.	(A)
18.	(B)
19.	(B)
20.	(A)
21.	(D)
22.	(A)
23.	(A)
24.	(C)
25.	(C)
26.	(A)
27.	(B)
28.	(A)
29.	(C)
30.	(A)
31.	(C)
32.	(D)
33.	(C)
34.	(B)
35.	(D)
36.	(A)
37.	(B)
38.	(C)
39.	(A)
40.	(D)

Question Number	Correct Answer
41.	(C)
42.	(A)
43.	(C)
44.	(B)
45.	(D)
46.	(D)
47.	(C)
48.	(A)
49.	(A)
50.	(A)
51.	(C)
52.	(D)
53.	(D)
54.	(A)
55.	(A)
56.	(B)
57.	(A)
58.	(B)
59.	(A)
60.	(A)
61.	(A)
62.	(C)
63.	(A)
64.	(D)
65.	(B)
66.	(C)
67.	(B)
68.	(D)
69.	(A)
70.	(D)
71.	(C)
72.	(A)
73.	(B)
74.	(C)

Question Number	Correct Answer
75.	(A)
76.	(A)
77.	(C)
78.	(C)
79.	(D)
80.	(A)
81.	(B)
82.	(A)
83.	(B)
84.	(C)
MATHEMATICS SECTION	
1.	(D)
2.	(C)
3.	(D)
4.	(D)
5.	(B)
6.	(A)
7.	(C)
8.	(B)
9.	(C)
10.	(B)
11.	(C)
12.	(C)
13.	(C)
14.	(B)
15.	(B)
16.	(A)
17.	(C)
18.	(D)
19.	(D)
20.	(C)
21.	(B)
22.	(D)
23.	(D)
24.	(C)

Question Number	Correct Answer
25.	(A)
26.	(B)
27.	(A)
28.	(A)
29.	(D)
30.	(B)
31.	(D)
32.	(D)
33.	(D)
34.	(B)
35.	(B)
36.	(A)
37.	(C)
38.	(A)
39.	(B)
40.	(C)
41.	(C)
42.	(C)
43.	(B)
44.	(D)
45.	(B)
46.	(C)
47.	(B)
48.	(A)
49.	(C)
50.	(A)

PRACTICE TEST 2 DETAILED EXPLANATIONS

PRACTICE TEST 2 DETAILED EXPLANATIONS

ENGLISH-LANGUAGE ARTS SECTION

Language Subtest

1. **(B)** had bought
Verb tense is tested in this question. "Boughten" is not a word. So both **(A)** and the original sentence are incorrect. Choice **(C)** is not a viable choice either, as "has" is not an option for the progressive verb "buying."

2. **(C)** There
Remember the difference between these tricky words! "Their" is a possessive and shows ownership. "They're" is a contraction for "they are."

3. **(A)** was sold
Because the core verb is in past tense ("sold" over "sell"), the helping verb is in past tense as well. Therefore, "was sold" is the best choice.

4. **(C)** was
The word "yesterday" gives you a clue on what tense the verb should be in the sentence. "Yesterday" is in the past, so "was" and "were" are two options. Because "yesterday" is singular, it takes a singular verb so "was" is the best choice.

5. **(D)** Correct as is.
This one is tricky! "Is" is a linking verb so it would take the predicate nominative (noun). That leaves the original choice ("I") and "me." If you remember from your reading, with linking verbs, you can flip the sentence around and it should still make sense. If you said "I have a dog," it would make sense. "Me have a dog" does not make sense.

6. **(B)** pulled
This is a simple verb choice. Because the sentence takes place "last year," the verb needs to be in the past tense. "Pulled" is the only past tense verb in the choice selection.

7. **(A)** its
"Its" is the only possessive that does *not* have an apostrophe. "It's" is a contraction of "it is," so in the possessive, "its" is irregular. This is a tricky question; more than likely, you will see one or more of these on the test!

PRACTICE TEST 2 DETAILED
EXPLANATIONS

8. **(D)** Correct as is.

"Holidays," a plural noun, is the subject of the sentence. Consequently, it takes a plural verb. "Is" is singular, so option **(A)** is not an option. "Spending" needs a helping verb for it to make sense in the sentence.

9. **(B)** My family and I went

"I" is always used as a subject option because "me" is always used as an object. Also, because the subject is plural, the option must have a plural verb. Therefore, "my family and I went" is the best choice.

10. **(C)** "Hey, what is that?" said Donny.

This sentence stresses comma and quotation rules. Remember that the punctuation to the quote goes inside the end quotation mark, not at the end of the full sentence. The following verb is in lowercase because the sentence isn't finished.

11. **(D)** Correct as is.

This question tests commas in a list. Remember to put a comma between each item and after the item before the "and."

12. **(C)** teams: Arsenal, Bayern-Munich, Juventus, and Benfica.

This question tests commas in a list. Remember to put a comma between each item and after the item before the "and." You would not put a comma between "Bayern" and "Munich" because, though they are two words, the hyphen means that they work together and should be counted together as one word.

13. **(B)** went

This sentence is in the past tense because it is "after the parade." Therefore, the verb should be in the past tense as well, making "went" the best choice.

14. **(C)** most dangerous

When comparing more than two things, the adjective must be superlative. If the adjective is one syllable, an "-est" is added to it. For example, "biggest" is in the superlative. If a word has two or more syllables, it is traditional to insert the word "most" before it. For example, "most genuine" is an example of the superlative. If you compare two items, the same rules apply, except you would use "-er" instead of "-est" and "more" instead of "most."

15. **(B)** his

A "captain" is a person; therefore, the correct pronoun should be masculine or feminine, not neuter, or "not gendered." Since the only gender specific pronoun is "his," that is the correct choice.

16. **(B)** belong to

"Oranges" is plural, so a plural verb is needed. Also, be careful and use the correct preposition. "In," as a preposition, infers going inside of something else. "To" is a better choice.

17. **(A)** more important
Because water is compared to food, only two items are used in the comparison. Consequently, you should use the comparative, not the superlative. Since "important" is more than two syllables, the correct form is "more" not "most."

18. **(C)** "Where is my history book?"
This question tests comma and end punctuation use in a quotation. Remember that when sentences are set up in this way (with the non-quoted material first), the comma comes first and then the open quotation mark. The end punctuation that fits the quoted statement goes inside the end quotation mark.

19. **(C)** isn't on
"Isn't" is a contraction of "is not," so the negative "not" is already used. It is poor English to use a "double negative" or, to say, "isn't not."

20. **(D)** Correct as is.
The semicolon is used as a conjunction in this sentence. It separates two independent clauses. There is no conjunction needed when you use a semicolon. Also, because the semicolon is a conjunction (like the word "and"), you would not capitalize "cake."

21. **(B)** he wanted
The first verb in this sentence is "practiced," a simple past tense verb. Since the verb has to agree in tense, you must choose a simple past tense verb from the choices.

22. **(C)** yelled, "You kids need to be quiet!"
This question tests comma and end punctuation use in a quotation. Remember that when sentences are set up in this way (with the non-quoted material first), the comma comes first and then the open quotation mark. The end punctuation that fits the quoted statement goes inside the end quotation mark.

23. **(B)** There is
"They're" is a contraction for "they are" and is easily confused with "there," a pronoun for a place, and "their," a possessive pronoun. Recognizing that "they're" is "they are," reading the sentence as "They are is a wonderful…." doesn't make any sense. The "there, their, and they're" homonyms are often confused, and these types of questions are common on the CHSPE.

24. **(B)** candy, an apple, and a bottle of water.
This question tests comma use with items in a list. Remember to place a comma after the last item before the word "and." In answer **(C)**, there is one added comma after the "and" which makes that choice incorrect.

25. **(A)** was repaired
The original sentence does not have a full verb, which make the "sentence" a fragment. It needs to have a helping verb for the sentence to make sense. Since computer is singular, it needs a singular verb and helping verb. Therefore, "was repaired" is the only choice.

PRACTICE TEST 2 DETAILED EXPLANATIONS

26. **(A)** to go
    Like "there, they're, and their," "to, too, and two" are often confused. "Too" is an adverb and means "in excess"; and "two" is a number. "To," in this sentence, is part of the infinitive "to go," and "to" is the only option.

27. **(D)** Correct as is.
    In the sentence, "travelers" is plural and, since the sentence is about something that happened in the past, the verb needs to be in the past tense. "Completed," the original word in the sentence, fulfills both of the sentence requirements.

28. **(B)** are important
    Though the sentence may look to be correct at first, it is important to recognize the word "parts." "Parts," being plural, changes how the word "important" is read in the sentence. Using the indefinite adjective "an" would make "parts" have to be singular. For example, if the sentence read "Vegetables are an important part of a healthy diet," that would be correct. However, because "parts" is plural, the "an" cannot appear before important.

29. **(C)** Chicago, Illinois.
    This question refers to the comma rule regarding the separation between a city and state. This rule is one of the easiest ones to remember, so be sure to get these right on the test.

30. **(B)** Some people are
    "People" is plural and needs to have a plural verb. "Some," in this sentence, is just an adjective and modifies "people." Therefore, **(B)** is the correct answer.

31. **(C)** to be valuable
    "Value" is either a noun or verb, depending on how it is used in a sentence. In this example, "value" cannot apply because it is being used as an adjective. The adjective form of "value" is valuable, which makes **(C)** the best choice.

32. **(C)** popular, but Jazz is
    The error in this sentence is how it is combined into one complete thought. The original sentence is a fragment because, after the colon, "Jazz" has no correct verb. In **(A)**, the separation of the semicolon is correct, but "Jazz" is singular and "are" is a plural verb. **(B)** is a comma splice; the two thoughts are shoved together without a correct conjunction. **(C)**, the correct answer, has an appropriate conjunction ("but"), and "Jazz" has the correct verb agreement.

33. **(B)** Ellington, a famous music composer, wrote
    The question tests the comma rule of appositives. An appositive, as you know, is a phrase that describes a noun in detail. It must be set off by commas. (Note: Appositives are always additional, not-really-needed information.) It can be picked up and removed from the sentence, and the sentence would still make sense. When looking at the options, it is important to remove the words inside the commas, read the sentence without them, and judge if the sentence is still grammatically correct. In **(B)**, if you removed the appositive, the sentence would read "Duke Ellington wrote that song." This is a grammatically correct sentence.

34. (C) our

"Are" and "our" are homophone, or two words that sound the same but have different meanings. Knowing the difference is important because "are" is a verb and "our" is a possessive adjective. Mixing them up makes a huge impact on the sentence!

35. (B) panda, who was named Billy, was

The question tests the comma rule of appositives. An appositive, as you know, is a phrase that describes a noun in detail. It must be set off by commas. (Note: Appositives are always additional, not-really-needed information.) It can be picked up and removed from the sentence, and the sentence would still make sense. When looking at the options, it is important to remove the words inside the commas, read the sentence without them, and judge if the sentence is still grammatically correct. In **(B)**, if you removed the appositive, the sentence would read "The panda was a crowd favorite." This is a grammatically correct sentence. **(C)** would not be correct because if you are talking about a panda in regards to one panda, the correct pronoun is "who." If you were talking about more than one, the correct pronoun would be "which," as in "which one."

36. (A) Michigan is a state that has many lakes.

This question tests a capitalization rule. All states are capitalized. They are proper nouns, and all proper nouns are capitalized to show distinction from common nouns.

37. (B) Charles Dickens wrote the book *The Tale of Two Cities*.

Because the entire title of the book is *The Tale of Two Cities*, the article "the" is capitalized in the beginning of the title. It is important to recognize the distinction between titles of books and titles of buildings or monuments. One monument, the Grand Canyon, only capitalizes "grand" and "canyon" as that is the actual name. We only use "the" as a definite article to describe it so it isn't capitalized.

38. (B) Lisa and I

"Me" is never used as part of a subject because it is an object pronoun. So, then, why isn't **(A)** correct? It is correct to always use "I" in the last subject position when there is more than one subject.

39. (C) pickles, cheese, mustard, and onions

This question tests commas in a list. Remember to put a comma between each item and after the item before the "and."

40. (A) He gave himself

"Self" pronouns are called reflexive pronouns. They are used to refer directly to the subject of the sentence. Because the subject is "he," the correct reflexive pronoun would be "himself."

41. (D) Correct as is.

This sentence stresses comma and quotation rules. Remember that the punctuation to the quote goes inside the end quotation mark, not at the end of the full sentence. The following verb is in lowercase because the sentence isn't finished.

42. **(B)** Walking is

"Walking" is a gerund. It looks like a verb, but it acts like a noun. "Walking" is singular; it is an act that is "done," which makes it a "thing" in the grammar "world." Since "walking" is singular, it would have a singular subject: "is."

43. **(A)** Male

The author makes the male reference in the first line of the piece. He writes that Jupiter makes "his appearance" in the sky.

44. **(D)** Correct as is.

You would not put a comma between "great" and "red" because, when you have adjectives in a list, you only use a comma if the word "and" would make sense. For example, it would be incorrect to say "a great AND red star," like in **(A)**. It doesn't even sound right! **(B)** is even worse: "a great red AND star." And **(C)** is funny: "a great AND red AND star." This is a good trick to help you with these types of questions.

45. **(D)** Fiery red, the startling sized stranger looks the more fateful.

With rewording sentences, it is easy to get caught up in arguing with yourself about which answer is best. This answer is deceptive. All of them, except for one, could possibly work. But which is the *best* one? The sentence is concise. It says, succinctly, that the planet is red, and the adjectives "startling sized" obviously modify "stranger."

46. **(B)** ... certainly, no one who had not followed in their courses what the Greeks so picturesquely called "the wanderers" would recognize in the apparition an orderly member of our own solar family.

This wordy sentence is a tough one. At first glance, you may have looked at the sentence and wondered why the phrase "who had not followed in their courses what the Greeks so picturesquely called 'the wanderers'" is not set off by commas like an appositive. The reason is because this bit of information is essential to the sentence; it is needed to explain the entire thought correctly. Therefore, it is not set off by commas. In the second part of the sentence, the phrase "an orderly member of our own solar family" is separated from the verb by the prepositional phrase "in the apparition." The subject, verb, and object of this sentence are "no one would recognize member." So, in the original sentence, the object of the sentence was separated from the main sentence as a fragment, which is completely incorrect.

47. **(C)** no one who had not followed in his/her courses

Because the author uses "no one," it is best to use a singular pronoun like "his" or "her." "Their" is a plural pronoun, and it is incorrect in this sentence. "Them," also a plural, is an object pronoun, and this sentence needs a possessive pronoun. "Those" does not refer back to "no one," so it is an incorrect option as well.

48. **(B)** a startled visitor

"Visitant" is a fancy way of saying "visitor." "Startling" is a fancy way of saying "startled." If you replaced the words in the options, **(B)** is the only viable option.

PRACTICE TEST 2 DETAILED EXPLANATIONS
ENGLISH-LANGUAGE ARTS SECTION
Writing Task

The following is an example of a well-written essay. **This essay would earn a 5–6 on the Writing Rubric.**

What does it mean to be adult? Most can agree that maturity and strength of character are the building blocks to adulthood. Therefore, juxtaposing drinking and voting to age limits is not an equal comparison.

When one asks what is needed to be a responsible drinker, one can agree that discretion is important. A person should be able to drink without causing harm to others or to oneself. However, in today's society, the media promotes and glorifies drinking in movies, television, and the Internet; in fact, several mainstream, recent comedies are based around drinking too much and the escapades that follow from such immature actions. The youth of today are more easily influenced by the media that others who have the life experience to make good, realistic judgments over what is seen on movie or television screens. Those three extra years of college or life experience are integral in helping younger adults to make sound decisions around drinking and the impact thoughtless decisions could make on others.

In regards to voting, 18 is the perfect age to become involved in the political system. One's schooling has hopefully provided political party background information, and a student is more able to understand political literature and discussions on the Internet and on television. Moreover, most 18 year olds have held jobs and have paid taxes for around two years. Because most of these young workers hold the lowest paying jobs in the nation, having the power to make decisions about taxes and the political system is an effective and appropriate means of voicing an opinion about the quality of one's life. In conclusion, 18 is the appropriate age for voting, but many of the same age still need to learn good judgment when it comes to drinking/partying with friends. Because most 18 year olds have had two years of working experience, they are more able to make a sound, informed decision when it comes to voting. Perhaps, three years after 18, when a person is 21, the same individuals will make respectable decisions in regards to drinking.

PRACTICE TEST 2 DETAILED EXPLANATIONS
ENGLISH-LANGUAGE ARTS SECTION
Reading Subtest

1. **(B)** member fees
   "Dues" is defined as an obligatory payment, and it is used as a noun. "Due" is a different word, a verb; therefore, **(B)** is the only acceptable choice.

2. **(A)** January
   You must look at the chart to make the right choice for this question. In this case, the cost per month for each year is about $60. If you look at just the month of December, you will see that it is $241. Obviously, $60 a month is much less expensive than $241. Therefore, purchasing membership in January is the most cost effective.

3. **(D)** Non-residents will not come as often
   Non-residents will not attend the club as often; therefore, they are a better investment for the club.

4. **(A)** Skills
   In this question, the best strategy would be to replace each word with "Arts." "Arts" are skills: whether they apply to painting, sculpting, dance, or music.

5. **(C)** ABCBBB
   The 2nd, 4th, 5th, and 6th lines all rhyme in each stanza.

6. **(A)** creepy
   Some of the words that clue you in to "creepy" over the other selections are "bleak," "dreary," "ghost," and "dying on the floor." Look at the adjectives in the selection when discerning tone.

7. **(A)** internal rhyme
   The 2nd and 4th lines of each stanza all have internal rhyme, something that gives this poem a definite, defined rhythm.

8. **(C)** Alliteration
   The repetition of "n" sounds is the give-away here. Assonance is the repetition of vowel sounds, and there is no obvious metaphor or simile present in the line given.

9. **(B)** A small, unusual old book of historical legends

"Quaint" means small, while "curious" can mean unusual or interesting. "Lore" is a term that is generally used for old historical legends.

10. **(D)** March

The darker elements of the chart show you where "your gas/oil boiler" produces the most heat. If you look at the months and compare them, March is significantly higher than the other three options.

11. **(C)** May

The lightly shaded area of the chart shows solar panel energy. Of the four choices, May is the highest.

12. **(C)** It is sunnier in those months so the panels can gather more energy.

This question is inferred by the chart. The lightly shaded area of the chart is much higher in the summer months. The most logical conclusion is because it is sunnier outside so the panels can gather more energy. Whether or not people use more hot water in the summer or winter does not matter, the solar panels work more efficiently because of the sun, not because of water use.

13. **(C)** Gas and oil are used more for hot water in those months.

This question is also inferred by the chart and what it measures. It would make sense that, in the winter and early spring, more gas and oil would be used to heat houses and water. The other answers do not reflect the purpose of solar panels.

14. **(B)** metaphor

Dr. King compares the rights or "promissory note" of African Americans to that of a check. When two unlike things are compared, without using "like" or "as," the comparison is a metaphor.

15. **(B)** Creators

"Architects," in this line, means the same thing as creators; he speaks about the creation of the Declaration of Independence and how "all" men would be given the same "inalienable" rights. Inserting any of the other choices into the "architects" space would not make any sense to the rest of the piece.

16. **(C)** The creators of the document signed a sort of promise to the American people.

The "promissory note" is a "sort of promise," and "heirs" are people who survive after others die, in this case, the American people for coming generations.

17. **(A)** Not able to be given away

An "alien" is a person who belongs to another place. "Inalienable" is an adjective that describes a sense of belonging or owning a place or rights to something. In this example, "inalienable rights" means the rights that belong to the people who belong to this country.

18. **(B)** worthy duty
    (B) is the best choice because in this sentence, it is the most appropriate answer. Though you may have thought that **(C)** would be a good choice because of the word "sacred," "holy" is too strong because of the religious connotations attached to it. Dr. King discusses in the text the duty of the American people to each other, no matter what the race. Therefore, "worthy duty" is the best choice.

19. **(B)** The government has not given African-American people the same opportunities as white people.
    This question refers back to the comparison of the promise America gave to African-Americans to that of an insufficient check. The other answers are off-base to the rest of the piece. There is nothing in the text about a bank giving African Americans bad checks or that, in general, America gives away bad checks, or that bad checks are only given out by Americans.

20. **(A)** African-American people have not been given what has been promised them by the American government.
    Main idea questions can be tricky. When you read the piece and apply the reading comprehension strategies, we know that Dr. King is talking about African Americans not getting what was promised them. **(B)** and **(D)** are both extreme in the sense that global generalizations are made about African Americans and people in general. **(C)** doesn't make sense in relation to the text because it was the government that did not keep their "sacred obligation," not the African-American people.

21. **(D)** Blocker
    The Blocker is the best option. Both the Warrior and the Blocker have the same options except for the hours of private coaching. If a person doesn't want private coaching, then the Blocker would be the best selection because it is more affordable at $1000.

22. **(A)** Champion
    At the most costly, the Champion option gives the most options. This option covers ten hours of private coaching and 25 dining room dinners, as well as the clothing, golf balls, and tournament fees.

23. **(A)** Basic
    The Basic option has no private coaching hours.

24. **(C)** Champion, Challenger, Warrior
    As the top three most costly options, the Champion, Challenger, and Warrior options include dining room options.

25. **(C)** complicated ideas
    "Abstract" means not concrete or tangible.

26. **(A)** combine
    The only word that could fit in this sentence and have it still make sense is "combine." If the rights "separated," the line wouldn't make sense. "Administer" and "scale" wouldn't make sense in the context of the sentence.

27. **(B)**   A promoter of uncensored literature
The author talks about how uncensored literature can "promote animated discussion and dialogue, and the texts also can encourage the student to think on more abstract levels because they have to interpret the content for themselves." This line shows that the author is for uncensored literature in classrooms.

28. **(A)**   parameters
"Axioms" are things we know to be true. In the second to last line, the author questions how education professionals should choose literature and if teachers should be overruled by administrators, like they have in the past. The last line questions if such overruling powers are appropriate and if these "truths" are really best for students.

29. **(C)**   Prejudice
The Foxes "persecute" the Geese; for what reason, we don't know. "Persecution" is most closely linked to "prejudice," the best choice for this answer.

30. **(A)**   the winner
In the second paragraph, the text said that the "victor" would stop for a feast. It wouldn't make sense to have a feast if you lost a battle. The best answer would be the winner of the battle. The other answer options do not make sense in the context of the text.

31. **(C)**   They are both beast and bird so they used both sides to their advantage.
Bats are flying mammals so they are the perfect combination of bird and beast. The bats didn't want to fight on a losing side, so they would wait and see which side was winning before they joined in.

32. **(D)**   bats
All of the other animals participated in the peace conference because they fought in the battle. Since the bats were the only ones who didn't fight in the wars, their fate was discussed by the other animals.

33. **(C)**   The other animals punished them, removing them from daylight "society."
The bats were exiled from the rest of the animals because they were two-faced and wouldn't choose allegiance to a side. Because of this fickle behavior, the other animals would not allow them to live in the new peace reached from the peace conference, and they banished them to only come out at night.

34. **(B)**   a moral
A moral is a lesson shown by a story or a fable. A summary is a shortened version of a text, usually one or two sentences long. A summary does not give a lesson. "Irony" and "characterization" are words commonly used to describe elements of literature.

35. **(D)**   lovers and madmen have similar minds
The entire passage is about how lovers, madmen, and poets are similar in how they view love.

36. **(A)** poets can write poems about dreams and fantasies
    The lines say that poets can take thoughts and dreams ("airy nothings") and give them form, or substance.

37. **(B)** shadows can seem real with an active imagination.
    When people are easily influenced, i.e., when in love or afraid, a bush in the night may be supposed a bear.

38. **(C)** Insane
    Though in some cases "seething" can mean angry, in this example, because the selection is about the insanity of love, insane is the best choice.

39. **(A)** compared
    Lovers, madmen, and poets are compared.

40. **(D)** ecstasy
    In this case, it would be the ecstasy of the insane.

41. **(C)** average percentage who drink more than two cups of coffee daily
    If looking at the percentages of people who drink more than two cups daily, you can see that the percentage on the right is an average of the age percentages. The other options have no validity in the information given.

42. **(A)** 29%
    The table shows that men aged 45–64 make up 29% of males who drink more than two cups daily.

43. **(C)** 25–34
    The table shows that women aged 25–34 make up 30% of females who drink more than two cups daily.

44. **(B)** Coffee consumption decreases in men and women after 65 because of health issues.
    This is the best assumption because the data drops off significantly after age 65. Health issues or concerns are realistic assumptions based on everyday knowledge.

45. **(D)** 33%
    Men aged 34–44 make up 33% of people drinking more than two cups daily.

46. **(D)** There is not enough information given to make a prediction.
    The chart does not give any information about why men drink more coffee than women. Remember that you can only answer questions based on given information and "common knowledge"; there are no additional clues given for the higher percentage of males drinking coffee.

47. **(C)** it was somewhat torn up by abuse.
    She describes the room with stripped off wallpaper all around the room as if it had been used as a gymnasium.

48. **(A)** Flashy

Flashy is the best choice because in her description, she says that the wallpaper has a large, swirling pattern in dark yellow. The other options are all defined as simple and dull.

49. **(A)** A creative crime

Artistic generally refers to creative genius or talent. A sin is a wrong-doing or injustice. In this case, "a crime of creativity" is the best selection, while the others are examples of "art" that aren't criminal or wrong.

50. **(A)** Personification

A pattern is not a living human being; therefore, it cannot "commit every artistic sin." Only something human could do that. Personification is defined as giving something in-human human characteristics.

51. **(C)** Flimsy

A and B both refer to "lame" in the sense of being physically lame, or handicapped. Choice **(D)** is lame defined in slang terms.

52. **(D)** Personification

Once again, curves cannot "commit suicide": that is a human action. Personification is defined as giving an animal, object, or abstraction human characteristics.

53. **(D)** Horrific

The character in the story hates the wallpaper, defining it as "lurid," "irritating," "unclean," and "repellent."

54. **(A)** Garish

Garish is loud and unseemly. Her description is "lurid orange in some places, a sickly sulphur tint in others." The other choices are dull, boring, and soft shades.

55. **(A)** right to publish a textual work

56. **(B)** serious

57. **(A)** crazy

58. **(B)** unclear

59. **(A)** beauty

60. **(A)** decency

61. **(A)** predict

62. **(C)** skinny

63. **(A)** charm

64. **(D)** crude

65. **(B)** holy

66. **(C)** influenced

67. **(B)** center

68. **(D)** formation

69. **(A)** obvious

70. **(D)** trench

71. **(C)** gestured

72. **(A)** housing

73. **(B)** sparkling quality

74. **(C)** vacation

75. **(A)** familiarize

76. **(A)** having no money

77. **(C)** highly decorated

78. **(C)** clear

79. **(D)** steep slope

80. **(A)** spacious

81. **(B)** absences without permission

82. **(A)** party

83. **(B)** foreshadowing

84. **(C)** ancestry

PRACTICE TEST 2 DETAILED EXPLANATIONS
MATHEMATICS SECTION

1. **(D)** This is scientific notation. Because the exponent is a 4, move the decimal point four places to the right and add zeros in the open spaces. The answer is 58,000.

2. **(C)** This is a factorial (!) problem. Multiply the given number by one less than that number; then multiply the resulting product by the next lower number, and repeat this process until you have multiplied by 1:

$$\frac{5!}{3!} = \frac{5 \times 4 \times 3 \times 2 \times 1}{3 \times 2 \times 1} = 20$$

3. **(D)** This is a simple percentage problem. Remember that 25% in decimal form is .25:

$28(.25) = \$7.00$

4. **(D)** The total number of jelly beans is 35:

10 blue jelly beans + 25 other-colored jelly beans = 35 jelly beans

So the ratio of blue jelly beans to all jelly beans is 10:35, which in simplest form is 2:7.

5. **(B)** Substitute each answer into the equation until you find a point that makes the equation true. $-3(10) + 7(5) = 5$ is true. So the answer is (10, 5).

6. **(A)** Plot the points on an x, y graph. Then connect the nearest points. This figure is a triangle.

7. **(C)** First, simplify the constants by dividing 64 by 8. Then simplify the x and y variables by subtracting the exponents on each:

$$\frac{64x^4y^7}{8xy^3} = 8x^3y^4$$

8. **(B)** The pattern is to double a number and then subtract 1. The last given number is 17, so the next number in the series is 33:

$17(2) - 1 = 33$

9. **(C)** First calculate the discount, and then subtract this from the regular price. Remember that 30% in decimal form is .3:

$$36(.3) = 10.8$$
$$36 - 10.8 = 25.2$$

The sale price is $25.20.

10. **(B)** The formula for slope is rise over run, or $\dfrac{y_1 - y_2}{x_1 - x_2}$, so plug in the given points—(6, 8) and (2, 3)—and evaluate:

$$\frac{8 - 3}{6 - 2} = \frac{5}{4}$$

The slope is $\dfrac{5}{4}$.

11. **(C)** $\dfrac{8}{48} = \dfrac{1}{6}$

12. **(C)** First round the numbers and then multiply:
$$300 \times 400 = 120,000$$

13. **(C)** The important parts in the equation of a line are the slope and the y-intercept. Remember that the general equation for a line is $y = mx + b$, where m is the slope and b is the y-intercept. Looking at the graph, you can see that the line intersects the y-axis at 3, so that gives you one part of the equation: $y = mx + 3$. Now, again looking at the graph, choose two points on the line and use the formula of rise over run, $\dfrac{y_1 - y_2}{x_1 - x_2}$, to find the slope. We'll use the points $(-1, 5)$ and $(0, 3)$:

$$\frac{5 - 3}{-1 - 0} = \frac{2}{-1} = -2$$

The slope of this line is -2 using rise over run. The y-intercept is 3. Therefore, the correct equation is $y = -2x + 3$.

14. **(B)** $\dfrac{xy \div 4}{6} + 10 = \dfrac{(9)(8) \div 4}{6} + 10 = 13$

15. **(B)** The absolute value of a number, other than 0, is positive. The absolute value of -2 is 2.

16. **(A)** There are five possible outcomes and two of them satisfy the question. So the probability of not getting a heart is $\dfrac{2}{5}$, or in decimal form, .40.

17. **(C)** Inspection of the graph shows that Bank A pays more than Bank B for balances of more than $3,000.

18. (D) This is asking for the number of permutations of five things from a set of five things. The answer is 5!:

$$5! = 5 \times 4 \times 3 \times 2 \times 1 = 120$$

19. (D)

$$10x - 5 = 3$$

$$10x = 3 + 5$$

$$10x = 8$$

$$\frac{10x}{10} = \frac{8}{10}$$

$$x = \frac{4}{5}$$

20. (C) Solving a system of linear equations involves finding the point at which two lines intersect. One approach to this problem is to substitute each answer, one at time, into the two formulas given. The correct answer is the one that makes both of the equations true. In this case, the point (8, 16) makes both equations true:

$$y = 3x - 8$$
$$16 = 3(8) - 8$$
$$y = 2x$$
$$16 = 2(8)$$

21. (B) Set this problem up as a proportion. Write a proportion for the corresponding sides. Let x represent the length of the missing side. Then solve for x:

$$\frac{x}{2} = \frac{12}{3}$$

$$x = \frac{12 \times 2}{3}$$

$$x = 8 \text{ inches}$$

22. (D) Use the formula for the slope of a line through two points:

$$m = \frac{y_2 - y_1}{x_2 - x_1}$$

$$m = \frac{13 - 5}{6 - 4} = \frac{8}{2} = 4$$

The slope is 4.

23. **(D)** Substitute the values given into the expression and simplify:

$$4a^3 + \frac{b}{3} - 5 = 4(2)^2 + \frac{21}{3} - 5 = 32 + 7 - 5 = 34$$

24. **(C)** Solve for x:

$$\frac{x}{5} - 7 = 8$$

$$\frac{x}{5} - 7 + 7 = 8 + 7$$

$$\frac{x}{5} = 15$$

$$\frac{5 \times x}{5} = 15 \times 5$$

$$x = 75$$

25. **(A)** As variable X increases, variable Y tends to decrease.

26. **(B)** The arrow is pointing in the greater-than direction and it has a solid dot. This number line represents greater than or equal to -4, or in symbol form, $x \geq -4$.

27. **(A)** The words "ten less than four times a number" can be turned into an expression. The part "ten less than" means "to subtract 10." "Four times a number" means "to multiply by 4." Let x represent the number. The correct expression is $4x - 10$.

28. **(A)** The average score for Peter is calculated by adding his four test scores and then dividing by 4:

$$10 + 7 + 5 + 6 = 28$$

$$\frac{28}{4} = 7$$

29. **(D)** There are four possible outcomes that can result from flipping a fair coin twice:

	Flip 1	Flip 2
Possible Outcome 1	Heads	Tails
Possible Outcome 2	Heads	Heads
Possible Outcome 3	Tails	Heads
Possible Outcome 4	Tails	Tails

As the chart shows, three of the outcomes include at least one head. So the probability of getting at least one head is $\frac{3}{4}$.

30. (B) The equation $y = -x$ is a line with a slope of -1 and a y-intercept of 0.

31. (D) The sum of the angles of a triangle must equal 180°. To find the missing value, first add the two known measurements together and then subtract from 180:

$$50 + 70 = 120$$
$$180 - 120 = 60°$$

32. (D) Solve using the Pythagorean theorem, $a^2 + b^2 = c^2$; remember that c represents the hypotenuse, the side opposite the right angle:

$$a^2 + b^2 = c^2$$
$$a^2 + 12^2 = 15^2$$
$$a^2 + 144 = 225$$
$$a^2 + 144 - 144 = 225 - 144$$
$$a^2 = 81$$
$$a = \sqrt{81} = 9$$

33. (D) Use the formula for the combination of five different things taken three at a time:

$$_nC_k = \frac{n!}{k!(n-k)!}$$

$$_5C_3 = \frac{5!}{3!(5-3)!}$$

$$_5C_3 = \frac{5!}{3!(2)!}$$

$$_5C_3 = \frac{120}{6(2)}$$

$$_5C_3 = \frac{120}{12} = 10$$

34. (B) To find the median score, the scores must be first ordered from smallest to largest:

0, 2, 2, 4, 6, 8, 9

The median score is the one in the middle. In this case, it is 4.

35. (B) There are six possible and equally likely outcomes from rolling one fair die. Rolling a 2 or a 6 would cover two out of the six possibilities. Therefore, the probability of rolling a 2 or a 6 would be $\frac{2}{6}$ or $\frac{1}{3}$.

36. (A) There are 36 possible outcomes from rolling two dice. Only one outcome results in rolling a 2. The probability is $\frac{1}{36}$.

37. (C) In the figure, $\angle q$ is equal to $\angle p$ because they are alternate interior angles of parallel lines. The measurement of $\angle p$ is equal to $\angle l$. Therefore, $\angle l$ equals 65°.

38. (A) The formula for volume is height times width times length:

$4 \times 6 \times 20 = 480$ cubic inches

39. (B) The formula for area is length times width:

$x(x + 2) = x^2 + 2x$

40. (C) The pattern that this data suggest is a straight line. If this imaginary line were extended down, the year 1997 would have a predicted value of 30,000.

41. (C) Find the side of the figure closest to the y-axis and measure the distance of this side from the y-axis. A reflection of the figure will put this side the same distance from the y-axis, but on the other side of the axis. Also, notice the point labeled "C." A reflection of this point across the y-axis will also be the same distance from the y-axis, but on the other side.

42. (C) Finding the fourth highest average monthly rainfall is simply a matter of looking for the fourth longest bar on the graph. May has the fourth longest bar and is therefore the correct answer.

43. (B) Imagine that this figure is a square with a triangle missing. First calculate the area of the missing triangle. Remember that the formula for the area of a triangle is $\frac{1}{2}$ the base times the height:

$\frac{1}{2}(9)(12) = \frac{1}{2}(108) = 54$

Then calculate the area of the imaginary square by multiplying length times width:

$15 \times 15 = 225$

Last, subtract the area of the triangle from the area of the square:

$225 - 54 = 171$

The area of the figure is 171 square units.

44. (D) The written expression, "the number of boys, b, is equal to two times the number of girls, g" can be written as $2 \times g = b$.

45. (B) The rule called order of operations tells us to do multiplication and division before addition and subtraction. Therefore, $41 + 9 \times 3 = 41 + 27 = 68$.

46. (C) First, calculate the area of the fish pond. Remember that each unit is equal to 10 feet, so the length of the fish pond is 4×10, or 40 feet, and its width is 3×10, or 30 feet:

Area $= 40 \times 30 = 1,200$ square feet

Next, calculate the area of the whole lot:

$80 \times 80 = 6,400$ square feet

Last, subtract the area for the fish pond from that of the entire lot to find the area of the flower garden:

6,400 − 1,200 = 5,200 square feet

47. (B) To find the area of a circle, use the formula πr^2. Pi (π) can be rounded to 3, and the given radius, 19.2, can be rounded up to 20:

πr^2

$3(20)^2 = 3(400) = 1,200$

The area of the circle is *approximately* 1,200 square centimeters.

48. (A) Solve using the Pythagorean theorem:

$$a^2 + b^2 = c^2$$
$$a^2 + 4^2 = 5^2$$
$$a^2 + 16 = 25$$
$$a^2 + 16 - 16 = 25 - 16$$
$$a^2 = 9$$
$$a = \sqrt{9} = 3$$

49. (C) The formula for the area of $\triangle$ is $\frac{1}{2}bh$, where b equals the base and h equals the height. First, find the area of each $\triangle$:

Area of $\triangle A = \frac{1}{2}(8)(6) = 24$

Area of $\triangle B = \frac{1}{2}(12)(6) = 36$

Now, divide the area of $\triangle A$ by the area of $\triangle B$, and put this fraction into lowest terms:

$$\frac{24}{36} = \frac{2}{3}$$

50. (A) Set this problem up as a proportion. Write a proportion for the corresponding sides. Let x represent the length of the missing side. Then solve for x:

$$\frac{x}{2} = \frac{16}{4}$$

$$x = \frac{16 \times 2}{4}$$

$$x = 8 \text{ feet}$$

ANSWER SHEET

Pretest

English-Language Arts Section

Language Subtest

1. Ⓐ Ⓑ Ⓒ Ⓓ	13. Ⓐ Ⓑ Ⓒ Ⓓ	25. Ⓐ Ⓑ Ⓒ Ⓓ	37. Ⓐ Ⓑ Ⓒ Ⓓ
2. Ⓐ Ⓑ Ⓒ Ⓓ	14. Ⓐ Ⓑ Ⓒ Ⓓ	26. Ⓐ Ⓑ Ⓒ Ⓓ	38. Ⓐ Ⓑ Ⓒ Ⓓ
3. Ⓐ Ⓑ Ⓒ Ⓓ	15. Ⓐ Ⓑ Ⓒ Ⓓ	27. Ⓐ Ⓑ Ⓒ Ⓓ	39. Ⓐ Ⓑ Ⓒ Ⓓ
4. Ⓐ Ⓑ Ⓒ Ⓓ	16. Ⓐ Ⓑ Ⓒ Ⓓ	28. Ⓐ Ⓑ Ⓒ Ⓓ	40. Ⓐ Ⓑ Ⓒ Ⓓ
5. Ⓐ Ⓑ Ⓒ Ⓓ	17. Ⓐ Ⓑ Ⓒ Ⓓ	29. Ⓐ Ⓑ Ⓒ Ⓓ	41. Ⓐ Ⓑ Ⓒ Ⓓ
6. Ⓐ Ⓑ Ⓒ Ⓓ	18. Ⓐ Ⓑ Ⓒ Ⓓ	30. Ⓐ Ⓑ Ⓒ Ⓓ	42. Ⓐ Ⓑ Ⓒ Ⓓ
7. Ⓐ Ⓑ Ⓒ Ⓓ	19. Ⓐ Ⓑ Ⓒ Ⓓ	31. Ⓐ Ⓑ Ⓒ Ⓓ	43. Ⓐ Ⓑ Ⓒ Ⓓ
8. Ⓐ Ⓑ Ⓒ Ⓓ	20. Ⓐ Ⓑ Ⓒ Ⓓ	32. Ⓐ Ⓑ Ⓒ Ⓓ	44. Ⓐ Ⓑ Ⓒ Ⓓ
9. Ⓐ Ⓑ Ⓒ Ⓓ	21. Ⓐ Ⓑ Ⓒ Ⓓ	33. Ⓐ Ⓑ Ⓒ Ⓓ	45. Ⓐ Ⓑ Ⓒ Ⓓ
10. Ⓐ Ⓑ Ⓒ Ⓓ	22. Ⓐ Ⓑ Ⓒ Ⓓ	34. Ⓐ Ⓑ Ⓒ Ⓓ	46. Ⓐ Ⓑ Ⓒ Ⓓ
11. Ⓐ Ⓑ Ⓒ Ⓓ	23. Ⓐ Ⓑ Ⓒ Ⓓ	35. Ⓐ Ⓑ Ⓒ Ⓓ	47. Ⓐ Ⓑ Ⓒ Ⓓ
12. Ⓐ Ⓑ Ⓒ Ⓓ	24. Ⓐ Ⓑ Ⓒ Ⓓ	36. Ⓐ Ⓑ Ⓒ Ⓓ	48. Ⓐ Ⓑ Ⓒ Ⓓ

Reading Subtest

1. Ⓐ Ⓑ Ⓒ Ⓓ	12. Ⓐ Ⓑ Ⓒ Ⓓ	23. Ⓐ Ⓑ Ⓒ Ⓓ	34. Ⓐ Ⓑ Ⓒ Ⓓ
2. Ⓐ Ⓑ Ⓒ Ⓓ	13. Ⓐ Ⓑ Ⓒ Ⓓ	24. Ⓐ Ⓑ Ⓒ Ⓓ	35. Ⓐ Ⓑ Ⓒ Ⓓ
3. Ⓐ Ⓑ Ⓒ Ⓓ	14. Ⓐ Ⓑ Ⓒ Ⓓ	25. Ⓐ Ⓑ Ⓒ Ⓓ	36. Ⓐ Ⓑ Ⓒ Ⓓ
4. Ⓐ Ⓑ Ⓒ Ⓓ	15. Ⓐ Ⓑ Ⓒ Ⓓ	26. Ⓐ Ⓑ Ⓒ Ⓓ	37. Ⓐ Ⓑ Ⓒ Ⓓ
5. Ⓐ Ⓑ Ⓒ Ⓓ	16. Ⓐ Ⓑ Ⓒ Ⓓ	27. Ⓐ Ⓑ Ⓒ Ⓓ	38. Ⓐ Ⓑ Ⓒ Ⓓ
6. Ⓐ Ⓑ Ⓒ Ⓓ	17. Ⓐ Ⓑ Ⓒ Ⓓ	28. Ⓐ Ⓑ Ⓒ Ⓓ	39. Ⓐ Ⓑ Ⓒ Ⓓ
7. Ⓐ Ⓑ Ⓒ Ⓓ	18. Ⓐ Ⓑ Ⓒ Ⓓ	29. Ⓐ Ⓑ Ⓒ Ⓓ	40. Ⓐ Ⓑ Ⓒ Ⓓ
8. Ⓐ Ⓑ Ⓒ Ⓓ	19. Ⓐ Ⓑ Ⓒ Ⓓ	30. Ⓐ Ⓑ Ⓒ Ⓓ	41. Ⓐ Ⓑ Ⓒ Ⓓ
9. Ⓐ Ⓑ Ⓒ Ⓓ	20. Ⓐ Ⓑ Ⓒ Ⓓ	31. Ⓐ Ⓑ Ⓒ Ⓓ	42. Ⓐ Ⓑ Ⓒ Ⓓ
10. Ⓐ Ⓑ Ⓒ Ⓓ	21. Ⓐ Ⓑ Ⓒ Ⓓ	32. Ⓐ Ⓑ Ⓒ Ⓓ	43. Ⓐ Ⓑ Ⓒ Ⓓ
11. Ⓐ Ⓑ Ⓒ Ⓓ	22. Ⓐ Ⓑ Ⓒ Ⓓ	33. Ⓐ Ⓑ Ⓒ Ⓓ	44. Ⓐ Ⓑ Ⓒ Ⓓ

45. Ⓐ Ⓑ Ⓒ Ⓓ
46. Ⓐ Ⓑ Ⓒ Ⓓ
47. Ⓐ Ⓑ Ⓒ Ⓓ
48. Ⓐ Ⓑ Ⓒ Ⓓ
49. Ⓐ Ⓑ Ⓒ Ⓓ
50. Ⓐ Ⓑ Ⓒ Ⓓ
51. Ⓐ Ⓑ Ⓒ Ⓓ
52. Ⓐ Ⓑ Ⓒ Ⓓ
53. Ⓐ Ⓑ Ⓒ Ⓓ
54. Ⓐ Ⓑ Ⓒ Ⓓ

55. Ⓐ Ⓑ Ⓒ Ⓓ
56. Ⓐ Ⓑ Ⓒ Ⓓ
57. Ⓐ Ⓑ Ⓒ Ⓓ
58. Ⓐ Ⓑ Ⓒ Ⓓ
59. Ⓐ Ⓑ Ⓒ Ⓓ
60. Ⓐ Ⓑ Ⓒ Ⓓ
61. Ⓐ Ⓑ Ⓒ Ⓓ
62. Ⓐ Ⓑ Ⓒ Ⓓ
63. Ⓐ Ⓑ Ⓒ Ⓓ
64. Ⓐ Ⓑ Ⓒ Ⓓ

65. Ⓐ Ⓑ Ⓒ Ⓓ
66. Ⓐ Ⓑ Ⓒ Ⓓ
67. Ⓐ Ⓑ Ⓒ Ⓓ
68. Ⓐ Ⓑ Ⓒ Ⓓ
69. Ⓐ Ⓑ Ⓒ Ⓓ
70. Ⓐ Ⓑ Ⓒ Ⓓ
71. Ⓐ Ⓑ Ⓒ Ⓓ
72. Ⓐ Ⓑ Ⓒ Ⓓ
73. Ⓐ Ⓑ Ⓒ Ⓓ
74. Ⓐ Ⓑ Ⓒ Ⓓ

75. Ⓐ Ⓑ Ⓒ Ⓓ
76. Ⓐ Ⓑ Ⓒ Ⓓ
77. Ⓐ Ⓑ Ⓒ Ⓓ
78. Ⓐ Ⓑ Ⓒ Ⓓ
79. Ⓐ Ⓑ Ⓒ Ⓓ
80. Ⓐ Ⓑ Ⓒ Ⓓ
81. Ⓐ Ⓑ Ⓒ Ⓓ
82. Ⓐ Ⓑ Ⓒ Ⓓ
83. Ⓐ Ⓑ Ⓒ Ⓓ
84. Ⓐ Ⓑ Ⓒ Ⓓ

Mathematics Section

1. Ⓐ Ⓑ Ⓒ Ⓓ
2. Ⓐ Ⓑ Ⓒ Ⓓ
3. Ⓐ Ⓑ Ⓒ Ⓓ
4. Ⓐ Ⓑ Ⓒ Ⓓ
5. Ⓐ Ⓑ Ⓒ Ⓓ
6. Ⓐ Ⓑ Ⓒ Ⓓ
7. Ⓐ Ⓑ Ⓒ Ⓓ
8. Ⓐ Ⓑ Ⓒ Ⓓ
9. Ⓐ Ⓑ Ⓒ Ⓓ
10. Ⓐ Ⓑ Ⓒ Ⓓ
11. Ⓐ Ⓑ Ⓒ Ⓓ
12. Ⓐ Ⓑ Ⓒ Ⓓ
13. Ⓐ Ⓑ Ⓒ Ⓓ

14. Ⓐ Ⓑ Ⓒ Ⓓ
15. Ⓐ Ⓑ Ⓒ Ⓓ
16. Ⓐ Ⓑ Ⓒ Ⓓ
17. Ⓐ Ⓑ Ⓒ Ⓓ
18. Ⓐ Ⓑ Ⓒ Ⓓ
19. Ⓐ Ⓑ Ⓒ Ⓓ
20. Ⓐ Ⓑ Ⓒ Ⓓ
21. Ⓐ Ⓑ Ⓒ Ⓓ
22. Ⓐ Ⓑ Ⓒ Ⓓ
23. Ⓐ Ⓑ Ⓒ Ⓓ
24. Ⓐ Ⓑ Ⓒ Ⓓ
25. Ⓐ Ⓑ Ⓒ Ⓓ
26. Ⓐ Ⓑ Ⓒ Ⓓ

27. Ⓐ Ⓑ Ⓒ Ⓓ
28. Ⓐ Ⓑ Ⓒ Ⓓ
29. Ⓐ Ⓑ Ⓒ Ⓓ
30. Ⓐ Ⓑ Ⓒ Ⓓ
31. Ⓐ Ⓑ Ⓒ Ⓓ
32. Ⓐ Ⓑ Ⓒ Ⓓ
33. Ⓐ Ⓑ Ⓒ Ⓓ
34. Ⓐ Ⓑ Ⓒ Ⓓ
35. Ⓐ Ⓑ Ⓒ Ⓓ
36. Ⓐ Ⓑ Ⓒ Ⓓ
37. Ⓐ Ⓑ Ⓒ Ⓓ
38. Ⓐ Ⓑ Ⓒ Ⓓ
39. Ⓐ Ⓑ Ⓒ Ⓓ

40. Ⓐ Ⓑ Ⓒ Ⓓ
41. Ⓐ Ⓑ Ⓒ Ⓓ
42. Ⓐ Ⓑ Ⓒ Ⓓ
43. Ⓐ Ⓑ Ⓒ Ⓓ
44. Ⓐ Ⓑ Ⓒ Ⓓ
45. Ⓐ Ⓑ Ⓒ Ⓓ
46. Ⓐ Ⓑ Ⓒ Ⓓ
47. Ⓐ Ⓑ Ⓒ Ⓓ
48. Ⓐ Ⓑ Ⓒ Ⓓ
49. Ⓐ Ⓑ Ⓒ Ⓓ
50. Ⓐ Ⓑ Ⓒ Ⓓ

ANSWER SHEET

Practice Test 1

English-Language Arts Section
Language Subtest

1. Ⓐ Ⓑ Ⓒ Ⓓ
2. Ⓐ Ⓑ Ⓒ Ⓓ
3. Ⓐ Ⓑ Ⓒ Ⓓ
4. Ⓐ Ⓑ Ⓒ Ⓓ
5. Ⓐ Ⓑ Ⓒ Ⓓ
6. Ⓐ Ⓑ Ⓒ Ⓓ
7. Ⓐ Ⓑ Ⓒ Ⓓ
8. Ⓐ Ⓑ Ⓒ Ⓓ
9. Ⓐ Ⓑ Ⓒ Ⓓ
10. Ⓐ Ⓑ Ⓒ Ⓓ
11. Ⓐ Ⓑ Ⓒ Ⓓ
12. Ⓐ Ⓑ Ⓒ Ⓓ

13. Ⓐ Ⓑ Ⓒ Ⓓ
14. Ⓐ Ⓑ Ⓒ Ⓓ
15. Ⓐ Ⓑ Ⓒ Ⓓ
16. Ⓐ Ⓑ Ⓒ Ⓓ
17. Ⓐ Ⓑ Ⓒ Ⓓ
18. Ⓐ Ⓑ Ⓒ Ⓓ
19. Ⓐ Ⓑ Ⓒ Ⓓ
20. Ⓐ Ⓑ Ⓒ Ⓓ
21. Ⓐ Ⓑ Ⓒ Ⓓ
22. Ⓐ Ⓑ Ⓒ Ⓓ
23. Ⓐ Ⓑ Ⓒ Ⓓ
24. Ⓐ Ⓑ Ⓒ Ⓓ

25. Ⓐ Ⓑ Ⓒ Ⓓ
26. Ⓐ Ⓑ Ⓒ Ⓓ
27. Ⓐ Ⓑ Ⓒ Ⓓ
28. Ⓐ Ⓑ Ⓒ Ⓓ
29. Ⓐ Ⓑ Ⓒ Ⓓ
30. Ⓐ Ⓑ Ⓒ Ⓓ
31. Ⓐ Ⓑ Ⓒ Ⓓ
32. Ⓐ Ⓑ Ⓒ Ⓓ
33. Ⓐ Ⓑ Ⓒ Ⓓ
34. Ⓐ Ⓑ Ⓒ Ⓓ
35. Ⓐ Ⓑ Ⓒ Ⓓ
36. Ⓐ Ⓑ Ⓒ Ⓓ

37. Ⓐ Ⓑ Ⓒ Ⓓ
38. Ⓐ Ⓑ Ⓒ Ⓓ
39. Ⓐ Ⓑ Ⓒ Ⓓ
40. Ⓐ Ⓑ Ⓒ Ⓓ
41. Ⓐ Ⓑ Ⓒ Ⓓ
42. Ⓐ Ⓑ Ⓒ Ⓓ
43. Ⓐ Ⓑ Ⓒ Ⓓ
44. Ⓐ Ⓑ Ⓒ Ⓓ
45. Ⓐ Ⓑ Ⓒ Ⓓ
46. Ⓐ Ⓑ Ⓒ Ⓓ
47. Ⓐ Ⓑ Ⓒ Ⓓ
48. Ⓐ Ⓑ Ⓒ Ⓓ

Reading Subtest

1. Ⓐ Ⓑ Ⓒ Ⓓ
2. Ⓐ Ⓑ Ⓒ Ⓓ
3. Ⓐ Ⓑ Ⓒ Ⓓ
4. Ⓐ Ⓑ Ⓒ Ⓓ
5. Ⓐ Ⓑ Ⓒ Ⓓ
6. Ⓐ Ⓑ Ⓒ Ⓓ
7. Ⓐ Ⓑ Ⓒ Ⓓ
8. Ⓐ Ⓑ Ⓒ Ⓓ
9. Ⓐ Ⓑ Ⓒ Ⓓ
10. Ⓐ Ⓑ Ⓒ Ⓓ
11. Ⓐ Ⓑ Ⓒ Ⓓ

12. Ⓐ Ⓑ Ⓒ Ⓓ
13. Ⓐ Ⓑ Ⓒ Ⓓ
14. Ⓐ Ⓑ Ⓒ Ⓓ
15. Ⓐ Ⓑ Ⓒ Ⓓ
16. Ⓐ Ⓑ Ⓒ Ⓓ
17. Ⓐ Ⓑ Ⓒ Ⓓ
18. Ⓐ Ⓑ Ⓒ Ⓓ
19. Ⓐ Ⓑ Ⓒ Ⓓ
20. Ⓐ Ⓑ Ⓒ Ⓓ
21. Ⓐ Ⓑ Ⓒ Ⓓ
22. Ⓐ Ⓑ Ⓒ Ⓓ

23. Ⓐ Ⓑ Ⓒ Ⓓ
24. Ⓐ Ⓑ Ⓒ Ⓓ
25. Ⓐ Ⓑ Ⓒ Ⓓ
26. Ⓐ Ⓑ Ⓒ Ⓓ
27. Ⓐ Ⓑ Ⓒ Ⓓ
28. Ⓐ Ⓑ Ⓒ Ⓓ
29. Ⓐ Ⓑ Ⓒ Ⓓ
30. Ⓐ Ⓑ Ⓒ Ⓓ
31. Ⓐ Ⓑ Ⓒ Ⓓ
32. Ⓐ Ⓑ Ⓒ Ⓓ
33. Ⓐ Ⓑ Ⓒ Ⓓ

34. Ⓐ Ⓑ Ⓒ Ⓓ
35. Ⓐ Ⓑ Ⓒ Ⓓ
36. Ⓐ Ⓑ Ⓒ Ⓓ
37. Ⓐ Ⓑ Ⓒ Ⓓ
38. Ⓐ Ⓑ Ⓒ Ⓓ
39. Ⓐ Ⓑ Ⓒ Ⓓ
40. Ⓐ Ⓑ Ⓒ Ⓓ
41. Ⓐ Ⓑ Ⓒ Ⓓ
42. Ⓐ Ⓑ Ⓒ Ⓓ
43. Ⓐ Ⓑ Ⓒ Ⓓ
44. Ⓐ Ⓑ Ⓒ Ⓓ

45. Ⓐ Ⓑ Ⓒ Ⓓ   55. Ⓐ Ⓑ Ⓒ Ⓓ   65. Ⓐ Ⓑ Ⓒ Ⓓ   75. Ⓐ Ⓑ Ⓒ Ⓓ
46. Ⓐ Ⓑ Ⓒ Ⓓ   56. Ⓐ Ⓑ Ⓒ Ⓓ   66. Ⓐ Ⓑ Ⓒ Ⓓ   76. Ⓐ Ⓑ Ⓒ Ⓓ
47. Ⓐ Ⓑ Ⓒ Ⓓ   57. Ⓐ Ⓑ Ⓒ Ⓓ   67. Ⓐ Ⓑ Ⓒ Ⓓ   77. Ⓐ Ⓑ Ⓒ Ⓓ
48. Ⓐ Ⓑ Ⓒ Ⓓ   58. Ⓐ Ⓑ Ⓒ Ⓓ   68. Ⓐ Ⓑ Ⓒ Ⓓ   78. Ⓐ Ⓑ Ⓒ Ⓓ
49. Ⓐ Ⓑ Ⓒ Ⓓ   59. Ⓐ Ⓑ Ⓒ Ⓓ   69. Ⓐ Ⓑ Ⓒ Ⓓ   79. Ⓐ Ⓑ Ⓒ Ⓓ
50. Ⓐ Ⓑ Ⓒ Ⓓ   60. Ⓐ Ⓑ Ⓒ Ⓓ   70. Ⓐ Ⓑ Ⓒ Ⓓ   80. Ⓐ Ⓑ Ⓒ Ⓓ
51. Ⓐ Ⓑ Ⓒ Ⓓ   61. Ⓐ Ⓑ Ⓒ Ⓓ   71. Ⓐ Ⓑ Ⓒ Ⓓ   81. Ⓐ Ⓑ Ⓒ Ⓓ
52. Ⓐ Ⓑ Ⓒ Ⓓ   62. Ⓐ Ⓑ Ⓒ Ⓓ   72. Ⓐ Ⓑ Ⓒ Ⓓ   82. Ⓐ Ⓑ Ⓒ Ⓓ
53. Ⓐ Ⓑ Ⓒ Ⓓ   63. Ⓐ Ⓑ Ⓒ Ⓓ   73. Ⓐ Ⓑ Ⓒ Ⓓ   83. Ⓐ Ⓑ Ⓒ Ⓓ
54. Ⓐ Ⓑ Ⓒ Ⓓ   64. Ⓐ Ⓑ Ⓒ Ⓓ   74. Ⓐ Ⓑ Ⓒ Ⓓ   84. Ⓐ Ⓑ Ⓒ Ⓓ

Mathematics Section

1. Ⓐ Ⓑ Ⓒ Ⓓ   14. Ⓐ Ⓑ Ⓒ Ⓓ   27. Ⓐ Ⓑ Ⓒ Ⓓ   40. Ⓐ Ⓑ Ⓒ Ⓓ
2. Ⓐ Ⓑ Ⓒ Ⓓ   15. Ⓐ Ⓑ Ⓒ Ⓓ   28. Ⓐ Ⓑ Ⓒ Ⓓ   41. Ⓐ Ⓑ Ⓒ Ⓓ
3. Ⓐ Ⓑ Ⓒ Ⓓ   16. Ⓐ Ⓑ Ⓒ Ⓓ   29. Ⓐ Ⓑ Ⓒ Ⓓ   42. Ⓐ Ⓑ Ⓒ Ⓓ
4. Ⓐ Ⓑ Ⓒ Ⓓ   17. Ⓐ Ⓑ Ⓒ Ⓓ   30. Ⓐ Ⓑ Ⓒ Ⓓ   43. Ⓐ Ⓑ Ⓒ Ⓓ
5. Ⓐ Ⓑ Ⓒ Ⓓ   18. Ⓐ Ⓑ Ⓒ Ⓓ   31. Ⓐ Ⓑ Ⓒ Ⓓ   44. Ⓐ Ⓑ Ⓒ Ⓓ
6. Ⓐ Ⓑ Ⓒ Ⓓ   19. Ⓐ Ⓑ Ⓒ Ⓓ   32. Ⓐ Ⓑ Ⓒ Ⓓ   45. Ⓐ Ⓑ Ⓒ Ⓓ
7. Ⓐ Ⓑ Ⓒ Ⓓ   20. Ⓐ Ⓑ Ⓒ Ⓓ   33. Ⓐ Ⓑ Ⓒ Ⓓ   46. Ⓐ Ⓑ Ⓒ Ⓓ
8. Ⓐ Ⓑ Ⓒ Ⓓ   21. Ⓐ Ⓑ Ⓒ Ⓓ   34. Ⓐ Ⓑ Ⓒ Ⓓ   47. Ⓐ Ⓑ Ⓒ Ⓓ
9. Ⓐ Ⓑ Ⓒ Ⓓ   22. Ⓐ Ⓑ Ⓒ Ⓓ   35. Ⓐ Ⓑ Ⓒ Ⓓ   48. Ⓐ Ⓑ Ⓒ Ⓓ
10. Ⓐ Ⓑ Ⓒ Ⓓ   23. Ⓐ Ⓑ Ⓒ Ⓓ   36. Ⓐ Ⓑ Ⓒ Ⓓ   49. Ⓐ Ⓑ Ⓒ Ⓓ
11. Ⓐ Ⓑ Ⓒ Ⓓ   24. Ⓐ Ⓑ Ⓒ Ⓓ   37. Ⓐ Ⓑ Ⓒ Ⓓ   50. Ⓐ Ⓑ Ⓒ Ⓓ
12. Ⓐ Ⓑ Ⓒ Ⓓ   25. Ⓐ Ⓑ Ⓒ Ⓓ   38. Ⓐ Ⓑ Ⓒ Ⓓ
13. Ⓐ Ⓑ Ⓒ Ⓓ   26. Ⓐ Ⓑ Ⓒ Ⓓ   39. Ⓐ Ⓑ Ⓒ Ⓓ

ANSWER SHEET

Practice Test 2

English-Language Arts Section

Language Subtest

1. Ⓐ Ⓑ Ⓒ Ⓓ	13. Ⓐ Ⓑ Ⓒ Ⓓ	25. Ⓐ Ⓑ Ⓒ Ⓓ	37. Ⓐ Ⓑ Ⓒ Ⓓ
2. Ⓐ Ⓑ Ⓒ Ⓓ	14. Ⓐ Ⓑ Ⓒ Ⓓ	26. Ⓐ Ⓑ Ⓒ Ⓓ	38. Ⓐ Ⓑ Ⓒ Ⓓ
3. Ⓐ Ⓑ Ⓒ Ⓓ	15. Ⓐ Ⓑ Ⓒ Ⓓ	27. Ⓐ Ⓑ Ⓒ Ⓓ	39. Ⓐ Ⓑ Ⓒ Ⓓ
4. Ⓐ Ⓑ Ⓒ Ⓓ	16. Ⓐ Ⓑ Ⓒ Ⓓ	28. Ⓐ Ⓑ Ⓒ Ⓓ	40. Ⓐ Ⓑ Ⓒ Ⓓ
5. Ⓐ Ⓑ Ⓒ Ⓓ	17. Ⓐ Ⓑ Ⓒ Ⓓ	29. Ⓐ Ⓑ Ⓒ Ⓓ	41. Ⓐ Ⓑ Ⓒ Ⓓ
6. Ⓐ Ⓑ Ⓒ Ⓓ	18. Ⓐ Ⓑ Ⓒ Ⓓ	30. Ⓐ Ⓑ Ⓒ Ⓓ	42. Ⓐ Ⓑ Ⓒ Ⓓ
7. Ⓐ Ⓑ Ⓒ Ⓓ	19. Ⓐ Ⓑ Ⓒ Ⓓ	31. Ⓐ Ⓑ Ⓒ Ⓓ	43. Ⓐ Ⓑ Ⓒ Ⓓ
8. Ⓐ Ⓑ Ⓒ Ⓓ	20. Ⓐ Ⓑ Ⓒ Ⓓ	32. Ⓐ Ⓑ Ⓒ Ⓓ	44. Ⓐ Ⓑ Ⓒ Ⓓ
9. Ⓐ Ⓑ Ⓒ Ⓓ	21. Ⓐ Ⓑ Ⓒ Ⓓ	33. Ⓐ Ⓑ Ⓒ Ⓓ	45. Ⓐ Ⓑ Ⓒ Ⓓ
10. Ⓐ Ⓑ Ⓒ Ⓓ	22. Ⓐ Ⓑ Ⓒ Ⓓ	34. Ⓐ Ⓑ Ⓒ Ⓓ	46. Ⓐ Ⓑ Ⓒ Ⓓ
11. Ⓐ Ⓑ Ⓒ Ⓓ	23. Ⓐ Ⓑ Ⓒ Ⓓ	35. Ⓐ Ⓑ Ⓒ Ⓓ	47. Ⓐ Ⓑ Ⓒ Ⓓ
12. Ⓐ Ⓑ Ⓒ Ⓓ	24. Ⓐ Ⓑ Ⓒ Ⓓ	36. Ⓐ Ⓑ Ⓒ Ⓓ	48. Ⓐ Ⓑ Ⓒ Ⓓ

Reading Subtest

1. Ⓐ Ⓑ Ⓒ Ⓓ	12. Ⓐ Ⓑ Ⓒ Ⓓ	23. Ⓐ Ⓑ Ⓒ Ⓓ	34. Ⓐ Ⓑ Ⓒ Ⓓ
2. Ⓐ Ⓑ Ⓒ Ⓓ	13. Ⓐ Ⓑ Ⓒ Ⓓ	24. Ⓐ Ⓑ Ⓒ Ⓓ	35. Ⓐ Ⓑ Ⓒ Ⓓ
3. Ⓐ Ⓑ Ⓒ Ⓓ	14. Ⓐ Ⓑ Ⓒ Ⓓ	25. Ⓐ Ⓑ Ⓒ Ⓓ	36. Ⓐ Ⓑ Ⓒ Ⓓ
4. Ⓐ Ⓑ Ⓒ Ⓓ	15. Ⓐ Ⓑ Ⓒ Ⓓ	26. Ⓐ Ⓑ Ⓒ Ⓓ	37. Ⓐ Ⓑ Ⓒ Ⓓ
5. Ⓐ Ⓑ Ⓒ Ⓓ	16. Ⓐ Ⓑ Ⓒ Ⓓ	27. Ⓐ Ⓑ Ⓒ Ⓓ	38. Ⓐ Ⓑ Ⓒ Ⓓ
6. Ⓐ Ⓑ Ⓒ Ⓓ	17. Ⓐ Ⓑ Ⓒ Ⓓ	28. Ⓐ Ⓑ Ⓒ Ⓓ	39. Ⓐ Ⓑ Ⓒ Ⓓ
7. Ⓐ Ⓑ Ⓒ Ⓓ	18. Ⓐ Ⓑ Ⓒ Ⓓ	29. Ⓐ Ⓑ Ⓒ Ⓓ	40. Ⓐ Ⓑ Ⓒ Ⓓ
8. Ⓐ Ⓑ Ⓒ Ⓓ	19. Ⓐ Ⓑ Ⓒ Ⓓ	30. Ⓐ Ⓑ Ⓒ Ⓓ	41. Ⓐ Ⓑ Ⓒ Ⓓ
9. Ⓐ Ⓑ Ⓒ Ⓓ	20. Ⓐ Ⓑ Ⓒ Ⓓ	31. Ⓐ Ⓑ Ⓒ Ⓓ	42. Ⓐ Ⓑ Ⓒ Ⓓ
10. Ⓐ Ⓑ Ⓒ Ⓓ	21. Ⓐ Ⓑ Ⓒ Ⓓ	32. Ⓐ Ⓑ Ⓒ Ⓓ	43. Ⓐ Ⓑ Ⓒ Ⓓ
11. Ⓐ Ⓑ Ⓒ Ⓓ	22. Ⓐ Ⓑ Ⓒ Ⓓ	33. Ⓐ Ⓑ Ⓒ Ⓓ	44. Ⓐ Ⓑ Ⓒ Ⓓ

45. Ⓐ Ⓑ Ⓒ Ⓓ	55. Ⓐ Ⓑ Ⓒ Ⓓ	65. Ⓐ Ⓑ Ⓒ Ⓓ	75. Ⓐ Ⓑ Ⓒ Ⓓ
46. Ⓐ Ⓑ Ⓒ Ⓓ	56. Ⓐ Ⓑ Ⓒ Ⓓ	66. Ⓐ Ⓑ Ⓒ Ⓓ	76. Ⓐ Ⓑ Ⓒ Ⓓ
47. Ⓐ Ⓑ Ⓒ Ⓓ	57. Ⓐ Ⓑ Ⓒ Ⓓ	67. Ⓐ Ⓑ Ⓒ Ⓓ	77. Ⓐ Ⓑ Ⓒ Ⓓ
48. Ⓐ Ⓑ Ⓒ Ⓓ	58. Ⓐ Ⓑ Ⓒ Ⓓ	68. Ⓐ Ⓑ Ⓒ Ⓓ	78. Ⓐ Ⓑ Ⓒ Ⓓ
49. Ⓐ Ⓑ Ⓒ Ⓓ	59. Ⓐ Ⓑ Ⓒ Ⓓ	69. Ⓐ Ⓑ Ⓒ Ⓓ	79. Ⓐ Ⓑ Ⓒ Ⓓ
50. Ⓐ Ⓑ Ⓒ Ⓓ	60. Ⓐ Ⓑ Ⓒ Ⓓ	70. Ⓐ Ⓑ Ⓒ Ⓓ	80. Ⓐ Ⓑ Ⓒ Ⓓ
51. Ⓐ Ⓑ Ⓒ Ⓓ	61. Ⓐ Ⓑ Ⓒ Ⓓ	71. Ⓐ Ⓑ Ⓒ Ⓓ	81. Ⓐ Ⓑ Ⓒ Ⓓ
52. Ⓐ Ⓑ Ⓒ Ⓓ	62. Ⓐ Ⓑ Ⓒ Ⓓ	72. Ⓐ Ⓑ Ⓒ Ⓓ	82. Ⓐ Ⓑ Ⓒ Ⓓ
53. Ⓐ Ⓑ Ⓒ Ⓓ	63. Ⓐ Ⓑ Ⓒ Ⓓ	73. Ⓐ Ⓑ Ⓒ Ⓓ	83. Ⓐ Ⓑ Ⓒ Ⓓ
54. Ⓐ Ⓑ Ⓒ Ⓓ	64. Ⓐ Ⓑ Ⓒ Ⓓ	74. Ⓐ Ⓑ Ⓒ Ⓓ	84. Ⓐ Ⓑ Ⓒ Ⓓ

Mathematics Section

1. Ⓐ Ⓑ Ⓒ Ⓓ	14. Ⓐ Ⓑ Ⓒ Ⓓ	27. Ⓐ Ⓑ Ⓒ Ⓓ	40. Ⓐ Ⓑ Ⓒ Ⓓ
2. Ⓐ Ⓑ Ⓒ Ⓓ	15. Ⓐ Ⓑ Ⓒ Ⓓ	28. Ⓐ Ⓑ Ⓒ Ⓓ	41. Ⓐ Ⓑ Ⓒ Ⓓ
3. Ⓐ Ⓑ Ⓒ Ⓓ	16. Ⓐ Ⓑ Ⓒ Ⓓ	29. Ⓐ Ⓑ Ⓒ Ⓓ	42. Ⓐ Ⓑ Ⓒ Ⓓ
4. Ⓐ Ⓑ Ⓒ Ⓓ	17. Ⓐ Ⓑ Ⓒ Ⓓ	30. Ⓐ Ⓑ Ⓒ Ⓓ	43. Ⓐ Ⓑ Ⓒ Ⓓ
5. Ⓐ Ⓑ Ⓒ Ⓓ	18. Ⓐ Ⓑ Ⓒ Ⓓ	31. Ⓐ Ⓑ Ⓒ Ⓓ	44. Ⓐ Ⓑ Ⓒ Ⓓ
6. Ⓐ Ⓑ Ⓒ Ⓓ	19. Ⓐ Ⓑ Ⓒ Ⓓ	32. Ⓐ Ⓑ Ⓒ Ⓓ	45. Ⓐ Ⓑ Ⓒ Ⓓ
7. Ⓐ Ⓑ Ⓒ Ⓓ	20. Ⓐ Ⓑ Ⓒ Ⓓ	33. Ⓐ Ⓑ Ⓒ Ⓓ	46. Ⓐ Ⓑ Ⓒ Ⓓ
8. Ⓐ Ⓑ Ⓒ Ⓓ	21. Ⓐ Ⓑ Ⓒ Ⓓ	34. Ⓐ Ⓑ Ⓒ Ⓓ	47. Ⓐ Ⓑ Ⓒ Ⓓ
9. Ⓐ Ⓑ Ⓒ Ⓓ	22. Ⓐ Ⓑ Ⓒ Ⓓ	35. Ⓐ Ⓑ Ⓒ Ⓓ	48. Ⓐ Ⓑ Ⓒ Ⓓ
10. Ⓐ Ⓑ Ⓒ Ⓓ	23. Ⓐ Ⓑ Ⓒ Ⓓ	36. Ⓐ Ⓑ Ⓒ Ⓓ	49. Ⓐ Ⓑ Ⓒ Ⓓ
11. Ⓐ Ⓑ Ⓒ Ⓓ	24. Ⓐ Ⓑ Ⓒ Ⓓ	37. Ⓐ Ⓑ Ⓒ Ⓓ	50. Ⓐ Ⓑ Ⓒ Ⓓ
12. Ⓐ Ⓑ Ⓒ Ⓓ	25. Ⓐ Ⓑ Ⓒ Ⓓ	38. Ⓐ Ⓑ Ⓒ Ⓓ	
13. Ⓐ Ⓑ Ⓒ Ⓓ	26. Ⓐ Ⓑ Ⓒ Ⓓ	39. Ⓐ Ⓑ Ⓒ Ⓓ	

INDEX

Index

REA's Study Guides

Review Books, Refreshers, and Comprehensive References

Problem Solvers®
Presenting an answer to the pressing need for easy-to-understand and up-to-date study guides detailing the wide world of mathematics and science.

High School Tutors®
In-depth guides that cover the length and breadth of the science and math subjects taught in high schools nationwide.

Essentials®
An insightful series of more useful, more practical, and more informative references comprehensively covering more than 150 subjects.

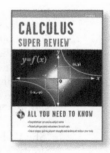

Super Reviews®
Don't miss a thing! Review it all thoroughly with this series of complete subject references at an affordable price.

Interactive Flashcard Books®
Flip through these essential, interactive study aids that go far beyond ordinary flashcards.

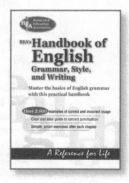

Reference
Explore dozens of clearly written, practical guides covering a wide scope of subjects from business to engineering to languages and many more.

For our complete title list,
visit www.rea.com

Research & Education Association

REA's Test Preps
The Best in Test Preparation

- REA Test Preps are **far more** comprehensive than any other test preparation series
- Each book contains full-length practice tests based on the most recent exams
- **Every** type of question likely to be given on the exams is included
- Answers are accompanied by **full** and **detailed** explanations

REA publishes hundreds of test prep books. Some of our titles include:

Advanced Placement Exams (APs)
Art History
Biology
Calculus AB & BC
Chemistry
Economics
English Language & Composition
English Literature & Composition
European History
French Language
Government & Politics
Latin Vergil
Physics B & C
Psychology
Spanish Language
Statistics
United States History
World History

College-Level Examination Program (CLEP)
American Government
College Algebra
General Examinations
History of the United States I
History of the United States II
Introduction to Educational Psychology
Human Growth and Development
Introductory Psychology
Introductory Sociology
Principles of Management
Principles of Marketing
Spanish
Western Civilization I
Western Civilization II

SAT Subject Tests
Biology E/M
Chemistry
French
German
Literature
Mathematics Level 1, 2
Physics
Spanish
United States History

Graduate Record Exams (GREs)
Biology
Chemistry
General
Literature in English
Mathematics
Physics
Psychology

ACT - ACT Assessment

ASVAB - Armed Services Vocational Aptitude Battery

CBEST - California Basic Educational Skills Test

CDL - Commercial Driver License Exam

COOP, HSPT & TACHS - Catholic High School Admission Tests

FE (EIT) - AM Exam

FTCE - Florida Teacher Certification Examinations

GED

GMAT - Graduate Management Admission Test

LSAT - Law School Admission Test

MAT - Miller Analogies Test

MCAT - Medical College Admission Test

MTEL - Massachusetts Tests for Educator Licensure

NJ HSPA - New Jersey High School Proficiency Assessment

NYSTCE - New York State Teacher Certification Examinations

PRAXIS PLT - Principles of Learning & Teaching Tests

PRAXIS PPST - Pre-Professional Skills Tests

PSAT/NMSQT

SAT

TExES - Texas Examinations of Educator Standards

THEA - Texas Higher Education Assessment

TOEFL - Test of English as a Foreign Language

USMLE Steps 1,2 - U.S. Medical Licensing Exams

For our complete title list,
visit www.rea.com

Research & Education Association

Installing REA's TestWare®

System Requirements

Microsoft Windows XP or later; 64 MB available RAM.

Installation

1. Insert the California High School Proficiency Exam (CHSPE) TestWare® CD into the CD-ROM drive.
2. If the installation doesn't begin automatically, from the Start Menu choose the RUN command. When the RUN dialog box appears, type d:\setup (where d is the letter of your CD-ROM drive) at the prompt and click OK.
3. The installation process will begin. A dialog box proposing the directory "C:\Program Files\REA\CHSPE" will appear. If the name and location are suitable, click OK. If you wish to specify a different name or location, type it in and click OK.
4. Start the CHSPE TestWare® application by double-clicking on the icon.

REA's CHSPE TestWare® is **EASY** to **LEARN AND USE**. To archieve maximum benefits, we recommend that you take a few minutes to go through the on-screen tutorial on your computer.

Technical Support

REA's TestWare® is backed by customer and technical support. For questions about **installation or operation of your software,** contact us at:

Research & Education Association
Phone: (732) 819-8880 (9 a.m. to 5 p.m. ET, Monday–Friday)
Fax: (732) 819-8808
Website: www.rea.com
E-mail: info@rea.com

Note: In order for the TestWare® to function properly, please install and run the application under the same computer administrator-level user account. Installing the TestWare® as one user and running it as another could cause file-access path conflicts.